Third Edition

COMPUTERS AND INFORMATION PROCESSING

William M. Fuori
Louis V. Gioia

Nassau Community College
Garden City, NY

PRENTICE HALL, Englewood Cliffs, NJ 07632

Library of Congress Cataloging-in-Publication Data

Fuori, William M.
    Computers and information processing/William M. Fuori, Louis
V. Gioia.—3rd ed.
        p. cm.
    Includes index.
    ISBN 0-13-173329-X
    1. Computers.   2. Electronic data processing.   I. Gioia, Louis
V. II. Title.
QA75.F86 1991
004—dc20   90-46901
                                                                CIP

Editorial/production supervision: bookworks
Interior design: Jayne Conte
Illustrations: Network Graphics
Cover design: Franklyn Graphics
Manufacturing buyer: Robert Anderson
Prepress buyer: Trudy Pisciotti
Page layout: Jayne Conte
Photo editor: Lorrinda Morris-Nantz
Photo research: Teri Stratford

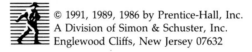 © 1991, 1989, 1986 by Prentice-Hall, Inc.
A Division of Simon & Schuster, Inc.
Englewood Cliffs, New Jersey 07632

Printed in the United States of America

10   9   8   7   6   5   4   3   2   1

ISBN 0-13-173329-X

Prentice-Hall International (UK) Limited, *London*
Prentice-Hall of Australia Pty. Limited, *Sydney*
Prentice-Hall Canada Inc., *Toronto*
Prentice-Hall Hispanoamericana, S.A., *Mexico*
Prentice-Hall of India Private Limited, *New Delhi*
Prentice-Hall of Japan, Inc., *Tokyo*
Simon & Schuster Asia Pte. Ltd., *Singapore*
Editora Prentice-Hall do Brasil, Ltda., *Rio de Janeiro*

*To my wife Elizabeth, and our children Elizabeth E. and Michael T.,
for the patience, consideration, and understanding you have exhibited
towards my writing endeavors over the past twenty years.*

To the memory of Ellen Fuori, my mother.

W.M.F.

*To Ellen, Kristine, and Amy, and to my parents Gloria, Michael,
Ann, and Thomas: Thank you for your patience, understanding, and
inspiration.*

L.V.G.

CONTENTS

5

THE PROCESSING UNIT
The Brain of the Mainframe 139 Probably will skip
Objectives 139

6 Easy Chapter

MICROCOMPUTERS
Computers In the Small 169
Objectives 169

Contents

12
WORD PROCESSING AND DESKTOP PUBLISHING
Putting It on Paper 359

13
MORE PACKAGED SOFTWARE
From the Spreadsheet to the Database and Beyond 395

15 *Will touch networking only*

UNIT V   THE COMPUTER MOVES YOUR WORLD

16 *Will not do*

17
COMPUTERS DOWN THE ROAD
A Glimpse at What Might Be 533

PREFACE

GENERAL PURPOSE

Today's educator must prepare each student to enter a world that has become heavily dependent on computers for its very survival. There can be little question that automation and the use of computers in every area of human endeavor is the driving force for change today. Educators at all levels, from the high school to the community college to the university, have recognized the impact of the computer and have had the foresight not only to recommend but, in many instances, to require that all students be instructed in the nature and uses of computers as an integral part of their formal education. To quote Dr. R. L. Bright, when he was Associate Commissioner for research of the United States Department of Health, Education, and Welfare, ". . . [anyone who graduates from a college or university] without being instructed in the use of computers has been severely cheated."

We have written from the premise that each student is a potential user of computers and will benefit from an understanding of computers. Students soon come to realize that with a little knowledge and understanding, the mystery and awe with which they might have viewed the computer will disappear, and the computer can begin to serve them as the useful and essential tool that it was intended to be. Therefore, this text provides a basic understanding of what a computer system is, what it can do, where and how it is currently being used. Perhaps more importantly, this book can help the student learn how to use a computer.

The first two editions of this text were a huge success. They were adopted by universities, two-year colleges, and vocational schools nationally and internationally. We feel the attraction was in a large part from the option the books provided the instructor to offer hands-on computer experience. Through the use of tutorials and other computer exercises, students became excited and encouraged as they learned the magic and power of a computer first hand. Therefore, in this third edition, we enhanced the hands-on aspect of our package by providing increased tutorial coverage in the companion applications book. This companion book, entitled, *Applications for Computers and Information Processing*, contains four tutorials that guide a student, step by step, through the popular microcomputer operating system DOS, and applications software such as Lotus 1-2-3, WordPerfect, and dBASE.

This text is recommended for use in a one-semester survey course or in an introductory computer course for general education, or for the business, computer science, or information processing student. Once the student has completed this one-semester course, he or she will be prepared to function effectively in our computerized world or pursue more advanced studies in the field of computers.

ATTRIBUTES OF THE TEXT

In addition to a thorough and comprehensive treatment of the subject matter, you will find the text contains the following attributes:

Hands-on Approach

Recognizing the importance of knowing how to use a computer, we have included four tutorials on the use of DOS, WordPerfect Versions 5.0 and 5.1, Lotus 1-2-3 Versions 2.01, 2.2, and 3.0, and dBASE III PLUS. Hands-on computer activities are provided at the end of each tutorial.

Currency

With new developments taking place daily in information processing, it is essential that the material presented in a textbook represent the state of the art. Current topics that are given extensive treatment in this edition are operating systems, artificial intelligence, expert systems, networking, wide area distributed data processing networks, local area networks, communications systems, the automated office, the integration of micros with mini- or mainframe computers in business and industry, lap-top microcomputers to mainframe supercomputers, fourth-generation languages, fifth-generation computers, and robotics! In addition, the *Third Edition* features new coverage of supermicros and workstations, the graphic user interface (GUI), computer assisted software engineering (CASE), desktop publishing, computer viruses, RISC computers, and the latest developments in microcomputer technology.

Readability

From the outset, we have tried to keep the student's needs and interests in mind. Realizing this material can sometimes seem dry and irrelevant to some, we have written in a lively and engaging manner. We want this edition of the text to be as meaningful and enjoyable to its readers as was the previous edition. Concepts, no matter how technical or complex, are explained in a simple, down-to-earth style with many references to real-life situations. When students see how computers can relate to their world, whether it's on the job or at home, they become interested; often, they get downright excited.

Flexibility

A top-down structured approach was used throughout that provides the instructor with the flexibility to alter the order of presentation of topics or modules within a chapter or unit, or to skip a particular topic or module altogether, without affecting the continuity and effectiveness of the overall presentation. This was accomplished by introducing concepts when needed to support a particular topic or module and not in a predetermined or set order. Terms are defined when they are introduced into a discussion. In the rare event that a term or concept that has not been adequately defined or explained in a previous topic or module, or covered in the instructor's presentation, is used in a module, an unprecedented glossary (of more than 450 terms) and index (in excess of 2000 entries) is at the student's disposal and should provide the needed assistance.

**Integration
of Microcomputers
Throughout**

The personal computer or microcomputer is no longer an interesting plaything for the computer hobbyist. It is fast becoming a familiar sight in homes and offices across the land. Many small businesses rely exclusively on microcomputers for their processing needs, while a number of larger companies continue to employ mini- or mainframe computers exclusively. The trend today is to network computers. Microcomputers are being hooked up to terminals and other micros in various networking schemes. Personal computers are being integrated into mini- and mainframe configurations to form more useful and powerful systems. Consequently, we have devoted an entire chapter to microcomputers and have emphasized micro-to-micro and micro-to-mainframe connections throughout.

One of the most asked questions today is, "What's the best microcomputer to buy?" The answer naturally depends on your needs. Realizing the need for help in this area, we have presented material concerning microcomputers in such a way that by the time the reader completes the book, he or she will be well prepared to go out and make a wise selection.

FEATURES OF THE TEXT

Tutorials

Recognizing the importance of prewritten, or packaged, commercial software like operating systems, word processing, electronic spreadsheets, and database management systems, we treat this all-important topic in three chapters in the text and in four complete tutorials (DOS, WordPerfect Versions 5.0 and 5.1, Lotus 1-2-3 Versions 2.01, 2.2, and 3.0, and dBASE III PLUS) in the companion applications book. From our own experiences as well as from research and comments received from instructors, business professionals, and students from all over the country, knowing how to use the computer as a tool has become at least as important as knowing about computers. This text is a response to that need.

We have spent much time and effort researching the topic and feel our treatment and presentation of prewritten software tutorials to be the most thorough of any introductory computer book yet published. Extra care was taken to present this material in a clear, natural, and easy-to-follow manner. Our writing assumes the reader has little or no prior knowledge of the subject matter. Teacher and student alike will find this timely information to be particularly interesting and of great practical value.

If a computer or software package is not available, each tutorial can still be used profitably and effectively. Because the illustrations shown in each tutorial are the computer screens produced by the actual software package, reproduced in exact detail, reading the step-by-step, keystroke-by-keystroke tutorial will be like looking over a friend's shoulder and directing him or her as to the steps to take—only the excitement of using the computer and the sensation of actually depressing the keys will be missing.

Boxed Features

To a degree, most books of this type are obsolete the day they are published. With this in mind, virtually every chapter contains boxed features composed of current material from a recent article or book. These materials were carefully selected to keep the reader informed about the latest computer-related topics and issues. Written in a motivational and entertaining manner, information of this type enriches the text material and relates the book's contents to the student's real world.

Computer Trivia

Most students enjoy reading about computer lore, culture, and fancy. We have included a number of tantalizing tidbits both to inform and to enliven and amuse. Readers will learn about the world's most expensive computer equipment, tips on computer safety, the greatest computer crime on record, the first computer "bug," some word about Elvis' whereabouts, and more.

UNIQUENESS

This book is different from others that appeal to students in the data processing, computer science, information processing, and related areas in several ways:

1. Understandably, instructors enjoy having the freedom to skip certain topics and to teach others out of order while maintaining continuity and cohesiveness in their overall presentation. This text affords instructors this capability to the greatest extent possible by virtue of its modular construction. Concepts are presented only as needed to support a particular topic or module and not in any arbitrary order.

2. As mentioned earlier, there is currently a nationwide outcry for people to learn how to use computers to perform all kinds of commercial and personal tasks.
   Chapters 12 and 13 provide a broad overview of word processing, desktop publishing, electronic spreadsheets, database management, computer graphics, and communications software. The tutorials presented in the applications book are designed to be used with a computer and corresponding software package. They will guide you step by step through the major functions of the software package in a simple, easy-to-follow manner. As we pointed out earlier, if a computer or the needed software is not available you will still reap most of the benefits of the tutorial, but only as an observer and not as a player.

3. The material presented in this text has been successfully field tested at Nassau Community College. The enthusiastic response has convinced the authors that the material is interesting, informative, and easy to understand.

4. The text includes a substantial number and variety of exercises at the end of each chapter. Included in these exercises are two different types of short answer questions (true/false, fill-in, multiple-choice, or matching), problems, research projects, and a crossword puzzle to reinforce the reader's understanding of the concepts and vocabulary presented in the chapter in a challenging and enjoyable

manner. The answers to the even-numbered short answer questions are included. The page number in the text where the correct information can be found is provided after each false answer.

5. Current and related topics are presented in highlighted boxes to acquaint the student with some of the more practical aspects of the subject matter as well as to stimulate interest in exploring the subject matter in greater depth.
6. Timely and related cartoons are integrated throughout the text. These have proven to be both interesting and informative in the authors' field testing of the material.
7. Amazing but true facts concerning the people and events surrounding the fascinating world of computers—a believe-it-or-not of computer trivia—are noted.

STRUCTURE OF THE TEXT

The text is organized to facilitate the student's comprehension of the relevance of information processing in business, science, and industry. To accomplish this end, we have divided the text into units as follows:

Unit I

In this unit, the brief but spectacular evolution of the computer is outlined and the impact of computers on business, science, and industry is graphically illustrated. This will help clarify why this study is being undertaken. Additional materials presented in this unit will prepare the student to begin a study of programming or to work with available software packages. Upon completion of this first unit, the instructor may freely choose if, when, and in what depth these topics will be presented.

Unit II

This unit describes the machines that comprise a data processing system and the programs that control them. A thorough and complete treatment of micro-computer and mainframe systems is provided. Particular attention is paid to the numerous conceptual and architectural similarities between the micro- and mainframe computer systems. In addition, this unit will focus on data-entry, input/output, file-processing, and data communications. The concepts and inter-relationship of distributed data processing including local area networks, multi-user systems, and bulletin boards are explained in detail.

Unit III

Unit III is devoted to an in-depth discussion of data structures and databases, operating systems, computer languages, program preparation, and problem solving concepts. Here we discuss the functions of an operating system and examples of operating systems used with the smallest microcomputers to the largest mainframes. Then we discuss structured programming and other top-down programming techniques used to produce clear, efficient, and well documented solutions to problems found in business, industry, and our daily lives. The student will learn how to prepare an application for programming, to logically analyze the problem to determine the sequence of operations that will efficiently solve it by computer, to represent this solution graphically utiliz-ing a program flowchart or pseudocode, and finally to use the flowchart or pseudocode to prepare a computer program.

Today, more than ever before, people are relying on packaged software to produce the greatest possible return from their computer for a minimum investment of time, effort, and money. These packages fall into certain distinct areas, namely word processing, desktop publishing, spreadsheet analysis, database design and implementation, computer graphics, and integrated software packages. We discuss each of these generally in Chapters 12 and 13. Tutorials on the three most popular of these packages (WordPerfect Versions 5.0 and 5.1, Lotus 1-2-3 Versions 2.01, 2.2, and 3.0, and dBASE III PLUS) are provided in the applications book.

Unit IV

In this unit we explore the more sophisticated topics of systems analysis and design and information systems. Application areas discussed include electronic mail, teleconferencing, videotext, telecommuting, and public utility services like THE SOURCE, PRODIGY, and CompuServe.

Unit V

In Unit V, we answer many of the questions asked by students in an introductory computer course. We answer such questions as "What careers are open to me if I pursue my studies in information processing? Where is this field headed? What lies ahead? Is HAL in Kubrick's production of 2001 or in 2010 a possibility? What is artificial intelligence? Can computers think and learn? Will I be able to carry on a conversation or speak to a computer in normal everyday English in the next decade or two?" We shall summarize what the experts see for our futures in their crystal balls.

Tutorials

The DOS, WordPerfect, Lotus 1-2-3, and dBASE tutorials contained in the applications book can be used by the instructor as a practical illustration of the software packages most commonly used in business today. How better can one understand the use of prepackaged software than by studying the biggest sellers in each respective area?

Appendixes

The appendixes include a discussion of computer number system and data representations, an extensive glossary of computer related terms, and answers to even exercises (including for each false answer a page reference(s) to where the correct information can be found).

INSTRUCTOR'S RESOURCE PACKAGE

Instructor's Resource Manual

To aid the instructor in structuring the course to fit the interests and backgrounds of his or her students, a teacher's resource manual is available. The manual is divided into four units.

Unit I includes, for each chapter:
    detailed guide to be used as a lecture outline
    discussion questions and class activities
    answers to the end of chapter activities
Unit II provides suggestions and outlines for presenting DOS, wordprocessing, electronic spreadsheets, and database software.
Unit III consists of suggestions for presenting BASIC.
Unit IV consists of a guide to the color transparencies with lecture hints on employing them effectively in the classroom.

Test Item File

Completely revised for the third edition, the test item file contains nearly 3000 test questions. The test bank is divided among multiple choice, fill-in, and essay questions. Each question has been rated according to level of difficulty. In addition, the corresponding text page is provided for each question to facilitate reference.

Test Bank

The Test Item File described above is provided on Prentice Hall's Test Manager. This computer program allows maximum flexibility in designing your tests. The Test Manager will allow you to construct tests using questions that you specify or draw at random from Prentice Hall's question files, or you can create your own question files containing test items keyed to each chapter in the text. You can print up to nine versions of the test using today's most popular wordprocessing programs.

Prentice Hall/New York Times Contemporary View Program

When the text is adopted, instructors and their students will receive a complimentary newspaper "student supplement" containing recent articles. These articles bring classroom topics to life and help expand a student's knowledge beyond the textbook and into the world in which we live.

The New Literacy: An Introduction to Computers

Developed by the Annenberg Foundation, this video series presents a comprehensive overview of the computer, data processing terminology, computer applications, and typical computing environments. In total, there are 26 segments contained on 13 video cassettes. Each institution is entitled to one video cassette per every 50 copies of the text adopted.

Video Professor Series

The Video Professor Series is a series of microcomputer software videos that provide step-by-step instructions on how to use today's most popular software programs. Adopters are eligible for these videos as an alternative to the *The New Literacy: An Introduction to Computers* series.

The ABC News/ Prentice Hall Video Library

The Library offers high-quality feature and documentary-style videos from any or all of the six programs included in this exclusive Prentice Hall agreement: *Nightline, World News Tonight/American Agenda, Business World, The Health Show, On Business,* and *This Week with David Brinkley.*

Study Guide

To assist the student in understanding and learning the material presented in the text, and to make the learning experience more enjoyable, a study guide is available and can be used. The study guide is subdivided into three units:

Unit I provides the following for each chapter:
A summary which emphasizes the main points of each chapter. Sufficient border space is available for student note taking during class lectures.
A vocabulary drill
Matching exercises
True/false exercises
A crossword puzzle utilizing chapter related terminology
Projects to be completed outside of class. These can be specifically assigned by the instructor or used as voluntary extra-credit assignments for the more enterprising students.

Unit II contains exercises that require the student to use the software packages of the type presented in the tutorials. Each exercise is designed to reduce anxiety, increase motivation, and provide a useful and meaningful experience for the student on a self-paced independent-learning basis. The exercises are of two types:
Performance exercises—distinct and clearly delineated tasks that can be carried out using the data files provided.
Project descriptions—descriptions of complete projects that can be fun to complete and of immediate benefit to the student.

Unit III contains answers to selected exercises in the Study Guide as well as solutions to the crossword puzzles.

Transparency Acetates

One hundred twenty full color transparencies are provided upon adoption of the text. Sixty of the acetates come directly from the text and the other 60 are from outside sources. The Instructor's Manual contains a complete guide to each transparency and how to use them effectively in the classroom.

Applications for Computers and Information Processing, 3/e

Written for the beginning student, *Applications for Computers and Information Processing*, 3/e will take you step by step through DOS, WordPerfect 5.1/5.0, Lotus 1-2-3, and dBASE III PLUS. This two-color, highly visual text introduces the student to the major skill areas in each package, skills which are then reinforced by a series of hands-on activities.

Basic Supplement

This supplement deals exclusively with the BASIC language. The BASIC instruction set presented is universal and is available in virtually every version of BASIC. This material is provided in five distinct lessons; the instructor can choose the most appropriate point(s) in the course to present the lessons.

A CONTEMPORARY VIEW

THE NEW YORK TIMES and PRENTICE HALL are sponsoring A CONTEMPORARY VIEW: a program designed to enhance student access to current information of relevance in the classroom.

Through this program, the core subject matter provided in the text is supplemented by a collection of time-sensitive articles from one of the world's most distinguished newspapers, THE NEW YORK TIMES. These articles demonstrate the vital, ongoing connection between what is learned in the classroom and what is happening in the world around us.

To enjoy the wealth of information of THE NEW YORK TIMES daily, a reduced subscription rate is available. For information, call toll-free: 1-800-631-1222.

PRENTICE HALL and THE NEW YORK TIMES are proud to co-sponsor A CONTEMPORARY VIEW. We hope it will make the reading of both textbooks and newspapers a more dynamic, involving process.

ACKNOWLEDGMENTS

It is with great pleasure and gratitude that we acknowledge the many people whose expertise and encouragement contributed immensely to the creation of this book. A project of this magnitude could not have been completed without the help of many talented and committed people.

We were indeed fortunate to have worked with the same extraordinary team of Prentice Hall publishing professionals who distinguished themselves throughout the production of the first edition of this book. The enthusiasm with which they accepted the challenge to create an even better third edition was truly inspiring. The cooperation, dedication, and perseverance of our friends and colleagues at Prentice Hall has been unwavering. Because of their collective efforts, this experience has been as rewarding and enjoyable as the previous editions. Our heartfelt thanks to all.

Among those we would like to individually recognize and thank are Dennis Hogan, Ted Werthman, Jeanne Hoeting, Mary Ann Gloriande, Caroline Ruddle, Leah Jewell, and Alison Reeves.

In any group of people, there are also those that distinguish themselves by going above and beyond. We were fortunate to have a number of these people on our team: Ted Werthman, editor, is to be thanked for his continued enthusiasm, support, and direction. Ted's ideas and foresight helped lay the groundwork for the completed project. Ted, thanks again for always being ready to help when we needed it. Jayne Conte, our designer, proved once again that she's the best. This is not only our opinion but one that is substantiated by the numerous design awards Jayne has received, including several for previous editions of this book. No one could have expected her to improve upon her previous award-winning designs, but we believe that she has done just that. Her inimitable brand of artistic talent is reflected on every page of the book. We have been extremely fortunate as recipients of her creative genius. Karen Fortgang, production editor, is to be congratulated for her exceptional efforts to coordinate the many facets of this project. Again, Karen was faced with a monumental coordination problem with the many books in the package being in different stages of production from raw manuscript to film proofs at one time. But, as the finished product attests, a true professional like Karen will always rise to the occasion. Thanks again for doing a great job of keeping the project together and on schedule. Kathy Marshak, copy editor, brought a personal commitment to the copy editing of this manuscript. Perhaps this is because Kathy will always have a place in her heart for this project, having been production editor on the first edition. Now her energies are principally directed to raising little David Marshak (born as the first edition was completed) and his sister Emma. Lorraine Abramson, Ron Weickart, and John Hargreaves from Network Graphics (Hauppauge, New York) deserve applause for their sophisticated yet exciting art renditions. Without question the best team of artists we have ever worked with, they are absolutely in a class by themselves. In a book of this type, sudden changes and new ideas are not unusual. They welcomed our ideas and were quick to respond to our suggestions. As you can see, the drawings and line art are simply beautiful. We were fortunate to have their services.

A special word of thanks to our colleagues at Nassau Community College for their contributions, helpful suggestions, and encouragement. We are especially indebted to Tony D'Arco, Joe Pacilio, Larry Aufiero, Mauro Cassano, Frank Avenoso, Stephen Solosky and Thomas Taylor, each of whom contributed their unique talents to the success of the project.

We are grateful to the many reviewers who helped improve our presentation. Many of their suggestions have been incorporated into the book. We are particularly indebted to Ray Fanselau, American River College; Barry Floyd, New York University; Mike Michaelson, Palomar College; Edward G. Oakie, Radford University; Leonard Presby, William Paterson College; Gayla Stewart, St. Louis Community College at Meramec; Jim Woolever, Cerritos College; and Margaret Zinky, Phoenix College.

We also appreciate the comments we received from William Fields, DeVry Institute of Technology-Atlanta; William Harrison, DeVry Institute of Technology-Atlanta; William Juchau, Florida Southern College; Susumu Kasai, St. Louis Community College at Meramec; Jan Lindholm, University of Central Florida; Loll Lomar, Florida Community College at Jacksonville; and George Ritler, Florida Community College at Jacksonville.

PHOTO CREDITS

The authors gratefully acknowledge the help of the numberous companies that supplied photographs and technical information. Credit lines for photographs used in this book appear below.

© Aldus Corp. 1988–1990
Courtesy of Amdek
Courtesy of American Airlines

Courtesy of Apple Computer, Inc.
Apple® is a registered trademark of Apple Computer, Inc.

Courtesy of AT&T Bell Laboratories
Courtesy of Burroughs Corporation
Courtesy of CalComp
Courtesy of Chemical Bank
Courtesy of Chrysler Corporation
Copyright 1988, *The Chronicle of Higher Education*. Reprinted with permission.
Courtesy of Cincinnati Milacron.
Copyright © 1989 by CMP Publications, Inc., 600 Community Drive, Manhasset, NY 11030. Reprinted from VARBUSINESS with permission.
Reprinted with permission of Compaq Computer Corp. All rights reserved.
Courtesy of CompuServe
Courtesy of the Computer Museum, Boston, MA
Courtesy of Control Data Corp.
Courtesy of Cray Research, Inc. Photo by Paul Shambroom.
Courtesy of Eastman Kodak Company
Courtesy of Electronic Associates, Incorporated
Courtesy of Epson America, Inc.
Courtesy of Ford Motor Company
Courtesy of General Motors.
Photos courtesy of Hayes Microcomputer Products, Inc.
Courtesy of Heath Company
Photos courtesy of Hewlett-Packard Company
Courtesy of International Business Machines Corporation
Courtesy of Intel Corporation
Courtesy of Mike Kirkpatrick.
Courtesy of Microsoft.

Reprinted by permission of *MIS Week*, March 5, 1990. Copyright Fairchild Publications 1990.
Courtesy of the National Aeronautics and Space Administration
Courtesy of National Computer Products
Courtesy of NCR Corporation
Courtesy of NEC Home Electronics (U.S.A.), Inc.
Courtesy of NEXT Inc.
Courtesy of PageMaker.
Reprinted from *PC Computing*, March 1990. Copyright © 1990, Ziff Communications Company.
Courtesy of *PC Magazine*
Courtesy of *PC World*
Reprinted with permission from *Portable Computer*. Copyright Miller Freeman Publication, Inc.
Courtesy of Quasar Company
By permission of the Trustees of the Science Museum, London
Courtesy of Source EDP.
Courtesy of Sperry Corporation
Courtesy of Tektronix, Inc.
Courtesy of Texaco, Inc.
Photos courtesy of Texas Instruments, Inc.
Courtesy of 3M Company
Courtesy of Unisys.
Courtesy of Wang Laboratories, Inc.
Courtesy of Western Electric
Courtesy of Xerox Corporation
Reprinted from *INFOSYSTEMS*, Aug. 1986, Jan. 1987, Feb. 1987, Mar. 1987. Copyright Hitchcock Publishing Company.

To those of you who will be reading and learning the many facts and concepts in our book, we hope you find the material exciting and challenging. Suggestions for improving the text or any of the supplemental materials will always be welcomed. Send them to:

Dr. William M. Fuori and Louis V. Gioia
% Nassau Community College.
Mathematics and Computer Processing Department
Stewart Avenue
Garden City, N.Y. 11530

We will respond to all correspondence.

William M. Fuori
Louis V. Gioia

1

INTRODUCTION TO THE WORLD OF COMPUTERS
What, Why, and How Did It Happen?

Objectives

- Appreciate the advantages of becoming computer literate.
- Discuss the factors contributing to the development of computers.
- Briefly trace the history of computers from their early beginnings to the present.
- Describe the characteristics of each computer generation.
- Discuss some of the more recent areas of computer application.
- List and describe the characteristics or problems suitable for a computerized solution.
- Describe how the computer has affected and will affect us individually and as a society.
- Discuss some of the problems brought on by the increased use of computers.
- Understand and use the key terms presented in the chapter.

It is said that an invention appears when it is needed. The *computer*—that awesome package of glass, plastic, metal, and wires—happened to explode onto the scene during our lifetime. The computer revolution predicted by futurists has arrived. This **information revolution** is bringing sweeping and dramatic changes in the way we live, work, and view the world—and it is still in its infancy. Advancements in computer technology will virtually ensure that this revolution will touch your life (if it hasn't already) in profound, far-reaching, and exciting ways (see Fig. 1-1).

The large, expensive, complex computers known as **mainframes** have been around for about forty years. In that time they have certainly played an increasingly important role in our lives, but for the most part, they have been doing it "behind the scenes," out of view. More recently, microminiature technology has made possible the personal, or **microcomputer.** The small size, nominal cost, and versatility of the microcomputer has been responsible for its universal appeal. What used to occupy an entire gymnasium can now fit in your lap, and if you don't own one yet, chances are you soon will.

Pessimists fear that the computer will have an increasingly dehumanizing effect and will tend to pull the family apart. Optimists believe that the computer will improve the world's culture by allowing people not only to be more productive but to have more free time to create. Many feel that the computer has already served to unify this generation, ridding it of the stigma of being "lost" and not having a cause to rally around. In any case, one thing is certain: for better or worse, our world will never be the same. We cannot evade the effects of computerization, but to harness and utilize the power of computers, we must know something about them.

WHY LEARN ABOUT COMPUTERS?

Computers are here to stay. Each day it becomes more difficult to get along without a basic understanding of what they are and how they are used. Some authorities have gone so far as to say that all students will need *four* basic

FIGURE 1-1
Virtually no place in the universe is too remote for the computers of today.

FIGURE 1-2
Soon all gradeschool classrooms will be equipped with mirocomputers as shown here.

skills in order to survive in today's high-tech world: readin', writin', 'rithmetic, and **computer literacy**—a basic knowledge of computers and their use (see Fig. 1-2). Although not everyone will have to know about computers, it is certain that as we move from an industrial society to an information society, the number of people needed to provide all kinds of information services is going to increase.

If you know a little about computers and what they can and cannot do, you will, in most cases, be more attractive to a prospective employer. You will be in greater demand if you can sit down and actually *use* a computer to do your bidding. Professional motives aside, computers can provide users with countless hours of fun and amusement.

Nothing to Fear

Computerphobia, the fear of computers, is apparently affecting more and more people as microcomputers continue to be plugged into more and more homes, schools, and offices throughout the land. This relatively recent phenomenon, also known as **cyberphobia,** occurs in a large proportion of students and professionals.

Some students have reportedly declined entering certain degree programs simply because the programs require taking one or more computer courses. Mere rumors that "the computers are coming" have been known to send some workers packing and looking for new jobs.

When the computer finally does arrive in the workplace, it is often seen as an intrusion. Some feel that computers are too difficult to learn; others worry about computers taking over their jobs. There are some who are afraid they might damage or "blow up" the computer, while others feel that they are too old to learn about computers or are threatened by the specter of depersonalization. People who know little or nothing about computers are mystified and often intimidated by computer jargon. Listening to a conversation involving two people who know something about computers can be enough to send shivers up the spine of the poor neophyte. In time, this computer anxiety should pass from society as new generations are born right into the lap of the computer.

Some of this fear is normal. It is human nature to be afraid of what we don't understand. One antidote to this malaise of computerphobia is computer education and training.

Are You A Computerphobe Or A Computerphile? According to a study by Professor Sanford Weinberg of St. Joseph's University, Philadelphia, at least 30 percent of the daily users of computers have some degree of **computerphobia** (fear of computers). Victims range from people afflicted by high blood pressure to a policeman who shot the computer console in his car.

Another Weinberg study shows **computerphiles** (compulsive computer users) to be no better off: they are usually friendless and single.

Computer Literacy   Although the term **computer literacy** means different things to different people, most would agree that a computer-literate person would:

- Have a basic *understanding* of what a computer can and cannot do.
- Be able to *use* a computer as a tool on a personal as well as a professional level.
- Be able to *interact* with a computer and use word-processing, database, spreadsheet, or similar business programs (these will be described fully later in the text).
- Have some idea of the social *implications* computer technology is posing now and what they might mean for the future.

Essentially, people who are computer literate will be able to unleash the power of the computer for their specific needs. As you read this book and apply what you learn, you will overcome any fear or inhibitions you presently have concerning computers. You will learn to work with microcomputers and become familiar with some of the most important business applications in existence today.

Hands-On Experience

Four hands-on **tutorials** are provided in the accompanying applications book. These include simple, keystroke-by-keystroke instructions that will guide you in the use of the personal computer operating system, PC DOS, and three of the most widely used commercial software packages on the market today: Word-Perfect, Lotus 1-2-3, and dBASE. WordPerfect and Lotus are divided into introductory and advanced lessons so that you may tailor them to your needs.

By completing these easy-to-follow tutorials, you will learn first-hand what a computer can and cannot do, and you will experience the excitement of having a computer's power at your fingertips. Each of these sessions will provide a worthwhile and enjoyable experience. Not only will you find these experiences useful in your professional endeavors, but we believe they will inspire you to further explore the magic and wonder of the computer.

INFORMATION PROCESSING

Since the beginning of recorded time, people have searched for more efficient means to obtain and process data. Every business and industry, regardless of its size or purpose, is concerned with processing facts—or **data**—in order to provide current, accurate **information.** Employees at every level within most companies use the computer or its output in the performance of their everyday duties. Scientists and engineers use it to perform complex mathematical calculations, and vast numbers of people employed in businesses use it to reduce the masses of data generated daily. Executive decisions are based on such data as operating expenses, market statistics, inventory levels, and other quantitative factors. Accurate and timely information can provide business management with a substantial edge over its competition.

However, like raw talent or raw materials, raw data are of limited use. Only after these data have been examined, classified, compared, analyzed, and summarized do they become usable information and take on real value. Nearly 1 trillion (1,000,000,000,000) pieces of paper filling over 100 million file drawers are generated annually by the nation's businesses. Papers piled up over the years in offices, warehouses, and storerooms throughout the nation amount to several trillion pieces. A large segment of the population, comparable in size to the U.S. Army and Navy combined, has as its daily chore the recording, processing, and analyzing of the factual data generated by industrial, professional, commercial, and governmental organizations. This army of white-collar workers, consisting of nearly 30 million people, does not buy, sell, manufacture, or even service goods but is concerned with the manual and automated processing of data relating to the design, production, and marketing of these goods in our complex civilization.

Need for More Efficient Processing Methods

With the advent of the Industrial Revolution, which brought ever-increasing amounts of data to be processed in shorter and shorter time, business and industry found that it needed faster, cheaper, more efficient methods of processing data.

To fill this need, various types of automated devices were developed and introduced. Most recent and foremost among them was the electronic digital computer, the fastest and most sophisticated tool yet devised for the processing of data (Fig. 1-3). Even with its tremendous initial speed advantage, the computer has continued to become even faster and cheaper (Fig. 1-4).

FIGURE 1-3
Evolution of automated devices used in business and industry.

Bookkeeping System—Pencil and Paper

Accounting with Key-Driven Machines

Punched Card Accounting

Large Centralized Data Processing System

Decentralized or Distributed Data Processing System

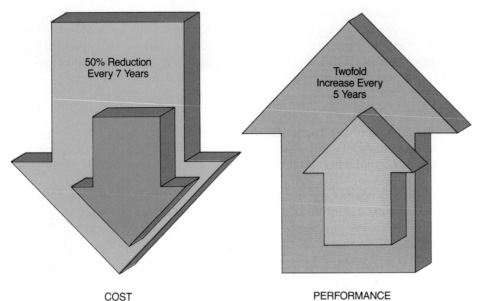

FIGURE 1-4
Cost/performance relationship for small business
computers (costing
<$20,000).

50% Reduction
Every 7 Years

Twofold
Increase Every
5 Years

COST

PERFORMANCE

For example, since the introduction of the first commercially available computer about forty years ago, the cost of processing data by computer has steadily decreased. Today it is a fraction of 1 percent of what it was originally. By way of comparison, if other costs had dropped proportionately, one would be able to take an airline trip around the world for less than $1. In addition to becoming even faster and cheaper, computers have decreased in size at an even more startling rate. Thirty-five years ago, to obtain the computing power available today with a briefcase-sized computer, one would have required a computer the size of the United Nations building in New York City!

COMPUTERS—FROM THEN TO NOW

In the Beginning

Many devices have been employed in the processing of data. The most appropriate place to begin our discussion of these devices is with the **abacus,** a mechanical calculating device first used around 2200 B.C. to add and subtract.

Because this device was so limited, scientists and mathematicians sought other means to aid their endeavors. About 1610, John Napier, a Scottish mathematician, developed a series of rods (commonly called **bones** because they were made of bone) that could be arranged in predetermined ways to produce the products of selected numbers (see Fig. 1-5). He used these rods or bones to produce the first table of logarithms.

The French mathematician Blaise Pascal improved on this concept and in 1645 produced the **Pascaline,** recognized by many to be the first commercially available mechanical calculator (see Fig. 1-6). Although more compact and easier to use than Napier's bones, the Pascaline was only capable of performing addition and subtraction.

Until 1820, all attempts to produce a calculator capable of performing all four arithmetic operations and producing mathematical tables quickly and accurately failed. Then, in France, Thomas de Colmar produced the **arithmometer,** the first four-function practical mechanical calculator.

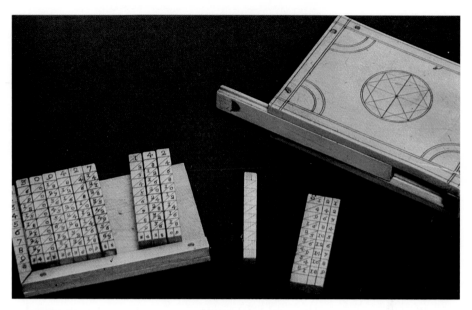

FIGURE 1-5
Napier's bones, a 17th-century mechanical aid to multiplication.

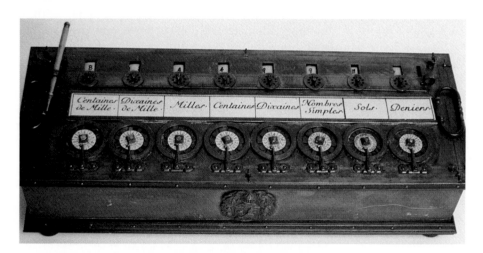

FIGURE 1-6
Pascal's Pascaline mechanical adding machine.

While Thomas was developing the arithmometer, a young genius named Charles Babbage, an English mathematician, was attending Cambridge University. There, Babbage gave much thought to the design of a device to produce mathematical and navigational tables and came upon a principle that used the "differences" between previous values in a table to produce new values. Babbage was unable to incorporate this concept into a working machine until 1822, when he had a working model constructed to illustrate the principle—the **difference engine** (see Fig. 1-7). Babbage commenced work on a steam-driven version of the difference engine capable of calculating and printing results at a rate of two twenty-digit numbers per minute.

FIGURE 1-7
A model of Babbage's difference engine.

Babbage succeeded in building part of the full-sized version but abandoned it in favor of a more powerful and versatile machine, the **analytical engine.** The analytical engine was to use coded punched cards to provide a constant flow of information through the machine's elaborate series of columns, gears, wheels, and levers. The analytical engine was to include all the functional parts of today's computers: input of data, arithmetic unit for computation, memory for data and instructions, and display for output. This was quite an ambitious undertaking during a time when electronics, transistors, and chips had not yet been heard of. The engine was a puzzle to all but a few mathematicians. It was considered by most to be preposterous, and consequently, it was never built. It wasn't until nearly a century later that a new generation of scientists and engineers equipped with new developments in theory and technology brought Babbage's vision back into focus to serve as a theoretical model for future computer technology advancements (see Fig. 1-8).

FIGURE 1-8
A model of the central processor of Babbage's analytical engine.

a

FIGURE 1-9
Herman Hollerith's census tabulator and card sorter (a), card puncher (b), and card reader (c).

b

c

Hollerith By 1890, Herman Hollerith had perfected his tabulating system, and in a census office speed contest, his statistical tabulator bested several rivals to win the 1890 census contract and become a new link in the chain of computer history.

Hollerith won prizes and praise for his invention and earned a doctorate from Columbia University. The company he formed was immediately and lastingly successful. After several mergers and name changes, Hollerith's company became known as International Business Machines Corporation, or IBM.

Little progress took place over the next decade. In the United States we were facing a serious problem indeed—the 1890 census was approaching, and there was no foreseeable way that it could be completed by 1900, as required in the U.S. Constitution. Recognizing this fact, Herman Hollerith, an employee of the Census Office in Washington, set out to develop an automated device capable of completing this task in the allotted ten years. The result was Hollerith's **census tabulator.** This device consisted of a manual card puncher, an electronic card reader, and an electromechanical card sorter (Fig. 1-9).

Skip

THE COUNTESS OF LOVELACE

That Babbage's work is remembered at all is a credit to Ada Byron King, the *Countess of Lovelace*. Together, they shared a clear vision of computers that even today experts are working to make a reality. The Countess translated and published Babbage's notes, illustrations, examples, and programs, and accurately explained all the technical aspects of the Difference Engine.

Considered to be the world's first programmer, Countess Lovelace, believing that Babbage's coded instruction cards were the framework for machine control, wrote actual programs for the machine. She recognized and documented the importance of two of the machine's features now standard to modern computers: the program **loop** and **conditional branching** (now known as **IF-THEN statements**). The Countess also pointed out that the machine could manipulate *words* as easily as *numbers*, thus foreseeing information processing.

The mechanical aspects of Babbage's analytical engine are considered archaic, and Ada Lovelace's programs are of little use to modern computer experts. Although they were trapped in the wrong century, their combined work reflects, with astonishing accuracy, the history and perhaps even the future of computer technology.

The nation has chosen to acknowledge the contributions of this unique individual by naming the programming language **ADA** in her honor.

Using his tabulator, Hollerith was able to complete the census count in only two years. In tallying the 62,622,250 people who lived in America at the time, Hollerith's machines counted approximately 2 billion punched holes. Hollerith's success paved the way for further research and development. A new class of computing devices emerged—**analog computers.** These calculating devices used electrical voltages to represent physical quantities; they functioned by establishing an analogy between a physical quantity and a voltage level (see Fig. 1-10). They were extremely fast but not sufficiently versatile, exact, or dependable.

FIGURE 1-10
An early analog computing device of the type used in the 1930s and 1940s.

IBM—THE BIRTH OF A GIANT

In 1941, under the leadership of *Thomas Watson Sr.*, a 67-year-old cash-register salesperson, the company grew into a multimillion-dollar concern that manufactured typewriters, desk calculators, and tabulating machines of the type devised by Herman Hollerith. With signs and slogans he exhorted his employees to "THINK," and he insisted that everyone wear neatly ironed shirts and ties.

An employee of IBM, *Howard Aiken*, frustrated by the enormous number of calculations required for his doctoral dissertation, wanted to build the kind of general-purpose programmable computer that Charles Babbage had envisioned. Babbage's original description of his analytical engine was all the guide Aiken needed. "If Babbage had lived 75 years later," said Aiken, "I would have been out of a job." In 1943, the largest electro-mechanical calculator, dubbed the **Mark 1**, was switched on. Relays served as the on-off switching devices, punched tape supplied the instructions, and the data was fed on IBM punched cards. It was an incredible 51 feet long and 8 feet high. The Mark 1 contained more than 750,000 parts strung together with 500 miles of wire. Parts of the system were on different floors, so users had to scurry up and down a flight of stairs, setting switches by hand in one place, and loading paper tape in another.

Most Famous Artificial Human Joseph Golem was created in 1580 by the high rabbi of Prague, Judah ben Loew. Golem was molded out of clay taken from the Moldau River and given life through prayer, incantation, and the inscription of the holy name on his forehead. As the story goes, only the rabbi was able to order Golem about, but even so, Golem eventually turned on his master and had to be destroyed.

Oddly enough, three of the greatest names in modern computer design and artificial intelligence trace their ancestry back to Rabbi Loew: John von Neumann, Marvin Minsky, and Norbert Weiner. Believe it or not!

In the early 1940s, the first electronic computers, the **ABC** (Atanasoff Berry Computer) and the **ENIAC** (Electronic Numerator, Integrator, Analyzer, and Computer) were built. The ABC, built by Atanasoff and Berry, was the first computer to calculate using vacuum tubes. It saw limited use. The ENIAC, built by Eckert and Mauchly, was a wartime special-purpose computer that was used extensively. Several years later, in 1949, at Cambridge, the first general-purpose electronic computer operating under the control of a stored program, the **EDSAC** (Electronic Delay Storage Automatic Computer), was completed. A **stored program** is a set of instructions stored internally that guide the computer, step by step, through a process.

While the EDSAC was being developed at Cambridge, John von Neumann, an originator of the stored-program concept, was developing the **IAS** (Institute for Advanced Study) computer at Princeton University (see Fig. 1-11). This machine was the embodiment of John von Neumann's ideas on computer design. Most computers built since that time have been "von Neumann" machines.

About the same time, a group of MIT scientists headed by Ken Olsen were developing the **Whirlwind** computer (see Fig. 1-12), more than twenty times faster than the ENIAC. Both the IAS and Whirlwind computers introduced computational innovations of astronomical proportions.

Until early 1951, computers were not available commercially. However, in 1951, the Sperry Rand Corporation built the **UNIVAC I** (Universal Automatic Computer). The UNIVAC I went into operation for the Bureau of Census, thus becoming the first commercially available computer. The first computer installation designed to handle business applications was set up in 1954 at General Electric Park, Louisville, Kentucky. In recognition of these events as the true advent of the computer age, the UNIVAC I is now on display in the Smithsonian Institution in Washington, D.C.

The race was on. Computers were becoming smaller, faster, and more powerful every day, and they were being applied to more and varied tasks. In 1956, MIT introduced its compact **TX-0** transistorized computer system. A few short years later, in 1960, the first **integrated circuit** was produced by

FIGURE 1-11
The Institute for Advanced Study (IAS) computer developed by von Neumann was the world's first stored-program parallel-processor computer. Instead of processing one binary digit at a time as other machines did, the IAS processed a word (a fixed number of binary digits) at one time. The IAS computer was retired in 1960 and put on display at the Smithsonian Institution in Washington, DC. Shown here is the processor of the IAS computer. The 20 cylinders along the bottom are storage tubes, each capable of storing 1,024 binary digits.

FIGURE 1-12
Around 1950, the Whirlwind computer was developed at MIT by Ken Olsen and others. It was the first computer to use magnetic core memory and is considered by some to be the world's first minicomputer. Whereas today's minis are about the size of a refrigerator, the Whirlwind was so huge that it filled a two-story building. Because the Whirlwind could calculate numbers in groups producing answers virtually immediately, it was considered the first example of real-time computing. It was also the first computer to be given "practical" jobs such as tracking missiles and assisting aircraft to land. Ken Olsen's work with the Whirlwind eventually led him to found DEC—Digital Equipment Corporation. Shown here are the Whirlwind computer's memory and magnetic drum storage units.

VON NEUMANN MACHINES

In 1946, John von Neumann, together with Arthur Burks and Herman Goldstein, presented the paper *Preliminary Discussion of the Logical Design of an Electronic Computing Instrument*. In this paper, von Neumann set forth, in detail, the logical design of the computer, the concept of instruction modification, and the details of the computer's electronic circuitry. The concepts set forth in this paper are employed in the design of most modern computers.

"Inasmuch as the completed device will be a general-purpose computing machine it should contain main organs relating to arithmetic, memory-storage, control and connection with the human operator. It is intended that the machine be fully automatic in character, i.e., independent of the human operator after the computation starts.

"It is evident that the machine must be capable of storing in some manner not only the digital information needed in a given computation . . . but also instructions which govern the actual routine to be performed on the numerical data. . . . [This is the basic idea of the stored program. The paper continues:]

"For an all-purpose machine it must be possible to instruct the device to carry out any computation that can be formulated in numerical terms. Hence there must be some organ capable of storing these program orders. [This is the memory unit.] There must, moreover, be a unit which can understand these instructions and order their execution.

"Conceptually we have discussed above two different forms of memory: storage of numbers and storage of orders. If, however, the orders to the machine are reduced to a numerical code and if the machine can in some fashion distinguish a number from an order, the memory organ can be used to store both numbers and orders. In other words, the machine should be able to store instructions and data in the same memory unit.

"If the memory for orders is merely a storage organ there must exist an organ which can automatically execute the orders stored in memory. We shall call this organ the Control.

"Inasmuch as the device is to be a computing machine, there must be an arithmetic organ in it which can perform certain of the elementary arithmetic operations. There will be, therefore, a unit capable of adding, subtracting, multiplying and dividing. It will be seen that it can also perform additional operations that occur quite frequently.

"The operations that the machine will view as elementary are clearly those which are wired into the machine. To illustrate, the operation of multiplication could be eliminated from the device as an elementary process if one were willing to view it as a properly ordered series of additions. Similar remarks apply to division. In general, the inner economy of the arithmetic unit is determined by a compromise between the desire for speed of operation—a nonelementary operation will generally take a long time to perform since it is constituted of a series of orders given by the control—and the desire for simplicity, or cheapness, of the machine.

"Lastly, there must exist devices, the input and output organ, whereby the human operator, and the machine can communicate with each other. . . [for example, a punched card reader or punch, a printer, or display device].

"In a discussion of the arithmetic organs of a computing machine one is naturally led to a consideration of the number system to be adopted. In spite of the long-standing tradition of building digital machines in the decimal system, we must feel strongly in favor of the binary system for our device. [Here is the proposal for the binary system of data representation.] Our fundamental unit of memory is naturally adapted to the binary system. . . . On magnetic wires or tapes and in acoustic delay line memories one is also content to recognize the presence or absence of a pulse or of a pulse train, or of the [algebraic] sign of a pulse . . . if one contemplates using the decimal system, one is forced into the binary coding of the decimal system—each decimal digit being represented by at least a tetrad [four] of binary digits. Thus an accuracy of ten decimal digits requires at least 40 binary digits. In a true binary representation of numbers, however, about 33 digits suffice to achieve a precision of 10^{10}. The use of the binary system is therefore somewhat more economical of equipment than is the decimal. . . . An important part of the machine is not arithmetical, but logical in nature. Now logic, being a yes–no system, is fundamentally binary. Therefore a binary arrangement of the arithmetic organs contributes very significantly towards producing a more homogenous machine, which can be better integrated and is more efficient.

"The one disadvantage of the binary system from the human point of view is the conversion problem. Since, however, it is completely known how to convert numbers from one base to another and since this conversion can be effected solely by the use of the usual arithmetic processes there is no reason why the computer itself cannot carry out this conversion."

THE FIRST INTEGRATED CIRCUIT

When *Jack Kilby*, a six-foot-six-inch Kansan, joined Texas Instruments, the company had already developed the first successful **silicon transistor** four years before. In 1958 Texas Instruments and Jack Kilby turned their attention toward a miniaturization scheme for the U.S. Army. The idea was to print electronic components on tiny ceramic wafers and then wire them together in a stack for a circuit. Kilby felt the plan was too complicated. While everyone else in the lab was on a two-week vacation, Kilby, knowing that resistors and the charge-holding components called capacitors could be made from the same semiconductor material as transistors, came to realize that these components could all be placed on the same piece of material—integrated on a single slice of semiconductor. The result was the world's first **integrated circuit,** or **IC.**

It was a thin wafer of germanium only two-fifths of an inch long. Tiny wires, which linked the components to one another and to the power supply, were simply soldered on, and the whole thing was held together by wax. One year later, Texas Instruments built for

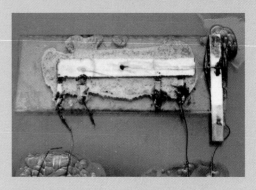

FIGURE 1-13
The first integrated circuit, produced by Jack Kilby of Texas Instruments.

the Air Force a computer that used 587 ICs; it occupied only 6.3 cubic inches, only 1/50 the space occupied by the machine it replaced! Soon afterward, as the size of each component on a circuit got smaller, ICs were soon nicknamed **chips.**

Jack Kilby of Texas Instruments (see Fig. 1-13), and the **DEC PDP-1** was being used with the first video game, "Space War" (see Fig. 1-14). In the mid-1960s, minicomputers began appearing (see Fig. 1-15), as did a forerunner of today's supercomputers—the **CDC 6600,** designed by Seymour Cray (see Fig. 1-16).

FIGURE 1-14
The first video game, "Space War," was programmed and played on the PDP-1.

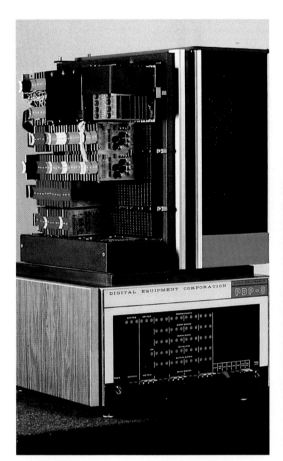

FIGURE 1-15
PDP-8, the first true minicomputer.

FIGURE 1-16
CDC 6600: console and processing unit designed by Seymour Cray in the mid-1960s.

Computer Generations

In the two decades after 1954, thousands of computers were put into operation, and today literally millions of computers are in use. Computer developments over the years have resulted in machines with greatly increased speeds, storage or memory, and overall computing power. These developments were so far-reaching and numerous that they have been categorized by generations. Each generation is initiated by significant advances in **computer hardware**—the equipment in a computer system—or **computer software**—the programs, or step-by-step instructions that run the machines.

First Generation (1942–1959)

"LIKE IT?IT'S MY NEW HOME COMPUTER..."

Early first-generation computers utilized **vacuum tubes** in their circuitry and for the storage of data and instructions. However, the vacuum tube was bulky, caused tremendous heat problems, and was never a completely reliable electronic device; it caused a great number of breakdowns and inefficient operations. Magnetic cores began to replace the vacuum tube as the principal memory device in these early machines (Fig. 1-17). Small, doughnut-shaped cores were strung on wires within the computer. Programming was principally done in **machine language**—machine operations expressed as combinations of the binary digits 0 and 1. The **bit,** or **b**inary dig**it,** will be fully described in detail later, but for now, you should know that it is the computer's way of representing data.

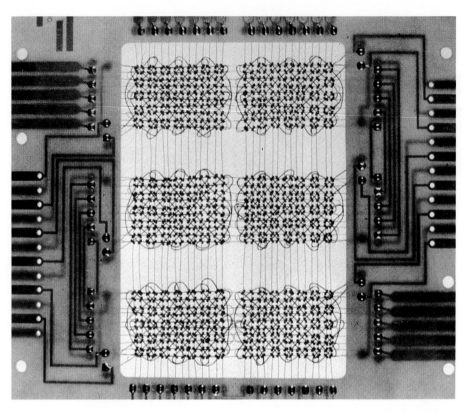

FIGURE 1-17
A magnetic core plane containing many small iron rings called "cores" strung together. Six separate cores were required to store one character of data. The core was first used in the Whirlwind computer in 1953.

Second Generation (1959–1965)

The second generation of computers saw the replacement of the vacuum tube in computer circuits with the transistor (Fig. 1-18). A **transistor** can be thought of as a switch, such as a light switch, but with no moving parts. Because of the speed with which the transistor can operate and its small size, computers were developed that were able to perform a single operation in **microseconds** (millionths of a second) and were capable of storing tens of thousands of characters.

Computer manufacturers began producing business-oriented computers with more efficient storage and faster input and output capabilities. Second-generation computers were extremely reliable, compact in size, and virtually free of heat problems.

Programs were written using both machine and **symbolic language.** Symbolic language utilized symbolic names or representations for computer commands and allowed the use of symbolic names for items of data.

Third Generation (1965–1970)

Third-generation computers were characterized by microminiaturized integrated circuits with components so small that in many cases they were hardly visible

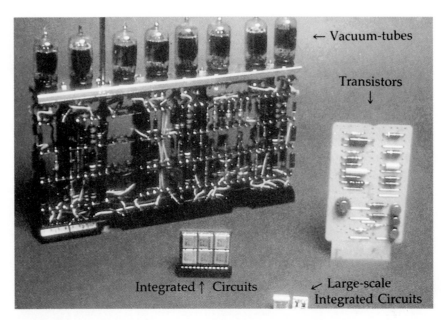

FIGURE 1-18
Comparison of components used in the first three computer generations.

to the naked eye. In addition to the actual components used in their construction, third-generation computers were characterized by increased input/output, storage, and processing capabilities.

Input/output devices were introduced that could communicate with computers over great distances via ordinary telephone lines or special communication lines, could scan a page and input the "observed" information directly into the computer, could display pictures on a television-like screen, could make musical sounds, and could even accept limited voice input and respond in kind.

Storage capabilities were increased to the point where millions of characters could be stored and randomly accessed by a computer in fractions of a second. With regard to processing speeds, third-generation computers could process instructions in **nanoseconds** (billionths of a second). In addition, computers were able to process several programs or sets of instructions concurrently.

Programmers were able to make use of high-level **problem-** and **procedure-oriented languages** that closely resembled the form of expression used by people (simple English, mathematical equations, and the like).

Fourth Generation (1970–   )

The fourth generation was responsible for still greater input, output, storage, and processing capabilities. In the fourth generation of computers monolithic storage devices were introduced (the components and surface that supports them utilize the same material, generally silicon; see Fig. 1-19), as well as improved and further miniaturized integrated logic circuits (Fig. 1-20), and an actual laser memory was constructed for the National Aeronautics and Space Administration. Predictions have been made that with laser storage we will soon be able to store more than 50 billion characters in the space occupied by

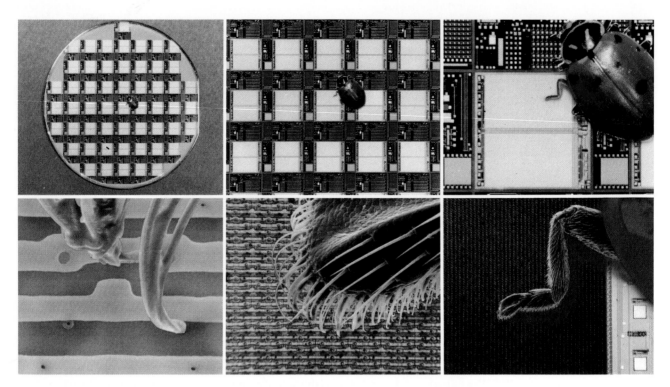

FIGURE 1-19
Various magnifications of a ladybug atop a fourth-generation monolithic storage circuit.

FIGURE 1-20
Integrated logic circuit.

a postage stamp. Concerning the potential of the laser, John M. Carrol wrote in *Theory of the Laser*, "The beam of the laser has the ability to carry all the conversations going on at one time on the planet Earth."

In the early 1970s, Burroughs, and later IBM, introduced the concept of **virtual storage** into their 5000 and 370 series of computers. Machines previously limited to a maximum internal storage capability of approximately 1 million characters now possessed a virtual storage capability in billions and trillions of characters. Thus, with this capability a machine could execute a program many times the size of the machine's actual memory capacity. We will investigate this concept in greater detail in Chapter 5.

More recently, the **compact disk (CD)** promises to become the data storage medium of choice. A compact disk read-only memory **(CD ROM)** is encoded

FIGURE 1-21
CD ROM (Compact Disk Read-Only
Memory) storage unit.

with a series of on and off bits (see Fig. 1-21). Bits are placed on the disk's aluminum surface as tiny pits at varying depths. The average CD can store an impressive 4,800 million bits or 600 million characters of data. This is approximately a quarter of a million pages of text or approximately 1000 textbooks—all on a $3\frac{1}{2}$-inch disk!

Perhaps the most significant advances have occurred with respect to **software,** the programs that are available with these computers. As a result of these changes, access to substantial computer power, previously only affordable by very large business concerns, is now economically feasible for the small business.

Fifth Generation (?)

Many believe that the fifth generation of computers is even now on the horizon. Fifth-generation computers will be unlike any computer we know today. They will be capable of reasoning, learning, making inferences, and otherwise behaving in ways usually considered the exclusive province of humans. These machines will be equipped with massive primary-storage capabilities and extremely fast processing speeds. Software will proliferate and get much cheaper. Hardware will continue to shrink in size while internal memory will increase dramatically. The vocabulary within computers will increase—"talking machines" will be heard across the globe. Voice-recognition, the ability for a machine to understand and obey spoken English, will also advance. Industrial and personal robots will roll and walk into our lives. Expert systems programs will place the knowledge of experts and consultants (such as doctors, lawyers, teachers) at our disposal. Huge computers will be linked in parallel offering computing power of an inconceivable magnitude.

IMPACT OF AUTOMATION

The computer revolution is, for all practical purposes, a second Industrial Revolution. And, as in the case of the Industrial Revolution, the computer revolution has opened many new careers for millions of people, making the automated processing of data into a big business. In 1980, for example, over 5 million people were employed in occupations resulting from and directly related to

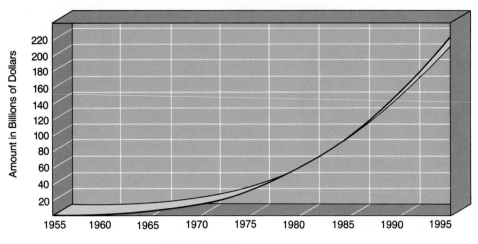

FIGURE 1-22
Value of computing equipment in use.

the computer. From an origin traceable to the abstractions of a few creative scientists (Charles Babbage, Herman Hollerith, and John von Neumann, for example), the concepts underlying electronic computers have grown into a multibillion dollar industry. In terms of capital investment alone, this represents an increase from $30 million in 1950 to over $150 billion in 1990 (Fig. 1-22). It

FIGURE 1-23
Computer equipment sold by type of application.

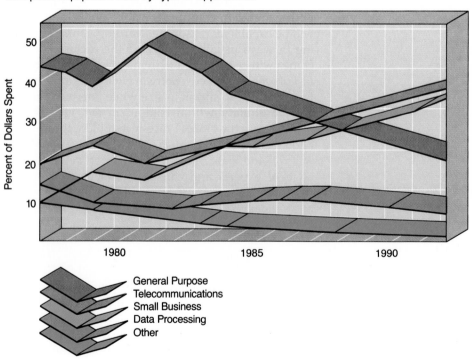

FIGURE 1-24
Cray supercomputer.

is expected that by 1995, over $20 billion will be expended each year for various types of computing equipment (Fig. 1-23).

These figures include computing systems ranging in price from a few hundred dollars for a small personal computer to over $10 million for a powerful Cray supercomputer. The Cray supercomputer is a six-foot-high, circular structure consisting of brightly colored panels and polished steel supports (Fig. 1-24). Behind this futuristic facade are dense circuits capable of carrying out over 100 million instructions per second (MIPS). To put this in perspective, these computers can perform literally 20 million calculations in the time it takes to blink an eye. Supercomputers such as these generally are applied only to the solution of very complex and sophisticated scientific problems.

There isn't an industry, a business, or home in North America that hasn't felt the impact of the computer. Computers are used to calculate gas and electric bills; to control electronic equipment during surgical operations; to control automobile traffic; to control the takeoff and landing of commercial aircraft, rockets, and space vehicles; to help teach children arithmetic; to control intricate or dangerous chemical processes; to predict enemy troop movements during a time of war; and to control the financial and management activities of business, to name but a few uses.

WHAT IS DATA PROCESSING?

Let us begin our analysis of data processing by answering the question: What is data processing? "Data" is the plural of "datum," which means "fact." **Data processing,** then, is simply the manipulating and using of facts to produce information. Accounts kept by the ancient Egyptians are examples of data processing. Much more recently, however, business and industry rely almost exclusively on computers to process their data (Fig. 1-25). It is for this reason that the term "data processing" and the concept of processing data by computer have become synonymous.

FIGURE 1-25
An automated airline reservation system.

AREAS OF COMPUTER APPLICATION

A computer is a very useful tool, but it is certainly not the answer to all of our problems. There are certain types of problems that a computer is equipped to handle more economically and efficiently than other devices or people.

Computers Do It Better

Computers are superfast. Because they can perform tasks a lot more quickly than we can, we spend less time waiting. This frees us up to do other things. Computers are capable of performing boring or dangerous tasks (and without complaining). Computers, believe it or not, are extremely dependable. When something goes wrong and service is disrupted or there is an error in your paycheck, statistics reveal that usually it is not the computer's fault; the problem generally lies elsewhere. "Sorry, the computer is down" usually translates into a human error, not a mechanical malfunction.

It should be apparent that computers are ideally suited to handle such primary business functions as payroll, personnel, accounting, and inventory, as each of these functions is justifiable, definable, repetitive, and deals with a large volume of data. New applications of computers are continually being discovered. If we were to attempt to produce a list of all the application areas to which computers are presently being applied, it would be obsolete before it could be completed. Some general areas that extensively employ computers are the following:

Unit 1   An Introduction to Data Processing

1. **General business:** accounts receivable, accounts payable, inventory, personnel accounting, payroll
2. **Banking:** account reconciliation, installment loan accounting, interest calculations, demand deposit accounting, trust services
3. **Education:** attendance and grade-card reports, computer-assisted instruction, research analysis, registration
4. **Government:** income tax return verification, motor vehicle registration, budget analysis, tax billing, property rolls.

Other areas of application include law enforcement, military affairs, sports, transportation, real estate, business forecasting, medicine, broadcasting, commercial arcade games, publishing, and personal use in the home, to mention but a few. The uses of computers are indeed boundless, and present applications are only a sample of things to come (Figs. 1-26 to 1-32).

FIGURE 1-26
The computer in the small business.

FIGURE 1-27
At Mt. Zion Hospital Hewlett Packard patient-monitoring neonatal equipment measures an infant's heart and lung functions.

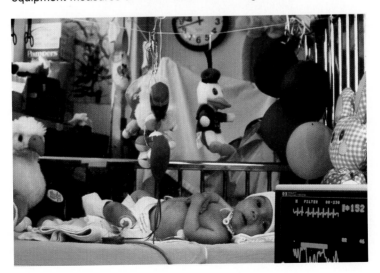

FIGURE 1-28
The computer in the laboratory.

FIGURE 1-29
The computer is used in the analysis of
complex electrical circuits.

FIGURE 1-30
Burroughs' family of universal workstations
help support and service
office personnel.

24

FIGURE 1-31
The computer in education.

FIGURE 1-32
The computer in the home.

COMPUTERS IN SOCIETY

Computers—Not For Lovers?
Computers will never make us better lovers. The more people work in the structured environment of the computer, the more this environment begins to rub off. An attempt to apply the computer's exactness to social relationships is an open invitation to rigid human relationships. The computer does exactly what it is told to do, while human relations are more often based on inference, context, silent understanding, and the fresh breath of the unexpected.

The initial applications of computers were in the areas of government research and in the solution of scientific and engineering problems. Subsequently, as a result of increased speeds and capabilities, greatly reduced costs, and commercial availability, computers were also applied to the solution of business problems. Today, either directly or indirectly, the computer affects the lives of every one of us (see Fig. 1-33). It benefits us by monitoring and controlling air and water pollution, improving weather forecasting, facilitating more effective urban planning and more efficient law enforcement techniques, making possible electronic advances that have been applied to improving household appliances, providing improved medical techniques for analysis and diagnosis, and on and on.

The 1970s brought into being the age of the micro, or personal, computer. For less than $1,000, a small but powerful computer system can be purchased for your home. Programs are readily available for these systems to do everything from balancing a checkbook to challenging the most capable user in a game of chess. If you can't find a program for what you want, you can write your own using the easily learned language BASIC. For the ardent fan, optional devices such as a voice synthesizer are available to allow the computer to talk to its user.

For those having only an occasional need or desire to use a computer, companies such as THE SOURCE (Source Telecomputing Association, McLean,

FINAL NOTICE!
I am your computer. No one but me knows you have not made payment. If I have not processed a payment in ten days, I will have to tell a human. Thank you very much.

FIGURE 1-33
A card typical of what people began to see in the late 1970s.

Virginia), PRODIGY (Interactive Personal Service by Sears and IBM), and CompuServe (Consumer Information Service, Columbus, Ohio) offer access to their computer systems for a few dollars per hour in intervals of one minute, including the cost of the call from anywhere in the continental United States. In addition, the user is given access to thousands of programs offering complete business packages, computer games, stock market quotations, professional sports information, movie guides, and more. All the user requires is a device to communicate commands and data to the desired computer system via telephone and a means to record or display the computer's responses.

PROBLEMS IN THE COMPUTER AGE

Computer Crime

Increased use of and dependence on computers has also brought about many new problems. Complete dependence on computers can lead to serious and often insurmountable problems when they malfunction or fail or when unauthorized parties gain access to data stored in the company's computer system. **Computer crime,** the unauthorized or misuse of stored data, is often difficult to detect and equally difficult to prosecute, as legislation is slow in coming. According to FBI figures, less than 10 percent of computer crimes are detected, and of those only a small percentage are reported. Compared to noncomputer white-collar crimes, the losses per occurrence are high; they range from $200 to almost $2 billion, with the average of $450,000, about 5 times higher than other white-collar crime.

Not all computer crimes are for profit. Malicious or deliberate damage to the data in a computer system can be just as costly and often harder to detect. One of the most serious types of malicious damage is the computer **virus,** a program designed to copy itself into other software and spread from computer to computer.

26

COMPUTER VIRUSES CAN MAKE YOUR COMPUTER SICK

Computer viruses are seemingly innocuous programs disguised as normal software. Their sole purpose, however, is to destroy programs and data on the computers of unsuspecting users.

Virus programs are commonly downloaded from computer bulletin boards where users can exchange public domain software. Unsuspecting users select the virus program, advertised on the bulletin board as a useful program or utility. When the program is executed, it proceeds to destroy any available information.

Virus programs can ruin all of the programs and data stored on a microcomputer's hard disk in less time than it takes to bring up the system. All of the computers on a large network can be "infected" in less than a minute and a multiuser system can be crashed in less than five minutes. Operators of computer bulletin boards have become so outraged by virus programs that they are warning board users by circulating a list of the disk-killing programs that have been identified. Computing center officials on college campuses and large businesses and organizations are warning users of the potential threat from virus programs.

Viruses come in two varieties. The simplest variety is exemplified by Egabtr. Claiming to be an innocent program to enhance screen graphics, it contained disk-destroying code. Such programs are fast and deadly. They immediately destroy information stored on disks. Software viruses can be even more treacherous. Such programs stay hidden for weeks or months, infecting hard disks and floppies alike. Then at a predetermined moment all contaminated software is disabled. Barry M. Simon, a professor at California Institute of Technology, told *The Chronicle of Higher Education* that "People who write viruses like to brag. They usually leave some clue that they've done something." Unfortunately, when their messages appear it is usually too late. Egabtr displays the words "Arf, Arf! Gotcha!" after it has destroyed disk information.

Computer pranksters have existed on college campuses for years. Unfortunately, the threat is no longer limited in scope. Viruses can affect computers everywhere. Any user that connects to a bulletin board, is part of a computer network, or shares disks with others is vulnerable. Some have suggested "computer celibacy" as a solution. However, such a solution eliminates one of the major advantages of modern computers: sharing of ideas and information. A less radical approach seems best. Program disks should be write-protected and backups should always be made. All programs received from acquaintances, bulletin boards, or networks should be tried with hard drives turned off and backup copies of the operating system available. Be vigilant. Programs making incredible claims may turn out to be quite different.

Solutions other than celibacy exist. A number of programs, including Data Physician, C4Bomb, and Disk Defender, have been designed to pretest software for viruses. However, no program can guarantee protection against all viruses. Vigilance and backup copies of software and critical data are the only guarantees against computer viruses.

The Chronicle of Higher Education. Reprinted with permission. C. J. H.

Computer Overuse

A growing concern observed by more than one astute observer is that computers, rather than saving time and increasing productivity, may, if they are not used wisely, actually waste time and *reduce* productivity. In their attempt to get things "just right," some computer users are guilty of **computer overuse.** For example, letters that were once handwritten now pass through endless reworkings using a word processing program; often, the changes are petty or completely unnecessary. Instead of creating the much hoped-for "paperless office," the computer can, if it is used without discretion, create mountains of paper.

Some computer programs have the ability to aid the user in decision-making. A manager may wisely turn to such a program to get assistance in deciding whether or not to invest in a certain venture to determine how profits will be affected by an increase in certain costs. Unfortunately, however, some are asking the computer to decide trivial issues that should never be given to a machine to decide or validate. One result of this abandonment of responsibility

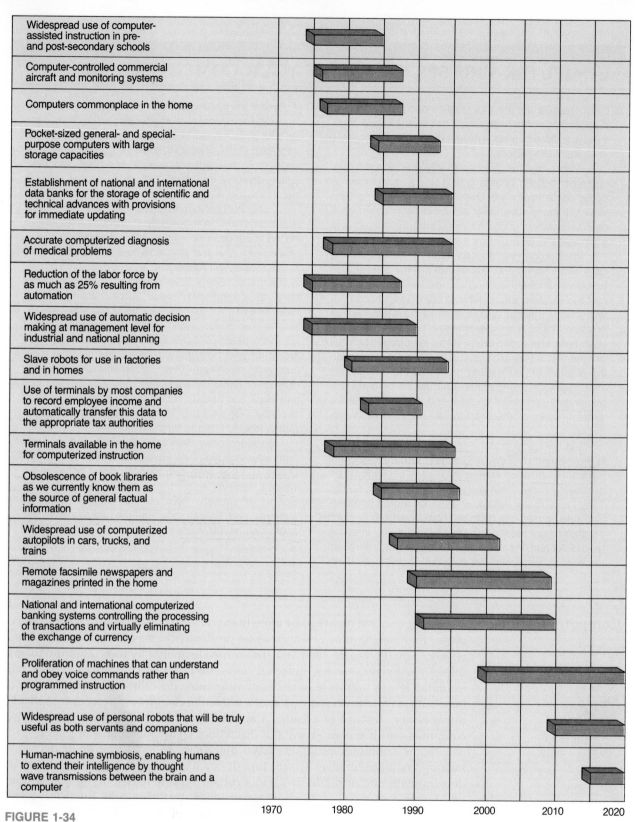

FIGURE 1-34
Computer applications by the year 2020.

28

could be the weakening or destruction of an individual's ability to make decisions. If overdependence upon the computer spreads, some argue, the problem could lead to a kind of universal "mental anemia."

Difficulty

"WELL,IT WILL REALLY SIMPLIFY BALANCING YOUR CHECKBOOK. FIRST, YOU WRITE DOWN THE AMOUNT...WHEN YOU GET HOME, SIMPLY INSERT THE PROPER PROGRAM, FEED IN YOUR PERSONAL ACCESS CODE, CALL UP YOUR BILLS PAYABLE REGISTER, RUN A SEARCH FOR YOUR LAST BALANCE........"

One of the biggest complaints voiced among microcomputer users is that computers are woefully difficult to use. Business and professional users don't have time to solve puzzles. They want a business tool that is dependable and easy to use. The simple and efficient typewriter or the easy-to-use adding machine are being looked at with renewed affection. Personal computers, by comparison, often seem to be obstinate and impersonal, requiring many hours of experimenting. Often, the result is frustration and lost productivity. A top-level manager doesn't have time to play with software that doesn't do what it's supposed to do, or tinker with a printer that doesn't work. If computer service and support is not prompt and effective (and for too many, it isn't), the old method of typing the weekly report is used. If the problem continues, the computer soon becomes an ornament.

A related problem involves the **documentation** that accompanies a computer system or software package (commercially available programs intended to perform a specified task). These trusted manuals, which are supposed to explain how to use the computer hardware or software and guide the user when problems arise, are notoriously inept. For many, they are simply incomprehensible; much of the documentation does not spell out in "plain English" what a computer novice needs to know.

Impersonalization and Invasion of Privacy

The practical advantages of using numbers or codes to identify people in computers has led to impersonalization whereby people are reduced to mere statistics. Many individuals are deeply concerned about their lack of control over information stored about themselves and the potential uses of this information by someone who may have access to the computer.

These are but a few of the problems that have accompanied the unprecedented growth in the number and diversity of computer applications. In light of the ever-increasing growth predicted by experts (see Fig. 1-34), it is imperative that we address ourselves to these problems now. We must formulate clearly defined policies concerning the application of computers and carefully delineate who may use the data contained in centralized data banks and for what purposes.

Only time will tell whether the use of the computer can be controlled to reduce, if not eliminate, the multitude of problems that have arisen and will continue to arise as new computer applications are discovered.

SUMMARY AND GLOSSARY OF KEY TERMS

- **Computerphobia** or **cyberphobia** is the fear of computers and is spreading as computer use increases.
- **Computer literacy** would enable a person to: have a basic *understanding* of what a computer can do, *use* a computer on a personal or professional level, *interact* with a computer using a prepackaged business program, and have some idea of the social *implications* caused by computer technology.

- Certain computers served as landmarks in the meteoric rise of the computer. Among them were the **ABC**, the first device to calculate using vacuum tubes; the **ENIAC**, the first special-purpose all-electronic computer; the **EDSAC**, the first general-purpose computer controlled by internally stored instructions **(stored-program);** and the **UNIVAC I,** the first commercially available computer.

- Because of the multitude of computers put into operation since the introduction of the ABC, computers have been categorized by **generations** according to **computer hardware** (equipment) and **computer software** (programs or sets of step-by-step instructions) employed.
- The **first generation** employed **vacuum tubes** and **magnetic cores** and was programmed in a language referred to as **machine language.**
- The **second generation** employed electronic switches referred to as **transistors** and could be programmed in machine language and **symbolic language**—a language utilizing symbolic representations for instructions and quantities of data.
- The **third generation,** utilizing **microminiaturized integrated circuits,** had increased input/output, storage, and processing capabilities. Input/output devices were capable of communicating with computers over great distances, could accept limited voice input, and could respond in kind. Storage capacities increased to millions of characters; processing speeds increased to nanoseconds.
- The **fourth generation** saw the introduction of further miniaturized **monolithic integrated circuits** and the introduction of **compact-disk (CD) read-only memory (ROM).** With the introduction of **virtual storage,** programs many times the size of a machine's memory could be executed.
- Experts tell us that the **fifth generation** is just around the corner. In the early 1990s we should start seeing computers capable of reasoning, learning, making inferences, and otherwise behaving in ways usually considered the exclusive province of humans.
- The computer revolution, like the Industrial Revolution, came about as a result of a need for increased productivity and brought with it substantial changes in society.
- The introduction of the computer has benefited mankind immeasurably, but not without some drawbacks. Some people resent the impersonalization and invasion of privacy that accompanied the computer revolution. Others find computers too difficult to use and go to extremes to avoid using them, and still others find them so powerful and easy to use that they tend to use them for everything—**computer overuse.** Everyone must guard against the criminal who would use computer technology for illicit gain or malicious purposes.

EXERCISES

True/False

_F_ 1. Commercial computers were not available before the 1960s.

_T_ 2. Third-generation computers supported voice response.

_F_ 3. Computer literate means that a person can read a message printed by a computer.

_T_ 4. Increased use of and dependence on the computer has brought about many new problems.

_T_ 5. Computers have provided a whole new way for people to break the law.

_F_ 6. The first all-electronic computer was the IAS. *ABC first*

_T_ 7. Every business has data to process.

_F_ 8. The laser is the most commonly used storage device in third-generation computers. *Fourth*

_T_ 9. The computer is part of the information revolution.

_F_ 10. The Cray is typical of the computer systems used by business concerns.

_T_ 11. The first commercially available computer was the UNIVAC I.

_T_ 12. Computer overuse is a serious problem that has accompanied the widespread use of computers.

_F_ 13. Video games were first played in 1978.

_F_ 14. Heat problems were prevalent until the third generation of computers. *Second*

_T_ 15. Some people expect the fifth generation computers to be able to reason as humans do.

_F_ 16. High-level procedure- and problem-oriented languages did not come into being until the fourth generation.

_T_ 17. CD ROM can store great amounts of data on small metal disks.

_T_ 18. Computer crime is one of the most serious problems associated with the introduction of computers in business.

_T_ 19. Computer programs exist that can pretest a disk for the presence of a computer virus.

Fill-in

1. Laser and bubble memories are the key hardware change that introduced the _fourth_ generation.

2. An analog computer system utilizes electrical _voltages_ to represent physical quantities.

3. Software for first-generation computers was written in _machine language_.

4. Using a computer to reach a decision that can be reasoned easily is an example of computer _over use_ .

5. The introduction of transistors occurred in the _second_ generation of computers.

6. One of the most costly problems associated with the introduction of the computer in business is _computer crime_

Problems

Skip

1. Is there a difference between raw data and information? Explain.
2. Discuss several applications of computers in business with which you are familiar from your reading or experience.
3. Why have business concerns been forced to resort to automatic data processing?
4. What are some of the social problems that have been brought about by the introduction of the computer?
5. Briefly comment on how the misuse of computers might cause possible violations of the following constitutional rights:
   a. Fifth and Fourteenth Amendment guarantees of "due process."
   b. Fifth Amendment protection against "self-incrimination."
   c. Fourth Amendment protection against "unreasonable search."
6. List three science fiction books, movies, or television programs that show computers in use. What capabilities do these computers possess that are not possible today? Which capabilities do you believe will soon be possible? To what unusual applications are these computers put?
7. What were some of the motivating forces responsible for the development of computers?

Projects

1. Go to your school or local library and examine the available computer-related literature to determine five areas of computer application that are not described in the text.
2. Visit a local computer store or read a current computer magazine and compile a list of available microcomputers and features. Which would you buy for yourself? Why? What applications would you intend to use it for?
3. Visit one of the organizations or agencies listed below and determine where, how, and for what the computer is used.

Internal Revenue Service	Bureau of Motor Vehicles
Bank	Credit card agency
Hospital	County or community center
College or University	Off-track Betting (OTB Corporation)
Local chain store	Other approved by your instructor

CROSSWORD PUZZLE

Across

1. A computer designed by von Neumann
2. The first computer system to use magnetic cores
3. The physical components of a computer system
4. We are in the midst of an _____
5. Raw facts
6. Replaced the vacuum tube as the principal memory device in the first generation
7. The language a computer understands
8. An engine designed by Babbage to produce tables
9. The first of these was invented by Jack Kilby
10. A set of instructions stored in the memory of a computer
11. As opposed to hardware
12. To be computer _____ , one must have a knowledge of and ability to use computers
13. One of the first electronic computers
14. Replaced the vacuum tube in computer circuits in the second generation
15. Computer _____ are initiated by advancements in computer hardware or software
16. The fear of computers
17. A storage medium that required a vacuum
18. Often referred to as the father of modern-day computers
19. A class of computer system that uses voltages to measure physical quantities
20. A pioneer who developed the Census Tabulator

Down

13. Designed the Mark I at Harvard University
21. A(n) _____ disk is a data storage medium with an aluminum surface
22. The largest type of computer
23. Computer _____ is a problem of the computer age
24. Smaller than a mainframe
25. A number system suggested by von Neumann for use in computers
26. A problem that has accompanied the use of computers in business
27. A memory device that uses the polarization of light
28. _____ storage allows a machine to execute programs larger than the actual memory in the machine
29. Problem that plagued the first generation of computers
30. A type of computer small enough to fit on your desk or in your lap
31. A set of instructions to solve a problem
32. A type of language used with second-generation computers
33. Short for binary digit
34. The first commercial computer
35. Designed the analytical engine
36. Not connected to a computer
37. The computer generation that first used microminiaturized integrated circuits
38. The computer generation that used only machine language

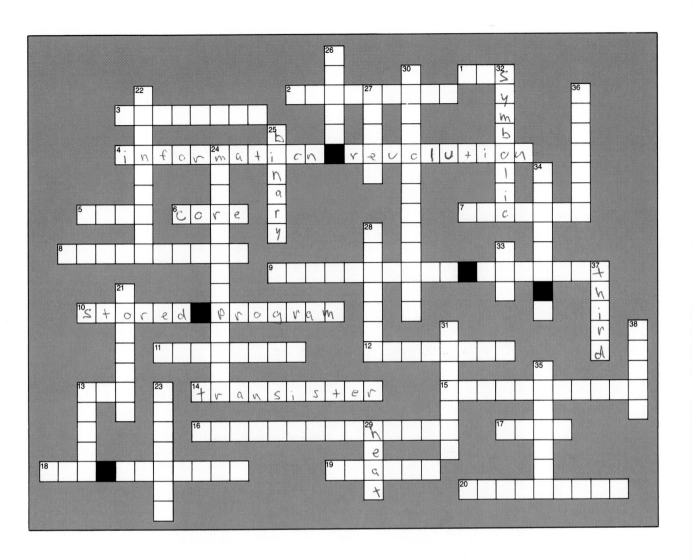

2

A COMPUTER SYSTEM
In a Nutshell

Objectives

- Define what a computer is and how it works.
- Describe and discuss the basic elements of a system designed to process data by computer.
- List and describe the nature and purpose of each of the hardware elements found in a computer installation.
- Name and discuss the most commonly employed methods for processing data by computer.
- Describe the factors that determine the classification of a computer system.
- Describe the categories into which computers are classified.
- Understand and use the key terms presented in this chapter.

oday, more than 60 percent of the work force in the United States is involved in the creation and dissemination of information. Think about it— the majority of the working people in this country either create, process, store, or transmit information. Computers have become the driving force behind the information explosion. Furthermore, the home computer has made it possible for some people to work out of their homes rather than in an office. Jobs in fields unheard of a few years ago, such as robotics, data communications, and artificial intelligence, are providing new employment opportunities every day.

Because of the widespread use and availability of computers, it is essential that future business people acquire an understanding of what computers are and how they work. This chapter will provide you with a basic understanding of what a computer system is and what it can do. We will introduce the data processing cycle, the elements of a computer system, the equipment comprising a computer system, processing methods, and the various sizes or categories of computers in use.

WHAT IS A COMPUTER?

Essentially, a computer is a machine that stores and manipulates, or **processes** data. It cannot think or reason. It can only carry out instructions given to it. A set of instructions that directs a computer's actions is called a **program** and is written by **programmers.** Obviously, different programs must be written to solve different problems. This ability to accept, store, and execute various sets of instructions or programs is what makes the computer the invaluable, all-purpose business tool that it is, and what sets it apart from the common calculator.

How Does It Work? The first step a computer takes in solving a problem is to access the desired program from a disk or other external storage medium and store it in its memory. Now the computer can begin carrying out the instructions in the program. Although the actual instructions will vary from program to program, they will generally direct the computer to perform the same basic three functions over and over again—input, processing, and output. These functions are shown in Figure 2-1 using a microcomputer, but they apply equally to larger systems. Collectively, these functions are referred to as the **data processing cycle.**

1. **Input:** input devices connected to the computer feed the computer "raw material"— facts or data to be processed
2. **Processing:** the control and storing of data, numerical comparisons, and arithmetic operations performed on the input data to produce the desired results
3. **Output:** the computer feeds the "finished product," processed data or information, to the output devices connected to it.

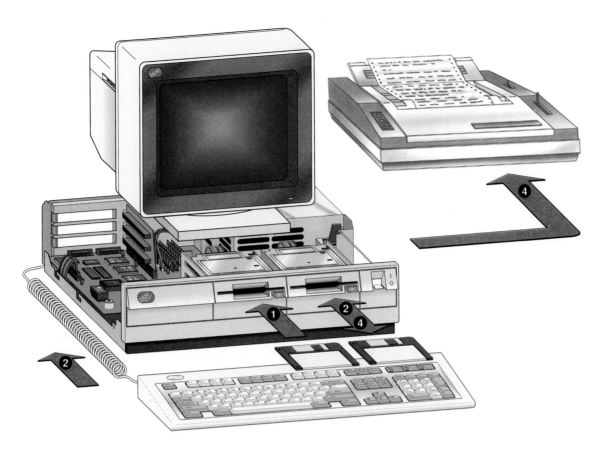

1 The computer reads a program and stores it in memory. The program instructions are carried out, causing the computer to:

2 Input data from the disk, the keyboard, or another device.

3 Process the data.

4 Output results to disk, the printer, the display screen, or another device.

FIGURE 2-1
Problem-solving with a microcomputer.

ELEMENTS OF A COMPUTER SYSTEM

A system intended to process data and solve problems must consist of more than just machines. A **computer system** must contain each of the following; hardware, software, peopleware, and procedures. Let us examine each of these briefly.

Hardware

The term **hardware** generally refers to the machines or physical equipment that performs the basic functions contained within the data processing cycle (see Fig. 2-2). In addition to the computer itself, auxiliary hardware devices are also required. These hardware components may be **offline**—detached and operating independently from the computer, or they may be **online**—directly connected to and controlled by the computer.

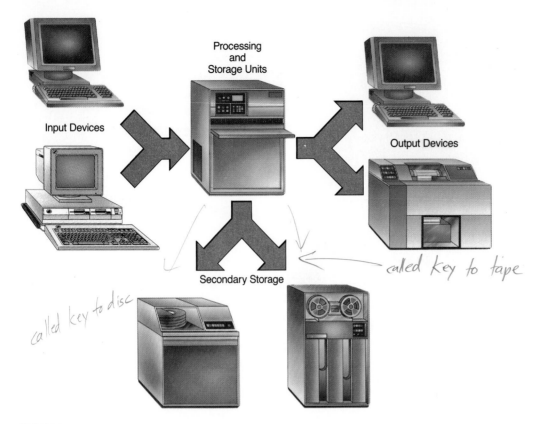

Processing and Storage Units

Input Devices

Output Devices

called key to tape

Secondary Storage

called key to disc

FIGURE 2-2
A large computer system is made up of many individual hardware components.

The particular devices required in a computer installation are determined by such factors as the size of the installation, the computer being used, and the type of data processing taking place at the installation. In general, every computer installation will contain hardware to perform the following functions:

- Data preparation and entry
- Processing
- Storage
- Input and output

Data Preparation and Entry

Computer programs and data must be in a computer-readable form before they can be input to a computer for processing. For large-volume general-purpose applications, such as payroll, budget analysis, accounts receivable, and accounts payable, the most commonly used media are magnetic tape and magnetic disk. Each of these media consists of a magnetically coated surface onto which data can be recorded, as one would record music on a home cassette tape. As with cassette tapes, computer tapes and disks can be written over once the data previously recorded on them is no longer needed.

Numerous devices are available to convert data from source documents to a computer-compatible media. Among them are the **key-to-tape** system, the **key-to-disk** system, and the **terminal.** Each of these systems, however,

"HONEY, I FINALLY HAVE THAT REPORT IN THE COMPUTER. IT TOOK FOUR HOURS AND I JUST HAVE TO PUT IT ON A DISK TO WRAP IT UP."

Unit 1   An Introduction to Data Processing

requires that the operator manually key in the data from original or **source documents.** As a result, they are each subject to all of the limitations and possible sources of error inherent in manual operations.

Therefore, it is not surprising that there is a trend toward eliminating these manual operations by creating a machine-readable form at the time the data is first recorded or by entering the data directly into a computer via a special purpose device. For example, many companies now use cash registers or other **point-of-sale** devices to transmit the data directly to the computer or record the transactions on a computer-acceptable medium while simultaneously producing a sales slip for the customer. In this way, the computer has immediate access to the data on which it must base inventory decisions. Also, in the case of an accounts receivable system, the data necessary to update a customer's account are immediately available to the computer.

For special-purpose applications, data-entry devices are available that can magnetically read data encoded using a special magnetic ink (used on personal checks), optically read special marks (used to record student answers on tests) and certain typewritten material, or "hear" and transmit the spoken word. Some of these devices are shown in Figure 2-3.

Processing

Every computer system must contain a processor unit whose primary purpose is to carry out instructions and process data. This unit is made up of millions of individual electrical components and is the control center of the entire computer system. It accepts and stores data from any of the various input devices, processes these data according to a programmer's instructions, and sends the results to a printer or other output device for recording. This unit must be capable of performing operations such as adding, subtracting, multiplying, dividing, moving data from one place in the computer to another, and comparing two quantities in a few millionths or billionths of a second. The processor unit consists of a **central processing unit (CPU)** and a **primary storage unit.**

Time Flies A nanosecond is to a second what a second is to 30 years. And a picosecond is to a second what a second is to 31,710 years.

THE CPU. The CPU of most early computer systems contained a control unit, an arithmetic/logic unit, and a primary storage unit. However, as the size and complexity of computer programs increased, so did the storage needed to support them. By the end of the third generation, the primary storage unit had grown to the point where it was no longer considered a part of the CPU but a separate unit apart from the CPU. Thus, the processor unit in today's computers contains a CPU (comprised of a control unit and an arithmetic/logic unit), and also a separate primary storage unit.

The principal purpose of the **control unit** within the CPU is to control and coordinate the activities of the computer system during the execution of a program. It doesn't actually process data; it selects, interprets, and oversees the execution of individual program instructions. It acts to control the other parts of the computer, as the central nervous system controls the muscles and other parts of the body to perform a particular activity.

The **arithmetic/logic unit,** commonly referred to as the **ALU,** performs such operations as data transfer, arithmetic, data editing, and decision making. Data transfer involves the copying of data from one location in the computer into another location in much the same manner as you might recall and transfer your telephone number from your memory onto a piece of paper for a friend.

a

b

c

d

FIGURE 2-3
Examples of data preparation and entry devices.

"THE PRICE INCLUDES AIR FARE TO JAPAN AND A SIX-WEEK COMPUTER REPAIR COURSE."

Storage

PRIMARY STORAGE. The **primary storage unit** (also known as **random access memory, RAM,** or **memory)** stores instructions and data as needed by the CPU for the program or programs currently being processed and for the overall operation of the computer system. It is basically a limited-capacity *temporary* storage area, not a permanent storage area. As soon as a program is no longer needed, its instructions and data are replaced by those of the next program.

BITS, BYTES, AND BINARY. Just *how* does a computer store and manipulate data in its main memory? Probably because humans have ten fingers, we began counting and using a decimal numbering system which uses the ten decimal digits 0 through 9. But computers don't have fingers, they use electronic circuits. Electronic circuits are either "on" or "off." It is therefore much easier and less expensive to build computers that use the **binary** number system, a system that uses only the two **binary digits** or **bits,** 0 and 1. Not only are numbers stored in memory as combinations of the bits 0 and 1, but so are letters and special characters.

Because a single bit is not sufficient to represent numbers, letters, and special characters, it has become commonplace to work with groups of eight bits. Each group of 8 bits, or **byte,** can represent one character of data—that is, a digit (7), a letter (L), or a special character (* or $). When you type a character on the keyboard, a specific bit pattern is electronically transferred to memory. The bit pattern transferred depends on the particular coding scheme used by the computer system. (A full and detailed treatment of the most common coding schemes is included in Appendix A of the text). To represent large numbers and strings of characters, most computers combine bytes to form **words.** Each word of storage is assigned a unique **address.** Microcomputers typically use word lengths of 2 bytes, or 16 bits; most mainframes and an increasing number of micros use 4 bytes, or 32 bits; and the larger "supercomputers" use word lengths of 8 bytes and larger. A few computer systems support a variable word length.

Know Computer manufacturers express the capacity of internal memory in terms of the letter **K,** or **kilobyte,** which equals approximately 1000 bytes (1K = 1024 bytes). A 256K machine would have approximately 256 kilobytes, or 256,000 bytes. Microcomputers are currently available with memories in the millions, *Know* or **megabytes** (1 megabyte = 1 million bytes). Modern supercomputers typically have billion or **gigabyte** (1 gigabyte = 1 billion bytes) memories, and the new fifth-generation supercomputers' memories are expected to be in **terabytes** (1 terabyte = 1 trillion bytes).

In most large computer systems, a **console,** consisting of a control panel and monitor, is also provided so that the computer operator can communicate with the computer system (see Fig. 2-4).

SECONDARY STORAGE. A more permanent storage area for instructions and data than available with primary storage is provided by one or more **auxiliary,** or **secondary, storage** devices (see Fig. 2-5). Any device that can do both input and output can be used to provide secondary storage. Magnetic disk devices are the most commonly used secondary storage devices. The particular

FIGURE 2-4
CPU with attached operator's consoles.

FIGURE 2-5
Computer magnetic tapes and disks.

secondary storage device used will depend on such factors as the amount of storage needed and whether the data can be accessed and processed directly without regard to sequence.

Programs and data stored on a secondary storage device are not immediately accessible to the central processing unit or to other devices in the system and hence must be routed through primary storage. Thus the processing of data contained in secondary storage first requires that these data be copied into primary storage, where they can then be processed by the CPU. For example, before the contents of an inventory record stored on disk can be updated, it must be read into primary storage. Once in memory, the record can be updated and stored back on disk. This process is shown in Figure 2-6. Table 2-1 illustrates some of the differences between primary and secondary storage.

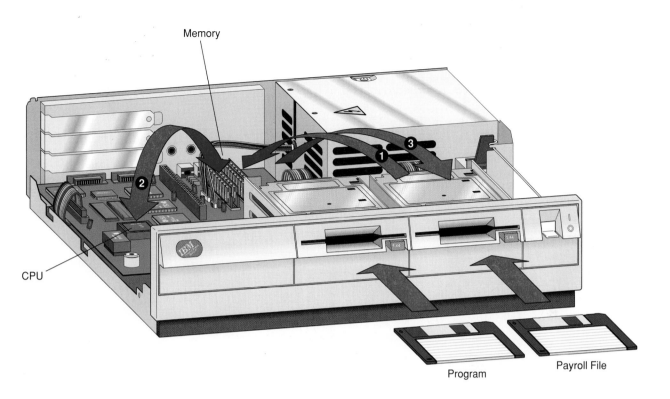

Memory

CPU

Program

Payroll File

❶ Read record from disk into memory.

❷ Update individual data items within the record using ALU.

❸ Write updated record back to disk.

FIGURE 2-6
Steps to update an employee record.

TABLE 2-1
Comparison of Primary and Secondary Storage

Floppy Drives

CHARACTERISTIC	PRIMARY STORAGE	SECONDARY STORAGE
Location with respect to the CPU	Outside of and directly accessible by CPU	Outside of and indirectly accessible by CPU
Cost *	Most expensive	Less expensive than primary storage
Capacity *	Up to several million characters	Billions of characters
Average access time *	In billionths of a second	In millionths of a second
Can data be processed directly from storage?	Yes	No, must first be moved into primary storage
Means of storing information	Microminiaturized integrated circuit, electrooptical, magnetic bubble, charged-coupled device	Magnetic disk, magnetic tape, mass storage system, optical disk

* These items will vary with manufacturers and computer systems.

Input and Output

Regardless of the type, size, color, or manufacturer of a computer, there is one thing about which we can be certain: Input devices must be available to accept recorded data and to transmit these data to the computer for processing. Some of the devices used to input instructions or data into a computer are shown in Figure 2-7.

FIGURE 2-7
Commonly used input and output devices.

a Disk Pack - inside huge hard drive

b Tape drives - good for backup

c - 3 point mouse

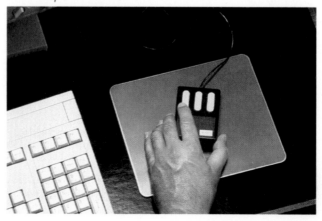

FIGURE 2-7 (*Continued*)

d

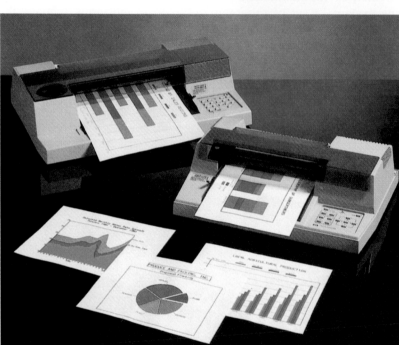

e

f

Similarly, output devices must be available to output processed data or information from the computer. Depending upon the particular device employed, data can be output from the computer onto magnetic tape, magnetic disk, or paper. Data may also be transmitted over communication networks, used to control analog devices, converted into visual or graphical displays or to microfilm images, or even converted to spoken words. The number and types of output devices that can be connected to a particular computer system are limited only by the design of the computer and the type of processing to be performed. Some commonly used output devices are shown in Figure 2-7. Note that a number of these devices can serve as both input and output devices as well as secondary storage devices.

Software

A **computer program** is a sequence of detailed instructions designed to direct a computer to perform certain functions. For a computer to input, store, make decisions, arithmetically manipulate, and output data in the correct sequence, it must have access to prewritten, stored programs for that purpose. Such programs are referred to as **software.** Every computer system must be supported by extensive software. Software is generally categorized as either systems software or applications software (see Fig. 2-8).

Systems software consists of programs designed to facilitate the use of the computer by the user. These programs, sometimes referred to as **utility programs,** perform such standard tasks as organizing and maintaining data files, translating programs written in various languages to a language acceptable to the computer, scheduling jobs through the computer, as well as aiding in other areas of general computer operations. Many of these programs are available to the user by the manufacturer of the computer system. Of all the systems software provided by the manufacturer of a computer, the most important is the **operating system**—a set of programs designed to efficiently manage the resources of the computer system. The operating system performs such functions as supervising input and output operations, communicating with the computer operator, and scheduling the computer's resources to allow for continuous operation with minimum manual intervention.

FIGURE 2-8
Computer systems of all sizes utilize systems software and applications software to support the hardware.

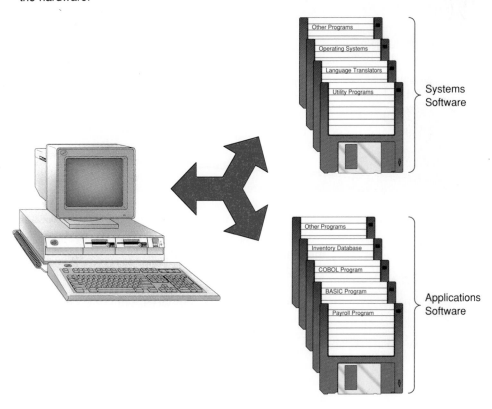

Unit 1 An Introduction to Data Processing

Applications software consists of a number of programs designed to perform specific user applications. A computer program giving instructions for the steps involved in preparing and printing employee paychecks is an example of applications software. These programs are either purchased or written in-house for specific applications.

Peopleware

Peopleware refers to the personnel required to design, program, and operate a computer installation. Although there are numerous categories of jobs or positions (see Chapter 16 on computer careers), the three principal positions required in a large computer installation are those of systems analyst, programmer, and computer operator. People in each of these areas generally perform special-purpose tasks under the supervision of a **director** or **manager** specially trained for this position.

The position of **systems analyst** requires the broadest background and most extensive training of the above three job categories. The principal task of the systems analyst is to study information and processing requirements. Specifically, a systems analyst defines the applications problem, determines systems specifications, recommends hardware and software changes, and designs information processing procedures. The analyst devises data verification methods and prepares program logic diagrams and data layouts from which the programmer can proceed (see Fig. 2-9).

The position of **programmer** requires a comprehensive knowledge of one or more programming languages and standard coding procedures, but does not require the broader understanding of the structure and inner workings of a business required of the systems analyst. The programmer's principal job is to code or prepare clearly defined programs based on the specifications set forth by the systems analyst (see Fig. 2-10).

The position of **computer operator** requires the least extensive background of the three categories. The computer operator must perform a series of fairly well defined tasks that will keep the computer operating at maximum efficiency. The operational efficiency of any computer installation is highly dependent on the quality and abilities of the operational staff (see Fig. 2-11).

Procedures

The operations of any data processing center require an extensive and clearly defined set of procedures for performing the essential functions of the installation (see Fig. 2-12). These functions will generally include obtaining, preparing, and entering of data into the computer, processing special and regularly scheduled jobs, initiating new programs and changing or deleting old ones, and so on. All such procedures must make provision for what actions are to be taken, and by whom, in the event a hardware or software malfunction occurs.

PROCESSING METHODS

The hardware and software capabilities of today's computer systems make possible a number of processing methods. This versatility allows a company to choose the processing that is most appropriate to each type of application. Among the most commonly employed methods are batch processing and interactive processing.

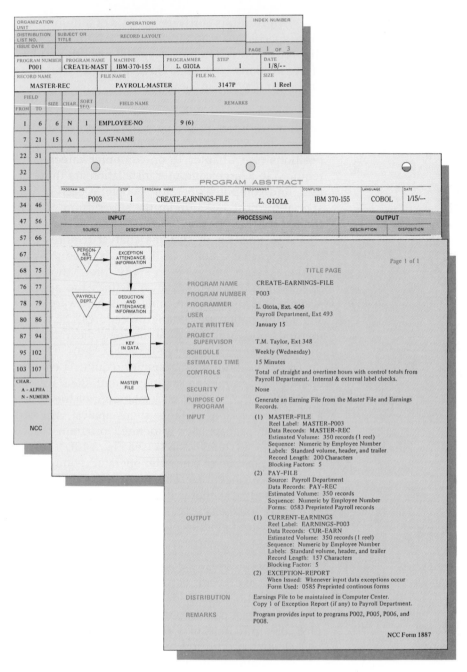

FIGURE 2-9
Reports typical of those produced by a systems analyst.

Batch Processing

Batch processing has been employed since computers were first used by business and industry. In a batch processing operation, data or transactions are collected into groups, or **batches,** before being processed by the computer. Processing a large volume of data through the computer generally results in lower processing costs per transaction than processing the transactions as they occur. Therefore,

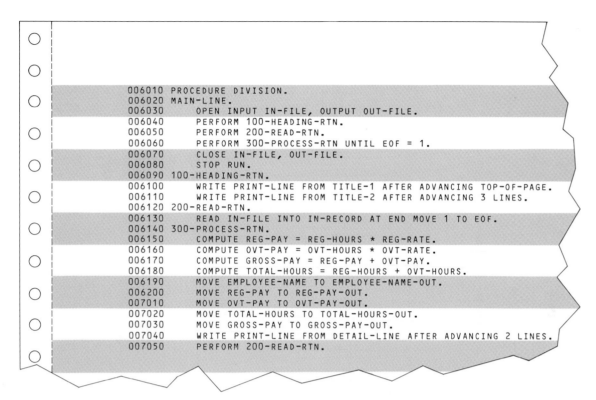

```
006010 PROCEDURE DIVISION.
006020 MAIN-LINE.
006030     OPEN INPUT IN-FILE, OUTPUT OUT-FILE.
006040     PERFORM 100-HEADING-RTN.
006050     PERFORM 200-READ-RTN.
006060     PERFORM 300-PROCESS-RTN UNTIL EOF = 1.
006070     CLOSE IN-FILE, OUT-FILE.
006080     STOP RUN.
006090 100-HEADING-RTN.
006100     WRITE PRINT-LINE FROM TITLE-1 AFTER ADVANCING TOP-OF-PAGE.
006110     WRITE PRINT-LINE FROM TITLE-2 AFTER ADVANCING 3 LINES.
006120 200-READ-RTN.
006130     READ IN-FILE INTO IN-RECORD AT END MOVE 1 TO EOF.
006140 300-PROCESS-RTN.
006150     COMPUTE REG-PAY = REG-HOURS * REG-RATE.
006160     COMPUTE OVT-PAY = OVT-HOURS * OVT-RATE.
006170     COMPUTE GROSS-PAY = REG-PAY + OVT-PAY.
006180     COMPUTE TOTAL-HOURS = REG-HOURS + OVT-HOURS.
006190     MOVE EMPLOYEE-NAME TO EMPLOYEE-NAME-OUT.
006200     MOVE REG-PAY TO REG-PAY-OUT.
007010     MOVE OVT-PAY TO OVT-PAY-OUT.
007020     MOVE TOTAL-HOURS TO TOTAL-HOURS-OUT.
007030     MOVE GROSS-PAY TO GROSS-PAY-OUT.
007040     WRITE PRINT-LINE FROM DETAIL-LINE AFTER ADVANCING 2 LINES.
007050     PERFORM 200-READ-RTN.
```

FIGURE 2-10
A segment of a program produced by a programmer.

FIGURE 2-11
Operations personnel at work in a computer center.

transactions are collected and held for processing until such time as it is most convenient or economical to do so. The transactions or data can be entered *offline*—into computers or terminals that are not even connected to the main computer. The delay between the time the transaction occurs and the time it is processed can vary from several minutes to hours, even to several days. Thus, batch processing is reserved for those applications where such a delay will not decrease the usefulness of the results.

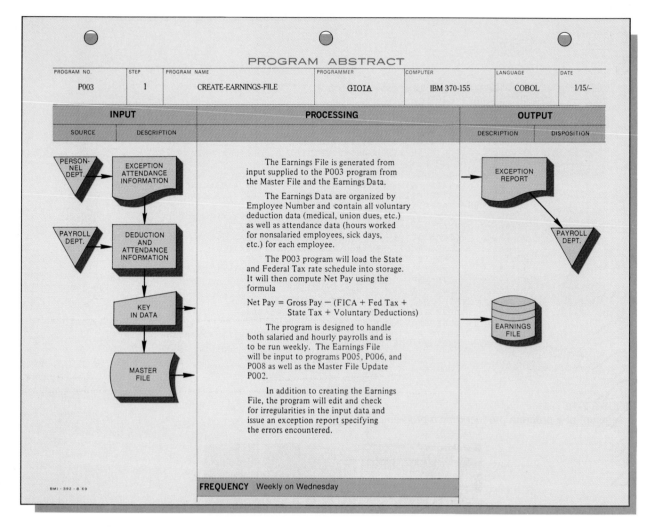

FIGURE 2-12
A sample page taken from a procedures manual.

A payroll application is ideally suited to batch processing. In a payroll application, hourly data is collected and stored for each employee over a fixed period of time. Then, at a prescribed point in time, every Thursday for example, the hourly data is placed *online* (placed on an input device connected to the CPU) and processed to produce weekly paychecks and associated reports (see Fig. 2-13).

Interactive Processing

There are many applications that require data be processed as it becomes available. This type of processing is referred to as **interactive processing** (see Fig. 2-14). In such cases, there can be no appreciable delay between the creation of the data to be processed and the actual processing of the data. This type of interactive processing is also referred to as **real-time** processing.

To facilitate interactive processing, the main computer must be online or linked to each terminal. In addition, a program must be resident in the CPU to process the data as it is input from the various terminals. Most forms of

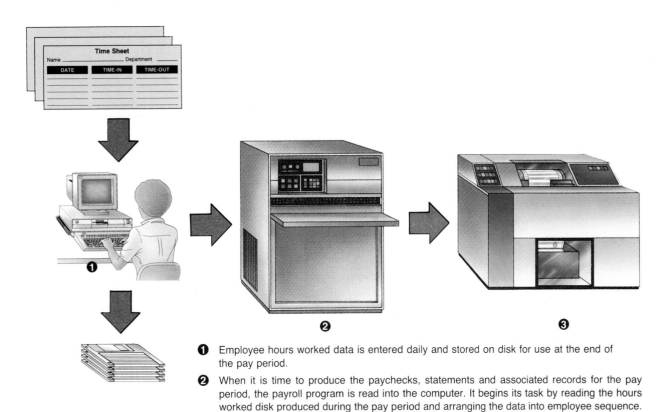

❶ Employee hours worked data is entered daily and stored on disk for use at the end of the pay period.

❷ When it is time to produce the paychecks, statements and associated records for the pay period, the payroll program is read into the computer. It begins its task by reading the hours worked disk produced during the pay period and arranging the data into employee sequence. The payroll program then calculates gross pay, deductions, net pay, year-to-date totals, and so on for each employee.

❸ The paychecks, deductions registers, and other associated reports are printed out.

FIGURE 2-13
A payroll application is ideally suited to batch processing.

FIGURE 2-14
Computer in a real-time processing mode.

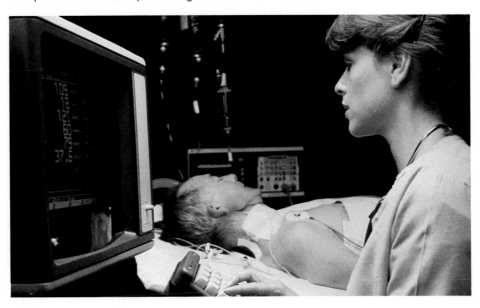

interactive processing take place in a **conversational mode.** That is, human-machine communications are maintained and the computer system is being used extensively to support remote terminals. In this mode a conversational "dialog" is maintained between the users and the computer system. Each statement or request input by the user is processed immediately and an appropriate reply is sent back to the user. Telephone lines are generally employed to link the computer system with geographically dispersed user terminals. This method of communicating is generally referred to a **telecommunications.** Some advantages of interactive processing in a conversational mode include immediate response to inquiries, ease of use, relatively low cost of terminal operation, and the ability to install terminals virtually anywhere.

Another form of interactive processing is **transaction processing.** In transaction processing, the user enters all data pertaining to a particular business event or transaction, then the computer performs the operations necessary to process that transaction. Figure 2-15 illustrates transaction processing being used in an airline reservation system. This represents interactive processing because data entered into the computer are *immediately* processed and output is created without appreciable delay. In addition, the data entered was sufficient to provide information for a complete transaction.

CLASSIFICATION OF COMPUTERS

Our discussion thus far has dealt with computer systems in general. It should be clear that computer systems are available in various sizes and with a variety of peripheral or support devices to cover just about every processing need. The variety of support devices will become even more apparent when we discuss these in detail in Chapter 3. Because of the variety of computer power and functions available, computers are classified as to purpose, type, and capacity.

Purpose

Computers are designed to be either special-purpose or general-purpose computing devices. **Special-purpose computers,** also known as **dedicated computers,** are designed around a specific application or type of application. Many such systems have a set of instructions permanently programmed into them that are designed to perform only one major function. For example, the Lunar Excursion Module (LEM), which landed the first man on the moon, had a special-purpose computer on board intended to do only one thing: control the altitude or relative position of the vehicle during descent and ascent to and from the moon. Special-purpose computers are also used in computer games, to control traffic lights, to control the collection of tolls on certain highways, and in automobiles, weapons, and appliances, to name but a few application areas (see Fig. 2-16). New applications are arising daily for which special-purpose computers are needed.

General-purpose computers are designed to handle a variety of tasks. This is possible by utilizing the **stored-program** concept. That is, a program or series of instructions is prepared for each application and input to and temporarily stored in the computer. Once stored in the computer's memory, this program can be executed, causing the computer to perform the specific function for

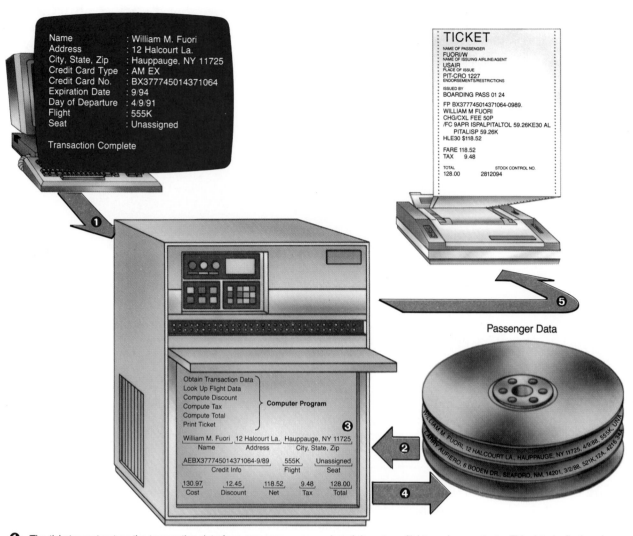

① The ticket agent enters the transaction data for a passenger: name, day of departure, flight number, seat, etc. This data is displayed on the agent's screen and is simultaneously entered into the computer's main memory.

② Without delay, a resident program accesses the appropriate record from disk and places it into the computer's memory.

③ Processing takes place; in this case, the new passenger is included and that seat is marked "booked" for that particular flight. If the seat had already been taken and was unavailable, an appropriate message would be displayed on the screen and a different seat or flight could be requested.

④ The updated record is written to disk on the master file. In this way, the master file is continuously updated by the entries made at the reservation counter.

⑤ Written confirmation of the reserved seat for that flight is printed out for the customer.

FIGURE 2-15
The SABRE system (Semi-Automatic Business Research Environment), a transaction processing system developed by American Airlines, allows a customer to obtain information and book flights, lodging, and car rentals over the telephone.

FIGURE 2-16
Special-purpose computer system in the engine room of a Texaco tanker.

which the program was intended. Upon completion of the execution of this program, another program can be input to the computer and the cycle repeated. Thus the same combination of hardware can be used to execute many different programs (see Fig. 2-17).

General-purpose computers have the advantage of versatility over special-purpose computers but typically are less efficient and slower than special-purpose computers when applied to the same task. In the case of the Lunar Excursion Module, for example, a general-purpose computer was not practical because it would have been much too slow.

Type

There are two types of computers currently available: analog and digital. So far we have been discussing only the digital computer. An **analog computer** represents variables or quantities by physical analogies (see Fig. 2-18). It functions by setting up physical situations that are analogous to mathematical situations. That is, it represents physical quantities, such as distance, velocity, acceleration, temperature, pressure, or angular position, as forces or voltages in mechanically or electrically equivalent circuits.

An automobile speedometer is an example of an analog computing device. It converts the rotational rate of the drive shaft of the automobile into a numerical approximation of the speed of the vehicle. Similarly, a thermometer functions as an analog device by converting the movement of a column of mercury into a numeric quantity or temperature.

World's Most Expensive Computer Equipment The "Underwater Manifold Center" developed by Exxon will roam about the ocean floor and enable ships, instead of permanent offshore rigs, to drill for oil. It will manage pumping the oil to the surface or to a master control rig 5 miles away. Even with a price tag of $667 million, the system will be cheaper than the platforms it replaces.

As data input to an analog computer results from a measuring process, these computers are ideal in situations where data can be accepted directly from a measuring instrument without having to convert it into numbers or codes. The analog computer's ability to collect data at high speeds, together with its ability to process these data at equally high speeds, makes it uniquely suited to controlling processes in oil refineries, steel mills, weapon systems, and similar operations. Analog computers do not require any storage capability because they measure and compare quantities in a single operation. Output

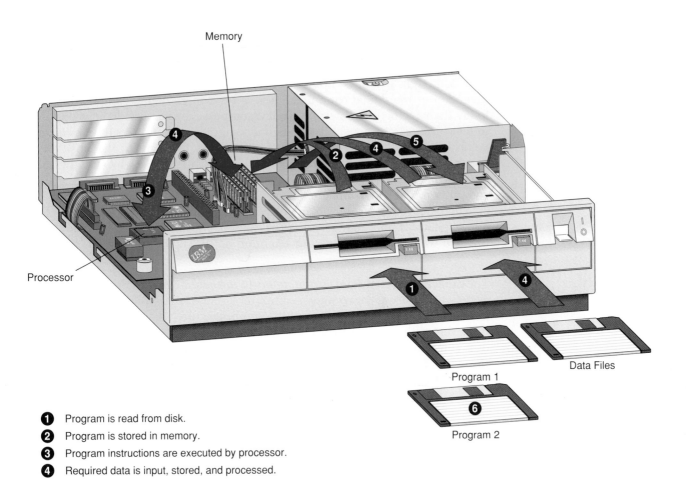

Memory

Processor

① Program is read from disk.
② Program is stored in memory.
③ Program instructions are executed by processor.
④ Required data is input, stored, and processed.
⑤ Results are output.
⑥ Next program is read from disk and the cycle is repeated.

Program 1

Data Files

Program 2

FIGURE 2-17
General-purpose digital computers utilize the stored-program concept.

FIGURE 2-18
Analog computer system used to simulate mechanical and electromechanical systems.

"I REALIZE IT'S VERY EFFICIENT, BUT I KICKED IT BECAUSE OF ITS KNOW-IT-ALL-ATTITUDE."

from an analog computer is generally in the form of readings on a series of dials (as in the case of the speedometer and odometer of a car) or a graph on a strip chart or cathode ray tube.

Although analog computers were in use some twenty years before the invention of the digital computer, there are far more digital computers in use today than analog computers. A **digital computer** counts discretely as opposed to measuring continuously. For a digital computer to plot the path of a moving vehicle, it would be necessary for the computer to calculate the position of the vehicle at various points in time and connect these points by straight lines. One of the principal differences between the digital computer and the analog computer is that results obtained from a digital computer are precise and repeatable, whereas the results obtained from an analog computer are only close approximations and generally are not exactly repeatable. For the remainder of this text we shall concentrate our attention on the digital computer.

Capacity

The **capacity** of a computer system refers to the volume of data that the computer system can process. Years ago, a computer's size was an indication of its capacity—the larger the physical size of the computer, the larger its capacity. Today, however, with the current state of microminiaturization, we measure the size of a computer by its **throughput**—the amount of processing that can be put through it in a given amount of time. Based on throughput, computer systems fall into three categories: microcomputers, minicomputers, and mainframe computer systems, with costs increasing proportional to size (see Table 2-2).

TABLE 2-2
Computer Cost Comparison Table

COMPUTER SIZE	APPROXIMATE PURCHASE COST	APPROXIMATE MONTHLY RENTAL
Microcomputer *	less than 10,000	$100–500
Minicomputer *	$10,000–150,000	$500–2,500
Mainframe computer †	$100,000 and up	$2,000 and up
		**($2,000–3,000 per hour)

* Generally purchased, not leased
† Generally leased, not purchased
** Shared access charge of a supercomputer

Microcomputers

Microcomputers were first introduced in the mid-1970s. They are small laptop or desktop systems that range in price from a few hundred dollars to nearly $10,000, depending on the input/output and secondary storage devices supporting it. The basis of the microcomputer is the **microprocessor,** a silicon chip containing the necessary circuitry to perform arithmetic/logic operations and to control input/output operations (see Figs. 2-19 and 2-20). The microprocessor is a complex electronic circuit consisting of thousands of transistors squeezed onto a tiny chip of silicon that is often little more than 3 or 4 millimeters square (one quarter the size of your pinky nail). The chip is then packaged as a single integrated circuit containing approximately forty leads or contacts. By adding an input/output capability and a memory to the microprocessor, a microcomputer **system** is formed.

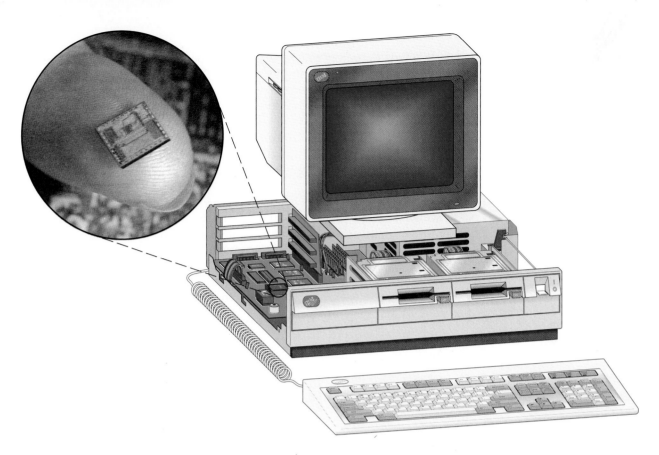

FIGURE 2-19
Microprocessor on a chip.

FIGURE 2-20
Close-up of an Intel 80386 microprocessor chip used in a Compaq 386 microcomputer.

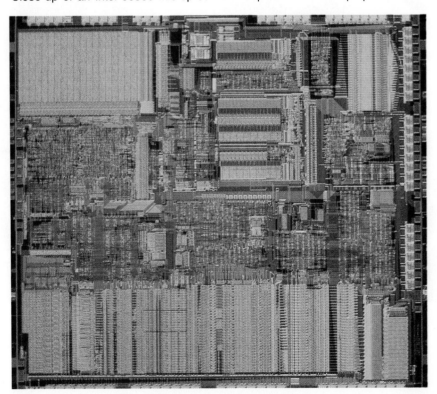

Early microcomputers offered a limited processing potential and an even more limited choice of input/output devices. Today, however, these devices have grown in number and processing capabilities and support a wide range of input/output devices. Microcomputers are available with a selection of input/output devices varying from a tape cassette recorder to a voice synthesizer. In addition to being used as general-purpose computation devices, microcomputers are used for special purposes in automobiles, airplanes, toys, clocks, appliances, and more. Figure 2-21 illustrates some of the many uses to which Apple microcomputers are put.

High-end **supermicros,** also known as **workstations,** are being introduced on the scene. The workstation represents the bridge between the micro- and minicomputer. Simply stated, it is a microcomputer with many of the capabilities of the larger minicomputers but costing much less. Initially designed for use by engineers and designers, today we find them being used in all aspects of society. These workstations are generally **multitasking** (they can run more than one application for a user) and **multiuser** (they can be shared by several users at the same time).

FIGURE 2-21
Apple computers in use (a) at home, (b) on the job, (c) in the office, and (d) just for fun.

a

b

c

d

Unit 1   An Introduction to Data Processing

FIGURE 2-22
Personal System/2 P70 386 portable computer system.

Minicomputers

Minicomputer systems perform the basic arithmetic and logic functions and support some of the programming languages used with large computer systems but are physically smaller, less expensive, and have a smaller storage capacity than mainframes. Minicomputer systems are ideally suited for processing tasks that do not require access to huge volumes of stored data. As a result of their low cost, ease of operation by non-computer-oriented personnel, and versatility, minicomputers have gained rapid acceptance from their infancy only a few years ago. Today, they represent a billion-dollar industry.

In late 1975, IBM shook the minicomputer market with its introduction of the IBM 5100 system (see Fig. 2-22). This computer system weighed only 50 pounds, was capable of storing up to 64,000 characters in its memory, supported several programming languages, and was equipped with a cathode ray tube monitor for displaying output and an optional 132 character per line printer—all for a cost of just over $8,000. By comparison, a large computer system at that time rented for as much as $100,000 per month. Today, however, a comparable system would be classified as a microcomputer system and would be available for less than $1,000. Some of the newer minicomputer systems are substantially more powerful and more expensive than this early system. For example, Figure 2-23 illustrates a minicomputer system from Sperry Corporation that costs more than $20,000; designed for the small business, it is capable of processing up to 16 jobs concurrently. Some of the larger and more expensive minicomputers are capable of supporting 20 or more terminals in a time-shared mode.

Chapter 2   A Computer System in a Nutshell

FIGURE 2-23
IBM AS/400 minicomputer system.

Mainframe Computers

Larger computers are generally constructed of modules mounted on a chassis or mainframe—hence the name **mainframe computers.** Mainframe computers vary in size, from those slightly larger than a minicomputer to supercomputers like the Cray and Control Data Cyber computers. Generally, mainframe computer systems offer substantial advantages over mini- or microcomputer systems. Some of these are: greater processing speeds, greater storage capacity (millions of characters), a larger variety of input/output devices, support for a number of high-speed secondary storage devices, multiprogramming, and time sharing. Figure 2-24 illustrates a mainframe computer system.

FIGURE 2-24
Mainframe computer system.

Unit 1   An Introduction to Data Processing

Because of the tremendous expense in operating a mainframe computer system, the system must be operated efficiently every moment that it is in use. To keep such a system operating at the required level of efficiency requires a very large and highly trained operations, programming, and systems staff. Such computer systems are generally used by large businesses, universities, governmental agencies, and the military. These systems are often coupled with other computer systems in a large network to provide enormous computing power to form what is referred to as a **distributed data processing network.**

Supercomputers

The largest and most powerful mainframe computer is called a **supercomputer.** The astronomical cost of these computers has limited their development to but a few hundred worldwide. The Cray X-MP shown in Figure 1–24 is an example of a supercomputer. Its maze of dense circuits can execute more than 100 million instructions per second (MIPS). Such supercomputers generally are applied only to the solution of very complex and sophisticated scientific problems and for national security purposes.

Smaller, less costly **minisupercomputers** have been developed by several United States computer manufacturers. These computers provide approximately half the power of the supercomputer but at a fraction of the cost. For example, a typical supercomputer will, on average, cost 10 million dollars while the average minisupercomputer costs about .5 million dollars. The relative low cost has made the minisupercomputer an attractive buy for mid-sized to large businesses. For example, many Wall Street brokerage firms have purchased one or more of these computers to speed up the processing of large financial models used by traders to keep track of securities that have tendencies to fluctuate greatly. These brokerage houses note that solutions are provided at a rate 50 times faster than that of the mainframe computers used to process the same models.

THE DAWN OF COMPUTER COMPATIBILITY

In 1964, IBM's Chairman, Thomas Watson Jr., claimed the company was about to make "the most important product announcement in company history." Time has shown he was correct. The corporation announced not just one machine, but a whole family of them. Called the **System/360,** the new line consisted of six models of varying size and price. Reportedly, the new project cost the company $5 billion to research, develop and manufacture—that's more than twice what the United States spent on the Manhattan Project to develop the atomic bomb.

In a typical, but daring fashion, the project centered around two untried concepts. The first was that the new machines would be capable of handling the full range of applications, from the arithmetic manipula-

tions, or "number crunching" required by the scientific community to the data-processing needs of the business world (the "360" represented this full, or 360-degree capability).

The second concept was that the new computers should be able to share programs and exchange data, that is, the computers were to be **compatible.**

System/360 proved to be everything IBM claimed it would. The new technology created the so-called plug-compatible industry. System/360 allowed IBM to lead the industry into a new, more freewheeling hardware technology. Even today, a large portion of IBM's gross income and earnings could be attributed to the direct descendants of System/360.

SUMMARY AND GLOSSARY OF KEY TERMS

- A **computer** is a machine that processes data. It is directed by a set of instructions or **program** written by a **programmer.**

- The functions performed by a computer system are collectively referred to as the **data processing cycle.** The data processing cycle consists of an **input** function during which data are gathered, converted to a machine-readable form, and transferred to the processor; a **processing** function, which is concerned with storing and manipulating data to produce meaningful results, and an **output** function, which puts the results of processing into a finished or edited form.

- The basic elements that constitute a system intended to process data by computer are **hardware, software, peopleware,** and **procedures.**

- The physical machines, or **hardware,** may operate **offline**—detached and operating independently from the computer, or **online**—directly connected to and controlled by the computer.

- The **processing** of data in a computer system is the function of the **central processing unit (CPU).** The CPU interacts with the primary storage unit to interpret and execute program instructions while communicating with the input/output and secondary storage units. The CPU consists of a **control unit,** which controls and coordinates the activities of the computer, and an **arithmetic/logic unit (ALU),** which performs the basic functions of data transfer, arithmetic operations, editing, and decision making. The **primary storage unit,** or **RAM,** or simply **memory,** is used to store the data and instructions being processed; it communicates directly with the CPU.

- **Auxiliary,** or **secondary, storage** is used to augment the primary storage capacity of a computer system. Data read from or written to secondary storage must pass through primary storage.

- A large variety of special- and general-purpose **data entry devices** and **input devices** are available to prepare and input data to a computer. There are equally as many **output devices** available for outputting the results of processing. The particular devices employed depend on the nature of the application.

- Computer programs, or **software,** are of two types: systems software and applications software.

- **Systems software** consists of **utility programs** designed to facilitate the use of the computer. The most important of these is the **operating system,** a set of programs designed to control the input and output operations of the computer, communicate with the operator, and schedule the resources of the computer with minimal manual intervention.

- **Applications software** consists of the programs generally designed and written in-house to perform specific user tasks.

- **Peopleware** refers to the personnel required to design, program, and support a computer installation. Typically, a medium-sized to large installation will contain a **director** or **manager,** who oversees the entire operation; several **systems analysts,** who study information and processing requirements and are responsible for designing and maintaining all software; a number of **programmers** to create and update programs; and **computer operators** to schedule jobs and keep the computer operating at maximum efficiency.

- **Procedures** must be established for the orderly and efficient processing of jobs by the computer system. Such procedures provide for recovery in the event of a hardware or software malfunction.

- The principal methods of processing data are **batch processing,** and **interactive processing.**

- **Batch processing** involves the collecting of transactions, online or offline, into groups or batches for processing at an appropriate time. Payroll is an application ideally suited to batch processing.

- With **interactive processing** the data are processed as they become available. The time delay between the creation and actual processing of data must be insignificant. This type of interactive processing is also called **real-time** processing. With interative processing the main computer must be online, and a program must be resident in the CPU as data are input through terminals.

- Most forms of interactive processing take place in **conversational mode.** In this mode telephone lines are generally used to maintain dialog between geographically dispersed user terminals and the computer. This method of communicating is called **telecommunications.**

- **Transaction processing** is a form of interactive processing that calls for the user to enter all data pertaining to a particular business event or transaction, then the computer performs the operations necessary to process that transaction. The American Airlines SABRE system is an example of transaction processing.

- Computers are classified according to purpose, type, and capacity. **Special-purpose** computers are designed for a special type of application, whereas **general-purpose** computers are designed to handle a variety of tasks.

- There are two general types of computers. **Analog computers** represent variables or physical quantities by physical analogies, whereas **digital computers** represent variables or physical quantities discretely in terms of numbers.
- The capacity of a computer system is a measure of its **throughput**—the amount of data that can be put through it in a given amount of time. Computer systems are classified according to capacity as **microcomputer, minicomputer,** and **mainframe computer** systems. Microcomputers represent the bulk of the personal computer market. A **workstation** bridges the gap between the microcomputer and the minicomputer. Minicomputers and mainframe computers are principally employed by businesses, governmental agencies, and so on. When enormous computer power and resources are required, a number of computer systems can be coupled together to form a **distributed data processing network. Supercomputers** are the largest, most powerful mainframe computers. They are used for scientific research and national security. The **minisupercomputer** is less expensive and provides approximately half the power of the supercomputer.

EXERCISES

True-False

_____ 1. The majority of working people today are not affected by the information explosion.

_____ 2. The basic elements which must be present in a system intended to process data by computer are hardware, software, peopleware, and procedures.

_____ 3. The parts of the computer that a person can touch are the hardware.

_____ 4. Software is generally further categorized as being either user-written or manufacturer-provided. *System software or Application software*

_____ 5. The computer center operates most efficiently when a set of procedures is followed closely.

_____ 6. The central processing unit contains the control unit and primary storage.

_____ 7. The CPU processes data according to a series of instructions contained in a stored program.

_____ 8. Data stored in secondary storage are immediately accessible to the central processing unit or to other devices in the system.

_____ 9. A printer is an input device.

_____ 10. In batch processing, data are collected into groups and then submitted to the computer for processing.

_____ 11. Two of the most commonly employed processing methods are interactive and batch processing.

_____ 12. A computer system with the capability of providing instantaneous access to any and all data is required of a real-time system.

_____ 13. Most interactive processing is done in a conversational mode.

_____ 14. To facilitate batch processing, the computer must be online.

_____ 15. A real-time system is inherently online.

_____ 16. Two types of computers are microcomputers and mainframe computers.

_____ 17. The stored program can be changed in a general-purpose digital computer.

_____ 18. Digital computers count discretely as opposed to analog computers that measure continuously.

_____ 19. Throughput refers to the amount of processing that can be put through a computer in a given amount of time.

_____ 20. The heart of the microcomputer is the microprocessor.

Problems

1. Name and describe the functions which constitute the data processing cycle.
2. Describe the basic elements of a system designed to process data by computer.
3. Give two examples of business applications to which each of the various processing methods is suited.
4. Distinguish those applications that are suited to an analog computer from those that are suited to a digital computer.
5. Construct a table which illustrates the similarities and differences between the various categories of computer systems.

Projects

1. Visit a computer center and make an inventory of the computer hardware utilized.
2. Determine the type of applications to which each of the hardware items listed in project 1 is applied.
3. Assume that you wish to purchase a personal computer. Visit your local computer store or examine some current computer magazines and determine what computer system you would buy. Justify your decision.

CROSSWORD PUZZLE

Across

1. An item of data contained in secondary storage
2. Eight bits
3. Input, processing, and output
4. Location of data in storage
5. Binary digits
6. A unit of the CPU
7. As opposed to offline
8. Central processing unit
9. Distributed data processing
10. Type of software consisting of utility programs
11. A computer smaller than a mainframe and bigger than a microcomputer
12. A set of programs designed to manage the resources of the computer system
13. A systems _____ is a computer professional requiring a broad background in computer systems
14. Not connected to a computer
15. A computer that represents variables or quantities by physical analogies
16. One thousand bytes
17. Cash register-type computer input devices
18. The unit within the CPU that handles arithmetic calculations

Down

19. The heart of a microcomputer
20. Memory
21. Most forms of interactive processing take place in this mode
22. A device used for data entry
23. A general-purpose device that can be used to enter data into a computer system manually
24. Data communication via telephone lines
25. A type of computer that counts discretely
26. One billion bytes
27. A unit of the CPU used to perform calculations
28. Computer designed to handle a variety of tasks
29. The largest mainframe computer is a _____ computer

Across:
4. address
10. system
12. operating system

Down:
21. conversational

3

INPUT/OUTPUT MEDIA AND DEVICES
What Goes in and What Comes out

Objectives

- Understand the importance of fast, efficient I/O devices.
- List and describe the more commonly used general- and special-purpose I/O devices.
- Identify the types of applications in which each type of general-purpose I/O device is used.
- Differentiate between the various types of printing devices.
- List and describe the functions performed by the various types of terminals.
- Describe some of the special-purpose I/O devices and their areas of application.
- Understand and use the key terms presented in this chapter.

Most likely, many of you have seen Kubrick's production of Arthur C. Clarke's *2001: A Space Odyssey*, in which HAL and Dave carry on the conversation,

Dave: HAL, give me manual hibernation control—on all units.

HAL: All of them, Dave?

Dave: Yes.

HAL: May I point out that only one replacement is required. The others are not due for revival for one hundred and twelve days.

Dave: HAL, switch to manual hibernation control.

HAL: I can tell from your voice harmonics, Dave, that you're badly upset. Why don't you take a stress pill and get some rest?

Dave: HAL, unless you obey my instructions I shall be forced to disconnect you.

HAL: O.K., Dave, you're certainly the boss. I was only trying to do what I thought best. Naturally, I will follow all your orders. You now have full manual hibernation control.

Clearly, we are not and will not be at this evolutionary stage of computer development for some time. Today, vending machines thank you for your patronage. Personal robots can carry on a limited conversation with you. Some of the latest model cars now tell you by voice when something requires attention, such as, "your key is in the ignition." These are examples of the fastest growing computer output technique, known as **voice response.** Similarly, there are input devices that allow you to command a computer's actions simply by talking to it as Dave did to HAL (see Fig. 3-1). These two rapidly developing input/output methods represent only a small fraction of the total number of ways we can communicate with computers.

In Chapter 2, you saw how input devices are needed to enter data into the internal memory of a computer while output devices are used to provide the user with useful information. In this chapter we discuss input/output media and devices. Computers are available in all sizes, shapes, and colors, and with few exceptions, no matter what type or size of business enterprise you consider, a suitable computer or computer service is available to handle its data-processing needs efficiently and economically. Furthermore, regardless of the type of computer, there is one thing about which we can be certain: there must be some means of feeding the computer data and getting back meaningful and useful information.

NEED FOR SPEED AND EFFICIENCY

Computer applications in business are characterized by their limited computations and by the large volume of data that are input to, and output from, the computer. Handling this volume of data is one of the functions of the **input/output (I/O) devices,** or **peripheral devices,** supporting a computer. These devices are responsible for sensing or reading data from the input medium and converting these data into a form that the computer can understand and process.

FIGURE 3-1
Texas Instruments microcomputer can accept direct voice commands.

At the other end of the system, they are also responsible for converting computer-stored data into information that can be read and understood.

I/O devices perform a significant function and are an indispensable part of a computer system. The faster and more efficiently we can input data to the computer, the more efficiently the computer will function and the faster we can obtain output. Thus we must become familiar with the various I/O devices so that we will know what devices are available to do various applications and when to use each. We shall also investigate the media used to record data associated with these input/output devices. Specific details, such as operating speeds, are presented only for purposes of comparison and need only be examined with this purpose in mind. Such specific information is included in the specifications available from hardware vendors.

INPUT DEVICES

On the Verge of Extinction

Since the time of Herman Hollerith, an early pioneer in the punched card industry, the punched card has served as an input medium to automated computational devices. It has undergone little or no change since that time, and most companies have phased out and replaced it with the more efficient data entry media. Among the punched-card devices still in use is the punched **card reader.** The reading of punched cards takes place at speeds ranging from 150 to more than 2,500 cards per minute.

SCRATCH-PAD COMPUTERS

Computer keyboards will some day be replaced by touch-sensitive pads designed to analyze your handwriting and convert it into computer type. Once converted to computer type, it can be printed or included with digitized graphics, then printed. Sony Corporation and Canon, Inc. have recently sold notebook-size machines that accomplish such a feat. They range in price from $500 to $2,300.

These battery-operated machines effectively eliminate the need for a keyboard. In fact, experts predict that in five to ten years this technology will make a computer the size of writing tablet, thus making it more approachable to people who do not type or who are intimidated by the thought of having to learn how to do so.

Key-to-Tape and Key-to-Disk Systems

In a **key-to-tape** system, data entered at a keyboard are recorded directly on magnetic tape (see Fig. 3-2). The magnetic tape used with these recorders is similar to the tape cartridge or cassette used with home recorders. Keying accuracy is verified by placing the recording tape into a magnetic tape verifier and having the original data retyped. Magnetic tape encoders and verifiers are generally housed in the same physical unit. Any errors detected are corrected simply by erasing the mistakes and substituting the correct character(s).

A multistation **key-to-disk** system generally consists of from 8 to 64 key stations, a magnetic disk, a control unit, a magnetic tape unit, and a micro- or minicomputer. The procedure involves keying in the source data at a key station keyboard, verifying the correctness of the data on a CRT (cathode ray tube) or monitor screen, editing the data by the computer, and temporarily recording the data on a fixed or rigid magnetic disk (see Fig. 3-3). Frequently used data

FIGURE 3-2
Key-to-tape process.

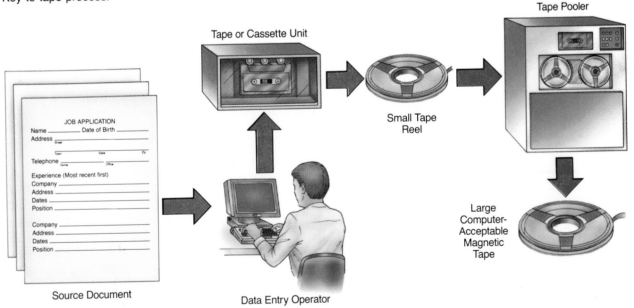

Tape Pooler

Tape or Cassette Unit

Small Tape Reel

JOB APPLICATION
Name _____ Date of Birth _____
Address _____

Telephone _____

Experience (Most recent first)
Company _____
Address _____
Dates _____
Position _____

Company _____
Address _____
Dates _____
Position _____

Large Computer-Acceptable Magnetic Tape

Source Document

Data Entry Operator

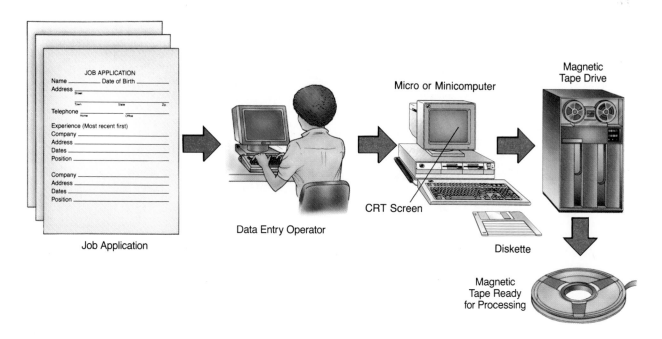

FIGURE 3-3
Key-to-disk process.

fields can also be stored on a disk and called up by an operator to eliminate unnecessary keying. For example, the name, address, and telephone number of employees can be stored by their employee numbers. The operator can then call up this information simply by typing in an employee number.

Character Readers

Character readers are capable of accepting printed or typed characters from source documents and converting these data into a computer-acceptable code for processing. Currently available high-speed character readers are capable of reading source documents at rates of up to 2,000 documents per minute and may cost several hundred thousand dollars. The three basic types of character readers are magnetic-ink, optical mark, and optical character readers.

Magnetic-ink Character Readers

The concept of **magnetic-ink character recognition (MICR)** was developed by the Stanford Research Institute for use by the world's largest bank, the Bank of America. This system was designed to read directly data prerecorded on checks and deposit slips with a special ferrite-impregnated ink that can be magnetized. The magnetized characters can be detected and interpreted by MICR equipment, allowing the input document to be mechanically processed (Fig. 3-4).

Figure 3-5 shows a canceled check containing, along the bottom, data relating to the individual bank's assigned number, the customer's account number, and the amount of the check. Obviously, the amount field is not coded by the bank until the check is received for payment at the bank.

FIGURE 3-4
A magnetic-ink character recognition (MICR) system.

FIGURE 3-5
Magnetic-ink characters and a typical application.

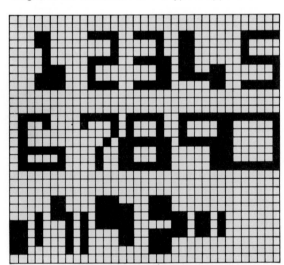

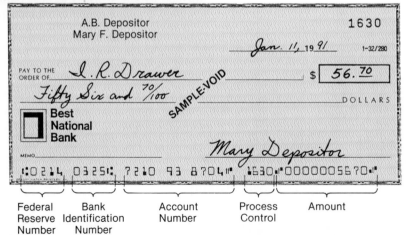

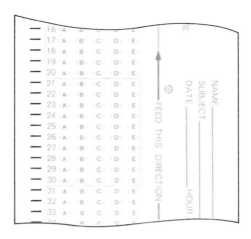

FIGURE 3-6
Portion of a special-purpose optical mark form typical of those used to grade examination papers.

Optical Mark and Character Readers

Optical mark readers (OMR) optically read pencil marks on special, carefully printed forms. Optical mark forms are relatively expensive, as they must be printed with exact tolerances so that the marks will line up under the optical sensing devices when read (Fig. 3-6). The most popular use of such devices is for scoring examinations in educational institutions.

Optical character recognition (OCR) devices can convert data from source documents to a machine-recognizable form (see Fig. 3-7). Current applications

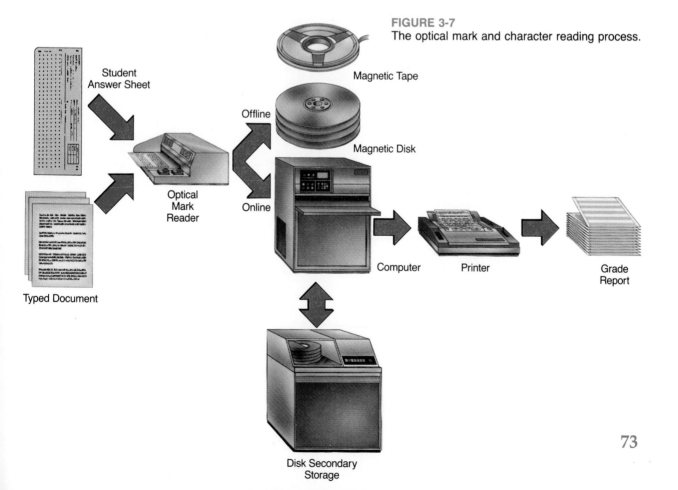

FIGURE 3-7
The optical mark and character reading process.

73

of optical scanning include billing, insurance premium notices, and charge sales invoices. It should be pointed out that, at present, no OCR device can reliably read and interpret script or handwriting. However, some are available that can read handwriting provided that certain general guidelines (see Fig. 3-8) are observed when the data are written. Generally, optical character readers are limited with respect to hand-written characters and can only read handwritten digits and some symbols. Many more OCR devices are available for the reading of machine-written or typed characters, including digits, letters, and some special characters. Not all printed characters can be read reliably on OCR readers. Generally, each reader is capable of reading only selected character styles, and then only with limited horizontal and vertical spacing (see Fig. 3-9).

Clearly, even if the character style and spacing are acceptable, errors can result from reading a character that was not written perfectly. To reduce such errors, OCR devices generally compare the pattern sensed or read with the patterns of all acceptable characters stored in the machine. The read character is assumed to be the character whose stored pattern most closely matches the read pattern. This process is shown in Figure 3-10.

FIGURE 3-8
Guidelines to be used when recording characters for optical character reading.

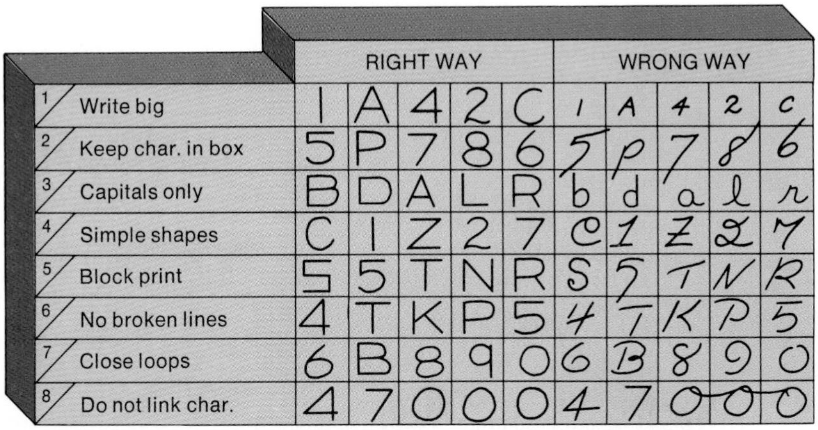

		RIGHT WAY					WRONG WAY			
1	Write big	I	A	4	2	C	ı	A	4	2	c
2	Keep char. in box	5	P	7	8	6	5	p	7	8	6
3	Capitals only	B	D	A	L	R	b	d	a	l	r
4	Simple shapes	C	I	Z	2	7	C	1	Z	2	7
5	Block print	5	5	T	N	R	S	5	T	N	R
6	No broken lines	4	T	K	P	5	4	T	K	P	5
7	Close loops	6	B	8	9	O	6	B	8	9	O
8	Do not link char.	4	7	O	O	O	4	7	O O O

FIGURE 3-9
Sample OCR fonts.

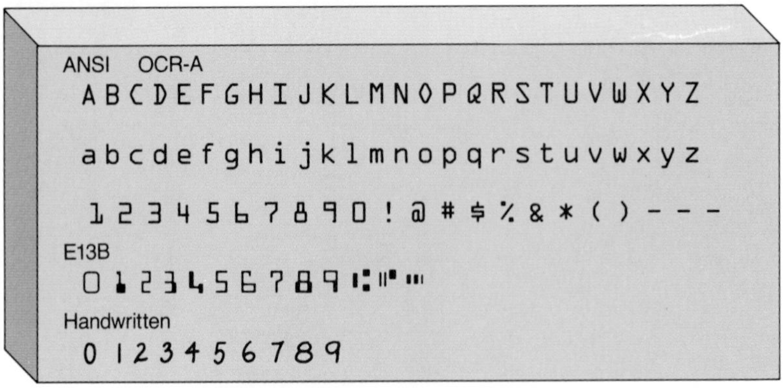

ANSI OCR-A
ABCDEFGHIJKLMNOPQRSTUVWXYZ

abcdefghijklmnopqrstuvwxyz

1234567890!@#$%&*()---
E13B
0123456789 ⑈⑈⑈⑈

Handwritten
0123456789

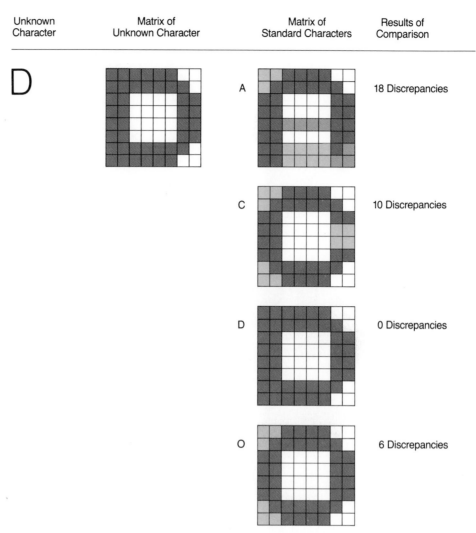

Unknown Character	Matrix of Unknown Character		Matrix of Standard Characters	Results of Comparison
D		A		18 Discrepancies
		C		10 Discrepancies
		D		0 Discrepancies
		O		6 Discrepancies

FIGURE 3-10
Character readers compare the digitized matrix of an unknown character against a stored set of templates. The templates with the fewest discrepancies is assumed to be the character read.

Because of the great cost of OCR devices, they are impractical unless a substantial number of documents are to be processed each day.

Pointing Systems

Computer users frequently find it easier to *point* to something on a display screen or at an item of text or graphical material they are entering into the computer. A number of devices are available to assist in fulfilling this need (see Fig. 3-11).

Light Pen

The earliest pointing device is the **light pen.** This device is placed close to a display screen or monitor and turned on. A photo sensor inside the light pen detects the scanning beam sweeping back and forth across the screen. Accompa-

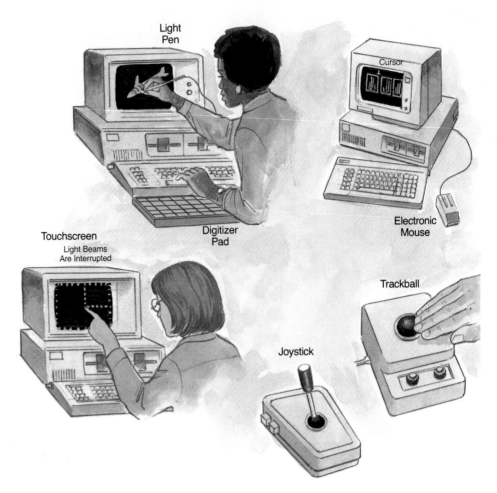

FIGURE 3-11
Various pointing input devices.

nying circuitry converts the pen's readings into the position of the pen on the screen. Light pens are used to select items from a list or **menu** displayed on the screen and to draw graphic displays on the video screen.

Digitizer Pad

A **digitizer pad** looks similar to a graph pad with a pointer. It functions like a light pen on a display screen except that the pad is mounted horizontally. As the pointer is moved on the pad, the corresponding point on the display screen is illuminated. The digitizer pad is particularly useful in converting graphic input, such as charts, graphs, and blueprints into patterns that can be manipulated and stored by the computer.

Mouse

A **mouse** is a hand-movable device that controls the position of the cursor on a video screen. It can be described as a box with buttons on the top and a ball on the bottom. The box is placed on a flat surface, with the user's hand over it. The ball's movement on the surface causes the cursor to move in a corresponding fashion on the screen. Various control information is sent to the computer depending on the application software being used.

Joystick and Trackball

Joysticks or game controllers are used with video games for user input. They are modeled after the controlling joysticks used in World War II fighter aircraft and thus take the same name. These devices may also be used to move the cursor around a video screen to facilitate input to a graphical display. A **trackball** is similar in operation to the joystick but uses a billiard-sized ball to position the cursor. Trackballs are becoming popular to the extent that several keyboard manufacturers have integrated them directly into their keyboards.

Touchscreen

Touch-sensitive display screens, **touchscreens** for short, detect the touch of a human finger. One popular technique used to detect the touch of a finger utilizes infrared light beams. In this technique, infrared light beams shine horizontally and vertically across the face of the screen. A pointing finger interrupts both horizontal and vertical beams, pinpointing its exact location.

OUTPUT DEVICES

Printers

Of all the output devices used in business, the **printer** is the most common. It provides the user with a permanent visual record of the data output from a computer. It is one of the few output devices capable of producing business reports and documents. Printers have been developed that are capable of printing from 150 to over 20,000 lines per minute, with each line having up to 150 characters (see Fig. 3-12). A quick calculation will reveal this to be a maximum printing speed of approximately 50,000 characters per second.

FIGURE 3-12
Inside this page printer, laser beams scan across the print drum to create text and graphics at speeds of over 20,000 lines per minute.

FIGURE 3-13
Continuous-form paper listing.

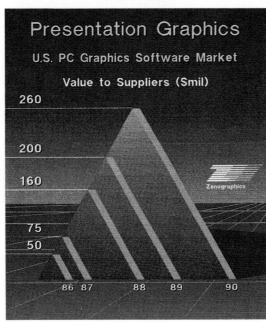

Printers can print on plain paper or on specially prepared single- or multiple-copy forms, such as invoices, stationery, labels, checks, bills, and other special-purpose forms used in business and industry (see Fig. 3-13). They can print both text and graphics in black and white or in color (see Fig. 3-14).

Printers can be subdivided into two broad categories, impact and nonimpact, with impact the most common.

Impact Printers

With **impact printers,** printing occurs as a result of a hammer striking a character form and the character form in turn striking an inked ribbon, causing the ribbon to press an image of the character onto paper.

Character printing devices (Fig. 3-15) print one character at a time at speeds of 10 to 500 characters per second. The fastest of these printers is the **wire-** or **dot-matrix** printer. It prints characters made up of a pattern of dots formed by the ends of small wires. Figure 3-16 shows the letter "A" as printed with different densities. By extending certain wires beyond the others, a dot

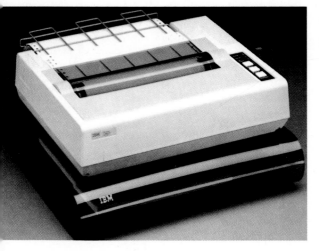 

FIGURE 3-15
Character printing devices.

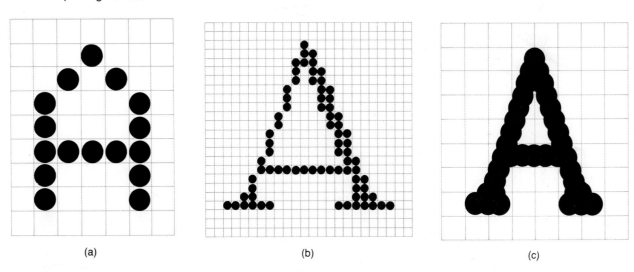

(a) (b) (c)

FIGURE 3-16
Dot-matrix printers form characters with an array of dots. Here the letter A is shown printed by (a) a 9-pin printer, (b) a 24-pin printer, (c) a 9-pin letter-quality dot-matrix printer capable of overlapped dot printing.

pattern can be created that gives the appearance of a number, letter, or special character. These extended wires are then pressed against an inked ribbon to print the character on the paper or form. Some slower and less expensive matrix printers print a character as a series of columns each one dot wide (see Fig. 3-17). Because of the nature of the matrix element, it can be used to print special character shapes that can be used with **graphics,** such as graphs and charts.

For those desiring a typewriter-quality output, a special dot-matrix or daisy-wheel printer may be employed. A **daisy-wheel** printer uses a single plastic or metal print element, similar in appearance to the arrangement of petals on a daisy flower (see Fig. 3-18). This element is rotated until the correct character is in position, and then pressed against an inked ribbon. The process is repeated

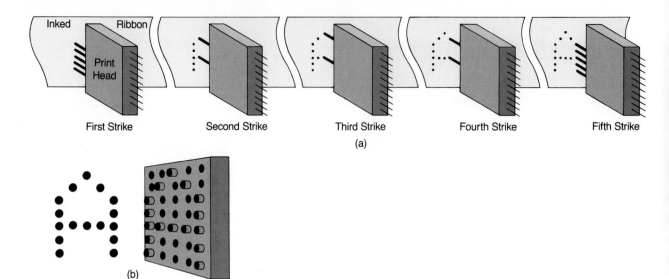

First Strike   Second Strike   Third Strike   Fourth Strike   Fifth Strike

(a)

(b)

FIGURE 3-17
(a) Some matrix printers print a character as a series of columns. This decreases both the number of elements in the print head and the cost of the printer. It also results in a substantial reduction in printing speed. (b) Other, faster matrix printers print the entire character in one operation.

FIGURE 3-18
Daisy-wheel elements.

for each character to be printed on a line. Typical speeds for such printers range from 25 to 100 characters per second.

Impact character printers are the most common hard-copy output devices used with personal and small business microcomputer systems. Their cost is significantly lower than that of line printers.

Impact line printers, capable of printing a whole line at a time, employ print wheels or a moving chain or drum (see Fig. 3-19). The **print-wheel** printer

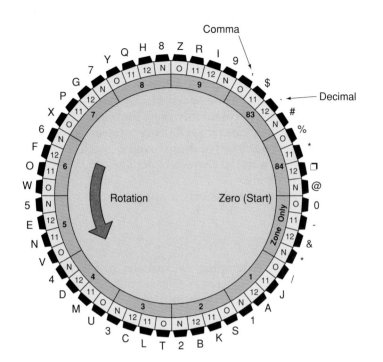

Comma
Decimal

Rotation
Zero (Start)

FIGURE 3-19
Print-wheel, drum, and chain elements.

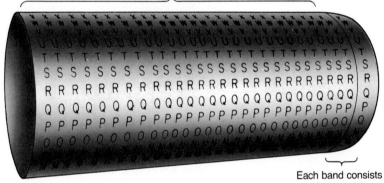

Number of bands corresponds
to number of printing positions

Each band consists
of all printing
characters available

Print Drum

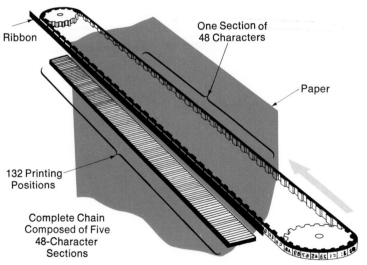

Ribbon

One Section of
48 Characters

Paper

132 Printing
Positions

Complete Chain
Composed of Five
48-Character
Sections

Print Chain

81

consists of a series of print wheels, each containing a full complement of digits and alphabetic characters in addition to a set of special characters. When printing, all print wheels are correctly positioned to represent the data to be printed on one line. They then impact simultaneously at a speed of 150 lines per minute.

The **chain** and **drum** printers are fast, commonly used, impact line printers. As the print chain (containing five 48-character sections or a lesser number of sections, each containing a larger character set) or drum revolves, each character is printed as it comes into position. Up to 150 characters per line can be printed at speeds of up to 2,500 lines per minute.

Impact line printers are used almost exclusively to support larger computer systems.

Nonimpact Printers

Nonimpact line printers, using laser, xerographic, electrostatic, or jet ink methods are the fastest and quietest printers. The Xerox 9700 laser printer, for example, is capable of printing more than 18,000 lines per minute. Before the development of the jet ink and laser printers, nonimpact printers were not heavily used, for several reasons:

1. Special, more expensive paper was required.
2. Printed output was not as sharp or as clear as with impact printers.
3. Only a single-part form can be printed at a time.
4. Output could not be easily or satisfactorily copied on office copiers.

With the exception that only single-part forms may be printed at a time, none of these limitations apply to the laser printers. Even this limitation is minor when one considers their improved quality and faster printing speed relative to most other available printers.

Electrostatic and **xerographic** printers place a pattern of the desired character on sensitized paper by means of an electric current or beam of light. The paper then passes through a powdery black substance called **toner,** which contains dry ink particles. As the ink particles are attracted to the exposed paper, the character becomes visible. These printers are capable of printing speeds of from 3,500 to 20,000 lines per minute.

LASER PRINTERS GIVE BIRTH TO DESKTOP PUBLISHING

The laser printer is extremely popular with small businesses. These devices provide hard-copy output of a quality previously requiring typesetting. The Apple *Laserwriter* and the Hewlett Packard *LaserJet* are two of the most popular laser printers. These devices print by using a laser beam reflected off a moving mirror to sensitize the surface of a photocopier drum. To date, most laser printers employ the Canon or Ricoh laser engine mechanisms. These devices print characters in the form of a dot matrix with a resolution of up to 90,000 dots per square inch. Once the surface has been sensitized, the device prints the results on plain paper using the same process employed by most photocopiers. This all takes place at the amazing rate of *8 pages per minute.*

In addition to the features provided by most other laser printers, the Laserwriter, equipped with a powerful 32-bit microprocessor and *PostScript* page description language, can produce output consisting of integrated text and graphics, and employing a wide variety of font types and sizes.

The **laser** printer utilizes a laser beam to form characters by projecting a dot-matrix pattern onto a drum surface. Toner is then attracted to the area exposed by the laser, brushed across the drum's photoconductive surface, and transferred to the paper. Finally, the paper is passed over a heating element which melts the toner to form a permanent character.

Many types of **jet ink** printers are available. The simplest of these contains a series of ink jet nozzles in the form of a matrix. Vibrating crystals force ink droplets, roughly the diameter of a human hair, from selected nozzles to form an image in the same manner as an image is formed by extending selected wires in a matrix printer. Different colored inks may be used and combined to form additional colors (see Fig. 3-20).

Several hundred nozzles are employed in the more sophisticated jet ink printers to direct a continuous stream of charged droplets across the page to form an image. These charged ink droplets travel at speeds of up to 40 miles per hour as they move between a set of plates that deflect the droplets. Droplets not needed are electrostatically attracted away from the paper and into a tiny gutter for reuse (see Fig. 3-21). A stream of more than 100,000 droplets can form approximately 200 characters per second.

FIGURE 3-20
Multicolor jet ink mechanism.

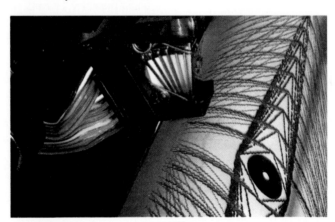

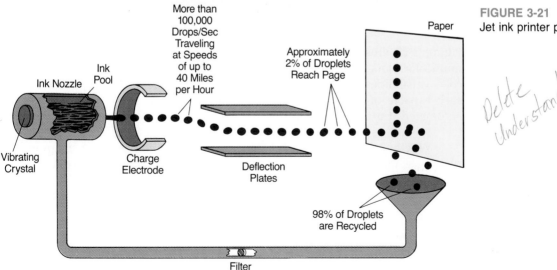

More than 100,000 Drops/Sec Traveling at Speeds of up to 40 Miles per Hour

Approximately 2% of Droplets Reach Page

Paper

FIGURE 3-21
Jet ink printer process.

Ink Nozzle

Ink Pool

Vibrating Crystal

Charge Electrode

Deflection Plates

98% of Droplets are Recycled

Filter

83

NONIMPACTS HAVE IMPACT

But Dot-Matrix Holds Its Own

The printers making a big impact are nonimpact, as buyers turn to laser and inkjet printers. By the end of 1989, 1.4 million nonimpact printers were sold to end users, according to research firm BIS CAP International, Norwell, Mass. The market will continue to grow, and in 1992 BIS CAP estimates there will be 2.4 million units sold to end users.

One is magnetography, a new nonimpact technology that is being marketed by Bull Peripherals Corp. of Waltham, Mass. Magnetographic printers transfer an image to a magnetized drum. The latent image is then transferred to paper using magnetized ink. Dave Crowley, marketing communications manager at Bull, says magnetography printers are a less expensive solution to high-volume printing than are laser printers. Chuck Rogers, president of CFR Associates Inc. in Haverhill, Mass., agrees. CFR is a VAR specializing in offering alternative products to users of Wang Laboratories Inc. products. He thinks the Bull printer is more reliable, as well as being less expensive to operate.

At this point magnetography is still a technology for the high end. Because its printing engine would be almost as expensive for a desktop system, according to a Bull spokesperson, there are no plans to downsize the technology to compete against the desktop laser and inkjet printers.

One feature that is migrating to the desktop is duplex printing—printing on both sides of the paper. Robert Parks, director of marketing for Kentek Information Systems Inc., a printer vendor in Allendale, N.J., says duplex printers are popular in the legal and publishing verticals. Meanwhile, sales of impact printers, while still substantial, will likely remain almost static. The news is pretty bad for an inflexible technology like daisy-wheel printers, which are limited to one font and type size. Although daisy-wheel printers are still being used in legal and government environments that require letter quality output, placements in the U.S. were halved from 306,000 in 1987 to a projected 152,000 by the end of this year, according to Keith Kmetz, market analyst with BIS CAP. In 1992 he expects sales to end users to plummet to 59,000 units.

Dot-matrix printers, on the other hand, are holding their own because they are adaptable enough to offer many of the features of laser and inkjet printers, such as different type fonts and sizes, at a fraction of the cost. "Approximately 5 million dot-matrix units will be shipped between the beginning of 1988 and the end of 1992," predicts Kmetz.

"Among dot-matrix end users there is a more-is-better mentality," Kmetz says, "and that is behind the shift from nine-pin to 24-pin dot-matrix machines. "And as impact printers, dot-matrix machines can imprint forms with "carbon" copies, something beyond the capability of their nonimpact rivals. Kmetz reports one study conducted by BIS CAP found large users insist the ability to do multiple forms is *essential* for their printers.

Although it is not clear how long they will be able to hold out in the wider market, impact printers like dot-matrix are likely to dominate important niche applications for some time to come.

Plotters

Figure 3-22 illustrates an inexpensive portable plotter capable of generating multicolor plots from data stored on magnetic tape or disk. Plotters with multicolor capabilities generally use a writing mechanism containing several pens, each capable of producing a different color (see Fig. 3-23). Some devices for automated drafting are equipped with plotting surfaces larger than 10 square feet and cost as much as a minicomputer system (Fig. 3-24).

Whether an application is a general one (such as designing, mapping, or plotting schematics) or more specialized (such as three-dimensional data presentation, structural analysis, contouring, or business charts), there's a plotter to do the trick.

FIGURE 3-23
Closeup of a CalComp 1070 plotter mechanism containing four color pens.

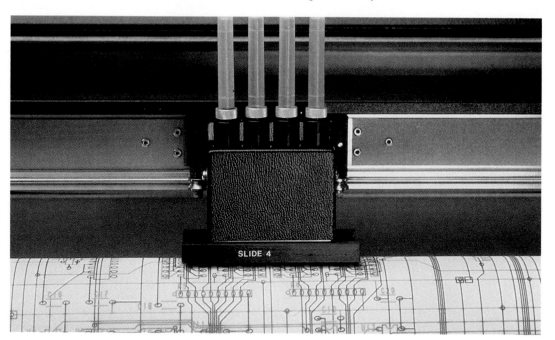

FIGURE 3-24
Two of CalComp's high-speed plotters. These plotters support head speeds as high as
52 inches per second with a resolution of .0005 inches.

Microfilm Devices

Computer output microfilm (COM) devices convert computer output to a human-readable form stored on rolls of microfilm (see Fig. 3-25) or as microfilm frames stored on cards called **microfiche** (see Fig. 3-26). At speeds of 10,000 to over 30,000 lines per minute, COM is one of the fastest computer output techniques—more than ten times faster than the fastest impact printer. A single

FIGURE 3-25
Kodak 16 mm microfilm cartridge.

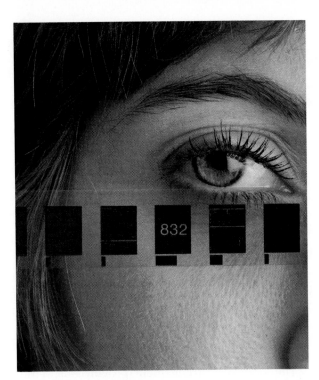

FIGURE 3-26
Documents as they appear on
microfilm.

roll of microfilm can store approximately 2000 frames and costs less than half the cost to print the same amount of data on paper.

Use of COM devices lessens the normally high demand on computer printers and frees them to produce reports for which microfilm is inappropriate. However, because of the high cost of COM equipment, it is generally only practical for larger businesses or industries generating approximately 1,000 to 10,000 documents per day. COM devices are commonly used in libraries, mail-order concerns, defense installations, government agencies, and similar, large operations (see Fig. 3-27).

FIGURE 3-27
Kodak's KAR-4000 information system.

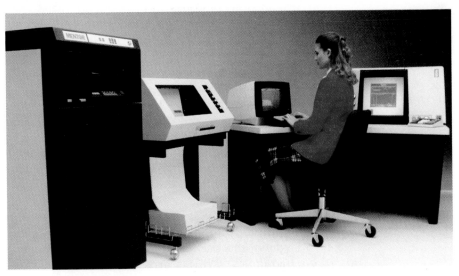

DEVICES THAT CAN BOTH INPUT AND OUTPUT

Terminals

The **terminal** is one of the most popular input/output devices. Terminals are used to facilitate two-way communications with the CPU or with other terminals that may be a few feet or thousands of miles away. Thus, with the aid of a terminal, a user can access computers around the world.

Terminals, sometimes called **workstations,** allow us to interact with a computer. We use a **keyboard** to enter data and receive output displayed on a **cathode ray tube (CRT)** display screen, or **monitor.** Because data must be keyed into these devices one character at a time, the possibility of error is high and the data transmission rate very low, thus limiting the use of these terminals to small-volume input and inquiries.

Keyboards

Keyboards today generally utilize integrated circuits to perform essential functions, such as determining the combination of 1s and 0s, or binary code, to send to the CPU, corresponding to each key depressed, switching between shifted and nonshifted keys, repeating a key code if a key is held down for a prolonged period of time, and temporarily storing or "buffering" input when keys are typed too fast.

The keyboard arrangement provided as standard on most keyboards is the **QWERTY** arrangement, named for the six letters beginning the row at the top left of the keyboard (see Fig. 3-28). This arrangement was chosen intentionally to slow down expert typists, since those who typed too fast would cause the keys on a mechanical typewriter to jam. Slowing down the typist was accomplished by scattering the most used keys around the keyboard, making frequently used combinations of letters awkward and slower to type. This QWERTY keyboard arrangement has been with us for nearly a century.

The **Dvorak simplified keyboard (DSK)** arrangement, designed in 1932 by August Dvorak, is the result of extensive ergonomic studies. Dvorak noted that with the QWERTY keyboard arrangement, typists used the weakest fourth and fifth fingers of their left hand a large proportion of the time. Thus, Dvorak rearranged the keyboard so that the five more frequently used vowels (a, o, e, u, and i) and the five most frequently used consonants (d, h, t, n, and s) were positioned on the home row where the fingers of the left and right hands rest, respectively (see Fig. 3-28). Thus, 70 percent of the typing is done on the home row. He then placed the next most frequently used characters in the row above the home row and the least frequently used characters in the row below the home row. This resulted in a reduction of finger movement of approximately 80 percent, and overall, an increase in productivity of nearly 40 percent.

Expert typists and word processors generally agree that using the Dvorak arrangement increases productivity while simultaneously decreasing fatigue. The world's fastest typing speed, nearly 200 words per minute, was achieved on a Dvorak keyboard. Despite these improvements the QWERTY keyboard arrangement is still the most common because of the difficulty of overcoming inertia and retraining.

In the meanwhile, some microcomputer manufacturers and software vendors are producing software that will convert your keyboard from QWERTY to Dvorak, and back again at will. To date, larger computer systems employ the traditional QWERTY arrangement only.

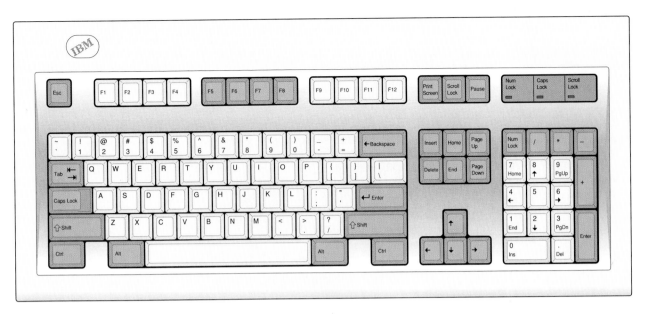

QWERTY Keyboard

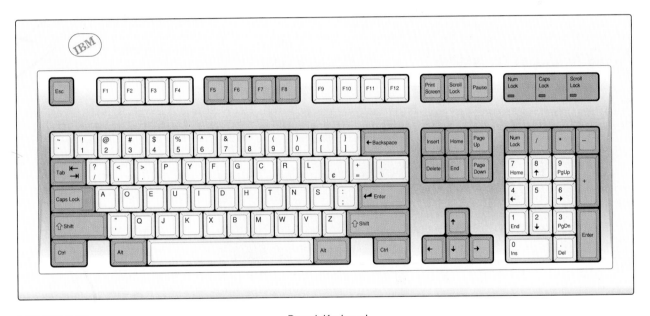

FIGURE 3-28
Dvorak Keyboard

QWERTY and Dvorak keyboard arrangements.

Terminal Functions

Some of the functions that can be performed using terminals are the following:

1. *Message switching*: The communication of information input at one terminal to one or more remote terminals. The system used by police departments, military installations, and businesses to communicate with one another represents such a function (see Fig. 3-29).

2. *Data collecting*: Data are input to one or more terminals and recorded on a secondary storage medium for subsequent processing (see Fig. 3-30). This eliminates the need to record the information on a source document and then to key the information from the source document into the computer.

3. *Inquiry or transaction processing*: Data stored in central data files can be accessed from remote terminals for updating or to determine answers to inquiries about information stored in these files. The system employed by most airlines to maintain and update flight information is an example of such a function (Fig. 3-31).

4. *Remote job processing*: Programs can be input from remote terminals directly to the CPU for processing. After execution, the results can be transmitted back to the terminal or to one or more other terminals for output (Fig. 3-32).

5. *Graphic display and design*: Data can be displayed in graphic form, and can also be manipulated and modified. Interactive graphic displays, from simple home video games displayed on a television set to sophisticated computerized systems, provide complex designs and three-dimensional displays in either black and white or color (Fig. 3-33).

Terminals are available with special features to suit the multitude of applications to which they are applied. In general, however, terminals are of three broad types: point-of-sale, interactive remote, and intelligent.

90

FIGURE 3-31
Terminal used to update air cargo records.

FIGURE 3-32
NEC-HE microcomputer serving as a remote job processing terminal.

FIGURE 3-33
A graphic display station.

Chapter 3   Input/Output Media and Devices

Point-of-Sale Terminals

In most retail firms, the majority of the raw data required for data processing operations originate at the point of sale. Therefore, if the data can be recorded on a computer-acceptable medium at the time of the transaction, the need for additional data-entry costs will be minimal. It is no wonder that **point-of-sale,** or **POS,** terminals are replacing the retailer's cash register (Fig. 3-34). POS terminals generally record the transactions on a self-contained cassette or are wired to a mini- or microcomputer, which records the data received from each of the terminals in the store (see Fig. 3-35). In the case of a large retail chain, often the data are communicated from the store's computer to a central computer that does the processing for the entire chain. To accomplish this, the data are converted to a form that can be transmitted over a telephone line by a controller located at the point of sale and are then converted back to a computer-acceptable medium by a controller at the site of the central computer system.

One of the advantages of a POS terminal being tied to a mini- or microcomputer is that once the item number has been entered, the computer can provide the correct price even though an incorrect price entry may have been made. Special documents, quantity prices, and similar information can also be programmed into the mini- or microcomputer.

Today, many consumer retail manufacturers premark their products with bar codes. Holographic scanners can read around the side of the object and detect the code no matter where it is located. This greatly reduces the need for a clerk to search out the code and pass it directly over the scanner (Fig. 3-36). Once the product-identifying data have been scanned, the terminal computer can provide the price and any other pertinent information. The computer also keeps track of each item sold and thus aids management in maintaining a current inventory status.

The particular bar code used can vary, as there is no single universally accepted code. The two principal codes are the **UPC (Universal Product Code)** and **Code 39** or **3-of-9 Code.** Even the UPC, used by most grocery and other

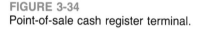

FIGURE 3-34
Point-of-sale cash register terminal.

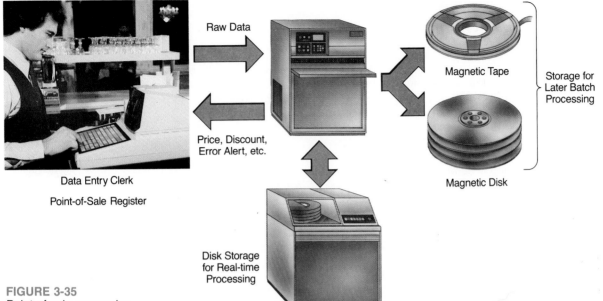

Raw Data

Price, Discount,
Error Alert, etc.

Data Entry Clerk

Point-of-Sale Register

Magnetic Tape

Magnetic Disk

Storage for
Later Batch
Processing

Disk Storage
for Real-time
Processing

FIGURE 3-35
Point-of-sale processing.

FIGURE 3-36
IBM's holograph point-of-sale terminal.

retail stores, is available in five slightly different versions. Code 39 is the only
bar code endorsed by the federal government.

Interactive Remote Terminals

An **interactive remote terminal** is a data entry device generally located at a
distance from a central computer system but online and operating under its
direct control. Typically, such devices generally consist of a keyboard and a
monitor to display messages received back from the central computer system

THE TWO MOST POPULAR BAR CODES—UPC AND CODE 39

The bar code shown is a version of the **Universal Product Code (UPC).** Information is enclosed as combinations of the binary digits 1 and 0 (represented by bars and spaces of a fixed width). The information contained on a typical label is comprised of nine individual parts. The first and last parts of the code are blank spaces equivalent in width to at least seven bars. In between, the **left guard band** alerts the scanner to receive coded data when the UPC code is scanned from left to right and that all data have been received when the UPC code is scanned from right to left; the **number system character** identifies which of the five UPC versions is used; the **manufacturer code** identifies Campbell as the product manufacturer; the **tall center bar** separates the manufacturer from the product half; the **product code** identifies a 10-¾ ounce can of Golden Mushroom Soup; the **modular check char-**

acter provides a check total when combined with the manufacturer and product codes scanned to ensure the correctness of the decoding process; and the **right guard band** signals the end or beginning of the coded information depending on the direction of scanning.

Note that the bit codes used to represent manufacturer digits are different from those used for product digits. This difference enables the scanner to determine the direction of scanning.

Each character encoded into **Code 39** or **3-of-9 Code** utilizes combinations of two wide and three narrow bars and one wide and three narrow spaces. That is, three of nine elements representing a character are wide bars or spaces. The dimensions of the bars and spaces must be precise to within .0017 inch. The blank space between characters and before and after the code must be multiples of the narrow bar or space width.

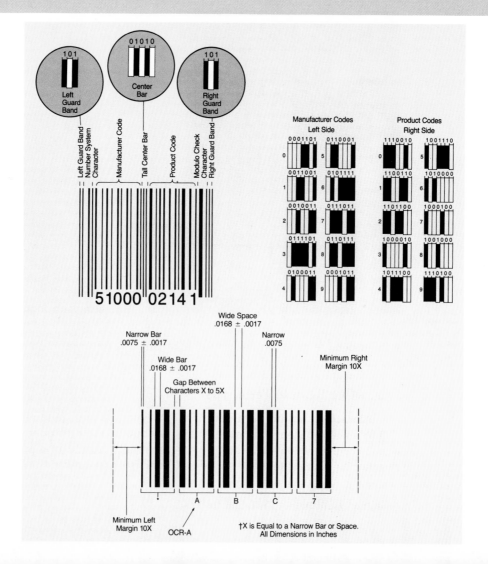

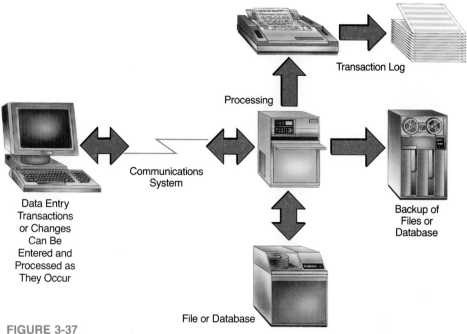

FIGURE 3-37
Interactive transaction processing.

(see Fig. 3-37). Currently, some monitors are capable of displaying as many as 2,000 characters at one time.

Once the data have been transmitted to the central computer, they can be edited, compared against predetermined limits, tested as to type, and so on. Errors detected by the central computer are reported back to the terminal for correction. Acceptable data are processed immediately or stored for future processing by the central computer system. A single central computer system can support numerous interactive remote terminals concurrently; thus the power of the central computer can be made available to many distant locations at the same time.

As seen in Fig. 3-38, data concerning a depositor at a savings bank is entered at a terminal, where it is fed directly into the bank's main computer. Under program control, the data entered by the user is used to calculate the new balance. As we learned earlier, processing of data fed to a computer in this manner is known as interactive processing. The computer then directs the output to a printer within the bank and also the bank's central database for updating.

If the interactive terminal has an ability to display graphical images in addition to text, it is often referred to as a **visual display terminal (VDT).**

Visual display stations are capable of displaying typed information, bar graphs, tables, and numerous other forms of visual output.

Interactive remote terminals are presently in use in the following areas:

1. *Airline reservation offices* for the purpose of accepting inquiries about available seats on scheduled airline flights and to display the computer's answer in a matter of seconds
2. *Commercial banks* to accept inquiries concerning the status of a consumer's account, possibly displaying the history of that account for the past several years, up to and including the instant the inquiry is made

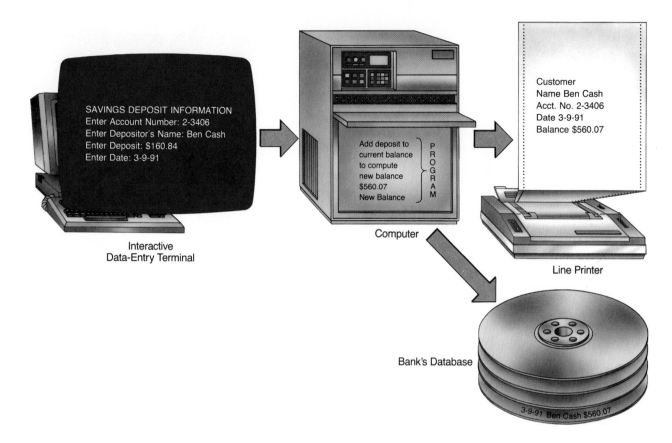

FIGURE 3-38
Interactive processing.

3. *Stock exchange brokerage houses* across the country to provide local offices with up-to-the-minute quotations of stock prices useful to customers

4. *Defense industry* for **CAD/CAM (computer-aided design/computer-aided manufacturing)** to aid scientists and engineers in the design and analysis of aircraft and space vehicles (see Fig. 3-39)

5. *Automobile industry* to aid in the design of automobiles (see Fig. 3-40)

Display stations such as the one shown in Fig. 3-41 are capable of displaying tables, graphs, charts, circuit diagrams, and alphanumeric data on a square screen containing more than 1 million display points. It can be equipped with a light pen that can be used alone or in conjunction with a keyboard to add, rearrange, or delete information displayed on the screen.

Intelligent Terminals

Intelligent, or smart terminals possess all of the capabilities of interactive remote terminals plus a processing capability. That is, an intelligent terminal can cue the operator by asking for information, and edit or process the data entered into it before transmitting the data to the central computer. This processing capability can vary from terminal to terminal, from abilities to format the data and perform limited editing to those of a complete mini- or microcomputer system. Some intelligent terminals have diskette storage attached. This enables the terminal to reconstruct information lost at or in transmission to the computer.

FIGURE 3-39
Computer graphics on a visual display terminal.

FIGURE 3-40
Visual display terminals are commonly used in automotive design. Positioned on this screen are the inner hood panel (white), dash panel (red), and engine parts with an oil pan (light blue).

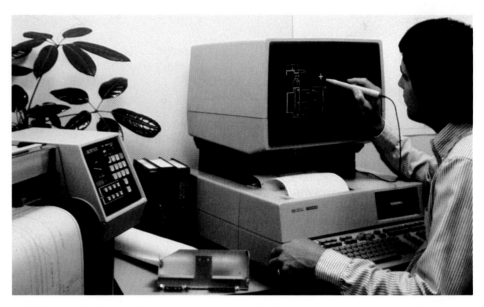

FIGURE 3-41
Light pen in hand, this engineer analyzes the control system of a jet aircraft prior to actual construction.

FIGURE 3-42
Quasar's intelligent terminal is available with a communications capability and a printer, all of which fit conveniently into a briefcase.

Intelligent terminals can function in either the real-time or batch processing modes. In the real-time mode, the data or transaction are communicated to the central computer as they are edited or processed. In a batch processing mode, the edited data are held or stored temporarily on disk at the terminal site. At some future time, the stored data can be loaded up **(uploaded)** to the central computer for processing.

Intelligent terminals are not generally used in applications where the primary concern is speed, but are used in those applications where accuracy is critical and where the operator must be familiar with the technical aspects of the application in order to interact with the central computer system. Such applications might include order processing, material control, text editing or word processing, and automatic bank tellers (Fig. 3-42).

Speech Recognition and Voice Response Devices

Speech recognition devices were introduced in the early 1970s. Typically, these systems contain a database of stored voice patterns for upwards of 250 words and the ten digits. This database of voice patterns is generally stored in a recognition unit or in secondary storage. A microphone, attached to the keyboard or recognition unit, records the spoken word patterns. A built-in microprocessor then compares, word by word, these patterns with the stored patterns and transmits the results of the comparisons to a computer for processing (see Figure 3-43). A sentence must be spoken as a series of disjointed words and numbers spoken as a series of digits and not as a single number. For example, the sentence, "The answer is 3,456." might be input as six separate voice patterns: "RESULT, EQUALS, THREE, FOUR, FIVE, SIX." Speech recognition devices are generally used in situations where access to a switch or control is not possible or where a user's hands are otherwise occupied.

Because voice patterns vary greatly from person to person, most speech recognition devices are **speaker-dependent** and must be fine-tuned to each operator. This is generally accomplished by having the operator speak each of the words or digits to be stored in the recognition unit dictionary in the unit several times. An average of the spoken voice patterns is taken and stored as the standard or **mask** against which future voice communications will be compared.

recognize one persons voice

Speaker-independent systems are less common and have a very restricted vocabulary—generally the ten digits and a "yes" or "no" response. Despite their restricted vocabulary, speaker-independent systems are widely usable since they do not have to be fine-tuned but can be understood by anyone. Clearly, speaker-independent systems are more desirable than speaker-dependent systems, but their great expense, large database requirements, and the limitations of current technology have made their development tiresomely slow.

Speech recognition devices are currently employed in the preparation of numeric control tapes and in airline baggage sorting. Manufacturers are beginning to offer very sophisticated speech recognition devices for the more popular microcomputers. For example, more than a dozen such devices are available for the IBM PC microcomputer alone.

Voice response devices are commonplace in today's automated world. It is not at all unusual to hear "Warning! Warning! Your oil pressure is low" being "spoken" by the voice response device in your car. The audio response

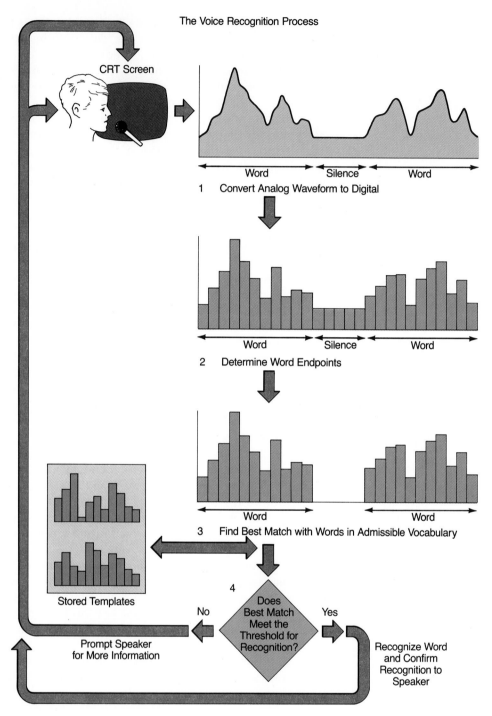

FIGURE 3-43
The speech recognition process.

100

is generally composed from a prerecorded vocabulary (selected from the most frequently used words associated with commercial and industrial applications) maintained on an external disk file. As an inquiry is received by the device, it is sent to the computer for decoding. The computer then decodes and evaluates the inquiry and, from the prerecorded vocabulary on disk, constructs an appropriate digitally coded voice message, which is sent back to the audio response unit. The audio response unit then converts this message to a vocal reply, which is "spoken" to the inquirer. Such systems are not limited to one language. Vortrax, for example, manufactures an audio response unit that is capable of speaking in English, French, German, and Spanish. Vortrax will custom make units to speak in virtually any language.

You may feel that computer-generated voice output is very "mechanical" or "artificial." This may be true, but the purpose of such a unit is expedience, not eloquence. It can be easily understood. It doesn't mumble, stutter, slur its words, or cough. These devices cannot reproduce the subtle shading of intonation commonly used in everyday speech. Their main advantage lies in the fact that they can be understood more than 99 percent of the time and that people respond more quickly to the spoken word than to the written word. Areas of application are generally characterized by situations that require responses to inquiries or verification of data entered directly into a computer system. Audio-response devices are typically used in banks for reporting bank account balance information, in large businesses for credit checking and inventory status reporting, and in experimental research to alert a worker who might otherwise be distracted or involved.

One of the strongest impacts made on the use of voice response has come from the manufacturers of microcomputers. They have brought the pricing and availability of voice response units down to a point where they are economically feasible for even the smallest concern. Voice response is no longer an isolated, esoteric discipline but another among the multitude of computer output techniques.

Vision Systems

For some, R2D2 and C3PO of Star Wars fame have forever changed our perception of all living creatures. Their ability to hear, feel, walk, talk, and especially to see has now brought all robotic "creatures" into our world of living creatures. Today's "real-life" robots have certainly not progressed to this extent, but are available with somewhat less sophisticated vision systems. A **vision system** utilizes a camera, digitizer, computer, and a technique known as image processing. **Image processing** is concerned with digitizing and storing of computer-processed images and with pattern recognition.

You are certainly familiar with examples of computer-processed images—computer-generated digitized portraits available for a few dollars at most amusement parks (see Fig. 3-44), computer-produced special effects in movies such as *Star Wars* and *Back to the Future, Parts II* and *III*, and digitized images of Jupiter and Saturn beamed from image processors onboard spacecraft to earthbound NASA computers where the images are reconstructed and displayed (see Fig. 3-45). The huge volume of data concerned with this latter operation forced NASA to construct a special supercomputer, the Massive Parallel Processor (MPP) computer, containing more than 16,000 individual processors.

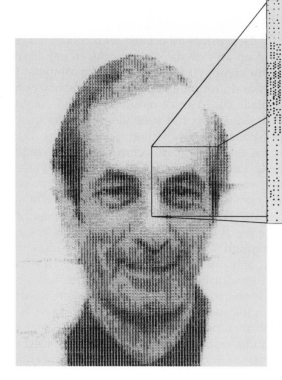

FIGURE 3-44
Computer-generated image.

FIGURE 3-45
NASA computer-generated photo of Saturn.

ARTIFICIAL VISION

The most important "sense" for a robot is sight. Sight enables robots to adjust to small changes in their work environment, giving them greater flexibility. The challenge is to develop a vision system that will enable a robot to see a part in a bin, recognize it, and pick it up. Picking parts out of a bin is trivial for humans but a giant step for a robot.

To date, artificial vision systems have no problem recognizing parts lying singly on a flat surface. Television cameras compare the image of what the robot "sees" to standard images stored in its memory. The television picture is digitized to reduce the number of bits of information required from 2.5 million to 10,000. The biggest drawbacks to these systems, besides being two-dimensional, are cost ($75,000 to $100,000) and speed (2 to 200 seconds to recognize a part). Continuing advances in microelectronics should make sight cheaper and faster as more memory becomes available to store higher quality images and the processors themselves become faster at "recognizing" objects.

The push to develop seeing robots is worldwide. Renault, the French auto maker, has developed a robot that can recognize each of 200 parts for transfer to the appropriate operations. Hughes Aircraft Company introduced a semiconductor-chip imaging system, called Omneye, that has "real-time" recognition capabilities using a digital camera.

Denny the Robot In the United States, robots nicknamed "Denny" are being considered for use as prison guards. These robots can "hear," "smell," and "see" approaching people. They can "shout" a warning and raise an alarm. They would be particularly useful for patrol duty at night.

All of these examples have one thing in common—their first step is to digitize an image. In a visual system, all images that must be recognized or interpreted must first be digitized and stored in a database. Only after the database has been established can the visual system be applied to pattern recognition. **Pattern recognition,** the process of interpreting images, begins when the system digitizes the image of the object to be interpreted. This digitized image is then compared to those in the database to determine a probable match. As it is unlikely that a perfect match will be achieved, there is always a small possibility of error. A robot at General Electric's Evandal, Ohio, engine plant uses a vision system to guide it during the welding of large steel plates. The very large size of these plates would make positioning them prior to welding virtually impossible by other means. In addition, GE's robot operates at speeds about twice those attainable by human operators, and with no loss in quality. As you might imagine, because of the tremendous storage requirements of the database, visual systems are only practical where the number of images is relatively small.

CAD/CAM

Two areas where personal computers are being used to improve productivity are **computer-aided design (CAD)** and **computer-aided manufacturing (CAM).** CAD permits architects and engineers to prepare complex drawings quickly and easily, greatly reducing the time they spend at the drawing board. Using light pens and specialized graphics terminals, workers can enter two- and three-dimensional drawings into a computer and have them displayed on the screen in full color (see Fig. 3-46). The designer may make changes to the drawing and have the computer analyze the displayed design. In this way, many different versions of a drawing can be examined and tested easily before the first prototype is actually manufactured.

FIGURE 3-46
In this computer-aided design (CAD) application, a grid pattern defines the compound shape of a body panel and the slope of a hood on a design model that has been measured by an electronic scanner. The three-dimensional measurements are stored and processed by a computer, which later directs a pen over a drawing board.

Each day, more and more factory operations are becoming automated. Computer-aided manufacturing (see Fig. 3-47) is often coupled with computer-aided design, and the interaction of the two is known as **CAD/CAM.**

Once a design has been entered into a computer with CAD, the calculations used to generate the design can be used by the computer to simulate the manufacturing process. For instance, after an automobile fender is drawn on the screen, a sander can be drawn next to it, and the entire sanding process can be simulated and recorded on magnetic tape or disk. The information on the tape or disk can then serve as the input needed to direct the movements of a computer-controlled machine, or robot to do the actual sanding.

CAD/CAM is an extremely dynamic field. People will be needed to fill the many positions that will be made available through the expansion of CAD/CAM applications. Computer-aided design and manufacturing have been used to great advantage in the automobile and aerospace industries to cut production time and improve product quality (see Fig. 3-48). Futurists see a time when CAD/CAM will enable computers of the future to design and build their own replacements. Won't that be interesting!

FIGURE 3-47
Computer-aided manufacturing (CAM).

FIGURE 3-48
CAD/CAM in operation.

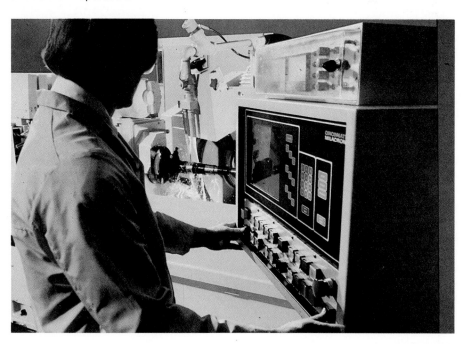

TABLE 3-1
A Summary of the Specifications of Selected Input/Output Devices

DEVICE	PURPOSE	MEDIUM	TYPICAL SPEED RANGES	CAPACITY	APPLICATION AREAS
Card Reader/Punch	Input/output of source data on 80- and 96-column punched cards	Punched card	150–2,500 cpm *reading, 8–600 cpm punching	80 or 96 characters per card	Low-volume applications in small or medium computer systems and for turnaround documents (telephone bills, etc.)
Paper Tape Reader/ Punch	Low-speed I/O of low-volume files	Paper tape	350–1,000 cps [†] reading, 15–150 cps punching	Up to 250,000 characters per tape; compact and easy to transport	Low-volume, long-term storage applications
Character Readers	Direct reading from source documents	Special paper or print	Up to 2,000 documents per minute		Installations requiring high-volume data input from source documents
Impact Line Printer	Low-volume hard-copy output	Regular paper	150–3,000 lines per minute	High-speed hard-copy output	Applications requiring low-volume reports, documentation, or results in printed form
Nonimpact Printer	High-volume hard-copy output	Regular or special paper	2,000–20,000 lines per minute	High-speed hard-copy output	For applications requiring a tremendous volume of hard-copy output
Computer Output Microfilm (COM)	Storage of large-volume output for subsequent remote use	Microfilm or micro-fiche	40,000–120,000 cps	Up to 2,000,000 lines of data	High-volume output for later use on a COM reader
CRT Display Devices	Keyboard entry of input data and inquiries; visual display of output on the CRT	Cathode ray tube	Up to 35,000,000 pixels (picture elements) per second	More than 1 million pixels per screen	Online inquiries and file updating; ideal in time-sharing and reservation systems

* cards per minute
[†] characters per second

SUMMARY AND GLOSSARY OF KEY TERMS

- The input/output devices that support a computer system are referred to as **peripheral devices.** The overall efficiency of a computer system is highly dependent on peripheral devices.

- **Key-to-tape** systems are used to transfer characters manually entered via a keyboard onto magnetic tape. **Key-to-disk** systems require mini- or microcomputer support and record data initially on disk.

- **Character readers** are capable of accepting printed or typed characters from source documents and converting these data into a computer-acceptable code for processing. The three principal character readers are **magnetic-ink** character readers, which read and interpret characters recorded with a special magnetic ink,

optical mark readers, which read and interpret pencil marks on special forms, and **optical character** readers, which read and interpret hand-printed or typed documents at rapid speeds.

- **COM (computer output microfilm)** converts computer output to a human-readable form stored on rolls of microfilm or microfilm frames stored on cards, referred to as **microfiche.**

- Many input devices provide information to the computer by *pointing* to something appearing on the display screen. Among the most popular pointing devices are the **light pen, digitizer pad, mouse, joystick, trackball,** and **touchscreen.**

- Printers are classified as **impact** or **nonimpact.** Impact printers are by far the most common, but nonimpact printers are faster and quieter.

- Impact printers are of two types: character printing devices and line printing devices. **Character printing devices** are similar to typewriters in operation and commonly use **dot-matrix** and **daisy wheel** elements. The output from daisy wheel printers is generally superior to that of dot-matrix printers, but they are also substantially slower than dot-matrix printers. Dot-matrix printers also have the distinct advantage of being able to handle **graphics** (graphs, plots, etc.). Character printers are commonly used with microcomputer systems.

- **Impact line printing devices** generally utilize **print wheels** or a moving **chain** or **drum.** The chain and drum printers are the most common of all impact printers. Line printers are principally used to support minicomputers and mainframe computer systems.

- Nonimpact printers, such as **laser, xerographic, electrostatic,** and **jet ink,** are the fastest of all printers. These printing devices are generally employed for special-purpose printing needs or where the volume of printing is great.

- **Plotters** range in size from the tiniest, intended for the home computer user, to the largest and most sophisticated plotting tables.

- **Terminals** are widely used data-entry devices. The **keyboard** is used to enter data, and the **CRT** or **monitor** displays output.

- Terminals can be used for **message switching, data collecting, inquiry** or **transaction processing, remote job processing,** and **graphical display** and **design.**

- **Point-of-sale terminals** can process transactions at remote locations by providing stored data to the user and at the same time updating previously stored data or storing new data concerning the transaction.

- **Interactive remote terminals** consist of a keyboard and a monitor and generally operate under the control of a remote central computer system.

- **Intelligent terminals** possess all the capabilities of interactive terminals *plus* a processing capability. They are most appropriate in applications where accuracy is primary and speed is secondary.

- **Speech recognition devices** generally contain voice patterns for upwards of 250 words and the ten digits. The unit simply compares spoken words to these stored patterns and transmits the result to a computer for processing. These devices are generally used where access to a switch or control is not possible or where a user's hands might be otherwise occupied.

- **Vision systems** provide a computer with "sight" via a camera, digitizer, processor, and a technique known as **image processing.** Image processing involves digitizing and storing selected images. Image processing is most commonly used for **pattern recognition.** The digitized image of an unknown object is compared against a database containing a number of previously stored patterns. The unknown object is assumed to be the item whose database pattern it most closely resembles.

- **CAD/CAM (computer-aided design** and **computer-aided manufacturing)** is among the most recent and most rapidly growing areas of computer applications in the automobile and aerospace industries.

EXERCISES

True/False

_____T___ 1. A light pen can be used to input data by simply touching the screen of a visual display terminal with a light pen.

_____T___ 2. Impact printers are more commonly used than nonimpact printers.

_____F___ 3. More flexibility in using special characters is possible with a daisy-wheel printer than with a dot-matrix printer.

_____T___ 4. Computer-aided manufacturing is generally performed in conjunction with computer-aided design.

_____T___ 5. OCR devices can recognize alphanumeric characters and convert those characters to machine-recognizable form.

_____T___ 6. Speech recognition devices compare spoken words to stored word patterns and respond accordingly.

_____T___ 7. MICR requires special ink that is magnetized.

_____F___ 8. All computer printers require special paper.

_____T___ 9. A visual display terminal serves as both an input and output device.

_T_ **10.** An audio response device usually has a prerecorded vocabulary.

_T_ **11.** The three most common impact line printers are the chain, drum, and print-wheel printers.

_T_ **12.** Point-of-sale terminals are rapidly replacing the cash register in retail stores.

_F_ **13.** OCR devices can read most handwriting styles.

_T_ **14.** OCR devices are generally impractical in installations processing less than several thousand documents per day.

_T_ **15.** Printers are subdivided into two broad categories, impact and nonimpact.

_T_ **16.** Input/output devices are commonly referred to as peripheral devices.

_F_ **17.** A fast and common type of impact line printer is the dot-matrix printer.

_T_ **18.** COM devices convert computer output to a form stored on rolls of microfilm or microfiche.

_T_ **19.** A terminal can be used for two-way communication with a computer which is near or far away.

_T_ **20.** Some POS terminals have optical scanning devices to read product codes.

_F_ **21.** The punch card reader is no longer in use.

_T_ **22.** Toner is typically used with xerographic and electrostatic printers.

_T_ **23.** Interactive remote terminals are used by commercial banks.

_T_ **24.** The most common computer output technique is printing.

_F_ **25.** The most typical keyboard arrangement is the Dvorak arrangement.

Fill-in

1. Printers are subdivided into two categories, _impact_ and _nonimpact_ .

2. COM stands for _Comp. output michrofilm_ .

3. The output technique known as _voice response_ uses devices that actually speak.

4. CRT is an abbreviation for _CRT_ .

5. Data and programs are usually entered into a terminal using a _keyboard_ .

6. A _daisey-wheel_ printer uses a single plastic or metal print element.

7. The fastest character printing device is the ~~non-impact line~~ _Dot Matrix_ printer.

8. Two industries where CAD/CAM has been used to cut production time and improve product quality are _Automobile_ and _aerospace_ .

9. A standard code used to premark products for point-of-sale terminal processing is the _UPS_ .

10. Character readers read _Hand_ characters from source documents and convert these data to a _Written_ form.

11. The primary users of MICR devices are _Banks_ .

12. _Optical mark readers_ requires that the data be recorded on special and carefully printed forms.

13. OCR stands for _optical character recognition_

108

14. Speech recognition devices can generally recognize the voice patterns for upwards of ___250___ words and ten digits.

15. The number 1,245 would be spoken into a speech recognition device as *one, two, four, five*

Problems

1. Contrast QWERTY and Dvorak keyboards.
2. Describe the different character readers in use. What types of applications are each used for?
3. What limitations are associated with speech recognition systems?
4. Contrast key-to-tape and key-to-disk data entry systems.
5. Briefly explain how point-of-sale recorders can be used.
6. How is MICR used by banks in check processing?
7. Discuss any recently introduced input or output devices about which you have read or heard. What do you believe to be their potential?
8. Determine whether each of the following devices or media are used for input only, output only, input/output, or as an offline device.
   - a. card reader
   - b. printer
   - c. visual display device
   - d. COM
   - e. audio device
   - f. terminal
   - g. plotter
   - h. keyboard
   - i. intelligent terminal
   - j. mouse
   - k. light pen
   - l. POS
   - m. touchscreen
9. Compare the similarities and differences of impact and nonimpact printers. Point out the advantages and disadvantages of each.
10. Discuss the role of the input and output devices in the overall performance of a computer system.
11. List three areas in which interactive remote terminals are being used.
12. In the past, laser printers and nonimpact printers were not heavily used. Explain why.
13. List some of the functions performed by terminals.
14. Explain how dot-matrix printers form characters.
15. What is the relationship that exists between laser printers and desktop publishing.

Projects

1. Visit a computer center and determine what input/output devices are being used. What new devices are being considered?
2. Examine a current issue of a computer-related magazine or newspaper and identify and describe an input/output device not described in the text.
3. Survey manufacturing companies in your area to determine those utilizing CAD/CAM and in what capacity.

Crossword Puzzle

Across

1. To transfer data from a terminal to a central computer
2. An impact printer that uses wires to form characters
3. A type of scanning device
4. A common code used to mark products
5. Data input device used with microcomputers
6. Character style
7. A process that uses magnetic ink
8. A type of character reader
9. Type of printer that uses a hammer
10. Hand held pointing device
11. The interpreting of human speech by a computer
12. Device that replaces the standard cash register
13. Can accept printed characters directly from source documents
14. An intelligent terminal
15. Not QWERTY but _____
16. A pointing device used to enter data

Down

17. High resolution nonimpact printer
18. I/O device
19. Printers that print characters without using a hammer
20. The type of output produced by audio-response devices
21. Computer aided design and manufacturing
22. Lets your fingers do the pointing
23. COM on film
24. Used in laser printers
25. Output device that uses microfilm
26. An automated system that sees
27. A terminal display screen
28. A type of impact line printer
29. Entering data from keyboard to disk

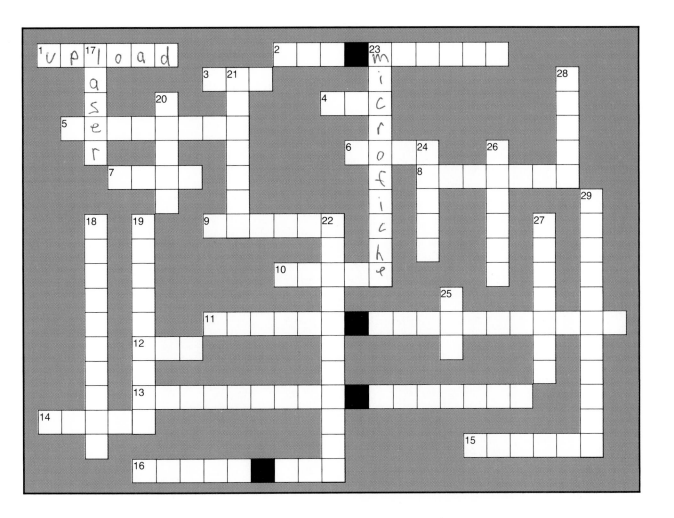

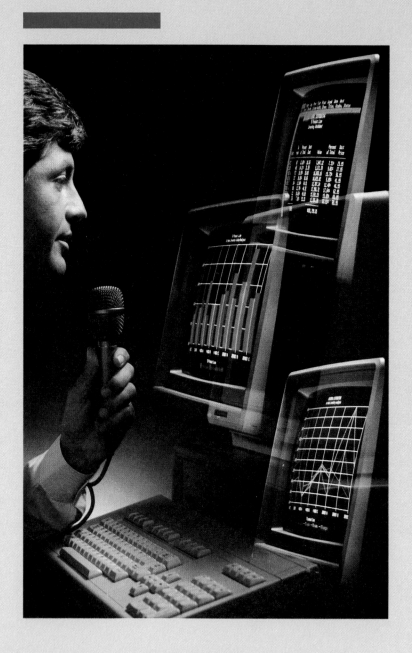

4

SECONDARY STORAGE AND FILE PROCESSING
The Computer's File Cabinet

Objectives

- List and describe commonly used secondary storage devices.
- Describe the characteristics of magnetic tape and disk secondary storage.
- Compare the advantages and disadvantages of magnetic tape and magnetic disk.
- Distinguish between the two types of files—master files and transaction files.
- Describe the principal factors to be considered in designing a file.
- Describe the three major file organizations and the advantages and disadvantages of each.
- Describe how data are processed when each type of file organization is used.
- Understand and use the key terms presented in this chapter.

arlier, we discussed the *information explosion* and how it is the direct result of the power and proliferation of the computer. The unprecedented volume of data being churned out every minute by millions of computers in businesses, universities, and everywhere across the land must be recorded and stored somewhere. If we were limited to paper storage as in the past, we would all be in danger of being displaced by loaded file cabinets. But fortunately, and in typical fashion, the very industry that has created the problem has also come up with the solution—for now anyway. Large amounts of programs and data are currently stored in compact form on various secondary storage media (see Fig. 4-1).

In this chapter we shall discuss the various types and capabilities of secondary storage devices as well as how data are organized, stored, and accessed from these devices.

PRIMARY VERSUS SECONDARY STORAGE

In Chapter 2 we learned that most computer systems contain both primary and secondary storage. **Primary storage,** or **RAM,** is a limited-capacity temporary storage area directly accessible to the CPU at high speed. It is used to store the program instructions and data currently being processed by the CPU. As soon as a program is no longer needed, its instructions and data are replaced by those of the next program.

Secondary storage, on the other hand, is a more permanent receptacle for program instructions and data. Virtually any device that can input, output, and store information can provide secondary storage. The limitation, however, is that before instructions or data contained in secondary storage can be processed, they must be routed through primary storage.

FIGURE 4-1
Row after row of disk storage devices are needed by some companies to store the enormous amounts of data processed routinely.

Why Use Secondary Storage?

A principal reason for using secondary storage is that it is **nonvolatile;** stored information is not lost when power is turned off.

In addition to permanence, secondary storage is cost-efficient. You can have a lot of secondary storage for the cost of a little RAM. Today, for example, 1 million bytes of secondary storage can be had for the price of 10 thousand bytes of RAM—a ratio of 100 to 1.

One reason for this cost difference is speed. As we said earlier, the computer transfers instructions and data between the CPU and RAM. These exchanges of instructions and data are taking place continually as the computer is used, regardless of the applications to which the computer is being put. The computer must also transfer instructions and data between RAM and secondary storage. However, these transfers are far less frequent, and hence they do not directly affect the overall performance of the system and can be somewhat slower. Transfers between the CPU and RAM are generally measured in **nanoseconds** (billionths of a second), whereas transfers between secondary storage and RAM are generally measured in **milliseconds** (thousandths of a second).

DATA ORGANIZATION TODAY

Since secondary storage is used to hold large amounts of information, it is essential that this information be organized to facilitate the greatest possible flexibility and access speed. Just how does a computer system organize its data?

The Data Hierarchy

Essentially, raw data is organized into characters, fields, files, and databases.

A **character** is a letter, number, or "special" character (*, %, $). Each character is normally represented by one byte (eight bits). Characters are grouped to form fields.

A **field** is a set of characters treated as a unit of information. The address *14 Tanwood Court* is a 16-character field consisting of related characters. Basically, there are three types of fields: alphabetic, numeric, and alphanumeric.

- **Alphabetic fields** only contain letters of the alphabet and spaces.
- **Numeric fields** typically consist of the digits 0–9, a decimal point (.), a plus sign (+), and a minus sign (−).
- **Alphanumeric fields** may consist of combinations of letters of the alphabet, digits, and special symbols like %, $, and !.

It should be mentioned at this time that within a field, numeric data are generally **right-justified,** and alphabetic or alphanumeric data are **left-justified.** That is, numeric data are placed as far right as possible within the field, and alphabetic and alphanumeric data are placed as far left as possible within the field. This is shown in Table 4-1.

TABLE 4-1
Examples of Different Type Fields

ALPHABETIC	NUMERIC	ALPHANUMERIC
JESSE	401076	GARDEN CITY,NY
Blanks	+43.1	+43.1
NET PROFIT	−711	$823.72
Data Name	3.459	ABCDEF
GARDEN CITY	80.07	99.44%

A **record** is a collection of logically related fields. A payroll record would normally contain fields for an employee's social security number, name, address, gross pay, and so on (see Fig. 4-2). Each field is of a *predetermined size*, sufficiently large enough to hold the required data.

A **file** is a collection of related records. The set of all employee records within a company could be organized into a single payroll file.

A **database** could be viewed as a set of logically related files, organized to facilitate access and to reduce redundancy (see Fig. 4-3). Databases will be discussed fully in Chapter 8.

Let us assume that a company records all transactions directly into a computer via a terminal (Fig. 4-4). As a terminal operator, you simply key the data as requested by the system directly onto a preformatted screen. The **cursor,** or blinking underscore, guides you by positioning itself at the beginning of the first field for which data are to be input. As you enter the data into the field, character by character, the cursor moves along with each character until either you complete the entry or the field is filled. The cursor then moves automatically to the next field, until you are given an opportunity to key data into each field of the record. You then verify the correctness of the data input, making any necessary changes. Once you have visually checked the record, you transmit the entire record to the computer to be processed or stored on a secondary storage medium for later processing. A screen format to assist a terminal operator is shown in Figure 4-5.

FIGURE 4-2
Fields make up records.

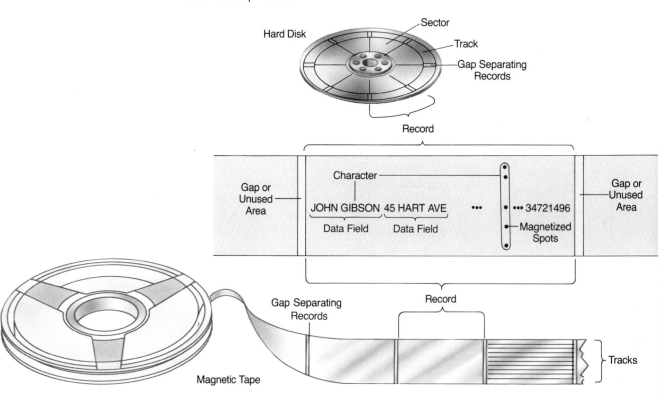

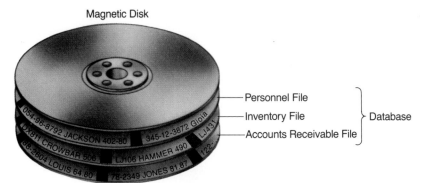

Magnetic Disk

Personnel File
Inventory File — Database
Accounts Receivable File

FIGURE 4-3
Records make up files; related files
make up a database.

FIGURE 4-4
A typical data-entry terminal in use.

FIGURE 4-5
A formatted screen for data entry.

TAPE STORAGE

Magnetic Tape Devices

Magnetic tape is a common secondary storage medium, used principally for storing large amounts of data in a predetermined orderly sequence. Its widespread use is due to its high **transfer rate** (characters that can be read or written per second), storage **density** (bytes or characters recorded per inch of tape), mass storage capability, compact size, and relatively low cost of operation. The IBM magnetic tape subsystem, for example, has a transfer rate of several million characters or bytes per second (see Fig. 4-6). This is extremely fast when compared to a high-speed impact printer capable of printing a maximum of approximately 6,000 characters per second.

Magnetic tape devices function as input storage and output units and may be operated under the control of the computer (online) or independently (offline) to perform routine conversions, such as tape-to-printer or disk-to-tape.

FIGURE 4-6
IBM 3480 magnetic tape cartridge and subsystem.

Figure 4-7 shows the manner in which data are recorded on tape. Notice that each character stored on the tape occupies one vertical column across the tape. Each column contains the combination of bits that represents the character in addition to a check bit. The check bit is used by the system to verify that the bits representing a character are not altered during the reading or processing of the tape. When data are initially recorded on a tape, the bit configuration for each character, including the check bits, is copied from primary storage and transferred to the tape.

The actual reading or writing of characters onto tape takes place while the tape is in motion. During these operations, the tape must be moving at a constant speed. Consequently, a blank space must be left on the tape before and after each record or **block** (two or more records) of data written. This space, referred to as an **interrecord gap (IRG)** when it separates individual records and as an **interblock gap (IBG)** when it separates blocks, serves three purposes:

1. While the tape is accelerating from rest to the constant speed at which the tape must be moving before data can be read or written, no data are lost.
2. While the tape is decelerating from constant speed after having read or written one record or block, no data are lost.
3. It physically separates records or blocks from one another.

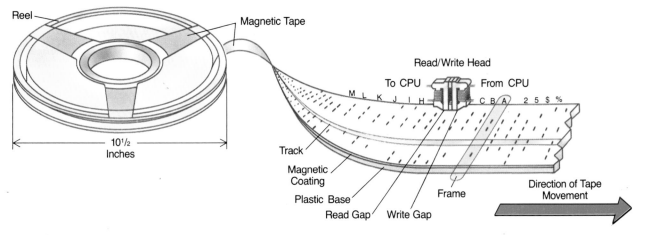

FIGURE 4-7
Magnetic tape is 1/2 inch wide and generally contains nine recording **tracks** running length-wise along the tape. A read/write recording head is positioned over each of the 9 (18 in a 3480 tape cartridge) tracks. A vertical section, or **frame,** of tape contains a combination of magnetic spots representing the character stored there. The **density** of the tape is a measure of the number of frames or characters that can be recorded per inch of tape. Magnetic tape densities can be as high as 6,250 bytes per inch (bpi) when using an iron-oxide coating and 38,000 bpi when using a chromium-dioxide coating. The rate at which data can be copied to or from magnetic tape, referred to as the **transfer rate,** can exceed 3,000,000 characters per second.

Tape IRGs or IBGs range in size from 0.6 to 0.75 inch, a space capable of otherwise storing thousands of characters.

Tape records are not limited to any fixed number of bytes, characters, or fields. A tape record can be any size, provided that the computer's memory is large enough to hold the record. Figure 4-8 illustrates some of the possible ways in which records can be recorded onto magnetic tape.

FIGURE 4-8
Records stored on magnetic tape are generally the same length and are recorded in groups (blocked records).

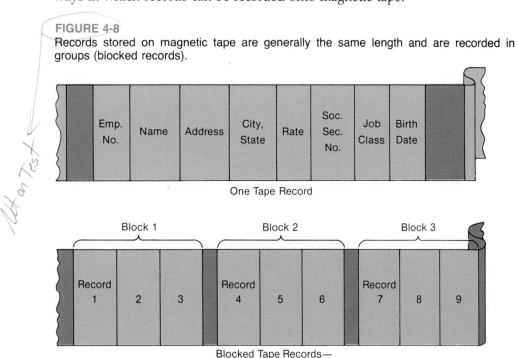

One Tape Record

Blocked Tape Records—
Blocked Three

Magnetic tape files can be easily protected against accidental erasure of data. The most common means is through the use of a **file protect ring.** This is a plastic ring that fits into a grove in the back of the magnetic tape reel. When it is installed, the tape can be read and written on. However, when the file protect ring is removed, the tape can no longer be written on but is still capable of being read. The jargon for this is "no ring, no write."

Limitations of Magnetic Tape

The use of magnetic tape does have some limitations. First and foremost is the fact that a magnetic tape may only be processed **sequentially.** That is, data must be recorded onto and read from a magnetic tape in a predetermined order. For example, if the magnetic tape were created containing a payroll record for each employee in a company in ascending sequence by employee number, the payroll records could only be read, or accessed, in that sequence. In other words, records would have to be accessed in numeric order, beginning with the record of the employee with the lowest employee number and ending with the record of the employee with the highest number. In addition, if one or more records are to be added to or deleted from those contained on the magnetic tape, it is usually necessary to recopy the entire tape.

For many applications, this limitation offers little or no problem. However, applications that require the ability to access a specific record quickly and directly without the need to access all previous records, cannot effectively utilize magnetic tape.

DIRECT-ACCESS STORAGE

Magnetic Disk

In addition to magnetic tape, several other media and devices are used to input data to and output it from a computer. These devices include the **magnetic disk** and mass storage system. Data are stored on these devices in the form of magnetic spots in much the same manner as they are stored on the surface of a magnetic tape. As with magnetic tape devices, these disks can be used to input and output data sequentially. But unlike magnetic tape devices, these devices can also input or output data records directly. That is, records do not have to be recorded on disks in a predetermined order, nor do they have to be accessed in any particular order. A single record can be read from or written directly onto any one of these devices without the need to read or write any previous records. This capability has led to these devices being referred to as **direct-access storage devices (DASDs)** (Fig. 4-9).

Magnetic disk storage consists of a series of thin, magnetically coated disks, similar in appearance to a stack of phonograph records. These disks are mounted on a vertical shaft, each disk separated from the disks above and below it by a small space. As the shaft rotates, it spins the disk at a very high but constant speed, generally more than 2,000 revolutions per minute. As these disks revolve about the center vertical shaft, read/write access arms are free to move in and out between the disks (Fig. 4-10). Each of these access arms contains several read/write heads that can read or write on the disk surface immediately above or below the heads (see Fig. 4-11).

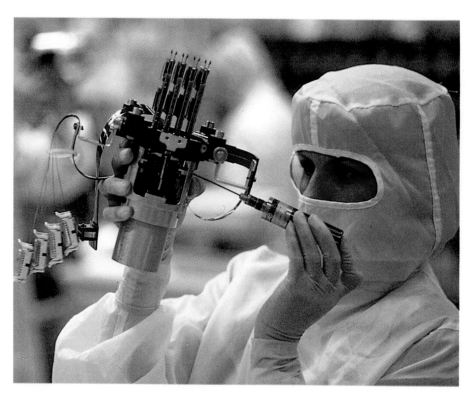

FIGURE 4-9
Technician adjusting access mechanism of a direct-access storage unit.

FIGURE 4-10
Magnetic disk access mechanism. The access arm is used to move the read/write heads over the tracks of a disk.

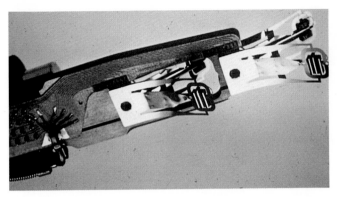

(a)

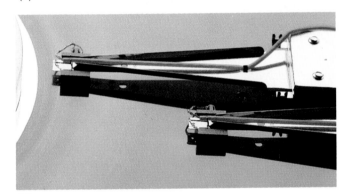

(b)

FIGURE 4-11
(a) One arm of a disk read/write mechanism containing a total of four read/write heads. (b) Read/write access heads riding over the surface of a disk.

Data are recorded on the surface of a disk magnetically in much the same way that they are recorded on magnetic tape or a magnetic drum. The recording surface of each disk is subdivided into concentric areas, or **tracks,** similar to the concentric circles that appear on an archery target. In one complete revolution of a disk, the read/write head assigned to a disk surface can completely read or write the entire track over which it is positioned. To read or write on a different track, the head would have to be moved in or out and positioned over the new track to be read or written on.

Data are recorded serially around a track, with individual data records separated by IRGs, as is done when records are recorded on magnetic tape. The storage capacity of each track on a disk is exactly the same. Thus data must be stored at greater and greater density as the data is located closer to the center of the disk. Some systems further subdivide the disk into **sectors,** but this is less common with the hard disks used with mainframe systems than it is with the floppy disks used with microcomputers.

Disks generally contain from 40 to over a thousand accessible tracks per surface. Each of these tracks can be uniquely accessed as the read/write heads are moved in and out. It should be noted, however, that all of the access arms containing the heads move in and out together. Thus, when a read/write head is positioned over a track on one disk surface, the other read/write heads are automatically positioned over the same track on the other disk surfaces. These vertically positioned tracks are collectively referred to as a **cylinder.** Data contained on any of the tracks constituting a cylinder may be accessed without any need to move the access arms in or out. Thus, to access a single track

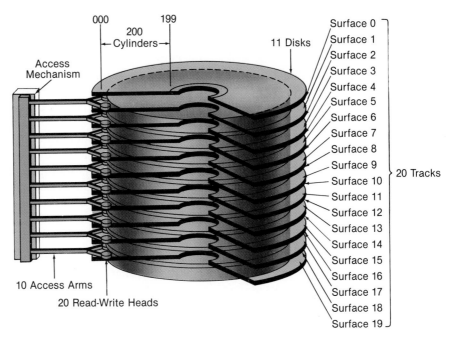

FIGURE 4-12
Organization of an 11-disk disk pack.

uniquely anywhere on the disk, one would have to provide the number of the cylinder containing the desired track and the disk surface on which the track is located (see Fig. 4-12).

Disks may be permanently attached to the drive unit or they may be made up as removable **disk packs** containing six or more disks each (see Fig. 4-13). Disk packs, depending on the particular model, can store tens of millions of characters.

FIGURE 4-13
Changing disk packs in a disk drive is a relatively simple task.

As is the case with magnetic tape, once the data have been recorded on a magnetic disk, they may be read an indefinite number of times and will remain on the disk until they are written over. Disk storage devices are capable of reading and writing data sequentially or directly, which makes them very flexible. Disk packs also provide the capability of easy removal and portability not available with primary storage.

For those organizations requiring more direct-access storage than is available with a single disk unit, a number of direct-access storage facilities are available. A disk storage facility contains multiple disk units and can provide direct-access storage in **gigabytes** (billion bytes), access any record stored in an average time of a few thousandths of a second, and transfer information between it and the CPU at a rate of more than 2 million bytes per second.

Mass Storage System

If you're really serious about storing *huge* amounts of data, you will be interested in a mass storage system. IBM markets a unit that can store several hundred gigabytes of data. This is comparable to the capacity of thousands of disk packs, or tens of thousands of reels of tape. This system combines the low cost of magnetic tape with the direct-access capability of magnetic disk.

The data are recorded on **cartridges,** each capable of storing over 50 megabytes of data. These data cartridges reside in cartridge storage cells from which they can be accessed by the cartridge access station (Fig. 4-14).

The mass storage facility can accept requests from several different computer systems. Upon receiving a request for data, it searches the inventory of cartridges and mass storage volumes to locate the cartridge on which the data are contained. Once located, the desired cartridge is retrieved by the access station, mounted on the read/write station, opened, and its contents transferred to a disk for processing. If the processing of the record causes it to be updated

FIGURE 4-14
Cartridge access station from an IBM mass storage system.

or changed, it is then written back on the tape over the old record, and then the cartridge can be returned to its cell. All this can be accomplished for any of several hundred gigabytes in a maximum of a few seconds.

FILE PROCESSING CONCEPTS

Earlier, we learned that a **file** is a collection of records composed of related items or fields. An inventory file, for example, would consist of a collection of inventory records, each record of which could describe an item in the company's inventory. Each record would, in turn, be composed of such fields as the name and number of the item, the number on hand, the order point, the minimum quantity order, the selling price, and the discount structure. Most file-processing systems use two types of files, master files and transaction files.

A **master file** contains data that are needed over a relatively long period of time. For example, a master file containing a bank's savings accounts would contain records consisting of a customer's name, account number, current balance, date, and so on. When a customer makes a deposit or a withdrawal, the file is *updated*, or modified, immediately to reflect the changes—in this case, a new balance. As this is an *interactive processing system*, it is necessary to update the master file at the time of the transaction. However, in a batch-processing system, transactions are saved on a **transaction** (or **detail**) **file** until some future time when the master file will be updated. Transaction files generally contain individual transactions or other data needed for a relatively short period of time.

Before an appropriate file storage medium can be selected or a file can be created, the *application* of the file must be carefully examined. Clearly, one major concern in this examination is the data to be recorded on the file. But an equally important and less obvious concern is *how* the data are to be placed on the file. To determine this, one must first know how the data are to be accessed from the file. For example, will the application allow for sequential processing of one record after the other, as a computer would read records from a magnetic tape, or will the application require the ability to access a specific record directly from the file without having to access all previous records, as a computer would access an item directly from its memory?

It is even possible that an application might require both of these methods. In this case, when the file is created the data records must be placed on it in such a way that they can be retrieved either directly or sequentially, as dictated by the nature of the application. To illustrate this concept, let us examine the organization of this textbook. When this book was created, it was organized so that you would have either sequential or direct-access capability. You could access the information contained in it sequentially by reading one page after the other. On the other hand, should you need a specific item of "data," you could refer to the index for the page on which the item is contained, then turn to that page and begin reading.

Organizational Considerations

The three principal factors that must be considered to determine an appropriate file organization are volatility, activity, and size.

Volatility is a measure of the frequency with which records are added to or deleted from a file. A **static** file is one in which there are relatively few additions or deletions, A **dynamic** file, on the other hand, is one in which there are a significant number of additions and deletions in a given period of time.

Activity refers to the average number of records that are processed during a single computer run. The ratio of accessed to nonaccessed records is high in an active file and low in an inactive file. In cases where the activity—the percentage of accessed records—is low, the file should be organized to allow a minimum access time to each record.

Size refers to the number of records on the file. This is an important consideration when a file is so large that it cannot fit in the available disk space. The file must be organized to minimize the time required to process the file.

After these factors have been carefully examined, one should have a clear picture of the processing requirements. It now remains to choose the specific file organization to be employed. Before this can be done, one must be familiar with the three commonly used file organizations: sequential, direct, indexed. Let us consider each of these.

Sequential Files

A **sequential file** is one in which the records have been arranged into ascending or descending sequence according to the value in a **key field** (see Fig. 4–15). In cases where several records may have the same value in their key fields, a secondary key field should be specified. Sequential files are generally maintained on magnetic tape, disk, or a mass storage system.

FIGURE 4-15
Records on a sequential file are arranged in key-field sequence.

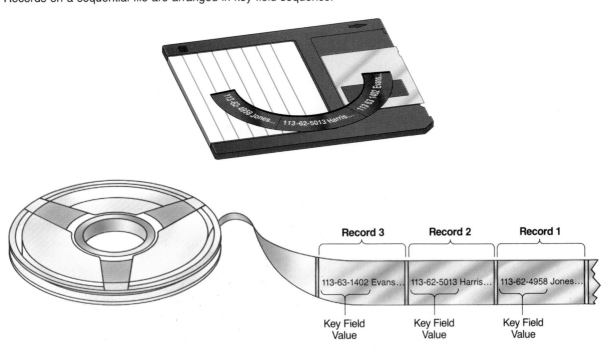

Unit 2   Computer Hardware

Processing Sequential Fields

With **sequential processing,** data or transactions are collected into groups, or batches, and then submitted to the computer for processing at certain designated times—usually at prescheduled intervals. Normally, this involves reading and processing the first record, then the second record, and so on until the last record in the file has been processed. For applications such as payroll, sequential processing is ideal.

The application illustrated in Figure 4-16 uses sequential processing with one of the programs that makes up a company's payroll system. In this application, a transaction file containing changes to the payroll master file is used to create a new or updated payroll master file and an employee change report.

Sequential processing is most efficient when the activity is high. Because each of the programs within a payroll system generally accesses a large percentage of the available records, sequential file processing represents a cost-effective approach to the problem (see Table 4-2).

TABLE 4-2
Sequential Files—An Appraisal

ADVANTAGES	DISADVANTAGES
■ Very efficient when a majority of the records are updated ■ Files easy to design ■ Can be stored on inexpensive storage media such as magnetic tape ■ Old master file and transaction files are automatic backup files since updating produces a new file	■ If only a few records need updating, entire file must still be processed and a new file written ■ Master files must be sorted into key field sequence ■ Transaction files must be sorted into same key field sequence as master files they are updating ■ Files are only current immediately after an update ■ Records cannot be accessed directly

Direct Files

As with a sequential file, each record in a **direct file** must contain a key field. However, the records need not appear on the file in key field sequence. In addition, any record stored on a direct file can be accessed if either its location or its address is known. Previous records need not be accessed. The problem, however, is to determine how to store data records so that, given the key field of the desired record, its storage location on the file can be found. It would be ideal if the key field could also be the location of the record on the file, but this is rarely possible. Therefore, before a direct-organized file can be created, a mathematical **randomizing** or **hashing** scheme must be devised to convert the key field value for a record to the address or location of the record on the file. The particular scheme or method is generally called an **algorithm.** The selection of the individual hashing algorithm varies from application to application and is beyond the scope of this text. It is sufficient to say that determining the most appropriate and efficient algorithm can be very complex and generally requires an expert.

In a direct-organized file, then, each record on the file is assigned to a storage address based on an algorithm, or mathematical relationship between the value of the key field for that record and the address of that record on the file. Clearly, this method is not used for processing an entire file, but where a

"THE JURY IS INSTRUCTED TO DISREGARD-- UH, ERASE -- THE WITNESS' CONCLUSIONS...."

Goes thru to algorithms to figure out where it goes on disc.

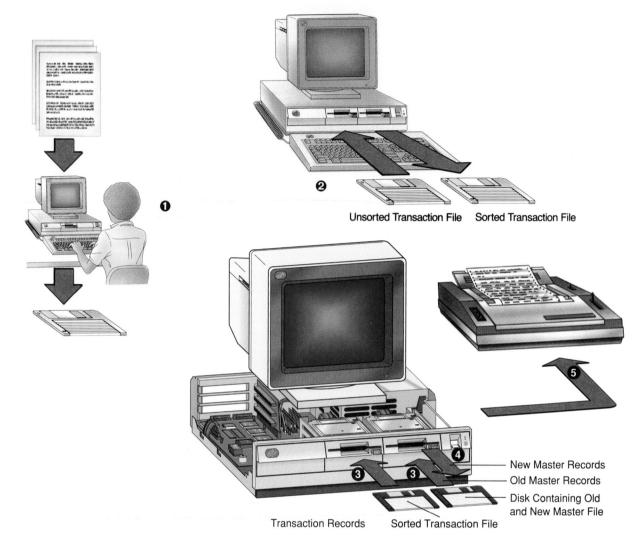

Unsorted Transaction File   Sorted Transaction File

New Master Records
Old Master Records
Disk Containing Old
and New Master File

Transaction Records   Sorted Transaction File

❶ Employee change data are entered via a terminal or computer and stored sequentially on tape or disk to form the **transaction file**.

❷ A program reads the transaction file and sorts the records into the same **key field** sequence as the master file, generally employee number sequence. The sorted transaction records are then written to tape or disk.

❸ A payroll change program reads a record from the payroll master file and/or sorted transaction file into memory.

❹ The program compares the value in the key field of each record. Unmatched master records are written directly to a **new** master file, matched records are updated and then written to the new master file.

❺ If a report, e.g., an employee change report is also to be produced, the appropriate data are edited and sent to the printer.

❻ Steps ③, ④, and ⑤ are repeated until both files have been completely read and processed.

❼ The transaction file and a copy of the "old" master file are kept for backup and the "new" master is used with payroll system programs until replaced by a "newer" master file.

FIGURE 4-16
Sequential update of a payroll master file maintained on magnetic disk.

TABLE 4-3
Direct Files—An Appraisal

ADVANTAGES	DISADVANTAGES
■ Terminals can be used to update files online as they occur, keeping the file current ■ No need for separate transaction files, as transactions are processed as they occur ■ Any record can be accessed in milliseconds ■ Not necessary to read entire file to update it; only master records to be updated need be accessed ■ Several files can be updated at the same time as transactions occur ■ Files do not have to be sorted into key field sequence	■ Backups must be created because updating destroys old records ■ Appropriate hashing algorithm often difficult to devise ■ Accidental destruction a problem ■ Security difficult to control because many users have access ■ More storage space may be required than for a sequential file ■ Does not facilitate sequential processing ■ Hardware and software requirements greater than for sequential files

limited number of records need to be accessed quickly and directly, as in the case of an online inquiry. This method of file organization is employed by airlines to obtain up-to-date flight information quickly and directly. All the agent needs to do is key in the flight number and the date of the flight (primary and secondary key field values), and the desired record is accessed and displayed on the agent's terminal screen virtually immediately. Direct-organized files are generally maintained on magnetic disk, optical disk (when the file is static), or on a mass storage system (see Table 4-3).

Indexed Files

An **indexed file** offers the simplicity of sequential file processing as well as a capability for direct access. In an indexed file, records are stored on the file in sequential order according to a key field. In addition, as the records are recorded on the file, the system establishes one or more **indexes** to associate the key field value(s) with the storage location of the record on the file. The system then uses these indexes to allow a record to be directly accessed. The indexes function in much the same manner as indexes function for a book of one or more volumes. That is, in order to access a particular record directly, the indexes are searched for the key value(s) of the desired record, which will then provide the address of the record to be accessed from the file. Indexed files are generally maintained on magnetic disk, optical disk (static files), or on a mass storage system (see Table 4-4).

TABLE 4-4
Indexed Files—An Appraisal

ADVANTAGES	DISADVANTAGES
■ Well suited for applications requiring both sequential and direct access ■ Access to specific records faster than with sequential files ■ Use of indexes eliminates need for a hashing algorithm as required with direct files	■ Storage requirements greater than with sequential files since space is required for the indexes ■ Random access slower than with a direct file ■ Require more complex hardware and software than needed with sequential files

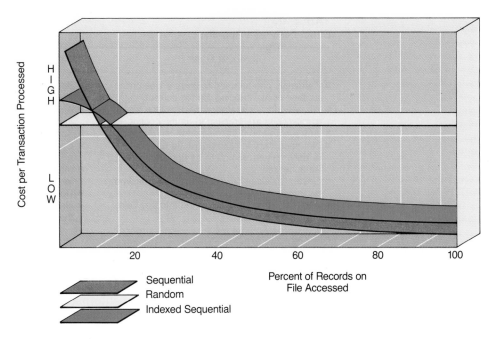

FIGURE 4-17
Cost versus activity for the three commonly used file organizations.

In summary, the primary differences between direct- and indexed-organized files are:

- Records may be accessed randomly from a direct-organized file, whereas records may be accessed sequentially *or* randomly from an indexed-organized file.
- Direct-organized files utilize a hashing algorithm to determine the location of a record, whereas indexed-organized files utilize indexes to locate a record to be randomly accessed.

Figure 4-17 illustrates the relationship between cost and activity for each of the three file organization systems, and Table 4-5 summarizes principal attributes.

Processing Direct or Indexed Files

Direct- or indexed-organized files are ideally suited for real-time applications involving interactive processing. You may recall that when **interactive processing** is used, data are entered into the computer and processed *immediately* to create output. There is no appreciable delay between the time the data are entered and when the output is generated. Thus, files used in these applications must be able to access any record in the file *directly*; preceding records need not be accessed. Typically, data are entered into the computer system from an online device such as a video display terminal or workstation.

When all of the data pertaining to a business transaction are entered and processed interactively, this is often referred to as **transaction-oriented processing.**

TABLE 4-5
File Organizations—A Comparison

FILE ORGANIZATION	TYPE OF ACCESS	STORAGE MEDIUM	FILE UPDATING	UP-TO-DATE DATA	ACTIVITY	VOLATILITY
Sequential	Records must be accessed sequentially	Tape,disk,* or mass storage system	Entire file must be processed and a new one created	No	High	Low
Direct	Records are accessed directly	Disk* or mass storage system	Records are updated in place	Yes	Low	High
Indexed	Records may be accessed sequentially or directly	Disk* or mass storage system	Records are updated in place	Yes	High	High

* Optical disks are being used for static files with large storage requirements.

SUMMARY AND GLOSSARY OF KEY TERMS

- The principal reason for using secondary storage is that stored information is not lost when power is turned off. It is also cost effective.

- Records are divided into **fields,** each of a fixed size and reserved for a unit of information. A field is described as a **numeric field** if it contains only digits or certain special characters (+, −, .); an **alphabetic field** if it contains only letters of the alphabet and blanks; or an **alphanumeric field** if it contains a combination of letters, digits, or special characters. Data is **right-justified** in a numeric field and **left-justified** within an alphabetic or alphanumeric field.

- A **file** is a collection of related records. A **database** can be viewed as a set of logically related files, organized to facilitate access and to reduce redundancy.

- Tape input/output devices utilize magnetized patterns in a magnetic material to record data. **Magnetic tape** is by far the most common tape medium due to the fact that it has a high **density** (characters per inch) and total capacity. In addition, the **transfer rate,** or number of characters per second that can be read from or written onto magnetic tape, is high. *when put on tape has gaps.*

- On magnetic tape records are separated by spaces called **interrecord gaps (IRGs);** groups of records, or **blocks,** are separated by **interblock gaps (IBGs).** To protect against the accidental writing over of data on a tape, a **file protect ring** is utilized. When this ring is removed, the tape can only be read ("no ring, no write").

- The principal disadvantage of tape is that it is only a **sequential** medium. That is, data records can only

be read and processed in the order in which they were written onto the medium. One record cannot be accessed without first accessing the records that precede the desired record. To read record number 100, for instance, you would first have to read records 1 through 99.

- **Magnetic disk,** the most popular storage medium, is a sequential or direct-access medium. Disk packs consist of a series of thin, magnetically coated disks that look like a stack of phonograph records. On each disk are a series of concentric paths, or **tracks,** each capable of storing the same amount of data. Reading and writing are accomplished magnetically and at high speeds. Data recorded on the surface can be accessed an indefinite number of times and are only removed when new data are recorded over them. Disk drives are available with fixed or removable **disk packs.**

- A **mass storage system** is a sequential or direct-access storage medium with a tremendous storage capacity (measured in gigabytes or billions of characters). The great speed possible with magnetic disk is sacrificed for the volume of data that can be stored.

- The manner in which these data are organized, stored, and accessed determines to a great extent the value that the results will have to a company, and the expense incurred in their production.

- **Master files** contain data that are needed and used over a relatively *long* period of time.

- **Transaction files** contain data needed for a relatively *short* period of time. Transaction files are used to update a corresponding master file.

- The three factors that must be considered to determine an appropriate file organization are **volatility,** the frequency with which records are added to or deleted from a file; **activity,** the average number of records processed during a single run; and **size,** the number of records on the file.

- On a **sequential file,** records are arranged in sequence (numeric, alphabetic, or alphanumeric) according to one or more **key fields.**

- With **sequential processing,** data are collected into groups, or batches, and then submitted to the computer for processing at certain prescheduled times.

- **Direct files** also make use of a key field in the data record. A record can be accessed directly from the file if its key field value is known. Records are placed into and retrieved from their locations on the file with the aid of an **algorithm.** An algorithm is a method for converting the key field value to a storage location on the file. Airlines utilize direct files to access information about particular flights. This file organization is generally not used when a large portion of the file must be accessed in a single application, that is, when the activity is high.

- The records on an **indexed file** are initially stored in sequential order according to one or more key fields. As the records are being recorded on the file, **indexes** are established by the system. These indexes associate the key field value(s) with the location of the record on the file. The system then uses these indexes to allow a record to be directly accessed. That is, the indexes are used to search for the key value(s) of the desired record. The key value will then provide the address of the record to be accessed from the file. Because the records were placed on the file in sequential order, the file may also be processed sequentially.

- Direct or indexed files are ideal for **interactive processing**—entering data directly into the computer where it is processed *immediately*. Records are located directly and are updated. When all of the data pertaining to a *complete* business transaction are entered and processed, it is referred to as **transaction-oriented processing.**

EXERCISES

True/False

＊ o̸ __F__ 1. A record is a collection of logically related files. *Data base*

__F__ 2. An alphanumeric field consists of numbers only. *#'s + letters*

__F__ 3. A record is another term for a large field.

__F__ 4. An algorithm is a method used to determine the location of a record in an indexed file.

__F__ 5. A master file contains data needed for a relatively short period of time.

__T__ 6. When interactive processing is used, data are entered into the computer and processed immediately to create output.

__T__ 7. Most file-processing systems use two types of files, master files and transaction files.

__T__ 8. Sequential processing is concerned with processing transactions in groups or batches.

__T__ 9. Magnetic tape can store more information than paper tape in the same length and width of tape.

__F__ 10. Sequential files never use more than one key field.

__F__ 11. It is generally a simple matter to determine an appropriate algorithm to convert key field data to the locations of the records on a direct organized file.

__T__ 12. Magnetic disk may be used for both sequential and direct-access processing.

__T__ 13. DASDs use magnetically coated surfaces to store data.

__T__ 14. Data stored on magnetic disk may be accessed sequentially.

__T__ 15. All tape media are inherently sequential.

__T__ 16. An advantage to using magnetic tape storage is that there is virtually no limit to the number of characters a record may contain.

132

_F_ 17. In order to file-protect a magnetic tape, the file-protect ring must be in place in the tape reel. *When it is removed*

_T_ 18. A cylinder consists of a series of tracks, each located the same distance from the center of each usable disk surface.

_T_ 19. Disk storage units are available with either fixed or removable disks.

_F_ 20. The surface of a disk is subdivided into concentric areas referred to as sectors. *Tracks*

_T_ 21. A distinct advantage of magnetic tape and disk is that they are reusable.

_T_ 22. Records on tape are separated by interrecord gaps.

Know gaps on Tape

_F_ 23. The direct-access storage device with the greatest capacity is the magnetic disk. *Mass storage System*

_T_ 24. Information is retrieved from magnetic disk via access arms which contain read/write heads.

_F_ 25. When transaction-oriented processing is used, only a portion of the total data needed for a complete business transaction is entered.

_F_ 26. Magnetic disk may not be used with sequential organized files.

_T_ 27. All data stored on a magnetic disk may be accessed randomly.

_F_ 28. A transaction file contains data needed for a relatively long period of time.

_T_ 29. Periodically, transaction files are used to update a corresponding master file with new data.

_T_ 30. With interactive processing, records can be accessed directly for updating; preceding records need not be accessed.

_F_ 31. Density refers to the speed with which characters can be read or written from tape or disk.

_T_ 32. The mass storage systems currently available can store data in the gigabyte range.

_T_ 33. Unlike magnetic tape devices, direct-access devices can input and output data directly.

_T_ 34. Magnetic tape devices operate at high speeds and provide the user with a low-cost medium for storing information.

_T_ 35. Data stored on magnetic tape are usually ordered by some key such as employee number.

Fill-in

1. A collection of related fields, independent of their physical environment, is a(n) *logical record*

2. Fields are classified, according to the type of information that they may contain, as *numeric* , *alphabetic* , or *alphanumeric* .

3. A tape medium currently in use is *magnetic tape*.

4. DASD is an abbreivation for *direct-access storage devices*

5. The three principal factors to be considered in order to determine an appropriate file organization are *volatility* , *activity* , and *size* .

6. A(n) *file* is a collection of related records.

7. A blinking underscore is called a(n) *cursor* .

8. A(n) *file protect ring* is used to protect against accidental erasure of data stored on magnetic tape.

9. Magnetic tape may only be processed *sequentially*.

10. ___Master___ files contain data that are needed over a relatively long period of time.

11. A(n) ___indexed___ organized file may be accessed sequentially or randomly.

12. Groups of records are separately by ___interblock gaps___

13. A(n) ___algorithms___ is a method for converting the key field value to a storage location on the file.

14. Concentric paths on a disk are called ___tracks___ .

15. A principal reason for using secondary storage is ___nonvolatile___ .

Multiple-Choice

___D___ 1. The principal factor that affects the organization of a file is
   a. Volatility
   b. Activity
   c. Size
   d. All the above
   e. None of the above

___B___ 2. Which of the following does not pertain to sequential or batch processing?
   a. Data are collected into groups before submission to the computer
   b. Data are submitted for processing immediately
   c. Is most efficient when the activity is high
   d. A transaction file is used to update a master file
   e. None of the above.

___E___ 3. The currently used file organizations include
   a. Sequential
   b. Direct
   c. Indexed
   d. Relative
   e. All the above

Wrong in back of book

___C___ 4. A storage medium that cannot be used for both direct-access and sequential-access applications is
   a. Mass storage system
   b. Optical disk
   c. Magnetic tape
   d. Magnetic disk
   e. None of the above

___C___ 5. Which of the following does not pertain to interactive processing?
   a. Data are entered into the computer immediately
   b. Also known as real-time processing
   c. Records are accessed sequentially
   d. No substantial delay between when the data are entered and when the output is generated
   e. None of the above

Problems

1. Define the following terms:

Algorithm	Key field
Direct-organized file	Master file
File	Sequential organized file
File organization	Transaction file
Index	Volatility
Interactive processing	

2. What is an interrecord gap? Why is it necessary in tape processing?
3. Name some business applications that would require interactive processing.
4. Describe and compare sequential-access storage with direct-access storage. Indicate what types of jobs would be best suited for each.
5. What are the advantages and disadvantages of an indexed file organization as compared to a sequential or direct file organization?
6. Compare the various types of storage media with respect to speed, cost, and data accessibility.
7. What is the purpose of the file protect ring?
8. What is meant by access time? Why is it an important consideration when selecting a secondary storage device?
9. Why is access time generally given in the form of an average?
10. In most computer systems several types of secondary storage devices are generally used. Why?

Projects

1. What kind of file organization do you think would be appropriate for each of the applications below? Visit local businesses to verify your choices.
   a. Payroll   b. Personnel
   c. Accounts payable   d. Accounts receivable
   e. Inventory
2. Choose one of the above application areas and determine what fields should be included in each data record contained on the file(s) employed. Be sure to indicate which field(s) should be the key field(s). Also indicate how many and what types of characters you would allocate to each field.
3. Visit the computer center in your school or at some other location. Investigate the type of processing going on there and describe it as either sequential or interactive.

CROSSWORD PUZZLE

Across

1. Not dynamic but _____
2. Organization of a tape file
3. No data loss when power is removed
4. A direct access storage device
5. Set of logically related files
6. Placement of numeric data within a field
7. A field containing digits
8. Blinking underscore
9. A field that determines the order in which records will appear
10. A section of a disk
11. A ring used to protect against accidental erasures

Down

6. A collection of logically related fields
12. One billion bytes
13. A static file
14. A part of a field
15. A collection of related records
16. Characters treated as a unit
17. Separates tape records
18. A file organizational consideration
19. A circular area on a disk
20. The number of characters that can be read or written per second
21. Characters per inch

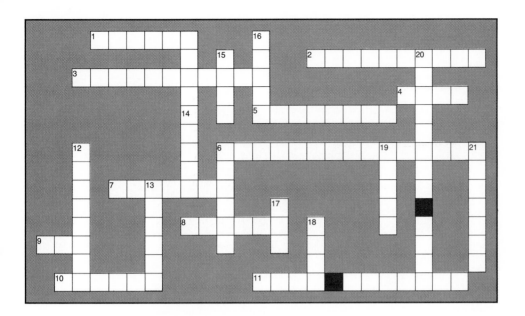

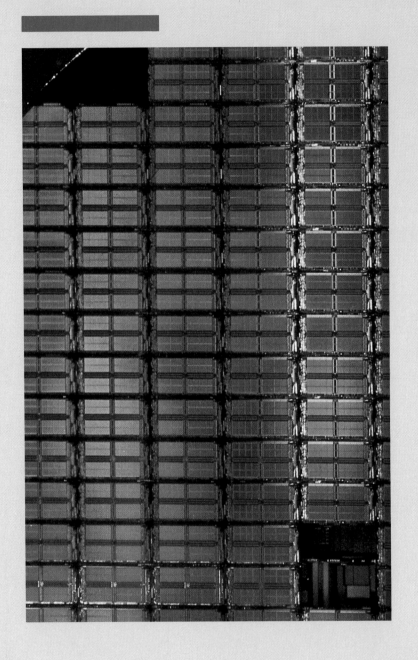

5

THE PROCESSOR UNIT
The Brain of the Mainframe

Objectives

- Describe the central processing unit (CPU).
- Explain the functions of the primary storage unit and the central processing unit.
- Describe the functions of the arithmetic/logic unit (ALU).
- Describe the basic components and functions of the control unit (CU).
- Describe current primary storage technology.
- Discuss the importance of the virtual storage concept.
- Describe how instructions are fetched from memory and executed within the CPU.
- Contrast fixed-length and variable-length words.
- Describe overlapped processing.
- Understand and use the key terms presented in this chapter.

$\mathbb{M}$ust you know how the internal combustion engine works in order to drive a car? Of course not. Is there value in knowing something about the inner workings of your car? Of course there is. Understanding something about how machines function—be they automobiles, lawn mowers, or computers—can help you in several ways. First, you will be in a better position to operate the equipment more efficiently. Second, if you know what is good and what is bad for a machine, you can take better care of it. If you take care of your computer, it will serve you faithfully for a long, long time. Third, the more familiar you are with the workings of the machine, the more adept you will be at spotting a malfunction should it occur. Last, should anything go wrong, you have a better chance of repairing it yourself (depending on how many thumbs you have) or you will be able to explain to the appropriate technician the nature of the problem.

Now that you have a fundamental understanding of what a computer system is and what it does, it's time to delve deeper into its inner chambers and learn a little more about how it works.

In this chapter we study the processor unit of a mainframe computer. It is in this unit that the execution of computer programs and the manipulation of data takes place. We will examine its principal components, the primary storage unit and the central processing unit, in detail. If you are not familiar with computer number systems and data representations, it would be helpful to familiarize yourself with the material in Appendix A before proceeding further.

PRIMARY STORAGE UNIT

Concepts

In Chapter 2 we learned that primary storage, or RAM, is a limited-capacity temporary storage area capable of providing stored information to the CPU at high speed. It is used to store the program instructions and data to be processed by the CPU.

These instructions and data can be input to the computer system as needed or they can be stored in secondary storage until needed. In either case, they must be brought into RAM before they can be processed. Once the set of instructions necessary to solve a problem is stored in RAM, the instructions may be recalled in sequence, together with the data they require, and executed. This set of instructions is referred to as a **stored program.** We perform a similar process every day. For example, when we go to work or school, we recall and execute a stored program—the sequence of instructions that gets us to our destination. This set of instructions constitutes a stored program, and a very complex one at that. For example, it must contain provisions for alternate actions depending on how late we arise, how much fuel we have in our car, weather conditions, traffic conditions, and so on.

If we were to attempt to list each of the instructions involved in handling all of these contingencies, we could fill a notebook. Programs stored in a computer can be equally long, if not longer. Thus an important consideration when select-

"I'M WORRIED ABOUT OUR COMPUTER. I THINK IT'S LOSING ITS MEMORY."

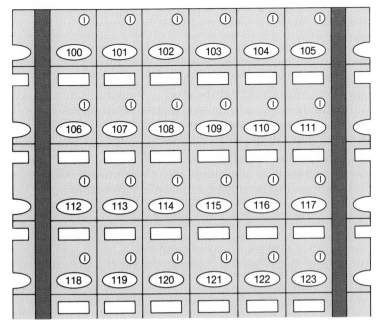

FIGURE 5-1
Primary storage cells are like post office mail boxes.

ing a computer system must be whether it has a primary storage capacity sufficient for the types of applications to which it will be put.

Computer primary storage consists of a large number of cells, each with a fixed capacity for storing data and each with a unique location, or **address.** The addresses of these cells can be likened to post office boxes in that each box has a unique location and designation (Fig. 5-1). Each storage cell is capable of holding a specific amount of data, and depending on the system, the unit of data may be a fixed number of binary digits, decimal digits, characters, words, or even an entire record.

The primary storage unit of some computer systems also includes a small, very fast, very expensive storage area referred to as **cache memory** (Fig. 5-2). This high-speed storage area is used temporarily to store instructions and data that will be accessed more frequently during the execution of a program. This area is also known as **scratch pad storage.**

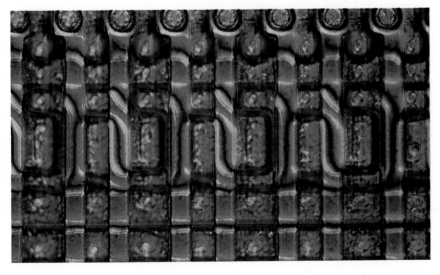

FIGURE 5-2
A highly magnified cache chip.

Know def.
cache memory
storage address

Storage Technologies

Early Storage Devices

Early computer memories utilized **vacuum tubes** similar to those used in early radio and television sets. Subsequently, the tubes in primary storage units were replaced by tiny iron rings called **ferrite cores.** The primary storage unit was composed of thousands of these tiny doughnut-shaped metal rings in which the direction of magnetization indicated a 1 or a 0 (Fig. 5-3). Each tiny core measured only a few thousandths of an inch in diameter and was capable of holding one **binary unit,** or **bit** of data.

Few of the new generation of computers still employ magnetic core in primary storage. Most computers currently being manufactured use more sophisticated components, such as those described below.

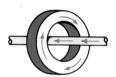

FIGURE 5-3
Magnetic states of a ferrite core.

"1"
Magnetized in a
Clockwise Direction

"0"
Magnetized in a
Counterclockwise
Direction

Right to the Core An Wang came to America from China in 1945 and became a U.S. citizen in 1954. Wang invented magnetic core memory and developed Wang Labs at an investment of $15,000. Today, Wang and his family have amassed a fortune worth nearly a billion dollars and head Wang Office Equipment Corporation.

Metal-Oxide Semiconductor (MOS) Storage Devices

Metal-oxide semiconductor (MOS) microminiaturized integrated circuit storage units began replacing the slower ferrite core units in the early 1970s. MOS chips have integrated circuits etched on them and can form as many as several hundred memory circuits (see Fig. 5-4). More recently, IBM has succeeded in storing 16 million bits, or approximately 2 million characters, on a single chip. MOS chips are used in the memories of most mini- and microcomputer systems (see Fig. 5-5).

Laser Storage Systems

While MOS memories were being developed and produced, research was directed toward the laser memory system, which employs the polarization of light in the same manner as the magnetic core employs magnetic polarization. Laser memory experiments resulted in a holographic storage system using a special optical plate to disperse laser beams as they pass through it (Fig. 5-6). In the 1970s a holographic memory was developed which could store more than 2,500 characters on a circular space only half a millimeter in diameter. The National Aeronautics and Space Administration subsequently succeeded in developing a *1-megabit* (1 million bits) all-optical laser storage device with access speeds ten times faster than existing devices and with a total primary storage capacity in the billions of characters. **Access time,** the time required to locate an item of data in storage and make it available for processing, is measured in microseconds and nanoseconds.

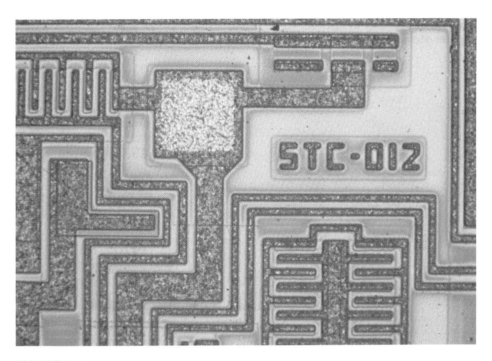

FIGURE 5-4
MOS miniaturized integrated circuits contain thousands of tiny transistors, shown here greatly enlarged, for the storage of data.

FIGURE 5-5
A chip developed by IBM that contains approximately 1 million separate memory cells.

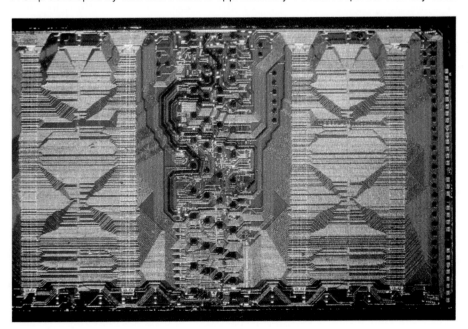

FIGURE 5-6
Special optical plate which disperses laser beams as they pass through it.

Magnetic Bubble Storage

Know

Bubble memory consists of a thin magnetic film in which cylindrical magnetic fields, or "bubbles," are generated that carry a polarization opposite to that of the film. One can think of this structure as negatively charged bubbles in a positively charged film (Fig. 5-7). These bubbles are generally a few thousandths of an inch in diameter. A single chip, approximately the size of a quarter, developed by Intel Magnetics Corporation in the late 1970s, was capable of storing 1 million binary digits. A very desirable characteristic of magnetic bubble storage is that it is **nonvolatile.** That is, it will not lose what is stored in it when power is removed.

Charged-Coupled Devices (CCD)

The **charged-coupled device (CCD)** is made up of microscopic MOS devices (capacitors) capable of holding an electrical charge for short periods of time. Data is stored on the CCD in the form of a charge on these capacitors. The presence of a charge represents a binary 1 and the absence of a charge represents a binary 0. Because these charges must be replenished continually, the device cannot hold data without power being available. Thus, CCDs are a **volatile** storage medium. Access time with CCDs is far shorter than that possible with any other auxiliary or secondary storage medium but somewhat longer than the access times attainable with other MOS primary storage devices. Roughly speaking, a CCD costs about one-fourth and has a storage density four times that of other storage devices (see Fig. 5-8). Because CCDs have faster access times than magnetic bubble devices, they have been used principally as secondary storage or sometimes as a means of extending existing magnetic bubble memory.

The principal disadvantages of the CCD for use in primary storage are its volatility and slow access time.

144

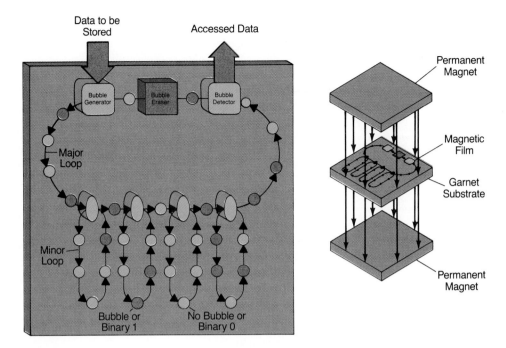

FIGURE 5-7

Bubble on the move. Bubble memory is made up of a naturally occurring orthoferrite material that contains alternating positive and negative bands in a zebra-like pattern. Passing a magnetic field close to the surface draws the closest band into a magnetic cylinder or "bubble" approximately .0005 inches in diameter. Once a magnetic bubble has been formed, it is put into motion and directed into a tiny circular loop. It remains in motion in this "minor" loop until it needs to be read or changed. When the computer needs to interrogate or change a bubble, it reroutes the bubble from its minor loop to a larger or major loop where it passes single file through a bubble read/write/erase circuit with all other bubbles in the major loop. The bubble detector or read circuit "reads" the bubbles in sequence as they pass by and sends a binary 1 or 0 to the computer for each bubble read.

A typical megabit bubble memory module consists of 2000 individual minor loops with each loop containing 500 bubbles.

FIGURE 5-8

Comparative costs for computer storage devices.

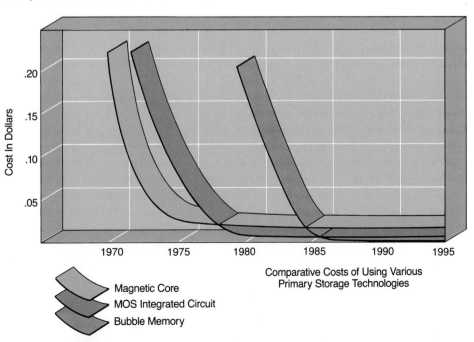

"HE SAYS HE'S WORKING ON THE ULTIMATE 'VIRTUAL MACHINE.' I THINK HE IS JUST GOOFING OFF."

Virtual Storage

Many modern computer systems employ a storage management technique called **virtual storage** (Fig. 5-9). This revolutionary storage technique, first introduced by Burroughs Corporation, allows the user of a computer system to process programs requiring more total storage capacity than is physically present in primary storage. Simply stated, virtual storage is a storage management technique that allows one to view the computer system as one containing many times the actual primary storage capacity. For example, a program previously requiring 100,000 storage locations can now be processed on a virtual storage computer containing fewer storage locations. This is accomplished by breaking the program up into segments, or **pages,** stored in secondary storage. As needed, these segments or groups of instructions are called into primary storage and executed. The remaining segments of the program reside on the direct-access secondary storage device until needed. When needed, a segment(s) is brought into memory replacing the segment(s) no longer being used.

FIGURE 5-9
Virtual storage concept.

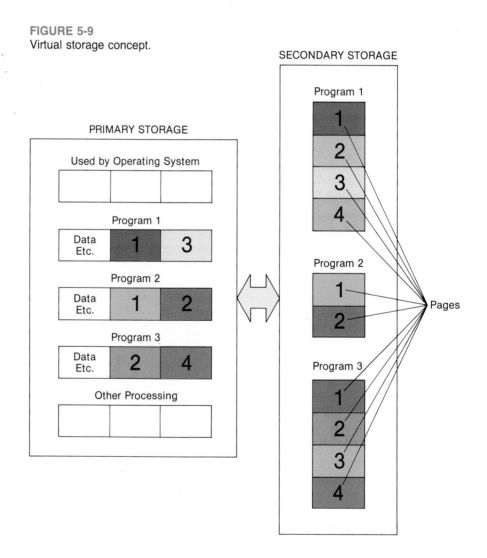

This process is very similar to that which takes place when we read a book. We begin by reading the first page of the book. When we have finished this page, we replace it with the next page by turning the page. This process can be continued until we have read all the pages in the book. If at any time it becomes necessary to refer back or ahead to a particular page, we can access it simply by turning to that page number. Throughout this process we have access to only one page of the book at a time. The factor that most affects our reading rate is the number of times we have to turn to a new page. So it is with virtual storage. The more movement there is of pages or sections of coding in and out of primary storage, the more time-consuming the process will be. The circuitry and control programs provided with virtual storage computer systems are designed to reduce this movement to a minimum.

Cryogenic Circuits

When metals are cooled to temperatures that are at or near absolute zero (-459.67 degrees Fahrenheit, or -273.15 degrees Celsius), all molecular motion stops. In **cryogenic circuits,** metal conductors of electricity that are cooled to such temperatures offer no resistance to the flow of electricity; the electrons making up the electric current will penetrate barriers that ordinarily would restrain them. This phenomenon is known as **superconductivity** and has led to experiments involving high-speed switching circuits.

CENTRAL PROCESSING UNIT

As we saw in Chapter 2, every computer system has a unit whose primary purpose is to process data. This unit is the control center of the entire computer system. It accepts data from the various input devices, processes these data, and sends the results to the printer or other output device under control of a stored program. This unit is referred to as the **microprocessor unit (MPU)** in a microcomputer and the **central processing unit (CPU)** in larger computer systems. Both units perform basically the same functions. We will defer our discussion of microcomputers until Chapter 6.

The processor of a modern computer contains two major components, the primary storage unit or memory, and the CPU. The CPU consists of an arithmetic/logic unit (ALU) and a control unit (CU) (see Fig. 5-10).

ARITHMETIC/LOGIC UNIT

The **arithmetic/logic unit (ALU)** is the computer's calculator. It performs all arithmetic operations, in addition to decision making and editing functions. A few special-purpose supercomputers use multiple ALUs to attain extremely high processing speeds. However, most computer systems have a single ALU.

Arithmetic Operations

Arithmetic operations include addition, subtraction, multiplication, and division. The data operated on can be stored in various forms (the binary, BCD, EBCDIC, and ASCII data representations are discussed in Appendix A), depending upon the hardware design and the type of arithmetic instructions being employed.

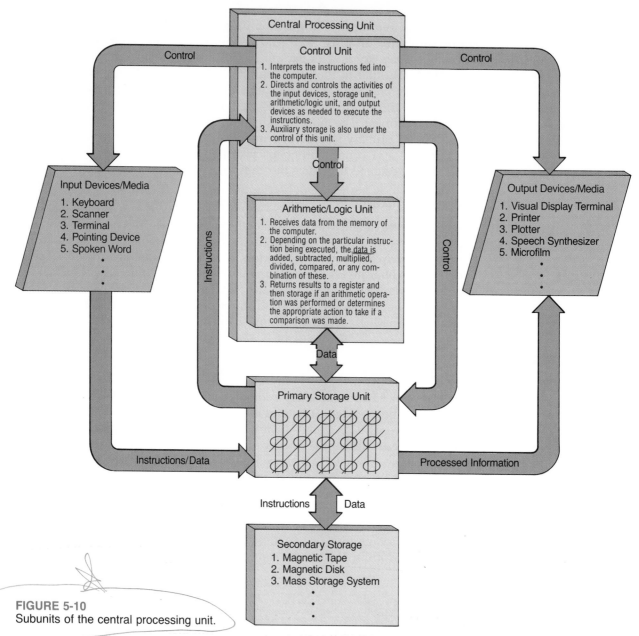

FIGURE 5-10
Subunits of the central processing unit.

When performing these operations, the ALU makes use of temporary storage areas referred to as **registers.** Data to be arithmetically manipulated are copied from storage and placed in registers for processing. Upon completion of the arithmetic operation, the result can be transferred from the register to storage, freeing the register for the next arithmetic operation. In addition to registers, the arithmetic unit uses one or more **adders,** devices that actually add, subtract, multiply, or divide the binary digits in the numbers (see Fig. 5-11).

Computers or computer ALUs are categorized according to the manner in which they carry out arithmetic operations. They are classified as either

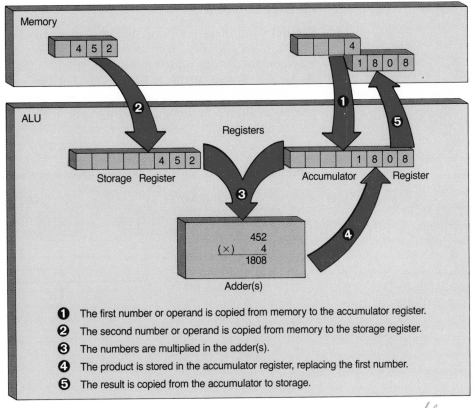

FIGURE 5-11
Performing arithmetic in the ALU. *Lotus a accounting best example*

① The first number or operand is copied from memory to the accumulator register.
② The second number or operand is copied from memory to the storage register.
③ The numbers are multiplied in the adder(s).
④ The product is stored in the accumulator register, replacing the first number.
⑤ The result is copied from the accumulator to storage.

serial or **parallel.** Let's examine these two techniques with respect to the process that takes place when the computer performs the following operation:

$$1234$$
$$(+)5678$$

Serial Computers

In a **serial** computer, the addition operation is performed digit by digit, much the same as we perform this operation manually with a pencil and paper (Fig. 5-12). Clearly, the time that it takes to complete a serial operation is dependent on the length of the numbers to be added. Adding two four-digit numbers together will take approximately twice as long as adding two two-digit numbers. This is not the case, however, in a parallel computer.

FIGURE 5-12
Serial addition.

Step	1	2	3	4
Addend	1 2 3 4	1 2 3 4	1 2 3 4	1 2 3 4
Augend	5 6 7 8	5 6 7 8	5 6 7 8	5 6 7 8
Sum	2	1 2	9 1 2	6 9 1 2
Carry	1	1	0	0

Parallel Computers

Parallel computers perform additions on **words.** Words are storage locations with a fixed capacity. Any two words, independent of the actual numbers they contain, can be added in one operation, including all carries. Thus this is by far the fastest of the two methods but the most complex to mechanize. Therefore, it is a trade-off—speed for hardware complexity and expense. This process is shown in schematic form in Fig. 5-13.

FIGURE 5-13
Schematic diagram of serial and parallel addition hardware.

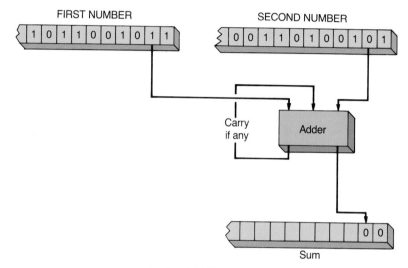

a. Serial Addition

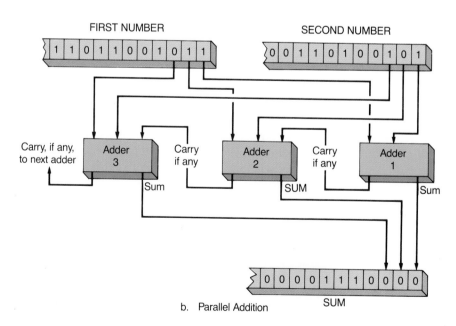

b. Parallel Addition

Other ALU Functions	## Decision Making

Other ALU Functions

Decision Making

Decision making is the ability to compare two quantities or numbers to determine, for example, if the first quantity is smaller than, equal to, or greater than the second quantity and to respond by taking an appropriate action based on the result of the comparison. For example, if the computer were asked, Is A > 100; the ALU would determine the answer as being either true or false depending on the memory contents of A. It is also possible to test for the existence of a condition encountered during the processing of an application and to alter the sequence of instructions accordingly.

Editing

Editing is generally performed on numeric data to accomplish such operations as the inserting of commas, decimal points, or dollar signs, or replacing of leading zeros with blanks. Typically, data items to be included in printed reports are edited before being output.

CONTROL UNIT

Concepts

The control unit is the computer's traffic cop. It coordinates and controls all operations occurring within the central processing unit. It does this much as the human brain coordinates and controls the activities of the human body. Table 5-1 illustrates how closely the control functions performed by the human brain relate to equivalent functions performed by the control unit of the CPU.

The control unit does not input, output, process, or store data; rather, it initiates and controls the sequence of these operations. In addition, the control unit communicates with input devices in order to begin the transfer of data or instructions into storage and with output devices in order to begin the transfer of results from storage. **Data transfer** involves the moving of data or instructions from one location in a computer to another. It is noteworthy that when an item of data is *stored* in a given location, it replaces the previous contents of that location, but when an item of data is *moved* from one location in storage to another, the item of data is not physically removed from its initial storage location; what does happen is that the data is *copied* to the new location. When

TABLE 5–1
Similarity between Control Functions Performed by the Human Brain and Those Performed by the Control Unit of the CPU

HUMAN BRAIN CONTROL FUNCTIONS	CONTROL UNIT CONTROL FUNCTIONS
Five basic senses	Uses input devices
Storing and retrieving of information from memory	Storing and retrieving of data from the storage unit
Ability to solve analytical problems and make decisions	The operations of the arithmetic/logic unit
Ability to communicate verbally, in writing, etc.	Uses output devices
Order in which we perform the above operations	Order in which instructions are to be executed

Chapter 5   The Processor Unit

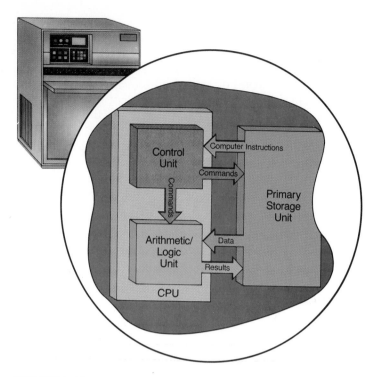

FIGURE 5-14

The CPU and primary storage unit work together to carry out program instructions. The process begins when the control unit fetches a program instruction from memory. The instruction is decoded, and if an arithmetic or logic operation is required, the control unit directs primary storage to make ready the data and the ALU to carry out the specific operation. After the ALU completes the operation and sends the result to memory, it returns control to the control unit which fetches another instruction.

the computer is executing a user program contained in primary storage, the control unit obtains the instructions in the sequence in which they will be executed, interprets these instructions, and issues signals or commands that cause other units of the system to execute them. To accomplish this, the control unit must communicate with both the arithmetic/logic unit and primary storage (see Fig. 5-14).

In executing an instruction, the control unit generally performs all or most of the following functions:

- Determines the instruction to be executed
- Determines the operation to be performed by the instruction
- Determines what data, if any, are needed and where they are stored
- Determines where any results are to be stored
- Determines where the next instruction is located
- Causes the instruction to be carried out or executed
- Transfers control to the next instruction

Machine Cycles

The activities of the control unit, as all other activities in a computer system, are actually composed of thousands of individual steps, each of which takes place in a fixed interval of time. These intervals are controlled by an internal **electronic clock** that emits regular electronic pulses at rates as high as one pulse every 0.00000001 seconds. Comparatively speaking, this would be approximately 10 million pulses in the blink of an eye. Clock speeds are generally measured in **megahertz (MHz)** or million pulses per second. Microcomputer systems currently have clock speeds in the 4- to 33-MHz range with faster systems being developed even as you read. Larger systems are even faster. No operation, regardless of how simple, can be performed in less time than transpires between clicks of this internal clock. In general, all operations within the CPU of the computer take place in terms of a fixed number of clock pulses. This fixed number of pulses determines the **machine cycle** for the computer. Within a machine cycle, the computer can perform one **machine operation.** The number of machine operations required to execute a single instruction will vary from instruction to instruction.

To illustrate this process, let us assume that the computer executes a *move* instruction (moving data from one place in the computer to another) and that this move instruction requires three separate machine operations for its completion. If we further assume that a machine cycle is made up of five clock pulses, then a quick computation would reveal that the move instruction takes place in fifteen ticks of the clock. Thus, the total time required to complete the move is fifteen times the time interval of a single clock pulse.

Execution of such instructions takes place under the direct supervision of the control unit. To understand this process, we must first examine the register and counter hardware elements and then the general format of an instruction contained within a stored program.

Registers

controlled by control unit

Registers are temporary storage locations that are used over and over again by the computer in the execution of stored-program instructions. They are not contained within primary storage but are generally within the CPU and controlled by the control unit. Their hardware makeup is similar to that of the storage locations found in primary storage, only they are faster and their uses are different.

Most computers contain both special-purpose and general-purpose registers. **Special-purpose registers** are used by the computer for only one purpose, whereas **general-purpose registers** may be used by the programmer or computer for different purposes. These registers can vary in both size and capacity from computer to computer or even within the same computer system. Registers generally have names that reflect their functions. For example, an accumulator register accumulates totals, a storage register contains information taken from or going to primary storage, and an instruction register contains the instruction or command being executed. Some of the registers available with a computer system may even have their contents continuously displayed on the computer console via a series of small lights. These lights indicate to the computer operator the contents of the register or a particular program's conditions.

Counters

Counters operate much like registers and may perform similar functions. Counters may be used to count up or down. A typical use of a counter is to maintain the storage address of the next instruction to be executed. For example, when program execution begins, the **instruction counter** is set to the address of the first program instruction. During the execution of this instruction, the counter is updated to contain the address of the next instruction to be executed. If,

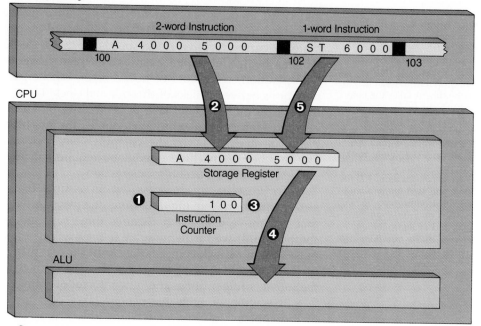

Primary Storage

2-word Instruction   1-word Instruction

A 4 0 0 0   5 0 0 0   S T 6 0 0 0
100   102   103

CPU

A 4 0 0 0   5 0 0 0
Storage Register

1 0 0
Instruction
Counter

ALU

❶ The instruction counter is set to 100 during execution of the previous instruction.

❷ The instruction stored in memory beginning at location 100 is fetched.

❸ The instruction counter is incremented by 2, the size of the instruction being executed. (100 will become 102).

❹ The instruction is decoded and executed.

❺ The next instruction is fetched.

FIGURE 5-15
The instruction counter.

for example, the first instruction was located at address 100, the instruction counter would initially be set to 100. If this instruction occupied one storage position, the instruction counter would be incremented to 101, the location of the next instruction. If the first instruction occupied two storage positions, the instruction counter would be incremented by two to 102, the location of the next instruction (see Fig. 5-15).

Counters may also have panel lights or other visual indicators on the computer console for the operator's use.

Instruction Format

All program instructions stored within memory must be in a machine-readable form. In general, these instructions consist of two distinct parts—an operation code and one or more operands. The **operation code,** or **op code** for short, tells the machine what task is to be performed; the **operands** specify what is to be used to perform the task. Operands can be: *2 parts of every instruction*

- The address of an item of data or an instruction in primary storage
- The address of an item of data or a program contained outside the CPU on a secondary storage device
- The address of an input or an output unit
- The address of a register or special-purpose temporary storage area

154

For example, the instruction

MV 4000 5000

contains the operation code MV and the operands 4000 and 5000. This could mean that the machine is to move the contents of storage location 4000 to storage location 5000. In addition to the address of an item of data in primary storage, an operand can be used to indicate the address of a register, the address of data stored outside of the computer in secondary storage, or even the address of an input or output unit.

Instruction Execution

As stated earlier, the actual execution of an instruction such as the move instruction described above, generally requires a number of machine cycles. The instruction must be retrieved from storage, interpreted, and executed. These functions generally require at least two machine cycles and are divided into an instruction cycle and an execution cycle.

Instruction Cycle

The **instruction cycle** represents the first machine cycle in the execution of an instruction. Four distinct steps are performed during the instruction cycle (Fig. 5-16). These are:

1. The instruction is retrieved or fetched from primary storage and placed in a register referred to as a **storage register.** This is accomplished by control circuits contained within the control unit. These circuits obtain from the instruction counter the address of the instruction to be executed, then they send appropriate signals to primary storage to locate and copy the instruction to the storage register. As we learned earlier, when program execution is initiated, the instruction counter is set to the address of the first program instruction. As instructions are executed, the instruction counter is updated so that it always contains the address of the next instruction to be executed.

FIGURE 5-16
The instruction cycle.

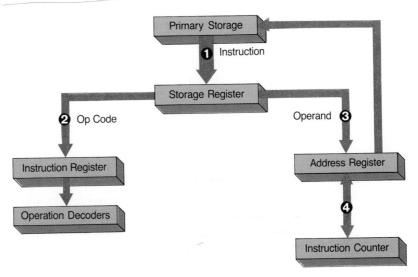

2. The operation code is moved to the instruction register and decoded. This is accomplished with the aid of operation decoders, which establish the circuit paths necessary to carry out the intent of the instruction.
3. The operands are placed in one or more address registers, depending on the number of operands in the instruction.
4. The address of the next instruction is determined. Normally, instructions are executed sequentially, one after the other. Thus, under normal circumstances, the next instruction will be located immediately after the current instruction in storage. Its address is simply the address of the current instruction plus the number of storage positions occupied by the current instruction. Under certain circumstances, it becomes necessary in a program to **branch,** or transfer control, to an instruction other than the next sequential instruction. In such cases, the current instruction must indicate the address of the next instruction. This address is then placed in the instruction counter, and the sequential processing of instructions is resumed until another branch instruction is encountered.

Figure 5-17 illustrates the contents of these registers during the instruction cycle for an ADD instruction. The total time required to accomplish these four steps is referred to as **I-time** (instruction time).

Execution Cycle

The **execution cycle** represents the remaining machine cycles in the execution of an instruction. Unlike the instruction cycle, the execution cycle can consist of more than one machine cycle, depending on the complexity of the instruction being executed. The time required to complete the execution cycle is referred to as **E-time** (execution time). Throughout this cycle, operations are controlled by the instruction register.

The actual steps performed in an execution cycle depend on the particular instruction being executed. To illustrate, let us assume that the program requires that two numbers be added (see Fig. 5-17). During the instruction cycle the control unit would have decoded the instruction and directed the ALU to perform an ADD. It would also have placed the addresses of the operands in address registers. The execution cycle would cause the following to take place:

1. The value of the operands would be obtained from the primary storage locations indicated in the address registers. One value would be placed in a storage register and the other would be placed in the accumulator register.
2. The ALU adders would then add these two numbers.
3. The sum would be stored in the accumulator register.

The instruction cycle of the next instruction would begin. This instruction would most likely involve moving the contents of the accumulator register (the sum of the two numbers) to a location in primary storage, freeing the accumulator register for use in subsequent instructions.

Fixed-Length and Variable-Length Words

Data can be addressed and processed by a computer system in three ways: using fixed-length words, variable-length words, or a combination of both (Fig. 5-18).

In computers that employ a **fixed-length word,** each word consists of a fixed number of bits, usually a multiple of eight, and is uniquely addressable. The actual number of bits or bytes (series of eight bits) that constitutes a word can vary from computer system to computer system. Whatever the size of the word, all manipulations within the computer will take place in terms of words.

156

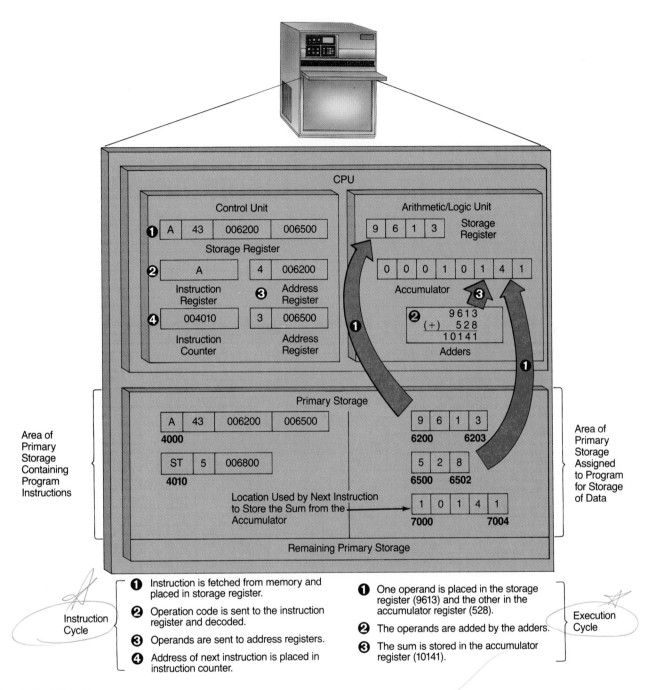

CPU

Control Unit

❶	A	43	006200	006500

Storage Register

❷	A		4	006200

Instruction Register   ❸   Address Register

❹	004010		3	006500

Instruction Counter   Address Register

Arithmetic/Logic Unit

9	6	1	3	Storage Register

0	0	0	1	0	1	4	1

Accumulator   ❸

```
❷      9 6 1 3
    (+)    5 2 8
       1 0 1 4 1
```

Adders

❶

❶

Primary Storage

A	43	006200	006500
4000

9	6	1	3
6200   6203

ST	5	006800
4010

5	2	8
6500   6502

Location Used by Next Instruction to Store the Sum from the Accumulator

1	0	1	4	1
7000   7004

Area of Primary Storage Containing Program Instructions

Area of Primary Storage Assigned to Program for Storage of Data

Remaining Primary Storage

Instruction Cycle

❶ Instruction is fetched from memory and placed in storage register.

❷ Operation code is sent to the instruction register and decoded.

❸ Operands are sent to address registers.

❹ Address of next instruction is placed in instruction counter.

Execution Cycle

❶ One operand is placed in the storage register (9613) and the other in the accumulator register (528).

❷ The operands are added by the adders.

❸ The sum is stored in the accumulator register (10141).

FIGURE 5-17
The instruction and execution cycles for an ADD instruction.

Registers, counters, accumulators, and storage are designed around the word. Computers that utilize only fixed-length words are therefore restricted in the number of significant digits that they can handle in a number. Clearly, this affects the accuracy with which such computers can perform arithmetic operations.

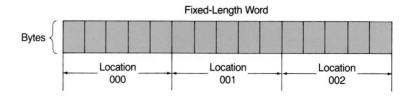

Fixed-Length Word

Bytes

Location 000   Location 001   Location 002

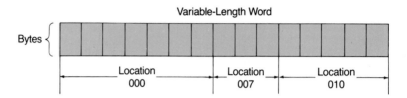

Variable-Length Word

Bytes

Location 000   Location 007   Location 010

FIGURE 5-18
Word lengths.

In computers that employ a **variable-length word,** data can be any practical length up to the size of the storage unit. Thus a number consisting of as many significant digits as the problem demands can be stored and processed. This is essential in commercial applications where the nature of the application dictates how many significant digits must be available. You can't tell depositors in a banking operation that their balance is too large for your computer to handle, nor can you carry out associated computations to a lesser accuracy than is allowable by law.

Because fixed- and variable-length words have advantages and disadvantages over one another (Fig. 5-19), most computer systems support both formats. To accomplish this, they generally have two sets of instructions, one for use with variable-length words and one for use with fixed-length words. In most IBM mainframes, for example, the fixed-length word is 32 bits, or 4 bytes. These words can be processed using parallel operations for speed and efficiency. These systems also support variable-length words from 1 byte up to more than 30,000 bytes in length; such words utilize serial operations.

FIGURE 5-19
Comparison of fixed- and variable-length words.

CHARACTERISTIC	FIXED-LENGTH WORD	VARIABLE-LENGTH WORD
Fastest arithmetic operations	x	
Best storage efficiency		x
Controllable accuracy in arithmetic computations		x
Highest internal transfer rate	x	

OVERLAPPED PROCESSING

Increasing the speed and efficiency of input/output devices has been the goal of computer designers and users since the advent of the computer. Slow and inefficient input/output devices often result in the computer's processing unit continually having to wait for input/output operations to be completed before processing can be resumed. This results in a reduction in the overall efficiency of the computer system and decreased throughput. The efforts of computer designers and users to increase the throughput and overall efficiency of a computer system have resulted in the concept known as **overlapped processing.**

All data processing applications involve the operations of input, processing, and output, with each of these requiring a specific amount of time for its completion. The time required to solve a problem completely, then, will be a combination of the times required to complete each of the three operations. However, the total time will depend heavily on how this is calculated. If, for example, only one of these operations could be performed at any one moment of time, the total required time for the completion of the job would be the sum of the times required to complete each input, processing, and output operation (nonoverlapped processing). Figure 5-20 illustrates how this might take place. Note that only three input-processing-output cycles are possible in the time period illustrated. In Fig. 5-21, however, in the same time period it is possible to perform more than seven input-processing-output cycles. This is accomplished by performing more than one operation at a time (overlapped processing). As you can clearly see, overlapped processing is more efficient than nonoverlapped processing, which is why most modern computers employ overlapped processing.

You have probably asked yourself how it is possible for the computer to do more than one thing at a time. The answer to this question is relatively simple. Attached to the computer are special devices, called **channels,** that control the input/output operations, thus freeing the processing unit to perform

FIGURE 5-20
Nonoverlapped processing.

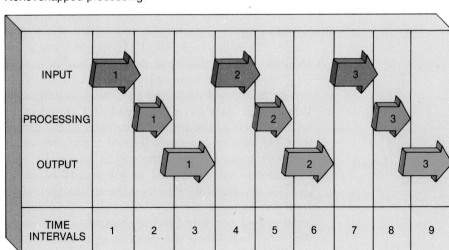

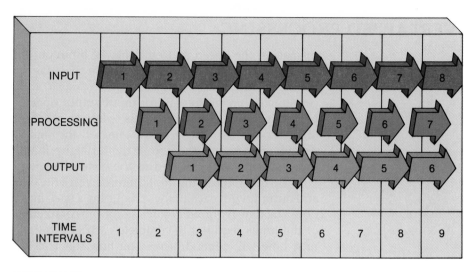

FIGURE 5-21
Overlapped processing.

other operations. At a given time, one channel can be controlling an input operation while a second channel could be used to control an output operation; the processor is then free to perform an arithmetic calculation. A computer system may have many channels attached to it, with each channel responsible for controlling one or more I/O devices.

Data channels are categorized as either selector or multiplexor channels. A **selector channel** can be used with one high-speed input or output device at a time. **Multiplexor channels,** on the other hand, are logically connected to several low-speed devices at the same time but are electronically connected to only one of these devices—the one transmitting or receiving at that instant. The multiplexor alternately selects a limited amount of data from the low-speed devices connected to it and transmits these data at high speeds to or from the CPU. Figure 5-22 illustrates one of the many possible arrangements and uses of channels.

What actually takes place between the input/output device, the channel, and the CPU is as follows. Let us assume that we wish to read several data records from an input device, perform a series of calculations, and output the results. To begin with, the CPU would issue a command to the appropriate channel to cause the input device to read one or more data records and store their contents in a temporary storage location, called a **buffer.** This operation can be performed while the CPU is busy with another operation or program. When these data have been read and stored in the buffer, a special **control unit** attached to the input device signals the channel, which, in turn, signals the CPU with an **interrupt.** (Input/output control units should not be confused with the control unit of the CPU.) Effectively, the channel is informing the CPU that it has completed its job and is awaiting another command. When the CPU becomes free to process these data, they will be called for and transmitted from the buffer to primary storage at a very rapid rate. The CPU then issues another *fetch* command to the channel to read more data so they will be ready when needed. When the processing of the input record has been completed, the CPU will transmit the results to an output buffer via the channel to which

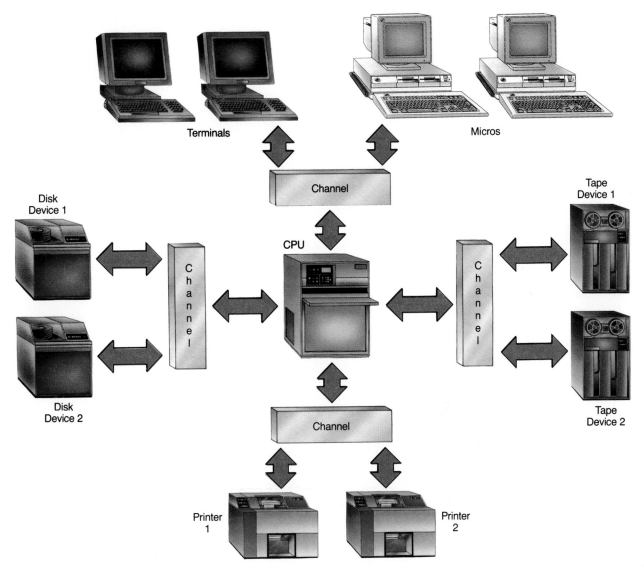

FIGURE 5-22
Schematic of an overlapped processing computer system.

the output device is connected. This channel will then issue a command to the control unit attached to the output device, which will accomplish the actual output.

What we have, then, is a condition where the relatively slow input and output operations are controlled by channels and input or output control units, allowing the CPU to process data and communicate with the channels at high speed (see Fig. 5-23). Thus, the idea of automatic interrupts, together with carefully preprogrammed commands to the channels and orders to the control units, leads to a far greater total amount of data handling per unit of time than would otherwise be possible. As a result, greater **throughput,** the amount of data input, processed, and output, is achieved.

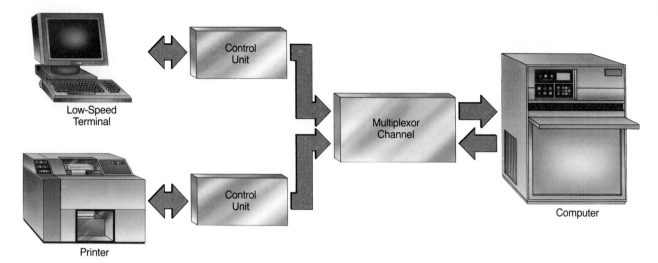

FIGURE 5-23
Path of input/output communications.

Besides housing the physical buffer(s), the control unit attached to an input or output unit generally houses the circuitry necessary to convert the data from a form acceptable to the device to a form compatible with the particular computer, and vice versa. For example, during an input operation the control unit associated with a low-speed terminal keyboard will convert the data being keyed in to binary, EBCDIC, ASCII, or whatever code is utilized by the CPU. These terms are more fully explained in Appendix A.

Multi-Programming

A **multiprogramming** system has the capability of executing two or more programs *concurrently* utilizing one central processing unit. A multiprogramming system generally consists of one CPU and several I/O units. I/O operations are generally not performed directly by the CPU. Instead, whenever a program requires either input or output, the CPU simply turns the task over to another device—**I/O channel**—for completion. This frees up the CPU so it can process another program while the channel takes care of the slower input or output operation. For example, while one program requires a search of a disk file to locate a needed record, requiring conceivably as much as half a second, a large computer could be performing hundreds or thousands of operations on other programs being processed concurrently. This multiprogramming capability makes it possible for the computer to juggle, or **swap** several jobs back and forth within its memory and mass data storage facilities. If a program being processed is awaiting the completion of an I/O operation, the CPU is idle, or **I/O bound.** In order not to waste time waiting for this operation to be completed, at the same time, the CPU transfers control to another program in the CPU that does not require the same I/O device. Then, when the first program's I/O operation is completed by the channel, the computer can resume processing the original program. In so doing, the output or productivity of the computer system can be multiplied by a factor of 5 or 10.

The proper operation of a multiprogramming system requires a supervisory program, or **supervisor,** that is usually provided by the computer manufacturer with the hardware. One of the prime functions of this program is to determine the order in which programs will be processed.

OPTICAL DISKS—TREMENDOUS GROWTH PREDICTED

The worldwide market for optical disk drives will top $2 billion at original equipment manufacturer (OEM) price levels in 1992, an 81 percent compounded growth rate from the $57 million value of the 1985 market, according to a recent market analysis published by Freeman Assoc. Annual shipments of the drives themselves exceeded 1 million units for the first time in 1991.

A report from Frost & Sullivan (F&S), *The PC Optical Disk Market in the US*, also predicts tremendous market growth over the next few years. F&S sees significant opportunities for both optical disk system manufacturers and retailers, as well as for manufacturers and retailers of optical media products.

What can an optical disk system do to warrant this kind of projected growth? Basically, using laser technology, it can store huge amounts of information for easy retrieval. Some systems have a storage capacity a thousand times that of diskettes.

The first encyclopedia encoded onto optical disks is being marketed at one-fourth the price of the 21-volume paper version, yet takes up a tiny fraction of the paper version's shelf space. Optical disk systems will eventually provide business microcomputer users with on-line storage capacity comparable to minicomputer and even mainframe storage systems. What is more, optical disks can store digital data of any form—video, audio, text and graphics—and interactive formats are being developed.

SUMMARY AND GLOSSARY OF KEY TERMS

- The **CPU (central processing unit)** is composed of two subunits—an **arithmetic/logic unit (ALU)** and a **control unit.** The **primary storage unit** is located outside the CPU.

- The functions performed by the ALU include **data transfer,** the moving of data from one location in the computer to another; **arithmetic operations,** the basic operations of addition, subtraction, multiplication, and division; **editing,** the preparation of data for output by inserting commas, decimal points, dollar signs, and so on; and **decision making,** the ability to compare two quantities or numbers to determine their numerical relationship to one another.

- The arithmetic/logic unit makes use of temporary storage locations referred to as **registers** during arithmetic operations. In addition to registers, the ALU also makes use of one or more **adders,** devices capable of adding binary digits.

- Computers are categorized according to the way they perform arithmetic operations. **Serial computers** perform arithmetic operations digit by digit, or serially. **Parallel computers** perform arithmetic operations on all digits in a word at the same time, or in parallel. Parallel operations are faster than serial operations but are much more expensive to mechanize.

- The primary storage unit is used to store both instructions and data. A set of stored instructions is referred to as a **stored program.** Each location in primary storage has a fixed capacity and a unique location or **address. Cache memory,** a high-speed storage area, is used to store instructions and data that will be accessed more frequently during program execution.

- Storage devices have evolved from **vacuum tubes** to the **ferrite core,** where each core is capable of holding a single binary digit or **bit,** to **MOS (metal-oxide semiconductor)** storage devices. A limited number of computer systems use **laser storage.** Other storage devices include **magnetic bubble storage** and **charged-coupled devices (CCDs).** Magnetic bubble storage is somewhat slower in access times than the CCDs, but it is **nonvolatile** (will not lose stored information when power is removed); CCDs are **volatile** (will lose stored information when power is removed). CCDs are cheaper and have greater storage capacities than most other storage devices.

- Many modern computer systems utilize **virtual storage,** a storage management technique that allows the computer to effectively utilize a storage capacity far in excess of its actual capacity. Essentially, programs are subdivided into segments, referred to as **pages,** which contain portions of a program and are stored outside the CPU in secondary storage. The program is then brought into primary storage a few pages at a time and processed. This eliminates the necessity to bring the entire program into the computer at one time.

- The **control unit** coordinates and controls all operations occurring within the CPU. The control unit performs its functions in steps of fixed time intervals that are determined by an internal **electronic clock.**

A fixed number of clock pulses represent a single **machine cycle.** Clock speeds are measured in **megahertz,** or million pulses per second. Within a machine cycle, the computer can perform one **machine operation.** One or more machine operations are necessary to carry out each instruction in a stored program.

- The control unit makes use of temporary storage locations, or **registers.** Registers are either **special-purpose** or **general-purpose.** These registers vary in size and capacity from computer to computer. In addition to registers, control units make use of **counters,** which can be used to count up and to count down. A commonly used counter is the **instruction counter,** which keeps track of the position of the next instruction to be executed.

- Computer instructions are made up of an **operation code** and one or more **operands.** Operation codes indicate what is to be done; and operands specify the data that is to be used in the operation.

- The execution of an instruction takes place in two steps—an **instruction cycle** and an **execution cycle.**

During the instruction cycle, the operation code is decoded and the machine is made ready to carry out or execute the instruction. After the instruction cycle is completed, the execution cycle commences and the instruction is carried out.

- **Overlapped processing** is a method of performing more than one input, processing, or output operation in the same time span, thereby increasing data throughput. This technique makes use of **channels** to control the input/output operations, freeing the CPU to perform other operations. Data channels are categorized as **selector**—used for one high-speed input/output device—or **multiplexor**—logically connected to several low-speed input/output devices. When an I/O operation is completed, the channel signals the CPU by means of an **interrupt.**

- A **multiprogramming** system is controlled by a **supervisor** program that allows the computer to **swap** several jobs between the CPU and storage. Two or more programs may be operated upon concurrently by the CPU.

EXERCISES

True/False

_____ 1. The ALU is where the internal processing of the data occurs.

_____ 2. When data is moved from one place in storage to another, the data is lost from the original location.

_____ 3. It is not possible for a condition encountered during the processing of an application to determine which sequence of instructions the computer should follow.

_____ 4. Multiple ALUs are possible with some computer systems.

_____ 5. MOS storage devices have been used in computer memories for over a decade.

_____ 6. A laser storage unit has not been constructed and used with a computer system.

_____ 7. Magnetic bubble memory is volatile.

_____ 8. The principal disadvantages of CCDs are that they are volatile and they are slower than other available primary storage components.

_____ 9. With virtual storage, primary storage is made to look bigger than it really is.

_____ 10. A computer can perform several machine operations in one machine cycle.

_____ 11. The op code tells what data to use in the instruction.

_____ 12. It is in the instruction cycle that an instruction is decoded.

_____ 13. During I-time, the instruction is brought from primary storage to an address register.

_____ 14. The execution cycle never requires more than one machine cycle for its completion.

_____ 15. Most computers support either fixed-length words or variable-length words, but not both.

_____ 16. Operations with variable-length words are generally performed more quickly than operations with fixed-length words.

164

_T_ **17.** Variable-length word machines provide controllable accuracy in arithmetic computations.

_T_ **18.** Attached to the computer are special devices called channels which facilitate input/output communications.

_T_ **19.** The control unit is like a supervisor or foreman.

_T_ **20.** The objective of all computer operations is to maximize throughput or the amount of data handling per unit of time.

Fill-in

1. Registers are _temporary storage locations_

2. The primary storage unit of a computer system is used to store both _data_ and _instructions_.

3. A set of computer instructions in primary storage is called a _storage program_

4. Each location in storage is assigned a unique _address_ .

5. I-time is the _____ .

6. The _control_ unit controls and coordinates all operations within the CPU.

7. The actual execution of an instruction takes place in two cycles: the _instruction_ cycle followed by the _execution_ cycle.

8. The ability of a computer to perform input, processing, and output operations at the same time is referred to as _overlap processing_

9. The special I/O devices used to facilitate overlapped processing are _channels & buffers_

10. Input/output units utilize temporary storage areas referred to as _buffers_ .

Problems

1. Describe and compare the storage technologies currently utilized in computers.

2. Describe the process which takes place during the execution of an instruction. What hardware elements are involved?

3. Describe the essential hardware elements necessary to facilitate overlapped processing. When is overlapped processing most advantageous?

Projects

1. Visit a computer center or store and make a list of the storage technologies employed in the computer system.

2. Visit your school or local library and determine a computer storage technology currently in use or planned for future use that is not discussed in the chapter.

CROSSWORD PUZZLE

Across

1. Each location in primary storage has a unique _____
2. Within a machine cycle, the computer can perform one _____ operation
3. Contains information taken from or going to primary storage
4. When an I/O operation is completed, the channel signals the CPU with an _____
5. Segments of a program when used with virtual storage
6. A storage management technique
7. The amount of data that can be processed by a computer in a unit of time
8. During this cycle the operation code is decoded
9. Short for operation code
10. After the instruction cycle the _____ commences and the instruction is carried out
11. _____ time—the time required to locate an item of data in storage and make it available for processing
12. Early internal storage device
13. A channel that handles several slow-speed devices
14. A temporary storage location used during I/O operations
15. The part of the CPU that controls and coordinates the operation of a computer

Down

2. Microprocessor unit
3. Computers that perform arithmetic operations digit by digit
16. Used to control I/O operations, freeing up the CPU
17. Decoded during the instruction cycle
18. Preparing data for output
19. The moving of data from one location in the computer to another
20. A mainframe MPU
21. Add numbers in the ALU
22. Replaced vacuum tubes
23. Temporary storage locations used by the control unit
24. A volatile storage device
25. A channel used with a high-speed I/O device
26. One million pulses per second
27. A small, very fast, very expensive storage area sometimes contained within memory
28. Retrieve an instruction
29. The instruction _____ keeps track of the address of the next instruction
30. Part of an instruction
31. A set of instructions
32. Must be updated as instructions are executed

6

MICROCOMPUTERS
Computers in the Small

Objectives

- Understand what constitutes a microcomputer system.
- Describe the organization of microcomputer memory and the type of hardware devices used.
- Describe the components and the basic functions of a typical microprocessor.
- Discuss how the microprocessing unit communicates with storage and with input/output devices.
- Be able to identify an input/output method as being programmed I/O, interrupt I/O, or direct memory access.
- Define telecommunications.
- Describe the many types of input/output devices designed specifically for microcomputers.
- Differentiate among major microcomputer software products, operating systems, utility and language translator programs, and canned or prewritten applications software.
- Name and describe some commonly used microcomputer systems.
- Understand and use the key terms presented in this chapter.

$\boxed{A}$s you will recall, UNIVAC I, the first computer produced in quantity for commercial data processing tasks, was first unveiled in 1951. It was huge. It fit snugly inside a large room and weighed over 30 tons. At that time, who would have ever imagined that three decades later you could purchase a computer that would be far superior to the UNIVAC I in every category, yet would be small enough to fit in your briefcase?

Computers have decreased in size and cost to the point where it is possible for millions of people to own them. Experts predict that by the mid 1990s, most homes in the United States will have at least one computer system. As the microcomputer, or personal computer, becomes more attractive and affordable to an ever-increasing segment of society, chances are excellent that if you don't already own one, you soon will.

In this chapter we examine the devices that generally make up a microcomputer, their purposes, and how they function. Some of the newest and most popular computer systems are also discussed. We also compare these functional parts with those found in larger systems.

GENERAL CONCEPTS

Most Chips Don't Work
That's right, most computer chips manufactured today don't work. The key to making money in the chip business is to make sure that at least 10 percent of any manufacturing run will function properly. Errors can be caused by imperfections in the silicon, misalignments in etching successive layers on the chip, faulty design, or introduction of foreign material. An employee at one of the major labs was actually fired for having dandruff.

Earlier we learned that a microcomputer is a small desk or laptop computing device. It can be a single, large-scale integrated circuit (LSI), or it can consist of many integrated circuits interconnected on one or more printed circuit boards (Fig. 6-1). Regardless of its actual physical makeup, it is a digital computer. As such, it must have the same basic elements as any of the larger digital computer systems: an arithmetic/logic unit, a control unit, a primary storage unit, and a capability to input and output data. Typically, input is accomplished through a typewriterlike keyboard and output is displayed on a display screen or simple printer. Logical and arithmetic operations, as well as overall control of the computer, are handled by a microprocessor and associated circuitry. The **microprocessor unit (MPU)** is generally an LSI or VLSI (very large-scale integrated) circuit central processing unit. Most microprocessors do not contain primary storage. This is generally provided on separate integrated circuits and is available in assorted sizes and types.

MICROCOMPUTER PRIMARY STORAGE

Organization

As with larger computer systems, microcomputers combine binary digits to form convenient size groups called **words.** The size of the word depends on the particular computer system used. Figure 6-2 illustrates the word sizes most commonly used with the various size computer systems. Only a few short years ago, IBM introduced their 8-bit word PC, followed a few years later by the 16-bit PC AT microcomputer, and already it has been replaced with a 32-bit word system. The advantage of the increased word size is that the machine

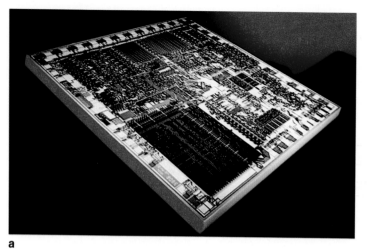
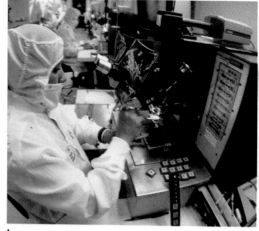

a   **b**

FIGURE 6-1
(a) A very large-scale integrated circuit. (b) A technician assembles an MC68020 32-bit microprocessor sometimes known as a "mainframe computer on a chip." The device is fabricated in a two-micron advanced HCMOS technology to squeeze 200,000 transistors on a ⅜-inch square chip. Accessing up to 4 billion bytes of memory, it provides sustained computing power of 2.5 million instructions per second (MIPS) and burst rates of 8 MIPS, equivalent to some mainframe computers.

is generally faster because it can process more bits of information in the same time span. Thus, the trend has been in the direction of the larger word.

Microcomputer memories are generally made up of many individual MOS (metal oxide semiconductor) chips and are available to perform different functions. The terms ROM, RAM, PROM, EPROM, and EEPROM are used in connection with the primary storage unit of a microcomputer.

ROM

ROM, or read only memory, is generally provided by the manufacturer of the microcomputer and is dedicated to a particular application. The data and program required by this application are **burned into,** or permanently stored on, the chip. Thus a user may read or access a program or data from ROM

FIGURE 6-2
Typical computer word lengths

WORD SIZE (BITS)	MICROCOMPUTERS	MINICOMPUTERS	MAINFRAME COMPUTER SYSTEMS
8	Many	None	None
12	None	A few	None
16	Most common	A few	A few
18	None	A few	A few
24	A few	A few	A few
32	Many	Most common	Most common
64	None	None	Only in the very largest

Chapter 6   Microcomputers

but may not write on ROM. The contents of ROM will not be altered when power is removed from the computer. It is therefore referred to as a **nonvolatile** storage medium. ROM is generally used to store **firmware,** manufacturer-supplied programs, routines, and language interpreters for immediate access by the user of the system. For example, many models of microcomputers come with ROM chips that contain the language BASIC.

RAM

RAM, or **random-access memory,** is general storage that can be read from or written on by the user (Fig. 6-3). RAM storage is used primarily to store user programs and data. Unlike ROM, however, the contents of RAM are generally **volatile,** and will be lost when power is removed. Because of this, when the system is powered up, programs and data to be used must be read into RAM via an input device. Access time for data stored in RAM generally ranges from a microsecond (millionth of a second) to a few nanoseconds (billionths of a second).

Laptop microcomputers such as IBM's Convertible computer utilize special MOS chips in RAM that draw almost no power and will preserve their contents indefinitely using a small internal battery. However, these low-power chips are substantially more expensive than their high-power counterparts.

PROM

PROM, or **programmable read only memory,** begins as blank chips which have nothing programmed or recorded on them. Once a series of instructions or data have been burned, or recorded onto the chip by a special programming

FIGURE 6-3
A technician inserting a 128K byte piggy-back memory chip into an IBM PC AT circuit board.

Unit 2   Computer Hardware

FIGURE 6-4
Erasable programmable read only
memory (EPROM) chip.

device, the PROM chip permanently stores this information and behaves like ROM. The programming of the PROM chip is generally done by the manufacturer of the computer system. PROM chips are used primarily to provide special-purpose programs such as games and graphics, which can be simply plugged into the main computer board or into a special outlet provided for this purpose.

EPROM and EEPROM

EPROM, or **erasable programmable read only memory,** chips can be programmed, as can PROM chips, but they differ in that they can be *erased* and reprogrammed by a special programming device should it become necessary or desirable. The previous contents of an EPROM chip can be erased by exposing it to an *ultraviolet light* (Fig. 6-4). The light passes through a quartz window in the plastic container and exposes the silicon chip that contains memory cells that are erased.

EEPROM, or **electrically erasable programmable read only memory,** is similar to EPROM except that it is erased by applying *electrical pulses* to the chip. Thus it is possible to reprogram an EEPROM chip via keyboard commands without the need to remove the chip from the computer.

MICROCOMPUTER SECONDARY STORAGE

Magnetic Tape Cassettes and Cartridges

A magnetic medium used with small home or personal computers is the tape **cassette** or **cartridge.** Computer audio cassettes are virtually the same as the standard variety of audio cassettes, they differ only in that computer cassettes generally do not have a leader or nonmagnetically coated beginning segment. Many micros are equipped with a standard circuit or interface to convert the cassette *audio* signals to computer-acceptable *binary* signals. Thus virtually any cassette player/recorder can be connected to a micro to record data onto or retrieve data from a cassette (Fig. 6-5).

These devices are capable of receiving and sending data at different rates, referred to as the **baud** rate. If the signal is changed every $\frac{1}{300}$ second, for example, the baud rate is 300. A baud rate of 300 (signals or bits per second, bps) is common, but baud rates of 500, 1,200, 2,400, and 9,600 are also used.

FIGURE 6-5
High-capacity (20 megabytes) magnetic tape cartridge compared to a high-capacity 5¼-inch diskette (1.2 megabytes) and EPROM.

In addition to the standard variety of audio cassettes and drives, some micros utilize digital cassettes. The digital cassette differs from the audio cassette only in how the data is recorded on it. Audio cassettes record data in the form of audio tones, whereas digital cassettes record the data in the form of magnetic spots that represent binary 1s and 0s. The capacity and cost of a digital cassette can be up to ten times that of an audio cassette. The principal use of digital cassettes is as a backup medium for high-capacity hard or fixed-disk storage units (see Fig. 6-5).

An important consideration when recording data on a magnetic medium such as a cassette or cartridge is the degree of protection that can be offered against accidental erasure. Any data stored on a magnetic medium can be lost if exposed to a strong magnetic field. Thus data stored on these media must be kept away from any such field (Fig. 6-6). In addition, it is also possible that a cassette or cartridge could be accidentally inserted into a cassette recorder/player and written on. To allow some degree of protection against this latter form of accidental erasure, it can be **file protected.** A small tab is provided on all cassettes and cartridges that, when broken off, will prevent it from being written on. Once this tab is removed, the cassette or cartridge may only be read.

The main advantages of the tape cassette or cartridge as a secondary storage medium are its simplicity and low cost. On the other hand, its disadvantages include its low speed, and the fact that it can only read and write sequentially.

Magnetic Floppy Disks

The principal advantage of the floppy disk, or **diskette,** over the cassette or cartridge is that the disk can be assessed directly. Any item of data or program stored on it can be accessed without the need to access all information stored previously. The floppy disk consists of a thin piece of magnetically coated mylar enclosed in a plastic or cardboard jacket (Fig. 6-7). Floppy disks are

174

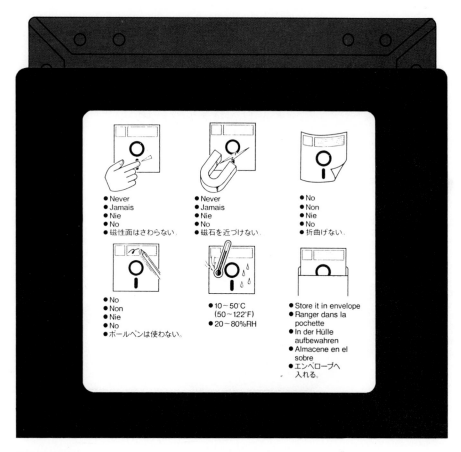

FIGURE 6-6
This multilingual warning label appearing on the back of a magnetic diskette jacket is typical of those used with any magnetic recording medium.

generally available in either a 5¼-inch diameter or a convenient pocket-sized 3½-inch floppy diskette. The 5¼-inch diameter standard floppy disk, typically used with IBM PC or compatible systems, is sometimes referred to as a **mini-floppy.** The 3½-inch diameter disk used with IBM PS/2s or compatibles, and Apple's Macintosh computers, is called a **micro-floppy.** Other than their outward appearance they are very similar.

When mounted in a disk drive, the floppy disk is held in the center by a motor-driven shaft that spins the disk within its protective jacket 300 to 360 rotations per minute (see Fig. 6-8). Data can be read from or written onto the disk by means of a read/write head, which can move in or out over the head-access slot in the jacket to access the different tracks on the surface of the disk.

As with magnetic tape cassettes, floppy disks can be file protected. Figure 6-7 illustrates a mini-floppy diskette with a small rectangular cutout that is used for this purpose. If the cutout is left open, the floppy is *not* file protected and can be read and written onto. If, however, this cutout is covered by a small piece of self-adhering foil or paper, the floppy is file protected and can be read but cannot be written on. A self-contained plastic slide is used to file protect a 3½-inch micro-floppy diskette.

"THE COMPUTER KNOWS WHO DID IT BUT IS IT LEGAL TO GRILL A FLOPPY DISK?"

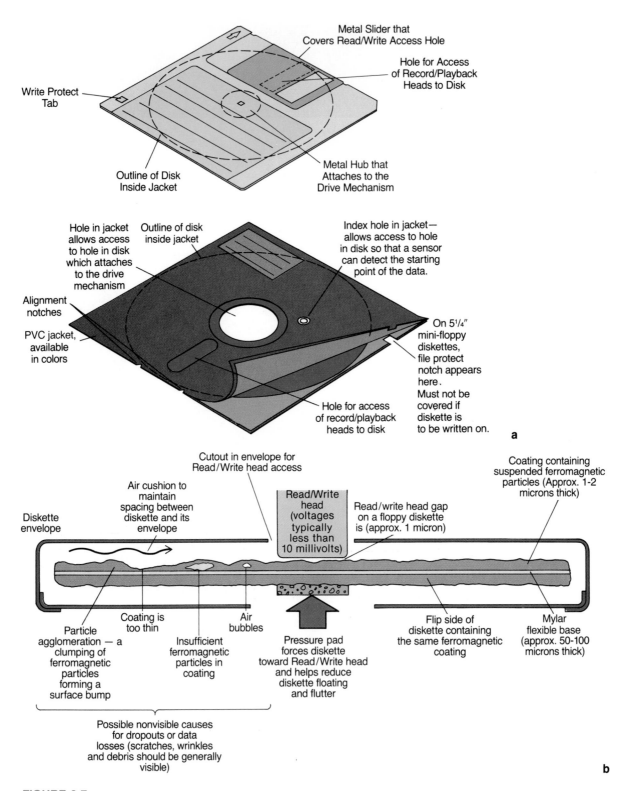

FIGURE 6-7
(a) Magnetic floppy disk physical characteristics.
(b) Composition of a floppy disk.

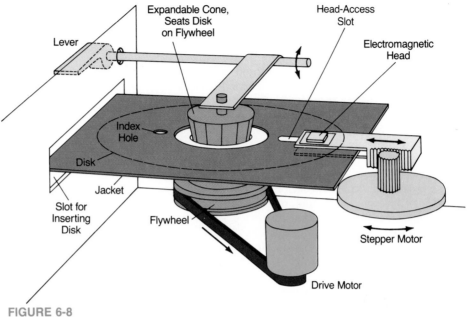

FIGURE 6-8
A floppy disk mounted in a floppy drive.

Floppy disks are subdivided into sides, tracks, and sectors, referred to as the **format** of the disk. A number of different formats are used with $3\frac{1}{2}$- and $5\frac{1}{4}$-inch diskettes. On an IBM PS/2, for example, the surface of a micro-diskette is subdivided into 80 concentric circular areas or **tracks,** each of which is subdivided into 9 or 18 pie-shaped segments, or **sectors** (Fig. 6-9). Each sector contains two fields: a **sector address field** containing information such as track, side, and sector numbers, and the **data field** containing the user data.

To access an item of data from a specific track and sector requires a number of individual steps (see Fig. 6-10). The average access time for this process with a soft-sectored mini-floppy is generally around 200 milliseconds but can be as low as 3 milliseconds when accessing adjacent sectors. This is relatively slow when compared to access times in the microsecond and nanosecond range possible with MOS RAM storage devices, but quite fast when compared to the sequential access capability available with cassettes. Access times with cassettes can be as much as several minutes.

Hard Disk

For more storage and faster access speeds than those available with floppy disks, fixed- or hard-disk storage is also available for use with microcomputers. The fixed or hard disk generally available for use with microcomputers ($3\frac{1}{2}$- or $5\frac{1}{4}$-inch) is similar to but somewhat smaller than those disks available with mini- and mainframe computer systems (usually 14-inch). However, unlike the hard disks for the larger computer systems, hard disks for the micros are generally not removable. Their storage capacity can range from 10 megabytes to more than 300 megabytes (Fig. 6-11).

Some manufacturers offer **disk cartridges,** which are removable hard disks housed within a cartridge. These cartridges are available in different capacities beginning with 10 megabytes, and at a substantially greater cost per megabyte

DISKETTE FORMATS

Most microcomputers use **soft-sectored** diskettes. These diskettes do not contain prerecorded sectors or tracks and must be **formatted** before they can be used. This process, described as **formatting a diskette,** uses a format program to establish the number of tracks and sectors per track, as well as the number of characters that can be stored in each sector. In addition, the format program verifies the usability of each sector and records the sector address at the beginning of the sector. **Hard-sectored** floppy disks differ in that one index hole is provided to mark the beginning of each of ten or sixteen sectors. These index holes are used by the hardware to uniquely address each sector on the diskette.

The number of characters that can be stored per sector on a disk drive is referred to as the **density.** Density is a function of the makeup of the diskette, the disk drive on which it is formatted, and format program used. The least dense storage format is referred to as **single-density.** The most commonly used density is referred to as **double-density** and offers double the capacity of single-density. On an IBM PC, for example, approximately 360,000 bytes or characters can be stored on a double-sided double-density (DS/DD) diskette.

Some manufacturers offer **high-capacity** disk drives. These drives record information at up to four times the density of DS/DD drives. This is achieved by increasing the number of sectors per track to 15, packing more bytes into each sector, and by increasing the number of tracks to 80. Thus each sector and each track on a high-capacity diskette is approximately half as wide as its double-density counterpart. High-capacity drives and diskettes are available in both the $5\frac{1}{4}$-inch (1.2 megabyte capacity) and $3\frac{1}{2}$-inch (1.44 megabyte capacity) sizes.

To increase the storage capacity of a diskette beyond high-capacity or quad-density, some manufacturers have introduced a new technology called **vertical axis recording.** This technique causes the magnetized spots to be stored vertically (like bar magnets standing on end) as opposed to the conventional method (like bar magnets lying flat on the surface). Again, a special recording medium is required. Instead of a magnetically coated mylar film, a cobalt chromium film containing minute iron particles is used. Densities up to fifty times greater are possible with substantially reduced access times.

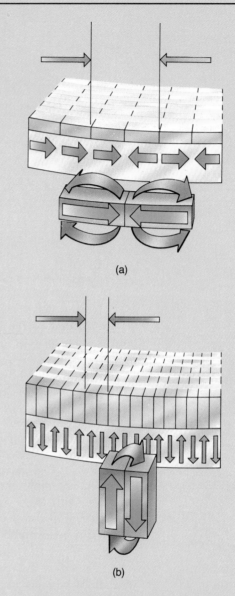

(a)

(b)

(a) Conventional technology, horizontal recording, attempts to squeeze magnets lengthwise, whereas (b) vertical recording squeezes magnets widthwise.

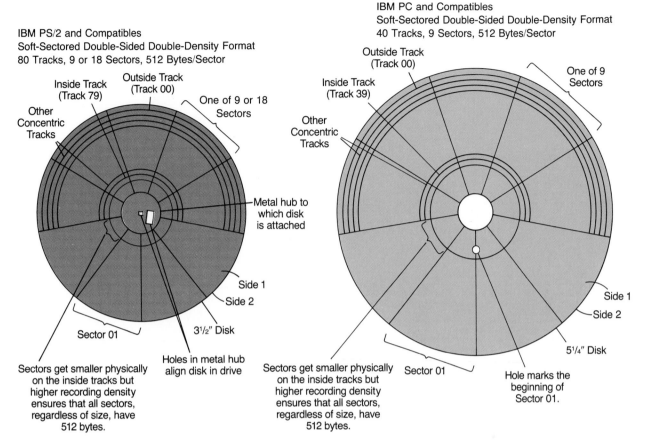

IBM PS/2 and Compatibles
Soft-Sectored Double-Sided Double-Density Format
80 Tracks, 9 or 18 Sectors, 512 Bytes/Sector

Inside Track (Track 79)
Outside Track (Track 00)
Other Concentric Tracks
One of 9 or 18 Sectors
Metal hub to which disk is attached
Side 1
Side 2
Sector 01
3½" Disk
Holes in metal hub align disk in drive
Sectors get smaller physically on the inside tracks but higher recording density ensures that all sectors, regardless of size, have 512 bytes.

IBM PC and Compatibles
Soft-Sectored Double-Sided Double-Density Format
40 Tracks, 9 Sectors, 512 Bytes/Sector

Outside Track (Track 00)
Inside Track (Track 39)
Other Concentric Tracks
One of 9 Sectors
Side 1
Side 2
5¼" Disk
Sector 01
Hole marks the beginning of Sector 01.
Sectors get smaller physically on the inside tracks but higher recording density ensures that all sectors, regardless of size, have 512 bytes.

FIGURE 6-9
The most common 3½-inch and 5¼-inch soft-sectored diskette formats are those used with IBM PC, PS/2, and compatible microcomputers.

than nonremovable units. It is also possible to obtain similar capacities with 3½-inch hard disks mounted on a **circuit board** that can be plugged directly into the computer. To date, disk cartridge and plug-in board units are not available as original equipment options but as "add-on" devices from other vendors.

RAM Disk

A RAM disk is not a disk at all. It is a block of memory treated by the operating system as a disk. A program must be used to install a RAM disk—to specify the size of the memory block allocated to the RAM disk and to assign a logical drive to the RAM disk. Any subsequent read or write to the RAM disk logical drive will be converted by the operating system to a read or write to the designated block of memory. To application programs and users, the RAM disk appears to be a super-fast floppy or hard disk. However, it is different from a disk in that it is volatile; its contents will be lost when power is removed. Therefore, one must always remember to *copy* the contents of the RAM disk to a floppy or hard disk before turning the computer off, if this is not done automatically.

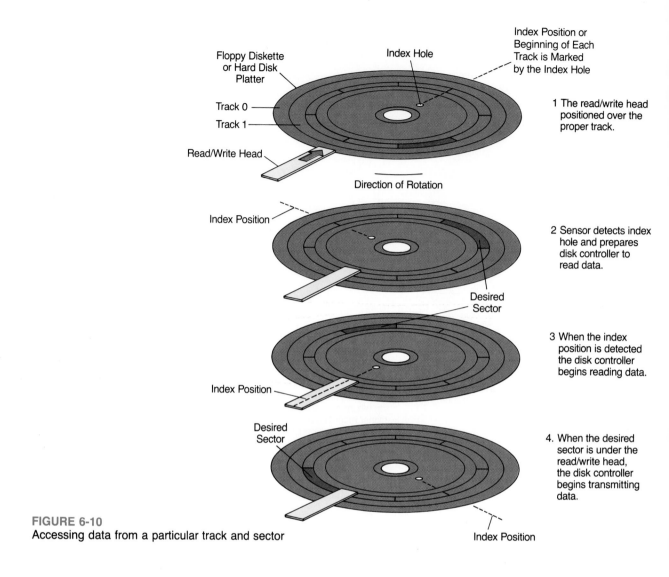

Floppy Diskette or Hard Disk Platter

Track 0

Track 1

Read/Write Head

Index Hole

Direction of Rotation

Index Position or Beginning of Each Track is Marked by the Index Hole

1 The read/write head positioned over the proper track.

Index Position

Desired Sector

2 Sensor detects index hole and prepares disk controller to read data.

Index Position

3 When the index position is detected the disk controller begins reading data.

Desired Sector

4. When the desired sector is under the read/write head, the disk controller begins transmitting data.

Index Position

FIGURE 6-10
Accessing data from a particular track and sector

FIGURE 6-11
IBM PS/2 computer system equipped with a hard and a floppy disk drive.

Optical Disk

Nonerasable Optical Disks

Although a relatively new entrant into the microcomputer secondary storage arena, **optical disks** have been used for music videos and audio recording for some time. The optical disk used with computers is similar to the magnetic disk in that data is recorded in sectors within tracks, but it is different in the method used to record the data. The recording technique most commonly used with optical disks prohibits new data from being recorded over the old. This is because the physical makeup of the disk is actually altered during the writing process.

Writing is accomplished by momentarily directing a laser beam onto the surface of the disk. This burst of light energy causes a change in the nature of the surface approximately one micron (millionth of an inch) in diameter. This change generally takes on one of two forms—it can be a small indentation in the surface of the disk, referred to as a **pit,** or it can be a **bubble** on the surface (see Fig. 6-12). To read an optical disk a light is focused on a tiny area of the surface of the disk passing below the read head. The intensity of the light reflected from this spot is monitored by a light sensor in the read head. If the light reflected from the spot is of a high intensity, the surface contains a pit or a bubble; otherwise it is smooth.

Optical systems are available that allow the user to write data once and read it many times. These systems are aptly called **write once read many (WORM)** systems. **CD-ROM (compact disk/read only memory)** systems are also available that can only read prerecorded disks. These systems are practical for large universally used common databases (documents and images).

CD-ROM USE GROWS

Imagine a futuristic library in which much of the reference material resides on PCs rather than books. Then stop imagining. In January, as part of a bid to build a presidential library on campus, officials at the University of Houston used CD-ROM and other multimedia technology to try to convince President George Bush to bequeath his presidential papers to the school.

But the pitch, say officials, was more than a presentation. "It was a demonstration of at least one aspect of what we think the next generation of presidential libraries will be like," says Robert Krauss, dean of the university's law school.

This is just one example of how CD-ROM and multimedia technology can help companies and institutions. As demonstrated at a recent Microsoft Corp.-sponsored CD-ROM conference in San Francisco, presentations and training are two areas in which CD-ROM is gaining acceptance. The interactive nature of the medium and the glitz of audio and video capabilities appeal to many companies.

"Multimedia makes the information more interesting and more accessible," says Fred Meyer, president of Meridian Data Inc., a Scotts Valley, Calif.-based developer of CD-ROM publishing systems.

At Aldrich Chemical Co. in Milwaukee, Wis., this value has translated into a whole new business. The company, which sells chemicals to pharmaceutical corporations and educational institutions, puts all its data on material safety—more than 35,000 sheets of information—onto CD-ROM and sells it to customers. Aldrich has also put its product catalogs on CD-ROM.

"We perceive this as a way of helping our customers," says Charles Pouchert, VP of Aldrich.

CD-ROM technology has begun to catch on. In 1989, an estimated 160,000 units were shipped, according to research firm Dataquest Inc. of San Jose, Calif., and the market is growing at 88% a year. Says Dataquest analyst Bob Gaskin, "People won't feel that a PC is complete unless it has one."

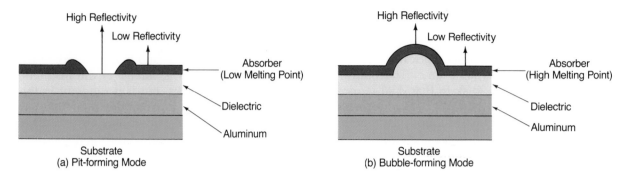

FIGURE 6-12
Result of laser burst in optical recording process.

In view of the nonerasable nature of these optical systems and the fact that access times are generally greater than with magnetic media, what makes the optical disk such an attractive secondary storage medium? First, the life expectancy of data stored optically is approximately three times the shelf life of magnetically recorded information. In addition, since there are no heads flying above the surface there will be no head crashes (heads colliding with the disk surface) or media wear. Secondly, optical media have an enormous storage capacity, ten to thirty times that of magnetic media. For example, RCA has an optical disk program in which lasers are used to store up to 100 gigabytes (1 gigabyte = 1 billion bytes) on a 14-inch disk. In terms of cost-effectiveness, the optical disk is ideal for storing large volumes of relatively permanent data such as high-resolution graphics, photographic images, or huge volumes of text.

Erasable Optical Disks

A new recording technique that combines optical and magnetic technologies has produced an *erasable* optical disk. This recording technique utilizes a laser beam to heat a minute spot on the surface of the disk, altering its properties so that it can be magnetized by a magnetic field that is applied simultaneously. Alone, a magnetic field will not affect the data stored on the surface of the disk. However, applying the laser beam to the surface without a magnetic field erases the data recorded within the range of the laser beam. The future

A DISK CACHE

A **disk cache** (pronounced *cash*) program works the same kind of memory magic as a RAM disk, but is somewhat more sophisticated. It, too, enables you to fence a tract of memory for the purpose of eliminating floppy disk access. But a disk cache, unlike a RAM disk, monitors the **frequency** and **location** of disk accesses and then automatically keeps the often-used portions of your floppy in memory (up to your defined limit) for quick access.

Disk cache software are sometimes included with memory expansion hardware, but are more often sold separately in packages. *Turbo-Charger* is a disk cache program that greatly speeds up program execution and other activities.

of these devices is not as a replacement for magnetic media, but as a replacement for microfilm, microfiche, and paper document storage, and for the storage of massive files and databases beyond the capacity of magnetic media.

Magnetic Bubble and Charged-Coupled Devices

Magnetic bubble and charged-coupled devices (CCDs) are used with some microcomputers. As we saw in Chapter 5, a magnetic bubble is a negatively charged magnetic field or bubble in a positively charged magnetic film. The charged-coupled device is made up of many microscopic capacitors capable of holding a charge for short periods of time. The presence of a charge represents a binary 1 and the absence of the charge represents a binary 0.

The reason for choosing these storage devices over the readily available electromechanical secondary storage devices, such as the tape cassette or floppy disk, are that bubble and CCD devices are not as affected by extreme environments (heat, cold, humidity, etc.), have a much lower incidence of maintenance, and are much faster. Of the two, bubble memory is more desirable because of its greater storage capacity and because of its nonvolatility. CCDs are volatile, but are even faster than magnetic bubble devices.

High-speed data acquisition and critical program storage are two typical areas of application for these secondary storage devices. In such applications, data can be collected as they become available and stored in the bubble. These data can then be loaded into RAM for subsequent processing, making the magnetic bubble ideally suited for use in a distributed data processing environment.

MICROPROCESSORS

Registers

As we learned earlier, a microprocessor is basically a CPU on a chip. As with larger computer systems, the MPU of a microcomputer is composed of an arithmetic/logic unit and a control unit. Both utilize temporary storage areas, or registers, to perform their functions. These include an accumulator, an instruction register, an address register, and other special- and general-purpose registers. All are present in larger systems and perform similar functions. Primary storage is available on separate integrated circuits but is logically and electronically connected to the microprocessor. A system of wires linking these internal components and capable of transmitting electrical impulses is referred to as a **bus.** Most microcomputers use one or more internal or **local buses** for communicating within the MPU and a common or **system bus** for communicating with components outside the MPU.

Arithmetic/Logic Unit

As in a CPU, the ALU of the microprocessor functions under the direct control of the control unit. The control unit determines when the services of the ALU are needed and it provides this unit with the data that it will need. The control unit also determines what is to be done with the results.

Control Unit

The control unit, in addition to overseeing the operations of the ALU, controls the orderly execution of program instructions. To understand how this is done, let's begin by examining the instructional formats used by MPUs.

THE 80486—MICRO HISTORY IN THE MAKING

In 1978, Intel developed the first in a line of illustrious computer chips—the **8086.** Besides being extremely powerful, fast, and efficient, the 8086 chip is most notable for having been the microprocessor selected by IBM for use in the first IBM personal computer. Since that first system, all IBM personal computers have been compatible—software written for the current system runs on the new system without modification. Compatibility has become so important that virtually every personal computer vendor now offers it to some degree. IBM compatibility depends on the ability to use the Intel 8086 instruction set. The much heralded **80486** (or simply 486) the latest microprocessor in the Intel family, uses all of the 8086 instructions plus it provides hundreds of new instructions to make use of the chip's expanded capabilities.

As far as microprocessors go, the 486 is a veritable blockbuster. It is a 32-bit processor that crams more than 1 million transistors into less than one square inch of silicon. Whereas the original IBM PC had a clock speed of 4.77 MHz, the 486 has a clock speed of 33 MHz, providing it with a capability to execute up to 4 million instructions per second. Another attribute of the 486 is that it can address 4 gigabytes (4 billion bytes) and can use 64 terabytes (64 trillion bytes) of virtual memory.

Modes of Operation

While the 486 was being designed, the millions of earlier Intel microprocessors were kept in mind. The 486 will run earlier applications without any major alterations. This is referred to as **backward compatibility.** To ensure compatibility but still provide a growth path for more powerful systems and applications software, three modes of operation were provided.

Real Mode

In the real mode every address is a *real* address as opposed to a virtual address. In this mode, none of the 486's multitasking or virtual memory features are used. However, the advantage is twofold. This mode will run up to 60 times faster than an 8088 processor, and any application or systems program written for an 8086/8088 will also run on the 486.

An Intel 80486 25-MHz microprocessor.

Protected Mode

Protection here refers to the ability to prevent two or more applications from wiping each other out through memory invasion. Multitasking is thus possible, with the concurrent execution of two or more programs by a single computer.

Virtual 486 Mode

In this mode, the 486 can run 8086 programs in real mode as well as in protected mode. That is, many separate applications can run concurrently.

The Memory Management Unit (MMU)

The MMU within the 486 chip permits both segmentation and paging, two important functions of virtual memory.

Segmentation is a memory-management technique for allocating and addressing memory. Segments are protected portions of memory that a program allocates; they are swapped in and out of memory. Managing this swapping is handled by the MMU.

Paging is a memory-management technique that maps pages from disk to real addresses in memory. Whereas segments are variable-length, pages are fixed-length blocks of memory—in the 486, a page is 4096 bytes. Segments can be compared to files, since they are variable-length blocks of data; and pages are similar to sectors on a disk—fixed-length units of data. A segment may be scattered over many noncontiguous pages.

CPU Power By the Year 2000
Intel's 10-year plan for its microprocessor calls for a 2 million transistor i586 by 1992, to be followed up with a 4 to 5 million transistor i686 in 1996. A 250MHz i786 CPU maintaining compatibility with the 80386/i486 instruction set is projected for the end of the decade.

Instructional Formats

Microprocessor instructions are of three types: one-word, two-word, and three-word instructions. A one-word instruction is generally 8 bits in length and specifies only an operation code, or **op code** for short. For example, an instruction to clear the accumulator would require no operand and therefore would consist of an op code only. A *clear* instruction would be an example of a one-word (8-bit) instruction. A two-word instruction would consist of an op code and one operand. For example, an instruction to *store* the contents of the accumulator would require an op code and the storage address where the data are to be placed. A three-word instruction would consist of an op code and two operands. The two operands are used together to represent an address in RAM larger than 255. Addresses larger than 255 cannot be expressed in one word (8 bits) and therefore require two words (16 bits).

Instruction Execution

As with larger computer systems, instruction execution takes place in two parts: the instruction cycle and the execution cycle. In the **instruction cycle,** the instruction is fetched from storage, the op code or first word of the instruction is placed in an instruction register, and the operand(s) is placed in the address buffer. The circuit paths necessary to carry out the instruction are then set up by the instruction decoder and the program counter is set to the address of the next instruction. In the **execution cycle,** the control unit causes the instruction to be executed. The next instruction is then fetched, and so on.

Clearly, the MPU of a microcomputer and the CPU of larger computer systems contain similar functional components and perform similar functions. Their principal differences lie in their size, speed, and overall capabilities. Because the words in larger computer systems are generally larger (Fig. 6-2), these systems are more versatile and are capable of supporting a larger primary storage capacity.

Reduced Instruction Set Computers (RISC)

RISC technology, an acronym for reduced instruction set computers (or computing) represents a recent development in the design of microprocessors. RISC CPUs have fewer and simpler instructions programmed into ROM yet still have the capability of performing complex tasks. This feat is accomplished by combining simple instructions to form more complex ones. The advantage of having a RISC architecture is speed, that is, processing time is greatly reduced. One currently finds RISC technology incorporated into the design of the CPUs used to drive workstations such as those developed by IBM and Sun Microsystems, Inc. (Fig. 6-13).

Coprocessors

Most modern microcomputers support the use of one or more **coprocessors.** A coprocessor is a special microprocessor chip or circuit board that is designed to perform one or more specific tasks. The most commonly used coprocessor is the math coprocessor. Its use will greatly speed up the carrying out of numerical calculations. Intel incorporated a math coprocessor into the design of its 80486 microprocessor chip.

Other available coprocessors will generally serve to enhance a computer's capabilities regarding the amount of systems and application software that will run on the computer.

FIGURE 6-13
IBM RISC System 6000 Powerserver
930 computer.

INPUT/OUTPUT OPERATIONS

In order to understand how input/output operations take place in a microcomputer, we must have a basic understanding of its physical arrangement.

Architecture of a Micro

The physical arrangement or **architecture** of most modern microcomputers utilizes a **motherboard,** a single large circuit board containing the MPU, ROM, RAM, and other associated circuitry. These elements are electronically linked through a series of parallel metal lines etched into the motherboard—the **system bus.**

The system bus carries three types of information—control, address, and data. Control information is carried by a series of **control lines,** addresses by a series of **address lines,** and data by **data lines.** However, the system bus can carry only one command, item of data, or address at a time. For example, when the MPU requests data from memory, they are fetched and sent to the system bus where they can be accessed and used by the MPU. However, while the data are being transmitted from memory to the MPU, no other data can be transmitted over the bus.

The size or **width** of the bus is important to the overall performance of the computer. The wider the bus, the more information that can be carried at one time and the greater the throughput of the system. Most 16-bit microcomputers use 8- or 16-bit buses, while 32-bit micros use 8-bit, 16-bit, and 32-bit buses.

A number of **expansion slots** provide access to the system bus (see Fig. 6-14). Virtually any input/output device can be connected to the microcomputer through one of these slots and an appropriate interface circuit board. These slots can also be used to expand the RAM capability of the system beyond the limits of the motherboard.

I/O Interface

All communications between an input/output device and the MPU take place through an interface. The **interface** is designed to convert the data from a form used by one of these devices to a form acceptable by the other. It must

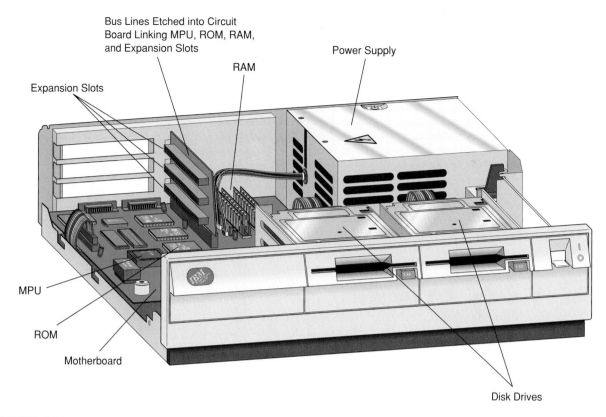

Bus Lines Etched into Circuit
Board Linking MPU, ROM, RAM,
and Expansion Slots

RAM

Power Supply

Expansion Slots

MPU

ROM

Motherboard

Disk Drives

FIGURE 6-14
Typical microcomputer architecture.

also adjust for any possible speed differences between the processor and the
other device. The interface circuits used in microcomputers correspond to the
I/O control units used on larger systems.

There are two general types of interface devices in use, serial and parallel.
A **serial** interface transmits a byte of data as a string of 8 bits, one bit after
the other, over a single wire. A **parallel** interface transmits data byte by byte
over a multiwire cable. That is, all 8 bits of a byte are transmitted simultaneously,
each over a separate wire. Parallel interface devices are clearly faster, but are
far more costly. The type of interface used must match the requirements of
the device it supports.

Figure 6-15 illustrates some of the I/O devices typically connected to a
microcomputer. It is important to understand that these devices are all linked
through a common system bus. All communications between these devices
must take place over this bus, under control of the processor. Thus, while the
bus is carrying data from a disk device to memory, for example, it cannot
carry data to or from the keyboard, monitor, or any other I/O device.

Microcomputers that use a **multiple-bus,** or **multibus** architecture similar
to that used on mini- or mainframe computer systems are being introduced.
These machines provide several independent paths between components instead
of linking all components by a common system bus. The MPU can now communicate I/O commands to a **channel** via a separate **command bus** (see Fig. 6-16).

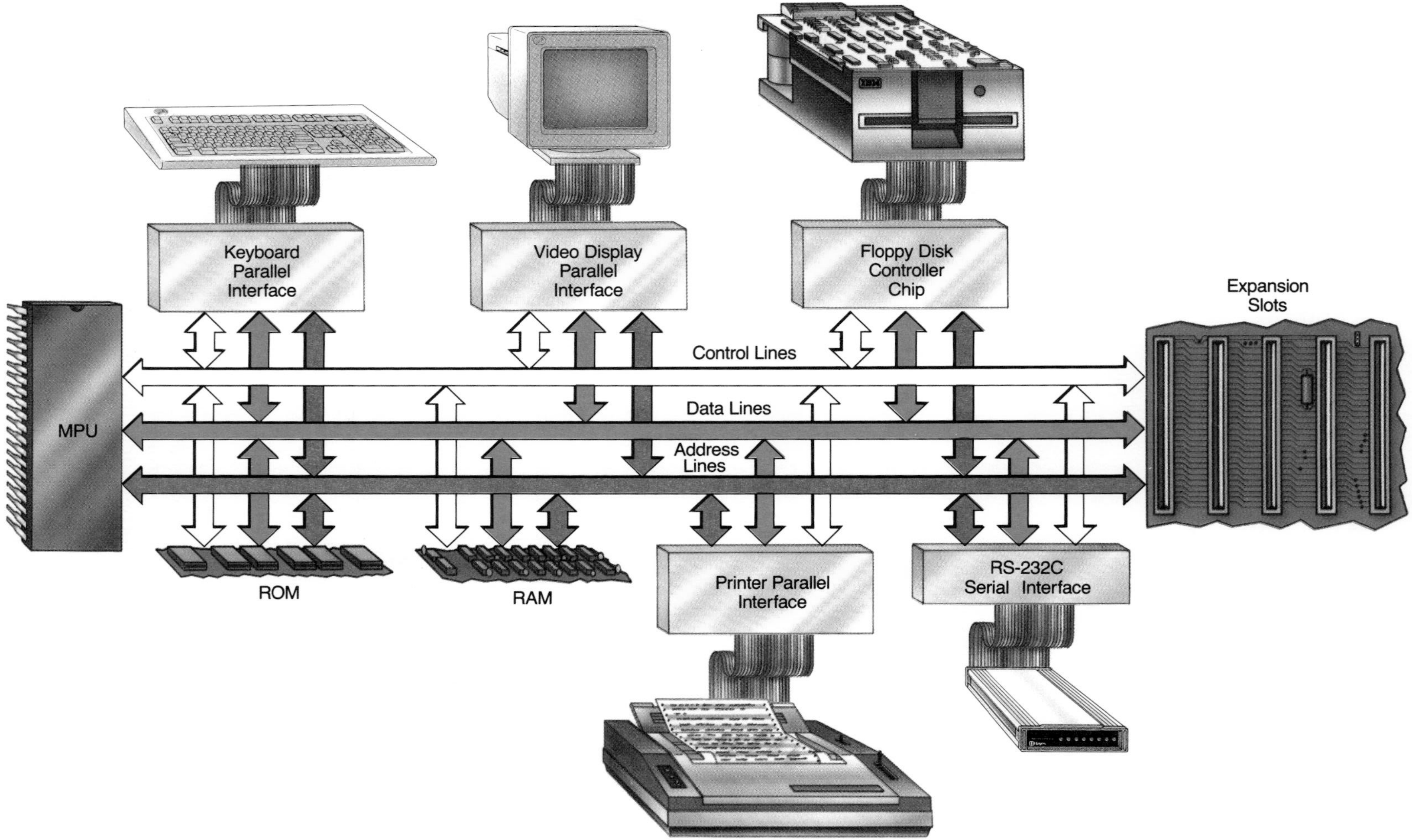

FIGURE 6-15
Interfacing various peripheral devices in a microcomputer.

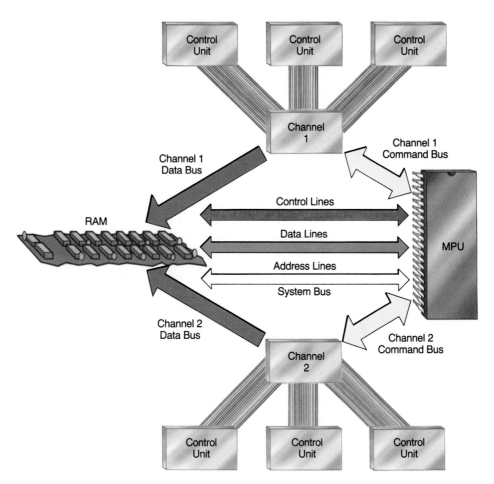

FIGURE 6-16
Multibus architecture microcomputer.

The channel then takes control of the I/O operation and monitors the transmission of data between the I/O device controller and memory via a **data bus.** During this time, the MPU might also be communicating with memory via another bus.

Some larger microcomputer systems use an **input/output control system (IOCS)** that contains a separate microprocessor to handle I/O operations. Additional buses link the IOCS to the MPU and to memory. This frees the MPU to perform non-I/O operations on other programs while the IOCS is handling the I/O operation for the current program—multiprogramming.

Input/Output Methods

There are three basic methods by which data can be input from or output to a peripheral device and RAM. These are referred to as programmed I/O, interrupt I/O, and direct memory access.

In **programmed I/O,** the MPU is in direct control of all data transfers and other I/O operations. This is accomplished with specific input or output instructions. When an input operation is desired, the MPU simply issues an input command and awaits the arrival of the data at the bus. From the bus the data is moved to memory. Similarly, if an output operation is desired, the

MPU transmits the data to the bus and issues a command to the output device through the appropriate interface. Once the data transfer is initiated, the MPU must wait for its completion and the bus to be freed up before beginning a new transfer. This method is commonly used in personal computers because it is effective and easily implemented.

In the **interrupt I/O** method, the MPU does not have to wait for the input/output devices to complete their tasks. This is because control of the operation is given to a *channel*. The channel signals the MPU when the operation has been completed. This is accomplished by means of an *interrupt*. The MPU is actually interrupted with the equivalent of "pardon me." Upon completion of the execution of the current instruction, the MPU may then initiate another I/O operation. This method requires a multibus architecture and is similar to overlapped processing in larger systems.

The **direct memory address** method is the fastest of the three methods. It requires a multibus architecture and allows the MPU to be bypassed completely. A special direct memory access controller is connected between RAM and an input or output device. This method is the most expensive of all to mechanize and therefore is not used except with very high-speed input/output devices and then only when absolutely necessary.

Telecommunications

Most microcomputers also support the intercomputer communication of data via telephone lines—telecommunications. This is facilitated by means of an add-on device referred to as a **modem** (see Fig. 6-17). In telecommunications, one computer or terminal issues a command, message, or some other form of output. This output from the computer, which is *digital*, is **modulated,** or converted to an *analog* signal that can be transmitted over telephone lines, by a modem interfaced to the sending computer. The signal is then carried over the telephone lines and received at another modem some distance away. This second modem then **demodulates,** or converts the *analog* signal back to a com-

FIGURE 6-17
Modem used atop a monitor to facilitate banking transactions directly from one's home.

Unit 2   Computer Hardware

puter-compatible *digital* signal. The name **modem** was chosen for this device simply because it performs the functions of modulation and demodulation.

Thus, with the aid of a modem and a serial interface to a microcomputer, communication can take place over great distances. The speed with which these communications take place is highly dependent on the modem employed. Modems support communications at 300, 1,200, or 2,400 bps; however, modems are available for 9,600 bps transmissions at substantially higher costs. These topics will be developed in Chapter 7.

Input/Output Devices

A number of input/output devices have been designed for use with the many types of microcomputer systems on the market. Many of these are simply less complex versions of I/O devices that have been available for larger computer systems for some time. The principal differences are that because they are intended for use with microcomputer systems they are significantly slower and substantially cheaper. Let us examine a few of these.

Keyboards

The simplest and most common of all the microcomputer input peripheral devices is the keyboard. Several versions of keyboards are currently available. The best, and most expensive, of these is the full-stroke keyboard (see Fig. 6-18)— ideal for word processing and other volume data and program entry activities that require a good touch. This is the type of keyboard that is available with most mainframe computer terminals or the more expensive microcomputer systems.

Some of the more popular microcomputers offer **enhanced** keyboards designed for easy entry of numbers. This is accomplished with a smaller group of keys known as a numeric keypad at the right of the standard keyboard. These keys generally consist of the digits, a decimal point, a negative sign, and an ENTER key. This type of keyboard is ideal for accounting operations, which require a large volume of numbers to be input.

FIGURE 6-18
IBM's full-stroke keyboard in use.

Monitors

The most commonly used microcomputer display device, the **monitor,** utilizes a cathode ray tube (CRT). CRT monitors generally produce images by the **raster-scan method.** In this method, a beam of electrons, varying in intensity, is moved back and forth horizontally across the face of the monitor. As the beam is directed to each spot on the phosphor-coated screen, it illuminates the spot in proportion to the voltage applied to the beam. Each spot represents a picture element or **pixel.** When the electron beam has scanned the entire screen and illuminated each pixel, we see a complete image although the complete image never appears on the screen at one time. The image we see is the one traced on the retinas of our eyes by the light beam. However, this image will fade unless it is *refreshed*. Thus the electron beam must scan the screen very rapidly, a minimum of sixty times per second, so that the intensity of the image we see will remain approximately the same and so that the screen will not appear to flicker.

The screen **resolution,** or detail, possible with a particular monitor is determined by the *number* of pixels that make up the screen. Monitors are currently available with from 64,000 to more than 2 million pixels per screen. The greater the resolution of a monitor the greater the storage demand on the computer since the image must be stored in memory before it can be displayed. Two techniques are used to store computer images: bit-mapped and character-addressable.

In a **bit-mapped display,** each pixel is uniquely addressable. One or more bits of information must be stored for each pixel on the screen. This technique puts the greatest demand on the computer's memory but provides the most detailed display. For graphical applications such as CAD/CAM, this detail is essential. However, for applications such as word processing, not requiring this detail, a **character-addressable display** is more appropriate. In a character-addressable display, the screen is divided into character positions, typically 80 characters per line and 25 lines per screen. Only the characters to be displayed are stored in memory. As each character is retrieved from memory, it is converted into a pattern of dots or pixels by a special character generator circuit and displayed.

MONOCHROME OR COLOR. Some monitors display images in only one color while others are capable of producing images in a rainbow of colors. **Monochrome monitors** use a single electron beam and display one color, generally green, amber, or white, on a black background. The phosphor composition of the screen determines the color produced. **Color monitors** produce multi-color images by combining the colors red, blue, and green in varying intensities. Each pixel is made up of three color dots—one red, one blue, and one green. It will appear to glow in different colors depending on the intensity of each individual dot in the pixel (see Fig. 6-19). Color monitors are commonly referred to as **RGB monitors** since they employ three electron beams, one for each color dot in a pixel. Color or RGB monitors are categorized as CGA, EGA, VGA and Super VGA depending on the resolution they offer. CGA monitors provide the least resolution (approximately 300×200 pixels) and Super VGA monitors provide the greatest resolution (1000×800 pixels and greater).

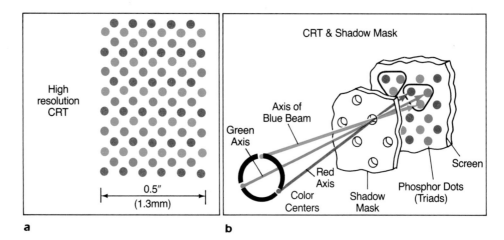

FIGURE 6-19
(a) The screen of a high-resolution color monitor is subdivided into red, blue, and green dots. (b) Dots are combined in differing intensities to produce different colored points called pixels.

MONITOR INTERFACE. A monitor by itself is of little value. As with other I/O devices, a monitor requires an appropriate interface to communicate with a computer. For example, a color graphics interface board is needed for an RGB monitor. This interface will generally not work with a monochrome monitor and might even damage it. Literally dozens of monitor interface boards are available for use with microcomputers, and caution must be exercised to match the interface to both the monitor and the computer used.

USING A TELEVISION. Some smaller microcomputer systems are designed to be used with a standard television. The basic difference between a monitor and a television set is that the resolution of a television is substantially less than that achieved with a monitor; also the television requires the use of a **modulator** to interface the computer output with the television. The modulator combines the separate audio and visual signals sent by the microcomputer into a single modulated signal as required by a television. Most inexpensive computer systems designed for use with a television set generally have a built-in modulator.

Flat-Panel Displays

With the introduction of laptop computers came the need for more compact, low-power, durable monitors. A number of flat-panel display technologies have filled this need. Among the most common are the plasma and liquid crystal displays.

PLASMA DISPLAYS. A **plasma display** consists of an ionized neon/argon gas (plasma) sealed between two glass plates. One glass plate encases a set of fine horizontal wires and the other a set of vertical wires. Pixels are formed by the intersections of the horizontal and vertical wires. A single pixel can be turned on by sending a current through its horizontal and vertical wire. This causes the gas between the wires to produce an amber glow. The images produced by plasma displays are generally very clear, detailed, and not subject to the flicker associated with raster-scan monochrome monitors. Plasma displays are generally more expensive than their CRT counterparts.

LIQUID CRYSTAL DISPLAYS. Liquid crystal displays (LCDs) have been used for several years in such commonly found items as calculators and digital watches. A thin layer of a liquid crystal substance is suspended between two sheets of polarized glass and separated by a wire grid into tiny square areas. Each square is a pixel. As current is applied to the wires surrounding a square or pixel the liquid crystal substance within the square changes from clear to opaque or black. The image produced is a pattern of thousands of clear and black squares.

The principal disadvantage of LCD displays is their lack of brightness and resolution as compared to CRT and plasma displays. In addition, the quality of the LCD display is dependent on the surrounding light and the viewing angle. It is sharpest and clearest when viewed in a well lighted room and from directly in front.

Specialized I/O Devices

A whole range of specialized I/O devices is available for use with microcomputer systems.

Speech synthesizers allow the computer to "talk" to its user. The speech pattern produced by most synthesizers is based on the spelling of the words to be spoken. Predetermined units of speech called **phonemes** are used to produce the sounds of a spoken word. The problem with this is that many words are not pronounced phonetically or as their spelling would indicate. Thus the words "spoken" by these devices are generally restricted to those that are pronounced phonetically. The word "read" in "He read the book" would probably be pronounced as if it contained a long e.

Other speech synthesizers store complete word patterns but are limited in that they can "say" only the stored words. As approximately one thousand bytes are required to store each word pattern, these devices are only practical for limited vocabulary applications. This may change as large-capacity, less expensive memory chips become available.

Speech recognition devices permit the recognition of the spoken word as input to the computer; they are still in their infancy and generally are capable of recognizing only up to 200 different words. This obviously limits their applications. In addition, speech recognition devices generally cost as much as the rest of the microcomputer system to which they are attached.

Plotters and **printers** capable of generating intricate plots in multiple colors, the **digitizer pad,** the **joystick,** and the **mouse** (Fig. 6-20) are other specialized devices available with microcomputers.

MICROCOMPUTER SOFTWARE

A multitude of software products are available for use with microcomputer systems. Basically, software can be divided into three areas—operating systems, utility and language translator programs, and canned, or prewritten, prepackaged software.

FIGURE 6-20
A mouse is used with applications software for making choices from the menu.

Operating Systems

An **operating system (OS)** can be described as a number of programs that control and coordinate the overall operation of a computer. Operating systems schedule programs for execution, control the use of I/O devices, and provide utility functions for all of the programs that run on the computer. They contribute significantly to the way the system appears to the user. Many available software packages are designed to appear to the user as an extension of DOS. Operating systems are described more fully in Chapter 9.

Utility and Language Translator Programs

Many utility and language translator programs are available to aid the user of a particular computer system. Among them one will usually find an assembler program and a BASIC language translator.

Most computer chips can understand only machine code—the set of machine instructions associated with that particular microprocessor chip. Machine code instructions are often difficult to learn and use. Therefore, we prefer to communicate with the microprocessor using **mnemonics**—letters and words instead of numbers. The symbolic language that uses mnemonics instead of numeric codes is referred to as **assembly language.** Because the machine can only understand machine code, an **assembler** is needed to translate the mnemonics into machine code. If one learns to use assembly language proficiently, the computer can be used to its fullest.

Since its inception at Dartmouth College, BASIC has become more and more popular to the point where today it is provided with virtually every microcomputer system produced. Some microcomputers provide a BASIC translator as a program that resides on an external storage medium; others provide a BASIC interpreter on a ROM chip.

In addition to supporting BASIC, many manufacturers make available **compilers,** or language translators, for higher-level languages such as Pascal, FORTRAN, and COBOL, to name but a few. High-level languages use compilers to translate to machine code (a process referred to as **compilation**), and assembly languages use assemblers to translate to machine code.

Canned or Prepackaged Programs

Among the **canned,** or prepackaged, ready-to-use programs are programs to do just about everything, from handling your financial affairs to playing video games to making your personal computer into a word processing system. The major classifications of canned software that are of general use include word processors, spreadsheets, databases, graphics, communications, and integrated software.

A **word processing** program accepts words typed into a computer and processes them to produce edited text. Characters, words, and whole paragraphs can be deleted, inserted or moved. These are only a few of many functions provided by word processors.

A **spreadsheet** program is a super calculator that provides you with a giant column-row table or spreadsheet on which you can enter numbers and store them in the memory of a computer. Once stored these numbers can be manipulated, causing simultaneous changes to take place in the corresponding spreadsheet.

A **database** package makes it easy for us to create and use a database—a set of logically related files organized to facilitate access by one or more application programs and to minimize data redundancy.

A **computer graphics** package allows us to convert data into meaningful diagrams or graphs. Graphics packages produce pie charts, graphs, bar charts, and so on.

A **communications** program allows your computer to "talk" to other computers and be understood. It makes certain your computer follows the rules for initializing a conversation, sending and receiving data, and maintaining a dialog with other computers.

Integrated software represents the most recent entry into the prepackaged software race. As the name implies, integrated software packages combine, or integrate, a number of individual software packages into a single larger program.

Canned software packages are covered in detail in Chapters 12 and 13.

POPULAR MICROCOMPUTER SYSTEMS

Today, there are literally hundreds of manufacturers of microcomputer systems. Companies that only a few years ago manufactured only computer components or peripherals now produce complete microcomputer systems. By and large the differences between these systems are subtle. A number of microcomputer systems marketed by different manufacturers are shown in Fig. 6-21. Channel option cards.

FIGURE 6-21
Pictured are some popular microcomputers offered by various computer manufacturers,
(a) AT&T, (b) Xerox, (c) Epson, (d) IBM PS/2, (e) Tektronix, (f) NEC-HE, (g) Apple Macintosh.

197

INTEL MICRO 2000: A COMPUTING REVOLUTION IN THE MAKING

By the end of this decade, Intel Corp. plans to produce a 250-MHz microprocessor containing up to 100 million transistors and performing 2 billion operations per second. And if that is not enough, Intel Senior Vice President David House said the chip will be 386-compatible.

Intel calls this project Micro 2000. If successful, such massive processing power, if available at a cost comparable to today's machines, promises to revolutionize computing.

"You are going to see microprocessor-based products displacing traditional minicomputer and mainframe products. We're going to find, by the end of the decade, that mainframes are going to be slower than microcomputers," House said.

What will users do with all this power?

"There is one primary area that will benefit most directly from this massive amount of power and that's the human interface. The problem we have in growing the computer business is that computers aren't friendly to use," House said.

As an example, he cited his own mother's unwillingness to use automated teller machines because she prefers to deal with a person instead.

"The reason is that, when you deal with a computer, you deal with it on its own terms," House said. Even today's "friendliest" graphical user interfaces require users essentially to work their way through a flowchart: making decisions and moving on to the next.

Although digital computers think this way, people do not. "People think by analogy and make intuitive links. They are able to recognize extremely complex patterns and trends. Maybe they don't carry things to the precision that a computer does, but they certainly have a much wider scope of reasoning," House said.

To truly integrate computers with humans, the computers will have to be made to think more like us, rather than vice versa. Such techniques as artificial intelligence, neural networks, common-sense knowledge bases and better user interfaces will all require significantly greater processing power, which Micro 2000 is aimed at providing.

How to Get There

Transistors have been shrinking and continue to get smaller. The total number of semiconductors which can be placed in a given area has been steadily increasing as a result of a decrease in the size of the devices themselves.

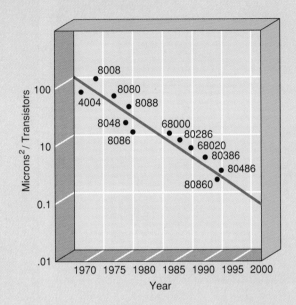

House said researchers have already demonstrated the ability to produce functional devices as small as 0.1 micron (see chart). These trends suggest that logic devices will contain at least 50 million transistors by the year 2000.

Because a higher percentage of the transistor count in microprocessors is being devoted to memory, it may be possible to develop a 100 million transistor microprocessor, House said.

Clock frequency, meanwhile, is dependent upon several factors. Among these are packaging, power consumption, interconnect technology and the amount of current required to drive the transistors.

"We will use multiple-layer interconnections, four or more, to optimize signal routing within a chip. These will be of a material with a much lower resistivity than those used today," House said.

The further miniaturization will also allow clock speeds to leap into the 250-Mhz range.

In trying to predict the future direction of microprocessors, Intel engineers noted an interesting trend. Engineer Pat Gelsinger postulated it as a new law of computing, namely, "Every good idea proven in the mainframe or minicomputer migrates on to the microprocessor."

For example, 1970s mainframe memory management first appeared in micros on the 286; paged virtual memory, first seen on the VAX line in the late 1970s, is now a common microprocessor feature.

Other examples include instruction and data caches, as well as pipelining. Thus far, this integration trend has focused on system bottlenecks outside the CPU. "But with each generation, the next system bottleneck migrates on to the microprocessor," House said.

The next mainframe concept likely to move to the micro is parallel processing. Multiple processors are already commonly used on mainframes and minis but are just beginning to be used on micros.

House predicted that multiple CPUs will eventually be built into a single microprocessor chip.

By the year 2000, House said he believes microprocessors will be executing multiple instructions per clock. Two or three instructions are possible today, and Intel expects a reduction of clocks per instruction.

If all this comes to pass, a single CPU would perform about 700 million instructions per second. Four such processors on a single chip could perform 2 billion instructions per second. Also, because so much processing power would be available, adding compatibility features would not be the burden it presents today, House said. He believes the chip will probably include on-board circuitry for processing full-motion video and stereo sound, features which are gradually working their way onto systems already.

Reprinted by permission of *MIS Week*, March 5, 1990. Copyright Fairchild Publications, 1990.

SUMMARY AND GLOSSARY OF KEY TERMS

- A microcomputer can consist of a single, **large-scale integrated (LSI)** circuit or several integrated circuits interconnected on one or more circuit boards.

- Regardless of the makeup of a microcomputer, it is a digital computer and must have an **arithmetic/logic unit,** a **control unit,** a **primary storage unit,** and a capability to **input** and **output** data.

- The heart of the microcomputer is the **microprocessor unit (MPU).** In most microcomputers, primary storage is not contained in the MPU, but is available on separate integrated circuits.

- Microcomputers utilize fixed-size units of storage referred to as **words.** Most microcomputer words are 8, 16, or 32-**bits** (1, 2, or 4 **bytes**) in length. Recently, microcomputers utilizing 24- and 32-bit words were introduced into the market. The larger the word, the faster the system, and the greater the cost.

- **ROM,** or **read only memory,** is generally provided by the manufacturer of the micro. ROM is dedicated to a particular application, may be read from but cannot be written over, and is nonvolatile. **Firmware** is manufacturer-supplied programs on ROM.

- **RAM,** or **random access memory,** is general storage that can be read from or written on. Access times for data stored on RAM can be from a few **nanoseconds** (billionths of a second) to 1 microsecond (millionth of a second).

- **PROM,** or **programmable read only memory,** are blank chips that can have programs or data permanently stored on them with a special programming device. Once programmed, these devices behave the same as ROM.

- **EPROM,** or **erasable programmable read only memory,** can be programmed as can PROM, but may be erased and reprogrammed. Once programmed, EPROMs behave the same as ROM. **EEPROM,** or **electrically erasable programmable read only memory,** is similar to EPROM but can be erased electrically.

- Magnetic tape **cassettes** or **cartridges** used with computers are the same as the standard variety of audio cassettes with the exception that they generally do not contain a leader. The cassette recorder is interfaced with the microcomputer via a standard circuit to convert the audio signals to binary signals. The rate at which these signals can be sent or received is referred to as the **baud rate.** Standard baud rates range from 300 signals or bits per second to 9,600 bits per second. Digital cassettes offer greater storage density but are not widely used because of their increased cost.

- The advantage of using magnetic tape cassettes or cartridges lies in their simplicity and low cost. Disadvantages include unreliability, low speed, and the fact that they can only be read or written on sequentially.

- **Floppy disks,** or **diskettes,** can be accessed sequentially or directly. Floppy disks are available in $5\frac{1}{4}$-inch (mini-floppy) and $3\frac{1}{2}$-inch (micro-floppy) diameters. Floppy disks are generally subdivided into sides, tracks, and sectors, referred to as the **format** of the disk. Disks are subdivided into concentric circular areas known as **tracks. Soft-sectored** disks record sector addresses on the disk; **hard-sectored** floppy disks utilize an index hole to mark each sector and the beginning of a record on the disk.

- Floppy disks are available in different **densities.** Today, floppies are available in single, double, and high-density formats.

- **Hard-disk** drives are available with some microcomputers. These disks are generally fixed in place, are faster than the floppy, and offer far more storage capacity than is available with floppy disk drives.
- The **RAM disk** is a block of *memory* treated as an extra "disk."
- The newest secondary storage devices to be used with the microcomputer are the **magnetic bubble, charged-coupled devices,** and **optical disk.** The advantage of the magnetic bubble and the optical disk over the charged-couple device is that the bubble and optical disk are nonvolatile, whereas the charged-coupled device is volatile. Many manufacturers are giving the optical disk careful consideration as a secondary storage medium for future machines. **WORM (write-once read many)** optical systems allow the user to record data once and read many times. **OROM (optical read only memory)** systems can only read prerecorded disks. The newer **erasable optical disks** make it possible for recorded data to be erased.
- A **microprocessor (MPU)** is a CPU on a chip. A **bus** is a system of wires that links the MPU with primary storage and peripheral devices.
- As with larger computer systems, the MPU makes use of **registers.** The **instruction register** and **program register** perform the same functions as they do in the larger systems. The **address buffer** is another name for an **address register.** In addition the MPU makes use of both **general-purpose** and **special-purpose** registers.
- The **ALU** functions under the direction of the **control unit.** Both the arithmetic/logic unit and the control units perform the same basic functions in a microcomputer as they do in the larger computer systems.
- There are three lengths of microprocessor instructions: one-word, two-word, and three-word instructions.
- In the **instruction cycle,** the instruction is fetched from storage, and the op code is placed in an *instruction register* and the operand(s) is (are) placed in the *address buffer.* In the **execution cycle,** the control unit causes the instructions to be executed.
- **RISCs** (reduced instruction set computers) utilize combinations of a small group of instructions to reduce processing times.
- A **coprocessor** is a special chip or circuit designed to perform one or more specific tasks. The most common coprocessor, the **math coprocessor,** is used to speed up numerical calculations.
- Communications between the MPU and primary storage, secondary storage, and other peripherals take place through one or more **interfaces.** An interface

converts data from a form acceptable to the sending device to a form acceptable to the receiving device and adjusts for any speed differences between these devices. A **serial interface** transmits a byte of data one bit at a time. A **parallel interface** transmits data byte by byte.
- The physical arrangement, or **architecture,** of a micro includes a **motherboard** (containing the MPU, ROM, and RAM) linked through a common or **system bus** to a series of **expansion slots.**
- The size or width of the bus determines the amount of data that can be carried through the system at one time. A 32-bit word microcomputer operates more efficiently with a 32-bit bus than with a 16-bit bus. **Multibus** machines provide independent paths between components, allowing the MPU to communicate I/O commands to a channel via a separate **command bus.** The channel takes control of the I/O operation and monitors the transmission of data between the I/O device controller and memory via a **data bus.**
- An **input/output control system (IOCS)** uses a separate microprocessor to handle I/O operations. This frees the MPU to perform non-I/O operations on other programs—multiprogramming.
- Three basic input/output methods by which data are transmitted between peripheral devices and RAM are programmed I/O, interrupt I/O, and direct memory access.
- In **programmed I/O,** the MPU is in direct control of all data transfers and I/O operations.
- The **interrupt I/O** method allows the MPU to carry on other activities while an input/output operation is taking place, and the control program or supervisor "interrupts" the MPU when the I/O operation is completed.
- The **direct memory address** method is the fastest and most expensive of the three methods, as the MPU is bypassed completely. A special controller is connected between the I/O device and RAM and controls the entire I/O data transfer operation. This method is only used with very high-speed I/O devices and only when maximum speed is essential.
- **Telecommunications** permits the communication of information between computers and between a remote terminal and a computer.
- The output of a computer is *digital*; it is **modulated** or converted to an *analog* signal so it can be transmitted over telephone lines. At the other end of the transmission, the analog signal is **demodulated** or converted back to a *digital* signal. The device that modulates or

demodulates signals for data transmission is called a **modem**.

- Microcomputer input/output devices include **keyboards** of various types, **monitors, speech synthesizers** that allow the computer to "talk" to a user, **speech recognition devices** capable of understanding and reacting to the spoken word, **plotters, printers, digitizer pads, joysticks,** and **mice.**
- Microcomputer software includes **operating systems,** the programs that supervise and control the operation of the computer.

- **Mnemonics** are the letters and words that comprise the commands of an **assembly language. Assemblers** translate the assembly language mnemonics into machine code—a process known as **assembly. Compilers** translate high-level languages into machine code, a process known as **compilation.**
- Popular **canned,** or prepackaged programs include **word processing, database, spreadsheet, graphics, communications,** and **integrated software** packages.

EXERCISES

True/False

_____ 1. The microprocessor incorporates the control and arithmetic/logic functions performed by the microcomputer.

_____ 2. MOS chips employed in microcomputer primary storage units are of five types: ROM, RAM, PROM, EPROM, and EEPROM.

_____ 3. ROM is volatile storage.

_____ 4. Once programmed, PROM and EPROM behave the same as ROM.

_____ 5. A baud rate of 300 means that the signal is changed every $\frac{1}{300}$ second.

_____ 6. The two types of cassettes used with microcomputers are $5\frac{1}{4}$-inch and $3\frac{1}{2}$-inch.

_____ 7. Advantages of tape cassettes are their low cost and simplicity.

_____ 8. The arrangement of tracks and sectors on the surface of a disk is referred to as the format of the disk.

__T__ 9. It is not possible to provide file protection for only part of the data on a floppy disk.

_____ 10. Two commonly used floppy-disk sizes are $5\frac{1}{4}$-inch and $3\frac{1}{2}$-inch.

_____ 11. Optical disks cannot be reused.

__F__ 12. Microcomputer primary storage is part of the MPU. *Separate from*

_____ 13. The ALU operates under the direction of the control unit.

__T__ 14. Registers are utilized in both the ALU and the control unit.

__F__ 15. The registers in microcomputers serve basically the same purposes as those in larger computer systems.

_____ 16. Instructions in microcomputers are of only two types: one-word and three-word. *one, two & three*

_____ 17. A three-word instruction format is needed for addresses in RAM larger than 255.

__T__ 18. A device that converts data to and from the MPU and the input/output devices is called an interface. *Brings 2 things together to communicate.*

_____ 19. In the programmed I/O method, the MPU is in direct control of all data transfers and other I/O operations.

_____ 20. In the direct memory address method, the MPU is bypassed.

_____ 21. Language translator programs are needed because the computer does not understand anything but numeric machine code, and that is not easy for humans to use.

_____ 22. An element on a letter-quality printer is referred to as a pixel.

_____ 23. Joysticks are specialized I/O devices used with microcomputers.

_____ 24. An operating system consists of programs that control and coordinate the operation of a computer.

_____ 25. Optical disks have more storage capacity than magnetic disks of the same size.

_____ 26. A RAM disk is a floppy diskette that can be added to some systems to increase the size of internal storage.

__F__ 27. Optical disk technology is expected to replace magnetic disk technology for secondary storage because it can provide the same features and the stored data last longer. *Can't write on it, features are diff!*

_____ 28. A system bus is a system of wires that links the MPU with components outside the MPU.

_____ 29. Usually, one-word instructions have an operand, but no op code.

_____ 30. During the instruction cycle, the instruction is executed.

_____ 31. An interface on a microcomputer corresponds to I/O control units on larger systems.

_____ 32. A 16-bit microprocessor requires a 16-bit bus to transfer data through the system.

_____ 33. The device which interfaces between a computer and the telephone line is called a modem.

_____ 34. Modems are used to modulate digital signals and demodulate analog signals.

_____ 35. Pictures on a monitor are made up of pixels.

Fill-in

1. The basic elements of a microcomputer are _____ .

2. The heart of the microcomputer is an LSI circuit referred to as a _____ .

3. The 3½-inch floppy disk format is referred to as _____ .

4. Microcomputer disk storage with larger storage capacities and faster access times than are possible with floppies can be obtained with _____ -disks.

5. ROM stands for _____ .

6. The smallest addressable unit in primary storage is the _____ .

7. EEPROM stands for _____ .

8. Any data stored on a magnetic medium can be lost if the medium is exposed to a _____ .

9. The surface of a disk is normally divided up into concentric circular areas known as _____ .

10. A block of memory that is treated by the computer as a disk is known as a _____ .

11. Optical disk systems that allow the user to write data once and read it many times are known as _____ systems.

12. A system of wires linking the MPU with primary storage and capable of transmitting electrical impulses is referred to as a _____ .

13. The system bus carries three types of information, _____,
    _____ , and _____ .

14. The architecture of a microcomputer generally includes a _____ , which
    contains the MPU, ROM, RAM, and other circuitry.

15. Memory expansion boards, floppy- and hard-disk controller boards, and serial and
    parallel interface boards can be plugged into _____ on a microcomputer.

16. When the channel has competed an I/O operation, it signals the MPU by means of
    a(n) _____ .

17. Output from a computer is in the form of digital signals. A(n) _____ is
    used to modulate or convert digital signals to _____ and vice versa.

18. The rate that data can be received from or sent to a device is measured in signals
    per second and is known as _____ rate.

19. The most commonly found output peripheral is the _____ .

20. In a bit-mapped display, each _____ is uniquely addressable.

21. _____ monitors display in only one color.

22. A(n) _____ converts computerized digital data into audible sounds allow-
    ing a computer to "talk" to its user.

23. _____ devices accept the spoken word as input to the computer.

24. A(n) _____ is a series of programs that control and coordinate the overall
    operation of a computer.

25. The computer language that uses mnemonics is referred to as _____ .

26. A(n) _____ is needed to translate the mnemonics of assembly language
    into machine code.

27. Language translators, or _____ translate high-level languages such as CO-
    BOL or BASIC into machine language.

28. A(n) _____ program is a supercalculator that provides a giant column-
    row table for the storage and manipulation of numbers.

29. To create a manuscript containing tables of numbers and graphical displays, one
    would use _____ .

30. A(n) _____ is a special hand-held input device that allows the user to
    simply point to icons, or graphic images on the screen.

Problems

1. Compare the MPU of the microcomputer and the CPU of the larger computer. List
   the similarities and the differences.
2. How does the variety of input/output devices available for use with microcomputers
   compare with those available for use with other computer systems?
3. For what types of applications would the microcomputer be ideally suited?
4. What are the principal advantages of a 16-bit microcomputer over an 8-bit microcomputer? Disadvantages?
5. Contrast the instruction and execution cycles of microcomputers with those of other
   computer systems.
6. Contrast the capabilities of a microcomputer system utilizing $5\frac{1}{4}$-inch disks with one
   using $3\frac{1}{2}$-inch disks.

Projects

1. Visit a computer store and make a list of what microprocessor and other integrated circuit components are readily available.
2. Visit a computer store and determine and describe the available microcomputer systems. Which are intended for a special use and which are general-purpose systems?
3. At your library, review the literature to determine five popular microcomputer systems other than those described in the text. List the features and intended uses of each.

CROSSWORD PUZZLE

Across

1. The arrangement of tracks and sectors on a diskette
2. A temporary storage area
3. Architecture that uses several independent paths to connect components
4. Disk drives capable of reading and writing at twice single-density
5. A motherboard is linked through a common system bus to a series of _____
6. A storage device that is written on by a burst of light energy
7. A signal from a channel to the MPU
8. The CPU in a microcomputer
9. A board that contains the MPU, ROM, and RAM
10. Graphic images used in place of menus
11. A modulator/demodulator of transmitted signals
12. Pie-shaped sections on a disk
13. Common microcomputer input device
14. The rate at which signals can be sent or received
15. Intercomputer communications via telephone

Down

1. Software contained on ROM
2. A block of memory treated as an extra "disk"
6. Optical read-only memory
11. A hand-held device to move the cursor
16. Internal memory that can be read from and written on
17. Fixed-size units of storage
18. Operating system
19. Memory that can only be read from
20. A system of wires that links primary storage with the MPU and peripheral devices
21. Allows communication between the MPU and a secondary storage device
22. Communicates I/O commands to the I/O device controllers
23. CRT monitors generally produce images by the raster-_____ _____ method
24. Abbreviation for a unit of a microprocessor
25. A three-gun color monitor
26. After the instruction cycle, the _____ is needed to carry out the instruction
27. A point on a monitor screen
28. A disk that is fixed, has more storage capacity, and is faster than a floppy disk
29. 8 bits
30. To convert digital data to a form that can be transmitted over telephone lines
31. The physical arrangement of components in a microcomputer

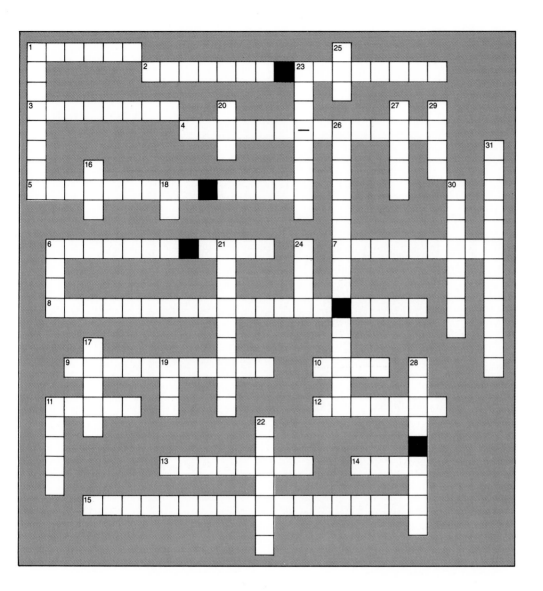

7

DATA COMMUNICATIONS
Bridging the Communications Gap

Objectives

- Compare and contrast the terms telecommunications, data communications, and teleprocessing.
- Discuss the major differences between data processing and data communications.
- Describe the major characteristics of data communications systems and list the elements that comprise a typical data communications configuration.
- Define basic terms and concepts related to the electronic transmission of data.
- Describe the necessary hardware needed to implement a data communications system and explain their function.
- Distinguish the various media currently used to transmit data and describe the various modes of transmission.
- Explain the various ways data communications is used in the office, home, and other places.
- Understand and use the key terms presented in the chapter.

The development of the printing press in the fifteenth century had a tremendous impact on the culture of that time. Whereas the creation of movable type caused the first information explosion, the rapidly evolving world of computer and communications technology is heralding the second information explosion. We are becoming increasingly dependent on the capability to transmit data and voice quickly from sender to receiver, whether the receiver is in the next room, in another section of the country, on the other side of the earth, or somewhere in outer space. With data communications, the tremendous power of a computer is no longer confined to one room; it can be made available to you wherever you happen to be.

WHAT IS DATA COMMUNICATIONS?

Before we begin to describe this fascinating field created by the union of computers and communications, you should understand certain terms.

The word **telecommunications** comes from the Greek word *tele*, meaning "far off." It describes the transmission of information over some distance without changing it. All telecommunications systems will contain the following components:

- A **sender,** which creates the information to be transmitted
- A **medium,** over which the information is sent
- A **receiver,** which receives the transmitted information *unchanged*

Figure 7-1 illustrates a simple telecommunications system.

Two people talking on the telephone would be an example of telecommunications in which the telephone line serves as the communications medium.

FIGURE 7-1
A simple telecommunications system.

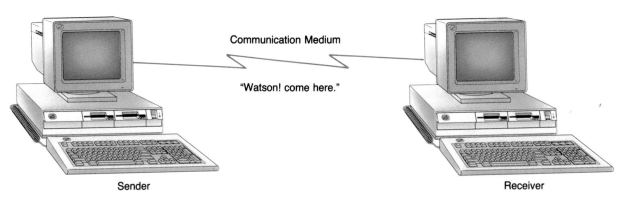

Communication Medium

"Watson! come here."

Sender   Receiver

Data communications comes from the words *data* processing and telecom-*munications*. In its broadest sense, data communications describes an environment in which data produced by a terminal or a computer are transported using some form of communications medium, such as phone lines, microwave or satellite systems, or fiber-optic channels.

Data communications, also known as **teleprocessing,** involves at least two hardware devices that can "talk" to one another over a communications network. For example, when you call an airline to make a reservation, the information is entered by an operator at a terminal and transported by telephone lines to the airline's computer. At the computer, the information may be *processed* or used in some way by the computer. The computer can then transmit an appropriate response back to the terminal where it will be displayed.

Data Processing or Data Communications?

In data processing data are somehow changed, and it is this change that adds value for the receiver or user. Data communications, on the other hand, adds value to data, not by changing it, but by the reliable and quick transmission of the data from one point to another.

Common Characteristics

All data communications systems contain the following common characteristics: online terminals, real-time processing, fast response time.

To obtain a high degree of efficiency, most data communications facilities can serve more than one user at the same time. For instance, when you deposit or withdraw money at an automatic teller machine, you might not be the only one using the system at that moment. The ability to handle users simultaneously is characteristic of most data communications systems.

Many large computer facilities perform both data communications and data processing functions. Such a facility, illustrated in Fig. 7-2, consists of the following elements:

- **Terminals** to transmit the data.
- **Terminal controllers** to handle the dialog with the computer.
- **Modems** or special devices to convert terminal or computer signals to signals that can be carried by telephone lines or some other media channel, and vice versa.
- **Communications management equipment (front-end processor)** to interface between a computer and other data communications elements, such as a modem. The purpose of this equipment is to optimize the flow of data to and from the computer.
- A **computer** to access, process, and store data.

The user enters data at the *terminal*, where the *controller* stores the data before they are transmitted. The *modem* converts the digital data generated by the terminal into an analog format that can be sent over a telephone line to another modem. The second modem converts the transmitted data back to a digital format for input to the front-end processor. The *front-end processor* accepts data from the modem and other devices connected to it and performs minor processing, data checking, and editing functions and passes the screened data *at high speed* to the computer for processing. A similar process takes place when the data originates at the computer and terminates at one or more terminals.

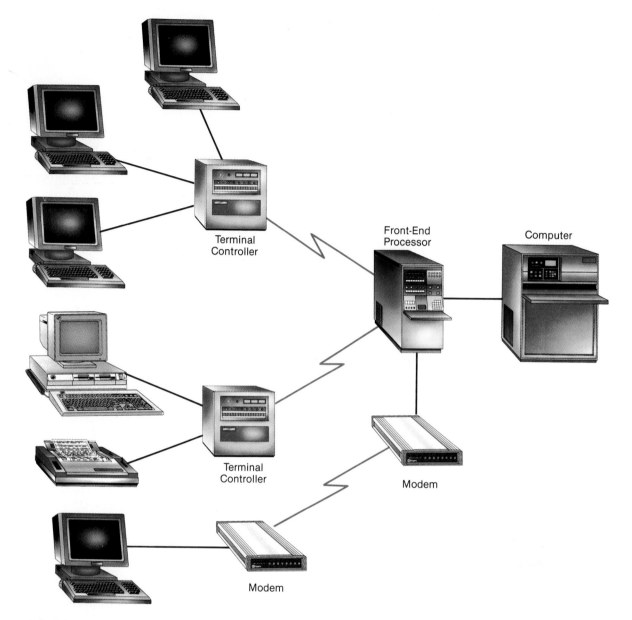

FIGURE 7-2
A computer facility capable of performing both data communications and data processing functions.

THE BASICS

**Serial
and Parallel
Transmission**

Earlier, we learned how data are stored in a computer in bytes or characters, and that it takes 8 bits to make 1 byte. The data transmission systems used by most computers and terminals are serial systems. **Serial systems** transmit data bit by bit in a serial stream over a single channel. With **parallel systems,** all 8 bits are sent out at once; that is, all 8 bits of data are transmitted over eight separate channels.

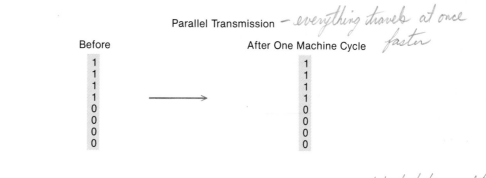

Parallel Transmission — *everything travels at once* *faster*

Before		After One Machine Cycle
1		1
1		1
1		1
1	⟶	1
0		0
0		0
0		0
0		0

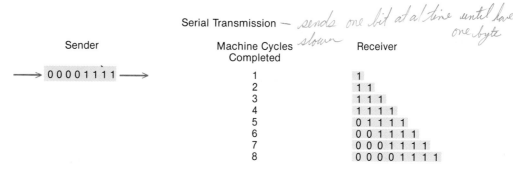

Serial Transmission — *sends one bit at a time until have one byte* *slower*

Sender	Machine Cycles Completed	Receiver
⟶ 0 0 0 0 1 1 1 1 ⟶	1	1
	2	1 1
	3	1 1 1
	4	1 1 1 1
	5	0 1 1 1 1
	6	0 0 1 1 1 1
	7	0 0 0 1 1 1 1
	8	0 0 0 0 1 1 1 1

FIGURE 7-3
Parallel versus serial transmission.

As you can see from Fig. 7-3, parallel transmission is much quicker than serial. But because telephone lines generally cannot support eight channels, bits must be passed out of the computer one at a time. At the receiving end, the bits are reconfigured from serial back to parallel.

Interface Standards

Bits going from parallel to serial can be viewed as cars traveling on an eight-lane highway being squeezed into a single lane. The electrical device that controls the parallel-to-serial conversion and serial-to-parallel conversion is known as a **universal asynchronous receiver/transmitter,** or **UART** for short (see Fig. 7-4).

Once the bits have been serialized, they are carried to the modem from the interface circuit or board. An **interface** connects two devices so that they can work or communicate with one another. It can adjust for slightly different transmission rates, amplitudes, codes, etc., so that one side of the interface can talk to the other side—much like an interpreter in the United Nations.

For the modem to understand the data being fed to it, it must be cabled to the interface. This may sound simple, but for computers using a nonstandard interface, this can be a difficult, even an impossible task. Some modems or other peripheral devices such as printers, plotters, and game controllers might not be able to accept or understand the data sent to them by the interface. For instance, the data could be sent at the wrong speed, or using the wrong

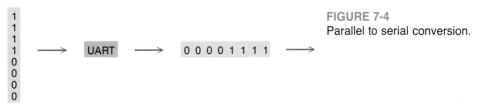

FIGURE 7-4
Parallel to serial conversion.

FIGURE 7-5
IBM PC showing RS-232-C serial interface.

codes. Whenever possible, make certain that the literature provided with the device lists your computer system and identifies the types of cable and plugs that must be used.

You ask, Wouldn't it be better if all manufacturers used the same interface? The answer is clearly yes, but some computer manufacturers want only devices manufactured by or for them to be used with their computers. Thus they use nonstandard hardware, special operating systems, and so on. However, the vast majority of manufacturers try to adhere to recognized standards.

A serial interface standard is Recommended Standard number 232, revision C, the **RS-232-C** serial interface developed by Electronics Industries of America (EIA). The RS-232-C interface is standard with respect to data transfer rates, control signals, the types of cables and plugs, and the placement of the various signal wires within the plug. A cable with a standard plug on each end is all that is necessary to connect a computer or terminal controller to a modem. Figure 7-5 illustrates this arrangement. Even when connecting two devices with a standard RS-232-C interface, it is possible that cabling or other problems might prevent you from using all the capabilities of the device. Your best bet is to contact the manufacturers or request a demonstration of the devices actually working together.

Codes

You will recall that computers use *codes* to represent data as strings of binary bits. Various codes have been developed for representing data for transmission over communications channels. In an effort to standardize the codes used for data communications, the American Standard Code for Information Interchange **(ASCII)** was developed. Most systems use one of the two standard ASCII codes for the transmission of data. Another popular code is the Extended Binary Coded Decimal Interchange Code **(EBCDIC)** developed by IBM. Other codes used are **Baudot** and **BCD.** ASCII uses 7 bits to represent a character, and

ASCII-8 and EBCDIC both use 8 bits. The 7-bit ASCII code is commonly used with micros, whereas the 8-bit ASCII-8 and EBCDIC codes are used with larger systems. Both codes employ an additional bit, a **parity** or **check bit,** to detect errors in data representation or data transmission. Parity or check bits are explained in Appendix A.

To understand how a character is transmitted, let's consider the letter *A.* The character A in ASCII is represented by 11000001, including a check bit. The data, or bit configuration, would be sent over a telephone wire by first sending two negative voltage pulses, which are translated as 1 bits in RS-232-C signaling, then by five positive pulses for the 0 bits, followed by a negative pulse for the last 1 bit.

Asynchronous and Synchronous Transmission

When characters are transmitted serially, they can be further classified as being either asynchronous or synchronous.

Asynchronous

Asynchronous transmission is sometimes referred to as start-stop transmission. One character at a time is transmitted. Each character or series of 8 bits (7 bits for the ASCII character representation and 1 check bit), is marked by a start bit and a stop bit. The start bit is a 0 bit which appears before the 8 bits of the transmitted character. The stop bit is a 1 bit which appears after the 8 character bits. Between characters, a stream of continuous 1s is transmitted. The presence of the next start bit activates the receiving mechanism. Figure 7-6 illustrates the asynchronous transmission of three ASCII characters.

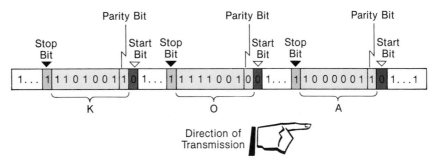

FIGURE 7-6
Asynchronous transmission.

Synchronous

With the **synchronous** transmission technique, it is not each single character that is marked off, instead, it is an entire block of characters that is marked. A block may consist of hundreds or thousands of characters. Each block is preceded by 1 or more **sync** bytes (see Fig. 7-7) and is transmitted at a steady rate, allowing the receiving device to get in step, or synchronize, with the sending device.

Although synchronous transmission is faster and more efficient than asynchronous, it requires more precise timing and is better suited to larger computer systems. Asynchronous transmission has become the standard mode used with microcomputer systems.

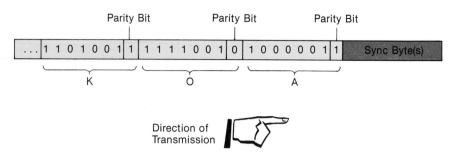

FIGURE 7-7
Synchronous transmission.

Protocols

To communicate verbally, we need more than just a common language. Successful communication requires a common set of rules, or **protocols,** to govern the exchange of information. Similarly, computer systems must follow certain protocols when sending and receiving information. Protocols are established and controlled by software which specifies character length, baud rate (speed of transmission), transmission mode, the number of bits separating characters, and parity (an error detection technique to assure that characters are received correctly). The continuing standardization of modems has made protocols less important than they once were.

The exchange of prearranged signals that indicate that two systems are compatible before actual data transmission occurs is known as **handshaking.** Just as a handshake between two people indicates that communication is about to take place, handshaking between two computers confirms that data transmission can take place.

Unfortunately, although everyone recognizes the need for standardized transmission, a uniform set of rules remains to be established. National and international groups have tried to establish and maintain standard protocols, but as yet, numerous rules and procedures are entirely incompatible.

Rate of Transmission

Transmission speeds are measured by baud rate or bits per second. The rate at which an analog signal can change in a communications facility is measured in **bauds.** If the signal can change every 1/2,400 second, the baud rate or number of signal changes per second is 2,400.

A more practical measure of the information actually moving through the system is measured in bits per second. **Bits per second (bps)** measure the rate at which information bits can be transmitted on a given line. It is possible, although somewhat expensive, to use signals that can carry more than 1 bit of information per signal change. This technique is employed principally on mainframe computer systems and results in a bps rate that is a multiple of the baud rate. The transfer of meaningful information is also referred to as **throughput.** Throughput is measured in bps, characters per second, or words per minute.

Now that we know a little about some of the basic terms and concepts related to data communications, let's take a closer look at the equipment necessary to implement a data communications system.

A CLOSER LOOK AT BPS AND BAUD

Contrary to popular belief, **baud** is not the same as **bits per second (bps),** except accidentally. A 1,200-bits-per-second modem, for instance, actually runs at 600 baud. So does a 2,400-bps modem.

The reason for the confusion is that, for a long time, modems that operate at 300 bits per second were the only kind available to personal computer users. It just so happens that a 300-bits-per-second modem is also a 300-baud modem. Many users assumed that "baud" stood for "bits per second" in the same way "hertz" stands for "cycles per second." Unfortunately, it isn't quite as simple as that.

Baud is a measure of the maxiumum number of data symbols, or electronic signals, that can be sent per second over a communications channel. Bits per second measures the information-carrying capacity of the channel. The trick to this situation is that each data symbol can represent more than one bit of information, depending on the transmission method.

A good analogy is a highway full of cars, with each car representing a baud and the passengers representing bits. If you put more passengers in each car, the highway can carry more people per hour.

If your modem is designed to use only two data symbols, then each data symbol can only represent one bit. The reason for this is that a bit must be either a 1 or a 0, since computers record information in binary code. Thus, with two data symbols, you can only send one bit per baud. A 1,200-bits-per-second modem, which runs at 600 baud, has four data symbols. With four symbols, each symbol can represent two bits (1 0, 0 1, 1 1 or 0 0), so the data transmission speed (bits per second) is equal to the symbol transmission speed times the number of bits per symbol (600 × 2 = 1200). A 2,400-bps modem also works at 600 baud, but the "alphabet" of this modem contains 16 data symbols, meaning each data symbol represents four bits.

When the difference is explained in that manner, it doesn't seem as if there would be much of a jump from 1,200 to 2,400 bps, but in fact there was. That's why 2,400-bits-per-second modems are only a few years old while 1200-bps modems have been around almost as long as personal computers.

The reason it took so long to advance from 1,200- to 2,400-bps modems was caused by the difficulty in developing inexpensive circuits that were sensitive enough to distinguish 16 different electronic signals and at the same time screen out noise on the telephone line. The quality of telephone lines is variable. Not only are there problems with noise on the telephone line, but the transmission characteristics of the lines differ with each call and they can even vary from minute to minute during the course of a phone call. To make matters even more complicated, most personal computer modems are full duplex. That means that these modems can send and receive data at the same time. It also means that some of the limited bandwidth has to be allocated to signals in both directions. (The alternative modem design, half duplex, can only send in one direction at a time. This design is rarely used today.)

The 1,200-bps modems can get by with preadjusted filters that will, among other things, amplify certain portions of the bandwidth. This is called **equalization.** But the 2,400-bps modems can't. They need to adjust to line characteristics continuously and automatically. This kind of adaptive equalization requires a microprocessor on the modem.

However, above 2,400-bps, adaptive equalization isn't enough. Because it is impractical to increase the data symbol alphabet above 16, the high-speed modems need ways of increasing the effective bandwidth of the channel—in the analogy, to put more cars on the freeway. Modem manufacturers employ a variety of methods, but all of them involve using microprocessors to make the modems smarter and able to send more information.

HARDWARE

The minimal components used in most data communications systems are depicted in Fig. 7-8.

Terminals and Controllers

Terminals, described earlier in this text, act as the interface between the user and the data communications system. They are the doorways of a computer system, allowing you to send to and receive messages from the outside world.

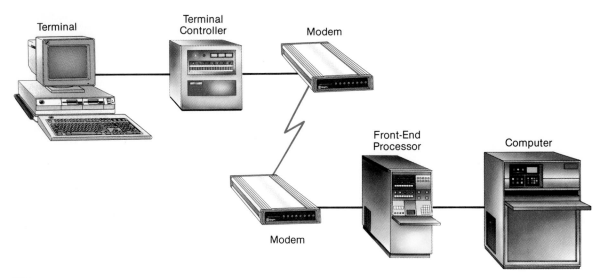

FIGURE 7-8
A basic data communications system.

Controllers

Large computer systems rely on controllers to handle the dialog with the computer. Controllers interface with such peripherals as tape drives, disk drives, printers, and video display terminals to manage the messages and communicate them to the computer. Controllers store information coming from terminals and peripheral devices and pass the information to the CPU or front-end processor when requested. In this way, the CPU is free to perform processing operations while the controller supervises the peripheral equipment.

As you can see from Fig. 7-9, tape controllers are used to supervise data traffic to and from tape drives and a CPU via the front-end processor. Disk controllers work with disk drives; terminal controllers coordinate terminals.

When a communications system has only one terminal placed on each line to a computer, the configuration is known as **point-to-point.** A point-to-point design may use either a leased line or a switched line to handle the data flow. A *leased line*, also known as a dedicated line, is a private line. Leased lines provide a permanent connection between the terminal and the computer. A *switched line*, also known as a dial-up line, is a public line. When you use the telephone to make a call, you are using a public line.

When several terminals are attached to the same line, the arrangement is called **multipoint.** A leased line is almost always used for multipoint designs. Figure 7-10 shows both configurations. Only one terminal can use a multipoint line at a time; a multiplexor or concentrator is necessary to facilitate simultaneous communications. These devices will be discussed shortly.

Polling and Contention

Terminals in a multipoint configuration must be managed in some way so that each gets a chance to send or receive information through the line. Two management techniques are polling and contention.

216

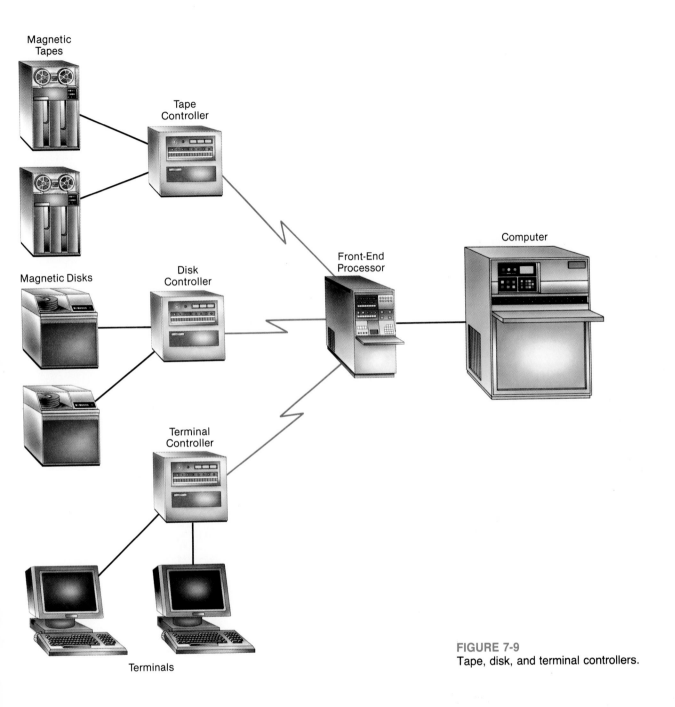

Magnetic
Tapes

Tape
Controller

Magnetic Disks

Disk
Controller

Front-End
Processor

Computer

Terminal
Controller

Terminals

FIGURE 7-9
Tape, disk, and terminal controllers.

POLLING. An invitation to send data is known as **polling.** With this technique, a terminal can transmit information only after the computer polls, or selects it. Selection is the process of choosing a particular terminal to send information. Once a terminal is polled, information may be transmitted to the computer. While the computer is processing data for the selected terminal and before the reply is sent back, the computer may poll other terminals, either in sequence or in some preselected order.

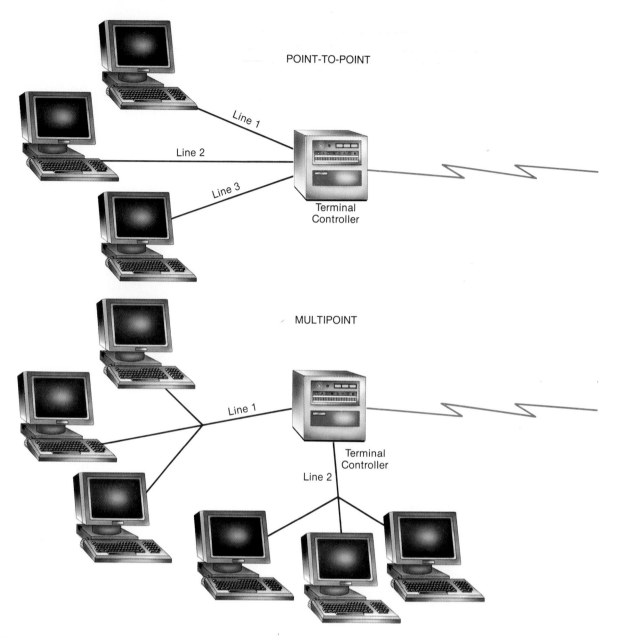

POINT-TO-POINT

Line 1

Line 2

Line 3

Terminal
Controller

MULTIPOINT

Line 1

Terminal
Controller

Line 2

FIGURE 7-10
Point-to-point and multipoint configurations.

CONTENTION. With **contention,** each terminal competes, or contends, for use of the line when it needs it. If the line is busy when a terminal attempts to use it, the terminal is given a busy signal and must wait and try again. Contention is the preferred method for a network that is not very active. In this situation, the line is made busy only when a terminal requests it. With polling, much time would be wasted in requesting information from terminals that are not active. It would be like a switchboard operator testing each line in succession to see if someone is there instead of waiting until a line rings for service.

218

The Microcomputer as a Terminal

Smart, or **intelligent,** terminals contain processing capabilities built right into their circuitry. A "brilliant" terminal has its own memory and operating programs and is programmable; it is a microcomputer.

Microcomputers are capable of performing terminal functions without the help of terminal controllers. To make a micro or personal computer serve as a terminal in a data communications network, you would generally need the following:

- A serial card and an interface (RS-232-C) to enable the parallel-to-serial bit conversion
- A software package that will enable your·computer (terminal) to send and receive information
- A modem, with access to a telephone line

Modems

Any data system that communicates via telephone lines needs a modem. The modem acts as an interface between the terminal on one side and the telephone line on the other. The terminal sends and receives digital signals consisting of patterns of 1s and 0s. Telephone lines, on the other hand, can only transmit voice or analog signals. Since most telephone lines are designed to transmit only *analog* signals (alternating current voltages), and computers and terminals work with digital or direct current voltages, a device to convert one form into the other is needed (see Fig. 7-11). Of course, if a telephone line was capable of transmitting digital signals, a modem would not be necessary; one such system is AT&T's Digital Dataphone Service (DDS).

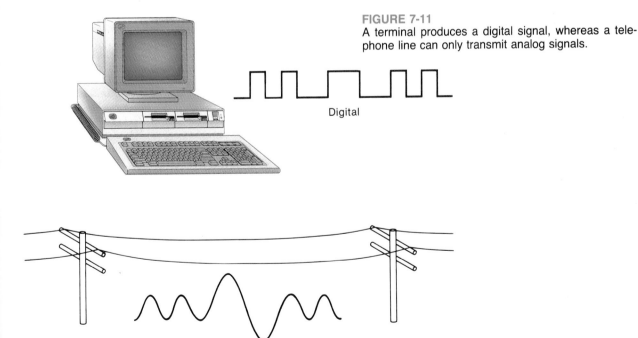

FIGURE 7-11
A terminal produces a digital signal, whereas a telephone line can only transmit analog signals.

Digital

Analog

A **modem** converts a signal from digital to analog on the sending side and from analog back to digital on the receiving side. The process of going from digital to analog signals is called **modulation,** and the reverse process is called **demodulation**—hence the name **modem** (*mo*dulate/*dem*odulate) (see Fig. 7-12).

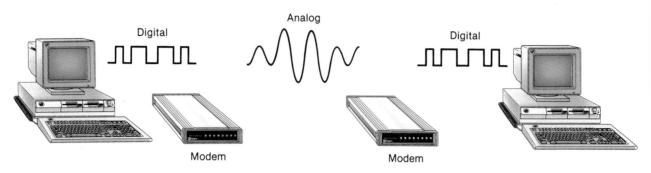

Digital

Analog

Digital

Modem

Modem

FIGURE 7-12
The use of modems to modulate and demodulate signals.

Amplitude Modulation

How can bits be represented by either analog or digital signals? As illustrated in Fig. 7-13, the strength of an analog or amplitude modulated signal indicates whether the signal is a 1 or a 0. Typically, a 1 is represented with a signal of higher strength and a 0 of lower strength. With digital signals, a pulse represents a 1 and no pulse represents a 0. Although other forms of modulation are sometimes used, amplitude modulation remains one of the most common.

FIGURE 7-13
Digital and amplitude modulated signals.

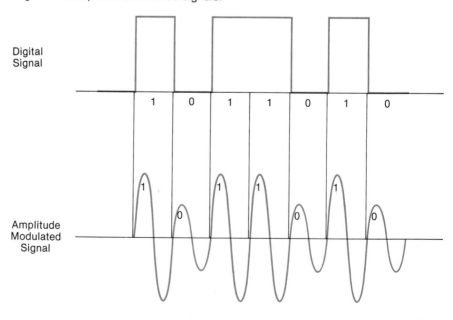

Digital
Signal

Amplitude
Modulated
Signal

Direct Connection and Acoustic Coupling

In most systems, the modems are directly connected to the terminal and the phone wire. The Hayes Smartmodem, shown in Fig. 7-14, is a direct connect modem. This very popular modem plugs directly into the telephone system. Some intelligent direct-connect modems contain their own microprocessors and operating systems; these are capable of monitoring the data system. Many come equipped with their own auto-answer and auto-dial capabilities.

In some cases, the modem is connected to the terminal with an acoustic coupler. An acoustic coupler uses a telephone handset to provide data transmission. Pictured in Fig. 7-15, this type of modem has a cradle that can hold a handset. When traveling with your system, as long as you can get to a telephone, you can communicate. The biggest problem of acoustic coupling is the filtering out of noise. When such sounds as voices, radios, or street or airplane sounds find their way into the transmission, the signal can be disrupted.

FIGURE 7-14
Direct-connect modem.

FIGURE 7-15
Acoustic coupler.

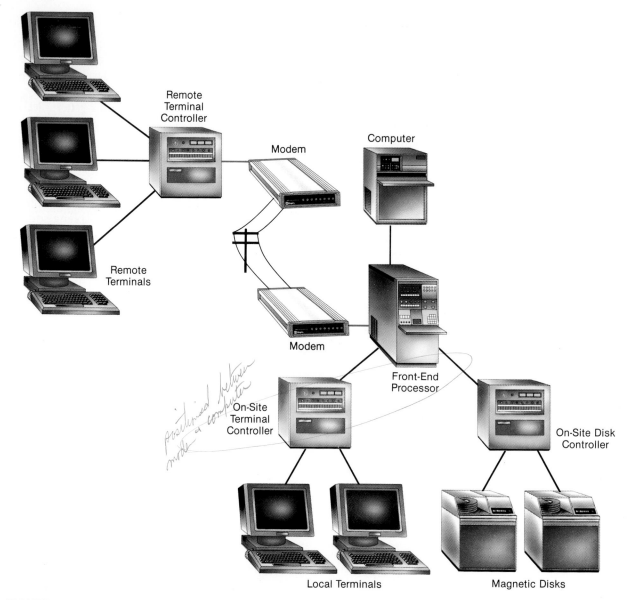

FIGURE 7-16
Front-end processing.

Front-End Processors

The **front-end processor (FEP)** is the next piece of equipment we might encounter in a data communications network. The FEP acts as an interface between a computer and other data communications equipment, as seen in Fig. 7-16.

Front-end processors are usually programmable minicomputers located near the main, or host computer. They are specifically designed and implemented to perform tasks that relieve the host of such communications functions as editing records, polling, and monitoring the network to permit only users with valid account. The host is then free to spend more of its valuable time on the processing of programs.

The Multiplexor

A **multiplexor** will permit more efficient use of communications channels. If, for example, a company needed four lines from several sites in Chicago to the CPU based in Dallas, a multiplexor could be used. Let's assume that four 300-bps (bits per second) lines were needed to transmit the information between the terminals and the computer. It might be more economical to have one high-speed multipoint line with a capacity of at least 1,200 bps between the locations instead of the separate, slow-speed 300-bps lines. Figure 7-17 illustrates how a multiplexor can facilitate communications between several terminals and a computer using a single high-speed communications line, thereby reducing costs.

Multiplexors are user-transparent. The terminals, FEP, and main computer are not aware that the information for separate terminals is being sent on the same telephone line.

The Concentrator

Functionally, **concentrators** are similar to multiplexors, but with an added storage buffer and a mini- or microprocessor. A multiplexor is essentially a hardware device; it cannot change either the structure or the content of the transmitted data. A concentrator has storage and logic capabilities to perform communica-

FIGURE 7-17
A communications network using a multiplexor.

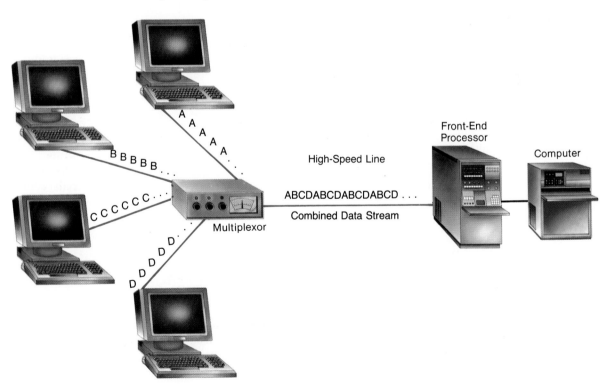

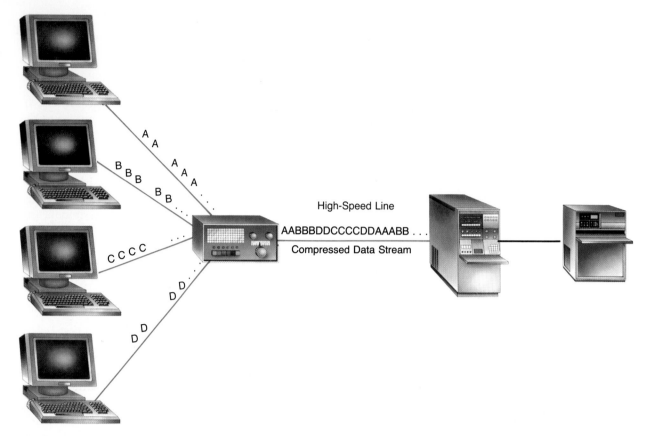

FIGURE 7-18
A communications network using a concentrator.

tions control functions and is normally located at the terminal or sending side of a long-distance line, as shown in Fig. 7-18.

With a concentrator in the line, it is possible to link inexpensive asynchronous terminal equipment with the more efficient synchronous transmission line to the computer. Slower, less expensive communications channels can be used between the terminal devices and the concentrator, and high-speed synchronous lines can be used to link the concentrator with the computer.

It is possible for the total capacity of all the lines feeding the concentrator to exceed the capacity of the high-speed line. Should the terminals generate more data than the concentrator can send out, the concentrator will store the data until the line is freed up to accept more data for transmission.

Unlike multiplexors, concentrators are not user-transparent. Once data transmitted on the high-speed line reaches the computer site, it is up to the FEP or the main computer to separate the information for different users.

Media—Making the Connection

Communications channels can be of various types. The media available to implement the transmission of information include

- Wire pairs
- Coaxial cables
- Microwave (terrestrial and satellite)
- Optical fibers

Wire pairs, also known as **twisted-pair wires,** consist of a twisted pair of copper (or copper-coated steel) wires. They represent the oldest electronic transmission

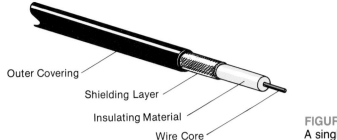

Outer Covering

Shielding Layer

Insulating Material

Wire Core

FIGURE 7-19
A single coaxial cable.

technology; normal telephone lines used by the telephone system are wire pairs. One pair of wires can serve only two points—two people or two devices—at a time. Currently, wire pairs are being replaced by other types of communications media for voice communications. The biggest advantage to using twisted wires in data communications today is that, since telephone lines already exist in virtually every corner of the globe, data may be transmitted to virtually any place in the world. Also, this method is relatively inexpensive.

Coaxial Cables

The increasing demand for faster transmission channels that are more interference-free has led to the rapid increase in the use of coaxial cables. A **coaxial cable** consists of a conductive cylindrical shield with a central wire or solid core held in place by an insulating material (see Fig. 7-19). Coaxial cables have very little distortion or signal loss and so are a more reliable medium for data transmission. Because they are shielded, these cables can be combined by the hundreds into larger cables without any noticeable interference. These larger cables have been used on the ocean floors for quite some time to provide intercontinental telephone communications. Coaxial cables are used for cable TV and are often the medium of choice to connect computers and terminals located in nearby buildings.

Microwave

Terrestrial **microwaves** are very high-frequency radio signals that are transmitted through open space. They are accurately beamed in **line-of-sight** transmission from one antenna to another. Antennas are positioned on mountain tops or on top of high towers or buildings, usually 25 to 50 miles apart. Microwave transmission is much faster than either telephone lines or coaxial cable transmission. At each antenna station, the signals are amplified and then relayed to the next antenna (see Fig. 7-20).

FIGURE 7-20
Microwave transmission.

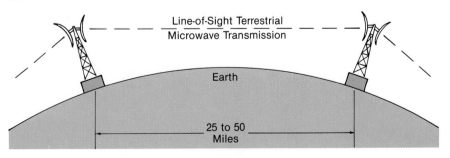

Line-of-Sight Terrestrial
Microwave Transmission

Earth

25 to 50
Miles

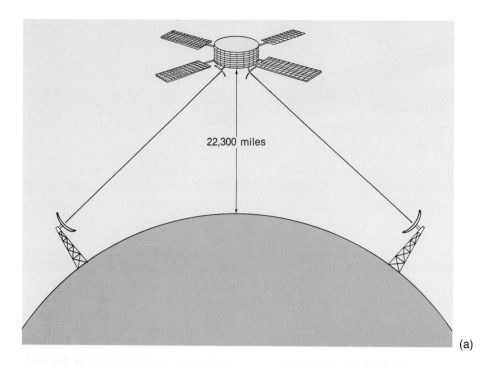
(a)

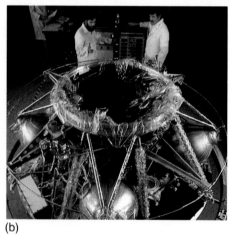
(b)

(c)

FIGURE 7-21
(a) Satellite transmission; (b) Telstar 3 under construction; (c) Telstar 3 in orbit around the earth; (d) earth-satellite transmission disk.

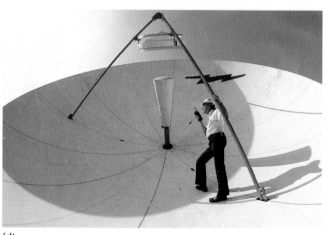
(d)

Communications satellites provide a special form of microwave transmission. A satellite is basically a microwave antenna that has been launched and placed in a geostationary orbit. That is, it is in an orbit approximately 22,300 miles (35,800 kilometers) above the earth and travels at the same speed as the earth's rotation, and thus appears to be stationary in relation to the earth (see Fig. 7-21). A typical satellite will house some twenty-four transponders—small amplifiers that can receive signals, amplify them, and retransmit them to earth. Three such satellites placed equidistantly around the earth will give communications coverage of the entire globe.

In addition to a satellite, a satellite communications system requires earth stations, or "dishes," that transmit and receive signals to and from the orbited satellite. Each transponder can carry one television channel, or 1,200 voice channels, or it can transmit a stream of data.

Satellites can relay signals over longer distances than is possible with a terrestrial microwave system because obstacles on the earth, as well as the planet's curvature, block line-of-sight transmission. Transmission by satellite allows large amounts of data to be transmitted long distances at great speeds. In spite of its tremendous cost (a mere $10 to $50 million to build and launch your own satellite, or more than $1 million per month to lease a satellite's transmission capabilities), more and more companies are opting to use satellite transmission in order to communicate with other continents because the unit cost is low and the reliability is good.

Optical Fibers

Fiber optics, also known as light-wave transmission, makes use of hair-like transparent strands to carry data in the form of light pulses. This medium is replacing conventional wire and cable for voice and data transmission, and for good reason. Fiber-optic cables use silica, one of the earth's most abundant resources, in contrast to copper, which is decreasing rapidly.

The advantages of using fiber optics instead of the traditional means of communication are many: freedom from electromagnetic and radio frequency interference, absolute security (no tapping), and inherent safety in explosive environments. But most importantly, the ability of fiber optics to transmit a multitude of information at higher rates makes this medium the communication medium of the future.

In today's information society, communications networks are being used to transfer written information, speech, drawings, photographs, moving pictures, and music. The telephone network is not used because currently the highest practical rate of transmission is only 9,600 bps (bits per second), even though the theoretical limit is several times this number. Television and video programs require a broadband network capable of rates of tens of megabits per second. Optical fiber is a medium that can handle these speeds. In fact, almost any conventional or traditional communication system can be adapted to incorporate optical-fiber transmission (see Fig. 7-22).

As you can see, various transmission media are available to send information from one place to another. The current trend is toward the use of optical fibers and microwave transmission, as these are faster and more reliable than more conventional methods that utilize twisted wires or coaxial cable.

FIGURE 7-22
Optical fiber cable.

Modes of Transmission

Communications lines can be categorized on the basis of their mode of data flow as either simplex, half-duplex, or full-duplex lines.

- **Simplex** lines permit data flow in *one* direction only. An example of this mode of transmission is the flow of a river—it is always in the same direction. Simplex lines are rarely used in data communications.
- **Half-duplex** lines allow transmission in both directions, but only in one direction at a time. CB radios utilize this type of data flow. Only when the transmitter button is pressed can your message be sent to a receiver. Only one person at a time can speak. The amount of time taken to switch the direction of the transmission is known as *turnaround time*. In this mode, data you enter at a terminal flow first to the computer. Data that the computer returns to you in response cannot flow until the line is free. Until the computer is through responding, you may not enter further data for transmission.
- **Full-duplex** lines permit data traffic in both directions simultaneously. Whereas half-duplex lines usually require two channels, full-duplex transmission normally requires four channels. Full-duplex lines eliminate turnaround time and are normally used when the sender and receiver are both composed of computer systems. Fig. 7-23 illustrates all three transmission modes.

Speed of Transmission

Bandwidth

The capacity of a communications channel to carry data is called the **bandwidth,** an interval equal to the difference between the upper and lower frequencies of the channel. The greater the bandwidth, or frequency interval, the greater the amount of data that can be transmitted per unit of time.

The bandwidth of a communications channel is a measure of its capacity to carry data. Currently, communications channels can transmit signals that vary in speed from approximately 100 bps (bits or signals per second) to more than 4 million bps. The speed of data transmission is directly proportional to the frequency range that the transmission medium can accommodate. From a speed perspective, media fall into three categories: narrowband, voice-grade, and wideband.

- **Narrowband** channels have a bandwidth of 300 and can transmit data at speeds up to 600 bits per second. These channels are used with low-speed devices such as teletypewriters.
- **Voice-grade** channels have a bandwidth of 3,000 and can transmit data at speeds in the range of 600 to 10,000 bits per second. The telephone company transmits signals that fall within this bandwidth.
- **Wideband** channels generally have bandwidths of more than 15,000 and can transmit data at speeds of more than 10,000 bits per second. **Basebands** (bandwidths

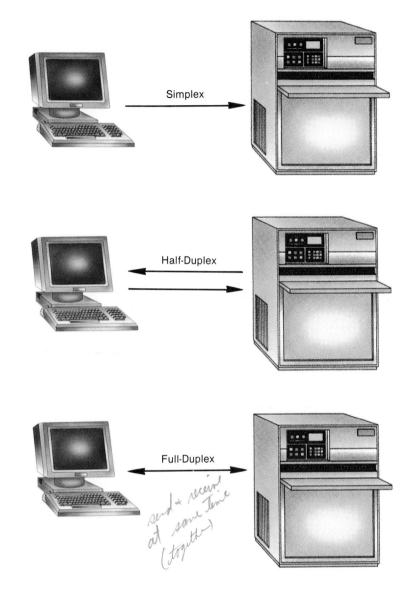

FIGURE 7-23
Simplex, half-duplex, and duplex transmissions.

generally under 50,000) are used for simplex transmissions, whereas **broadbands** (bandwidths typically 300,000 or more) are used for duplex transmissions. Because of their large bandwidths, multiple transmissions can take place simultaneously over subchannels of a broadband channel. Communications satellites and fiber optic cables are generally broadband channels and can carry as many as 4 billion bits per second.

Common Carriers

Just how do companies or private individuals go about procuring data communications services? **Common carriers** are companies that offer communications services to the public. These companies must be licensed and are regulated by the government. Because data communications is regulated by both state and federal governments, any organization desiring to offer communications services must have their approval. The organization must describe its services and accompanying prices and submit the list to the Federal Communications Commission (FCC). This list of services and prices is called a **tariff** and must be approved before a license will be granted.

The transmission links used in most communications networks are provided by the regulated common carriers. An example of a common carrier that offers sale of equipment (terminals and modems), transmission service, and voice and data systems is American Telephone and Telegraph (AT&T).

Value-added Networks

Value-added networks, or **VANs,** are also available for the user. An organization offering VANs "adds value" to a common carrier's communications service by providing computer processing capabilities. Essentially, the VAN vendor leases the facilities of a common carrier, enhances the services, and then offers it to users on a time-shared basis. That is, several users might share the same line and the cost without any noticeable loss in service.

DATA COMMUNICATIONS IN ACTION

Some of the applications mentioned earlier in our text involve data communications technology. Any time someone enters data at a terminal or computer and sends it via one of the transmission lines, data communications is involved. When you think of the millions of telephones installed throughout the world, you can begin to get an idea of the potential this form of communication holds. As more companies lease satellite facilities, the globe will continue to shrink at an ever-increasing rate.

Let's take a closer look at some of the ways networking and data communications are affecting the way we function in the office and in the home.

The Automated Office

A few short years ago, this section would have been entitled "The Office of the Future." But for many organizations, the future is now. What we describe here are applications that are being used today by the thousands. The trend for many companies is away from simple terminals and toward the use of individual computers. Workstations consisting of microcomputers tied to peripherals, such as terminals, printers, and disk drives, are popping up in offices everywhere (see Fig. 7-24).

Upload/Download Capabilities

The power of a microcomputer is enhanced when it is connected to a mainframe computer and its database. **Uploading** is the process of sending a file from your personal computer "up" to the mainframe. **Downloading** is the reverse process—capturing information that comes streaming "down" from a database into your personal computer and onto the screen. With this arrangement you can, for example, type a document at your computer and, when it is finished, upload it to the mainframe. This capability allows you to create a file and correct it inexpensively offline, and only when you actually upload do you tie up the main computer.

230

FIGURE 7-24
The uncluttered and spacious automated office of the future.

Electronic Mail

Electronic mail permits the transmission of letters, memos, and other documents from one terminal or computer to another in a different office, city, state, or country. Using a **facsimile** or **FAX** machine, pictures and drawings as well as text may be transmitted.

When using services like electronic mail, you interact with the computer either by typing simple commands or by making selections from menus presented on the screen. Initially, menus help the neophyte to learn the system. Once you become a pro, you can dispense with menus and get quicker action by using direct commands.

What would you have to do to mail a letter to X? Typically, you would first log on and type a command to initiate the "mail" operation, and follow it with X's account number. You would then enter your text and send it with another command. Want to send it express? Need copies sent to other people? No problem! Type a few simple commands and your wishes will be carried out.

Because the mail is sent and stored, the recipient cannot miss your "call." The intended receiver, also a subscriber of the same information utility, can read the stored mail at any time. After reading it, the mail may be filed, deleted, or forwarded to another subscriber.

Electronic Message Services

Elvis You Had Better Check Your Electronic Mail

Although many people claim to have seen and talked to Elvis, one company, Starbridge Communications of Los Angeles, CA, has set up a 900 telephone number for the king of rock 'n' roll. According to the *Wall Street Journal* this system will let an individual record a personal message to Elvis. Of course, there is no evidence that Elvis has returned any of these calls.

Electronic message or bulletin board services, mentioned earlier, differ in detail, but they usually perform several standard functions. Whereas electronic *mail* is intended for a designated recipient, *messages* are placed on public bulletin boards.

These services normally screen the caller by requesting some form of identification. After being cleared, the caller may send messages. Earlier, message systems were used primarily by computer buffs who wanted a place to leave notes to friends. Today, message systems allow users to keep private mailboxes, scan huge bulletin boards that are divided into many categories, and select particular areas of interest, run programs, and advertise products. Tired of going to dating services to meet people? Use a message service to post a description of yourself and include your address or phone number. You never know!

Closely related to electronic mail and message systems is **voice mail.** Voice messages are spoken into a telephone, digitized, recorded, and transmitted. They may be played back when the intended receiver assesses his or her "mailbox." Once a message has been recorded, it can be sent to any number of recipients. Sales managers could use this technology to send the same message to several salespersons at their regional offices.

Teleconferencing and Videoconferencing

Business travel as we know it may be coming to an end. Why hop on a plane and travel hundreds or thousands of miles to participate in a conference when you can speak to an entire group of people while sitting in your own home office? **Teleconferencing** utilizes special telephone equipment to permit one or more persons to talk to groups of people in remote locations. **Videoconferencing** permits groups in different geographical locations to see as well as hear one another. This technology utilizes a special telephone hookup for the transmission of voice and satellite links for video transmission (see Fig. 7-25).

Many organizations use one-way video and two-way audio teleconferences. Some companies, for example, are sending recruiters to colleges and universities

FIGURE 7-25
A teleconference in action.

armed with this form of communications capability. Graduating students get an inside view of the company while the company's representative answers students' questions and narrates what is being shown. This is an example of one-way video transmission. Whereas one-way video transmission can take advantage of mobile equipment, two-way video can presently only be accomplished in specially set up conference rooms.

The biggest advantage to using tele- and videoconferencing is the saving of corporate dollars. The cost of a videoconference, including equipment, camera crews, satellite time, consultant fees, rental of hotel conference rooms, and the services of a professional moderator could be as high as $75,000. As high as this amount might appear, it generally represents a savings over the amount that would otherwise have been spent on airfares, hotel rooms, and meals, not to mention the loss of services of the participants while they are away from the office. However, these advantages have not proven sufficient to generate the widespread acceptance of these techniques that was first anticipated. Many people still prefer the personal interaction possible only when people meet in the same room.

Computer conferencing is closely related to teleconferencing but offers some distinct advantages. Users communicate by typing messages and comments to each other while online. When desired, a printed record of the conversation of the participants may be obtained. This record, or log, allows interested parties to keep track of *who* said *what* and *when*.

Computer conference participants need not be located in a designated conference room, as is necessary with videoconferencing. To take part in a computer conversation, a participant simply logs on to a computer and converses via the keyboard with other participants. Of course, microcomputers with the requisite data communications equipment may also communicate with one another.

Telecommuting

How would you like to get up for work about 10 A.M., have breakfast, and walk 40 feet to your office to begin your workday? There is no boss to look over your shoulder, no punch-in or punch-out time, and no one will say anything if you take a little nap after lunch (see Fig. 7-26).

This scenario is not a dream but a reality for thousands of employees in the United States who work at home. The word **telecommuting** was first coined by Jack Nilles, director of the Center of Futures Research at the University of Southern California, to describe the growing number of workers and professionals who use data communications to telecommute their work to an office. Using a terminal or personal computer, these employees avoid the fatigue and frustrations that accompany commuting to work every day. Essentially, they are liberated from the nine-to-five grind.

According to a recent survey by Electronic Services Unlimited (ESU), a New York City research firm, approximately 400 companies have employees who work at home, and this figure does not include those who are self-employed telecommuters. Prime candidates for telecommuting are people who supply an information service—accountants, writers, reservation agents, contract computer programmers, and researchers represent only a few.

The advantages of being a "computer commuter" for the employee are savings in transportation, food, clothing, and most of all, time. Mothers with

FIGURE 7-26
Neither rain, sleet, nor snow can prevent telecommuters from the performance of their jobs.

small children and the physically impaired are among those who have the most to gain. The advantages of instituting telecommuting for the employer include more available office space and, believe it or not, increased productivity (according to a recent ESU survey).

But, alas, telecommuting is not without its problems. Some telecommuters have complained that working at home brings loneliness and isolation. After all, with whom can the employee socialize? Others fear being away from the "action" at the office lessens their chance of getting a deserved promotion or raise. And one of the biggest drawbacks is that upper management, for the most part, is finding it difficult to relinquish control over people, thinking, how can we be sure our employees are doing their best, if we can't even see what they're doing?

Despite its critics, most experts predict that approximately 20 percent of the nation's information work force—about 10 million people—will be involved with telecommuting at least part of the time by the end of the decade.

Personal Networks

Most of the network services being used within the automated office are also available to anyone who owns a personal computer with a data communications capability. Whether you own a tiny laptop or a fully equipped Apple Macintosh, you can communicate with any other machine as long as you have the following five components.

- A plug-in communications card to convert parallel to serial communications
- A modem
- An RS-232-C serial interface cable to connect the modem to the communications card (see Fig. 7-27)
- A communications software package
- A telephone

234

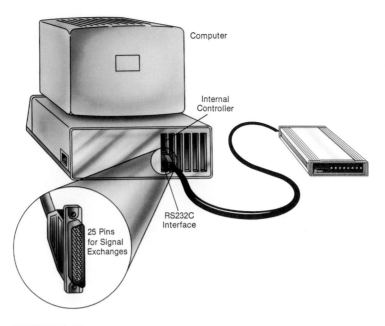

Computer

Internal
Controller

RS232C
Interface

25 Pins
for Signal
Exchanges

FIGURE 7-27
Personal computer showing an RS-232-C standard serial interface
cable which connects an internal communications controller card to
a modem or other serial devices such as a serial printer.

Earlier, we mentioned the worldwide information explosion. In this section
you will see how your home computer can be used as a veritable window to
a world of information. Before we discuss home computer applications, however,
we should take a look at one area of computing that does not require that
you own your own computer.

Electronic Funds Transfer

At this point in time, every banking institution in the United States uses the
computer in some way. Perhaps you have used a bank's **automated teller machine (ATM)** located on the outside walls of many bank buildings. If you have,
you know you can walk up to an ATM terminal at *any* time, day or night,
insert a plastic card, enter your personal identification number (PIN), and make
withdrawals, deposits, and other transactions—all automatically—with the aid
of a computer. Obviously, this makes banking easier and more convenient
(see Fig. 7-28).

ATMs are just one instance of **electronic funds transfer (EFT),** a way for
you to pay for goods and services without paper. Transactions from your checking and savings accounts are performed electronically, using computer technology. For example, using EFT, you could arrange to have a portion of your
paycheck deposited directly into a savings account each pay period. On certain
predesignated dates, you might have payments for some of your monthly bills
transferred from that savings account to your checking account. Instead of
paying cash for items you want to buy, you present your bank card to the
cashier, who inserts it into a terminal and checks your balance. The purchase
amount is electronically subtracted from your bank account. The procedure is
fast and convenient, and requires no paperwork.

FIGURE 7-28
An automated teller machine.

A FACSIMILE SYSTEM

A facsimile system is made up of three components—the telephone system, two or more facsimile terminals, and an interface device that links the terminals to the telephone system. These three components make up a communications system that is as easy to operate as a photocopier or a telephone.

Perhaps the most convenient feature of a facsimile communications system is that it will generally work with your existing system. You need to add additional telephone lines for the facsimile terminals only if you wish to dedicate those lines to the facsimile devices.

A facsimile terminal functions like a photocopier, except that the copy is produced at a remote location. The terminal scans the surface of a document and converts the image into an electronic signal that is transmitted by a telephone system to the receiving unit. The receiving device converts the signal into an exact replica of the original and produces a print. Most facsimile terminals can both send and receive documents, and some can perform both functions simultaneously.

An interface device connects the facsimile terminal to the telephone system. With some terminals, this can simply be a jack that plugs into the telephone system. With others, an acoustic coupler or data coupler is required. The interface equipment required is readily available either from facsimile suppliers or from the telephone company.

Facsimile System Operation

Great strides have been made in the past few years in making facsimile systems convenient and easy to use. The steps required to make a facsimile transmission are:

1. Telephone the number of the receiving location
2. Answer the telephone at the receiving location
3. Feed the document into the sending unit and transmit
4. Verify reception at the receiving unit and make a print
5. Terminate the telephone call.

While the degree of automation varies from unit to unit, today's facsimile terminals can perform most, if not all, of their intended functions automatically. The operation of today's facsimile communications system, therefore, is not much more complicated than that of a photocopier.

Computer Shopping

You have been wondering what to buy your father for his birthday and can't decide. Worse yet, you hate to shop. Ah, a way out. You turn to your microcomputer or terminal. Because it is linked to a modem and the necessary peripheral equipment to permit data communications, you dial a local number. After you type in your account number and password, your screen displays

WELCOME TO COMP-U-STORE

You can now begin to shop, even though it's 1:00 in the morning.

Comp-U-Store is the nation's leading 24-hour home shopping service. From the convenience of your own home, and with no traveling or crowds to contend with, you can purchase brand-name products at hefty discounts, normally up to 40 percent off the list price. Shopping is a breeze (it's always easy to spend money, but Comp-U-Store makes it even easier). To locate what you want, you type in responses to questions. The choices are narrowed down until the item you want is identified. You pay for your merchandise through Master Card, Visa, or a personal check. Did you ever believe shopping could be so easy and so much fun?

Information Utilities—Database Power

A growing number of home computer users are discovering how they can transform their personal computers into virtual sponges capable of sucking up the wisdom of the inner sanctums of powerful mainframes. Home computers can provide the enthralled user with all kinds of valuable information and convenient services.

Networking with information utilities will enable you to have quick and easy access to the following:

- Stock market reports
- Encyclopedias of all types and sizes
- Train and airline schedules
- Business analyses
- Extensive information related to special interest groups like doctors, lawyers, researchers, snail breeders, or coffee producers
- Computer games
- Government publications and news articles

The list goes on.

In addition, you can use a database to bank at home (EFT), shop at home, send electronic mail, and use all sorts of programming languages. You can also converse with other subscribers fortunate enough to have the same networking capabilities.

How can you make this type of service your own? To use a database, a subscriber must have the necessary hardware and software to engage in data communications. Database subscription fees average $50—normally a one-time fee—plus some nominal hourly usage fee. Some are actually free. After calling up the database, the user types in a password. The database then displays instructions telling the subscriber how to go about getting the information or service desired.

Two of the most popular databases are *CompuServe* and *THE SOURCE.* Both of these are actually collections of dozens of different databases. Stepping out? You can use either of these utilities to read movie reviews or check restaurant guides. If you are staying at home, you can call up the latest news releases or see how well your stocks and bonds are doing. *THE SOURCE* now offers a database containing reviews of commercial software—a long awaited and much needed service.

Doctors can access one of the many medical information databanks like *AMA/NET* to get information on the latest drugs or receive help in diagnosing diseases. Lawyers can tap a database like *LEXIS*, which provides a collection of laws, regulations, and court decisions.

Teletex and Videotex

Often, the services known as teletex and videotex are confused with public information utilities, but there is a difference. Both teletex and videotex provide subscribers with information that is piped into their homes; however, rather than a microcomputer serving as the prime receiver of information, the central component is a television set.

Teletex uses a home television set and telephone line to link the subscriber with a database. The user makes entries to a host computer with a keyboard. Signals are carried via telephone lines and the information is displayed on the TV screen. This is a true interactive system (see Fig. 7-29).

Videotex uses the home television set but not the telephone line or keyboard. The information is transmitted by the host television station, constituting a one-way system. The user doesn't use a keyboard to make selections, but instead must watch the screen until the desired page of information is transmitted, at which time he makes his selection. This is not an interactive system.

HOW TO FILE YOUR TAXES ELECTRONICALLY

Filing tax returns with the IRS electronically can be great for harried taxpayers. Electronic returns yield refunds in three weeks, as opposed to five to eight weeks for paper returns. And if you specify a direct deposit for the refund, you can have your cash on hand in two weeks. The IRS also acknowledges receipt of all electronically filed returns and can spot errors and advise the filer accordingly within a day of the return's filing.

Unfortunately, you can't do it yourself. According to spokesperson Frank Keith, the IRS accepts electronic returns only from preapproved transmitters, in batches of 50 or more, and only if a refund is due to the taxpayer. So if you want to circumvent the "paper pipeline" at the IRS, you must submit your return through a third party, and you must have a refund coming to you.

Although the IRS is working on a "balance due" enhancement, the agency has no timetable for incorporating it into its electronic system. Nor does it plan to allow individuals to transmit their own returns.

If your tax-prep package offers electronic filing as an option, the vendor has selected a third-party "transmitter" for you and has included a utility to convert your return file into a format that the transmitter can read. Filing entails either mailing a disk or sending files via modem to the licensed transmitter.

Nelco, a Green Bay, Wisconsin-based company, handles tax returns that have been prepared with ChipSoft's TurboTax, at a cost of $6.50 to the filer. If you're using MECA's TaxCut, you can file through Universal Tax Systems, in Fredericksburg, Virginia, for $20. Ten-Key can transmit returns that its package, Tax Shop, generates; the fee is $12 (after the first transmission). Users of Softview's MacInTax for Windows can file through InstaTax, of San Diego, at a cost of $29.95.

You can often offset the surcharge with the interest you gain by getting your refund into the bank earlier. But for most people, the sheer convenience makes it worthwhile. For more information about electronic filing and accepted transmitters, contact the IRS at 1-800-424-1040.

FIGURE 7-29

In Florida, participating families obtain news and other information from a central database. They also use the Bell Labs-developed teletext system to pay bills, shop, and buy entertainment tickets.

SUMMARY AND GLOSSARY OF KEY TERMS

- A **telecommunications** system consists of the following components: a **sender,** a **medium,** and a **receiver.** The term **data communications** is derived from the words *data* processing and tele*communications*. Data communications (sometimes referred to as **teleprocessing**) involves at least two hardware devices that can "talk" to one another over a communications **network.**

- Data processing operates on information to increase its worth to the end user by summarizing, manipulating, or in some way changing the data. **Data communi-** cations does not change information but adds value to it by the reliable and quick transmission of data from one point to another. When the purpose is to change information, the system is data processing. When the purpose is to transmit data, it is called data communications.

- Common characteristics of all data communications systems are **online terminals, real-time processing,** and **fast response times.** Most large companies use the same computer system for both data processing and data communications. Such a system will generally consist of **terminals, terminal controllers, modems, communications management equipment (front-end processor),** and a **computer.**

- The data transmission systems used by most computers and terminals are **serial systems,** which transmit data bit by bit over one channel, and **parallel systems,** which generally transmit data one byte at a time (8 bits simultaneously over 8 channels).

- Computers use codes to represent data as strings of bits transmitted over communications lines. The most popular codes are the 7-bit **ASCII** code and the 8-bit **ASCII-8** and **EBCDIC** codes.

- When transmitted serially, characters can be further classified as **synchronous** or **asynchronous.** A **start bit** and **stop bit** frame each character sent in asynchronous transmission. Blocks of characters are separated by one or more **sync bytes** when the synchronous transmission technique is used.

- To communicate, computers must use a common set of rules known as **protocols.** The exchange of prearranged signals that indicate two systems are compatible before actual transmission occurs is called **handshaking.**

- Transmission speeds are measured by signal changes per second (**baud rate**) or bits per second (**bps**). The amount of meaningful information transmitted per unit of time is sometimes referred to as **throughput.**

- A **terminal** acts as an interface between the user and the data communications system. The terminal allows you to transmit and receive data. A single terminal placed on one line is a **point-to-point** link to the computer. Several terminals may be placed on one line to the computer with a **multipoint** line. **Polling** and **contention** are techniques used to manage terminals on a multipoint line.

- Large computer systems rely on **controllers.** Controllers interface with peripherals to manage messages and communicate them to the computer.

- A programmable terminal with its own memory and operating programs is called an **intelligent terminal.**

- A data system communicating over voice-grade telephone lines needs a **modem.** A modem **modulates** the **digital** signals of a computer into **analog** signals sent over phone lines. The reverse process is called **demodulation.** The **amplitude,** or strength, of an analog signal determines the digital value to which it will be converted. Most modems are directly connected to a terminal and phone lines. **Acoustical couplers** use telephone handsets to provide data transmission.

- A **front-end processor (FEP)** is usually a programmable minicomputer. It acts as an interface between a computer and other teleprocessing equipment. It performs tasks to relieve the main CPU of various communications functions.

- Efficient use of communications channels can be permitted by a **multiplexor.** It enables several channels of communications to be carried over one multipoint communications line. A **concentrator** is similar to a multiplexor, but it also has storage and logic capabilities to perform communications control functions.

- Common types of communications media include **wire pairs, coaxial cables, microwave,** and **optical fibers.** The use of **light-wave transmission** over optical fibers should increase in the future. A special form of microwave transmission is provided with **communications satellites.**

- Communications traffic may flow over lines in several modes: **simplex, half-duplex,** and **full-duplex.** The speed of transmission can be classified with **bandwidth.** From slowest to fastest are **narrowband, voicegrade,** and **wideband.**

- Communications services are offered through **common carriers** such as AT&T. **Value-added networks (VANs)** lease the facilities of common carriers, enhance services, and offer them to users on a timeshared basis.

- The power of a microcomputer is enhanced when it is connected to a mainframe and its database. Files stored on the mainframe system can be **downloaded,** or transferred to the microcomputer, and microcomputer files can be **uploaded,** or transferred to the mainframe system.

- **Voice mail, electronic mail,** and **electronic message services** (called **bulletin boards**) are made possible with data communications. Bulletin boards allow anyone with a microcomputer and data communications equipment to access publicly-posted electronic messages.

- Through data communications, businesses have taken advantage of **teleconferencing, videoconferencing,** and **computer conferencing. Automatic teller machines** and **electronic funds transfer (EFT)** have provided services not possible before teleprocessing techniques became available. Other applications of data communications are **computer shopping, videotex,** and **teletex.** To those with computer systems that support data communications, vast amounts of information are available through **information utilities** and **databases.**

EXERCISES

True/False

_T_ 1. Synchronous transmission is faster than asynchronous transmission.

_F_ 2. A single set of rules and protocols has been established to make teleprocessing as standardized as possible.

_T_ *Test? K* 3. Data communications is also known as teleprocessing.

_F_ 4. The terms "data communications" and "data processing" essentially have the same meaning.

_F_ *Not* 5. Data communications systems may serve only one user at any time.

_T_ *Test?* 6. The front-end processor interfaces with the main, or host, computer and data communications elements.

_T_ 7. Bit-by-bit transmission is called serial transmission, whereas parallel transmission is sent blocks at a time.

_T_ 8. A parity bit helps to detect an error in a transmitted character.

_T_ *K.* 9. Point-to-point lines may be leased or switched lines.

_F_ 10. The process of changing analog signals to digital signals is called modulation. *demodulation*

_T_ 11. An example of a public line is a dial-up line.

_T_ 12. An acoustical coupler must be used in a relatively quiet or noise-free environment or it may not operate properly. *Many makes it true*

_F_ 13. It would be economically feasible for a company using one remote communications terminal to use a multiplexor.

_T_ 14. Advantages of optical fibers for light-wave transmission are that the medium is cheaper, faster, and less subject to distortion than other communications media.

_T_ *Test?* 15. Two-way concurrent transmission is called duplex transmission.

_F_ 16. Satellite and light-wave transmission would probably use a narrowband bandwidth.

_T_ 17. Downloading allows programs and data to be sent from a mainframe computer to an intelligent terminal for subsequent processing.

_F_ 18. Because telecommuting offers many advantages and no disadvantages, it will be welcomed by everyone.

_F_ 19. EFT actually transfers paper currency over communications lines.

_T_ 20. Videotex and teletex are relatively inexpensive communications systems and are available for the home.

Fill-in

1. Telecommunications systems contain the following components: _sender, medium, & receiver_.

2. All data communications systems have the following common characteristics: _online terminals, real-time processing, & fast response times_

3. A(n) _modem_ can convert digital signals to analog signals.

4. A(n) _UART_ controls the parallel-to-serial conversion and serial-to-parallel conversion of data. _Universal asynchronous receiver/transmitter_

K. 5. Common data transmission codes are: _ASCII, Epcidic (ASCII)_

K. 6. Data speeds may be measured by _bits per second, baud rate,_ *cf. 593 for more*

Chapter 7 Data Communications

241

7. The _controller_ [Front-End] supervises the peripheral equipment, freeing up the CPU to perform processing tasks.

8. A dedicated line with only one terminal attached to it is called a _point-to-point_ line.

9. Several terminals may be attached to a computer with a single line called a _multipoint_ line.

10. A programmable computer terminal with its own memory and operating system is known as a(n) _intelligent terminal_

11. Transferring data from a mainframe database into your personal computer is called _down loading_.

12. A(n) _acoustic coupler_ uses a telephone handset to provide data communications.

13. _Front-end processor_ acts as a monitor to the CPU to handle communications and leave other processing to the CPU.

_p. 224_ 14. The four common types of transmission media are _wire pairs_, _coaxial cables_, _Microwave_, and _Optical fibers_.

15. The different modes of data transmission are the following: _simplex, half-duplex, full-duplex_

16. A vendor offering access to a library research database using AT&T's transmission services is called a(n) _value-added_ network. _VAN_

17. Pictures and documents may be sent over communications lines with a(n) _fascimile or fax machine_

18. Meetings can take place even if the participants are miles away with the aid of _teleconferencing, video conferencing, + computer conferencing._

19. The 24-hour banking machine is known as a(n) _ATM automatic teller machine_

20. To use videotex and teletex, the following elements must be present: _television, telephone, & keyboard_

Problems

1. How could you set up your own personal communications system at home? What equipment would you need?

2. List the elements found in a combined data processing/data communications system.

3. What is meant by protocol? Why is it important to have standard protocols in communications?

4. What are the advantages of using an acoustical coupler over a direct-connect modem in teleprocessing?

5. How are terminals on a multipoint line managed to transmit and receive data?

6. What transmission media would you use in the following networks:
   a. A small banking firm with seven offices located in the same city
   b. A real estate office making four computer inquiries a day to a larger computer
   c. A large international commodities trading firm
   d. A national airline

7. With information utilities and databases available, what new applications can you think of for the computer in the home? At the workplace? In school?

Projects

1. What would you have to do to set up a popular personal microcomputer to communicate with information sources such as CompuServe? Research and find out exactly what you would need and the associated costs with implementing such a system.

2. Arrange to meet with someone from a local bank who can tell you how banking uses telecommunications to implement such things as EFT and automatic teller machines. Prepare a research paper.

CROSSWORD PUZZLE

Across

1. Converts between analog and digital
2. Transmission of information over great distances
3. Transmissions carried out bit by bit
4. Transmission technique that utilizes sync bytes
5. _____-duplex lines facilitate transmission in both directions at the same time
6. Front-end processor
7. Type of signal transmitted from modem to modem
8. A smart terminal
9. A public transmission line sometimes referred to as a dial-up line
10. The number of signals that a communication channel can transmit per second
11. An invitation by the computer to a terminal to send data
12. Transfer of funds electronically
13. A communications line capable of transmitting in only one direction
14. A multiplexor with storage and a processing capability
15. The oldest electronic transmission medium
16. A bandwidth commonly used by telephone companies
17. Allows several individuals to both see and hear one another
18. Electronic message service

Down

19. Can be used to connect several low-speed lines to one high-speed line
20. One-to-group or group-to-group verbal communications
21. Two hardware devices "talking" to one another over a communications network
22. High-frequency line-of-sight radio wave
23. _____ interface between peripherals and the computer.
24. Used to detect errors in data representation or transmission
25. A dedicated communications line
26. Standard serial interface
27. A nondirect-connect modem
28. The exchange of prearranged signals
29. Measure of transmission speed
30. Added value to a common carrier communications service
31. Transferring data from a microcomputer to a mainframe computer

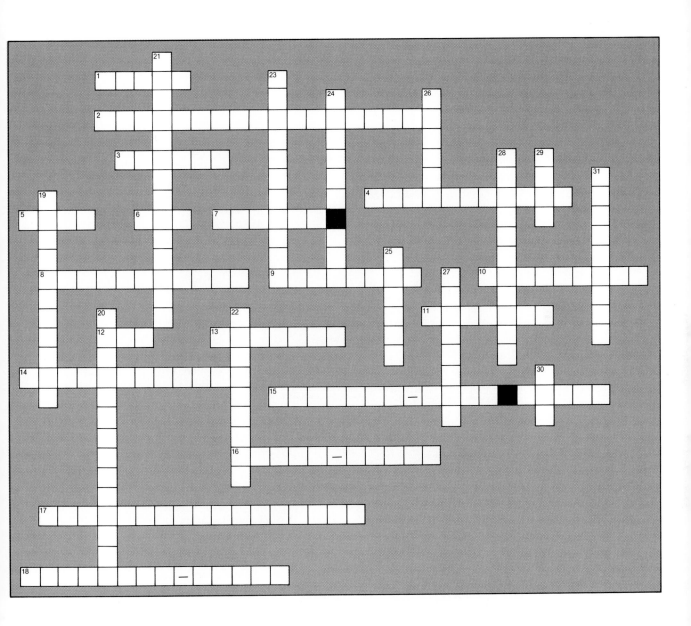

8

DATABASE AND DATA STRUCTURES
Let's Get Organized

Objectives

- Define a database
- List and describe the considerations when designing a database management system
- Explain the need for and uses of a data dictionary
- Describe the difference between the physical and logical structure of a database
- Name and describe the characteristics of each database structure
- Illustrate possible uses for each of the database structures
- Understand and use the key terms in the chapter

In the beginning, the data used by an information system was stored on individual files. The organization selected for each of these files was only dependent on the nature of the application(s) for which it was used. Payroll files were created containing all the data pertinent to a company's payroll system. Similarly, individual files were created for use with the company's personnel, accounts payable, accounts receivable, inventory, and other systems. If the data on these files were not carefully delineated, the same data very likely appeared on several files. In other words, these files would contain **redundant data**. For example, both a company's personnel and payroll master files could contain the name and address of each employee. This would mean that a simple change of address would have to be processed twice and possibly three or four times, depending on the number of other files on which these data appeared. Perhaps the greatest drawback to processing with many individual files is that it does not provide easy access to all data. Only the data contained on the files being processed are accessible.

Clearly, these problems would be eliminated if it were possible to store a data item *once* and still have it accessible to all application programs. Such a set of *data* items would provide a *base* for many applications. It was with these goals in mind that database technology was developed.

In this chapter, we will examine databases and database processing.

WHAT IS A DATABASE?

A **database** can be thought of as a set of logically related files organized to facilitate access by one or more application programs and to minimize data redundancy. This concept does not imply that *all* data relating to a company's business should be contained on a single database, but simply that all records in a database should be related and that redundant data should be minimized.

General Objectives

The elimination of data redundancy is only one of many reasons for establishing a database. Others include:

- Integrate existing data files.
- Share data among all users.
- Incorporate changes easily and quickly.
- Simplify the use of data files.
- Lower the cost of storing and retrieving data.
- Improve accuracy and consistency.
- Provide data security from unauthorized use.
- Exercise central control over standards.

A DATABASE MANAGEMENT SYSTEM

In addition to the database itself, a set of programs is necessary to facilitate adding new data as well as modifying and retrieving of existing data within a database. This set of programs is referred to as a **database management system (DBMS).**

The design of a DBMS involves three considerations:

- Users' needs or application programs
- Database processing system
- Database itself

Generally, the user of a database management system accesses the database via a special query language or via application programs written in a high-level language, such as COBOL, FORTRAN, or C (see Fig. 8-1). Application programs are written in much the same way as if they were accessing a discrete file. The difference when using a DBMS is that the application program utilizes special **host** or **command-language** instructions to communicate requests for data to the portion of the DBMS referred to as the **database processing system,** which acts as the link between the user program and the database itself. Basically, the database processing system consists of a series of programs that translate requests from users or user programs into the instructions necessary to access,

FIGURE 8-1

Relationship between DBMS and application programs.

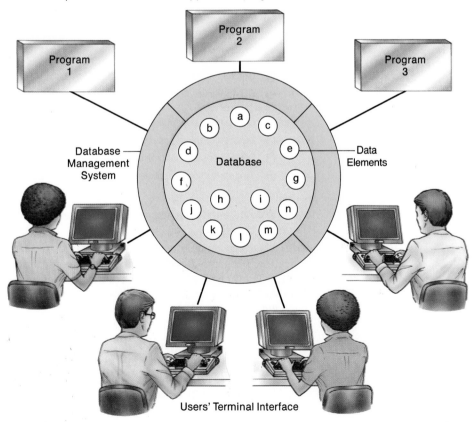

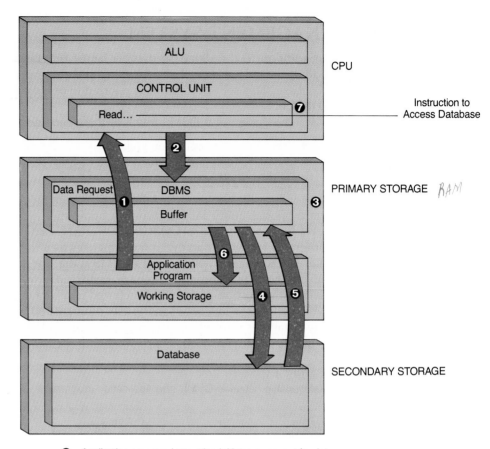

- ❶ Application program instruction initiates a request for data.
- ❷ Control unit transfers control to DBMS.
- ❸ DBMS verifies that the request is valid and determines location of data element in database.
- ❹ DBMS issues command to access data from secondary storage.
- ❺ Data element is accessed and stored in a buffer of the DBMS.
- ❻ DBMS transfers data element to application program storage area .
- ❼ Next instruction in application program is accessed and executed.

FIGURE 8-2
Accessing data from a database in response to an application program request.

add to, change, or delete records or items of data from the database. Thus an application program need only include a command to access the desired data element. The actual mechanics of locating and accessing the data element are accomplished by the database processing programs. This process is shown in Figure 8-2.

Data Dictionary

You might have asked yourself, How does the DBMS keep track of all the data elements involved? The answer is, it maintains a data dictionary. A **data dictionary** is simply a repository for information about the database—data definitions and characteristics such as usage, physical representations, ownership, authorization, and security.

The DBMS can access the data dictionary to determine the information it needs to operate. For example, the DBMS can access the data dictionary to:

1. Determine if a data element already exists before adding. This reduces data redundancy.
2. Change the description of a data field. For example, to change the description of a 20-position alphanumeric field to a 25-character alphanumeric field, only the description in the data dictionary need be modified.
3. Determine what relationships exist between data elements.
4. Determine what applications programs can access what data elements.

The data dictionary is also useful to programmers and systems analysts:

1. A programmer can copy a definition directly from the data dictionary for use in an applications program. This guarantees greater accuracy with less work from the programmer.
2. If a data description is changed, the data dictionary can be consulted to determine all affected application programs.

Query Language

In addition to a data dictionary, most DBMSs also provide a query language that enables a user to request and receive information directly from the database system. The complexity of this query language and the level of difficulty using it varies greatly with the DBMS. Some query languages are procedural and require step-by-step instructions to be written, as with a high-level language. Others accept Englishlike commands or guide the user with a series of fill-in questions, or even display a menu on the terminal monitor from which the user must select a desired command.

Query languages supplied with microcomputer database packages (such as dBASE III PLUS (see Fig. 8-3), which is discussed in Tutorial 4 of the accompanying applications book, are almost always used to interact with the database and provide built-in help for novice users.

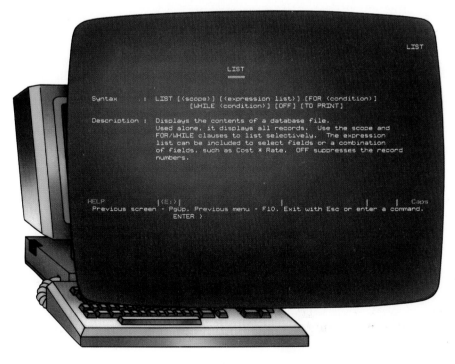

FIGURE 8-3
A typical dBASE III PLUS help screen.

Database Software Packages

In Chapter 13 we will discuss those prewritten software packages currently available for creating and using databases. In Tutorial 4, we will learn how to use the most popular microcomputer database package, dBASE III PLUS.

DATA STRUCTURES

The structure of the data within a database can be viewed in two different ways, physically and logically.

The **physical data structure** refers to the physical arrangement of the data on the secondary storage device, usually disk. Typically, this physical structure is the concern of specialists who design DBMSs. Analysts, programmers, and users are generally less concerned with the physical structure than with the logical structure.

The **logical data structure** concerns how the data "seems" to be arranged and the meanings of the data elements in relation to one another. This structure or **model** is generally defined in terms of a **schema**—an overall conceptual view of the logical relationships between the data elements in the database. It includes the names of the major elements, their attributes, and the logical relationships between them. Figure 8-4 shows a schema that might apply to the database of an autoparts store. Although greatly simplified, it illustrates that relationships exist between part numbers, types of cars, models, and manufacturers. The connecting lines indicate links and the arrows the type of relationship. For example, in this schema, *manufacturer* is linked to *part number*, and the relationship is one-to-many (a double-headed arrow implies many and a single-headed arrow one). That is, one manufacturer produces many part numbers, but each part number has only one manufacturer. There are also indirect links indicated. A part number, for example, is linked to type vehicle through model.

FIGURE 8-4
Schema for an autoparts store.

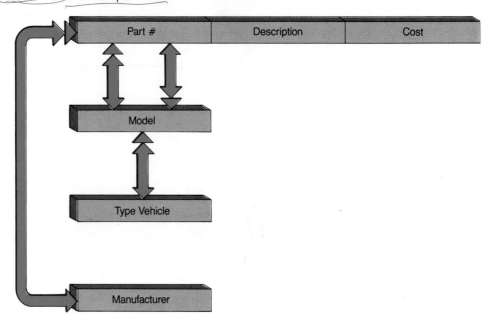

In a large database, the relationships are far more complex than those shown in Fig. 8-4. Typically, each user or application program is concerned with only a small part or subset of the data elements in the schema. The subset of the database schema required by a particular application program is referred to as a **subschema** or **user's view.** The subschema of a payroll program would be different from the subschema of an accounts payable program, and so on. This logical arrangement not only clarifies the user's view of the database, but it serves to enhance data security by providing access to limited data elements on a need-to-know basis. A programmer working on an inventory program, for example, would have no need to access employee salary data.

Several logical data structures are used to express the relationships between individual data elements or records in a database. Common logical data structures are hierarchical, network, and relational, with relational being the most predominant.

Hierarchical Structure

In a **hierarchical structure** (see Fig. 8-5), sometimes referred to as a **tree structure,** the stored data gets more and more detailed as one branches further and further out on the tree. Each **segment,** or **node,** may be subdivided into two or more subordinate nodes which can be further subdivided into two or more additional nodes. However, each node can emanate from only one "parent." To the user, each record resembles an organizational chart in which the segments or nodes fit into a well-defined hierarchy or tree. There is only one segment, or **root,** at the top.

Application programs process hierarchical databases one record at a time, as with conventional file structures. Hierarchical database structures are commonly used with large mainframe computer systems.

Figure 8-6 represents a hierarchical database that might be used at a college. The college illustrated has several departments, each department has several teachers, and each teacher has several courses.

The only problem with this model is that it does not provide for a teacher teaching in more than one department or for several teachers team-teaching a single course. We could resolve these problems, should they occur, by including the teacher as a node of each department and the course as a node of each teacher. However, this would introduce data redundancy, the same data item in more than one place—a situation that DBMSs were intended to eliminate. A possible solution might be to consider another structure, perhaps a network structure.

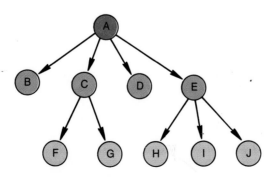

FIGURE 8-5
Hierarchy structure.

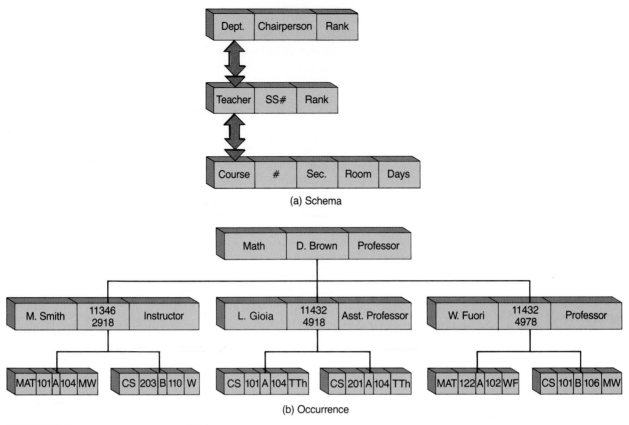

(a) Schema

(b) Occurrence

FIGURE 8-6
(a) Hierarchy database schema, (b) an occurrence.

Network Structure

The **network structure** (Fig. 8-7) is similar to the hierarchical structure with the exception that in the network structure a node may have more than one parent. The trade-off between the simplicity of design of a hierarchical structure and the storage efficiency of a network structure is a very important consideration in database implementation. Network structures are most commonly used with mainframe and minicomputer systems, rarely with microcomputers.

In the college example above, a network structure could handle the special cases mentioned without introducing redundant data. A teacher could belong to several departments and a course could belong to several teachers (see Fig. 8-8). In this example MAT 109 belongs to teachers Gioia and Fuori, and teacher Fuori belongs to departments Math and Business.

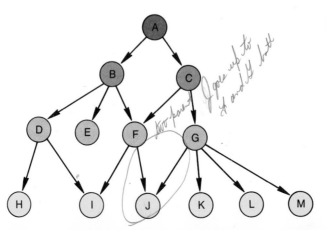

FIGURE 8-7
Network database structure.

254

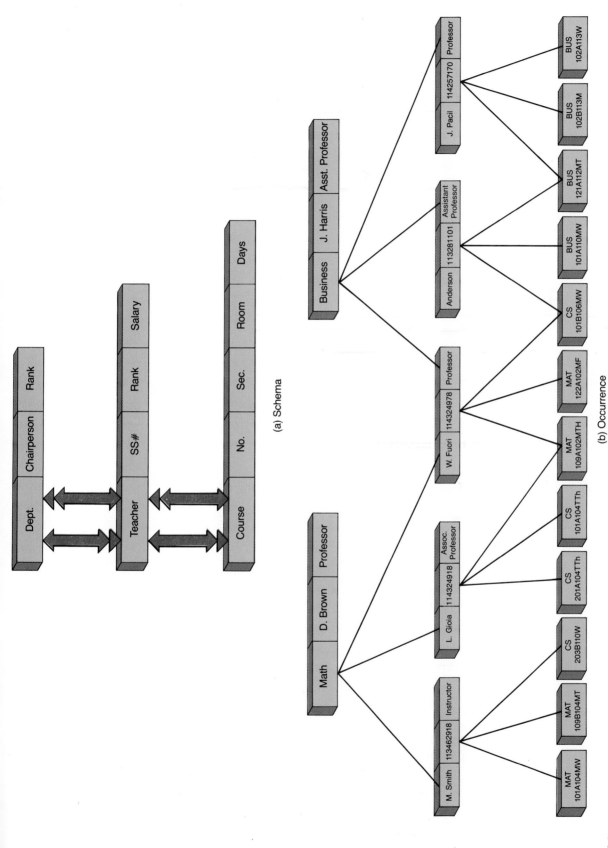

(a) Schema

(b) Occurrence

FIGURE 8-8
(a) Network database schema, (b) an occurrence.

255

The **relational structure** organizes data in terms of two-dimensional tables (Fig. 8-9). These tables offer great flexibility and a high degree of data security. The relational structure uses relatively little memory or secondary storage. Unfortunately, the process of creating these tables is rather elaborate. Another disadvantage of this structure is that it generally requires more time to access information than either of the other two structures. This is because much more information must be searched in order to answer queries posed to the system. In addition, some implementations use a fixed amount of storage for each field, resulting in inefficient storage utilization. In spite of these disadvantages, the relational structure has gained rapid acceptance and is currently the most popular of the three structures. This structure is used almost exclusively with microcomputer systems and is increasingly being applied to minicomputer and mainframe systems. Many experts predict that it will eventually replace the other structures completely.

FIGURE 8–9
Relational structure.

STUDENT NAME	ADDRESS	OTHER DATA
Adams, J.	14 Spruce St.	. . . . .
Bass, C.	112 15th St.	. . . . .
Jones, T.	641 Spencer Dr.	. . . . .
Ross, J.	12 Pine Ave.	. . . . .
Trumble, A.	133 Aston Pl.	. . . . .

(a) Student Name–Address Table

Student Name	Student Number	Other Data
Adams, J.	113245436	. . . . .
Bass, C.	114346789	. . . . .
Jones, T.	087453190	. . . . .
Ross, J.	114280834	. . . . .
Trumble, A.	086453321	. . . . .

(b) Student Name–Student Number Table

Student Number	Major	Other Data
113245436	Data Processing	. . . . .
114346789	Computer Science	. . . . .
087453190	Mathematics	. . . . .
114280834	Physics	. . . . .
086453321	Accounting	. . . . .

(c) Student Number–Major Table

Figure 8-10 illustrates how the traditional approach to data organization compares to a database management approach. Figure 8-11 illustrates a database implementation procedure.

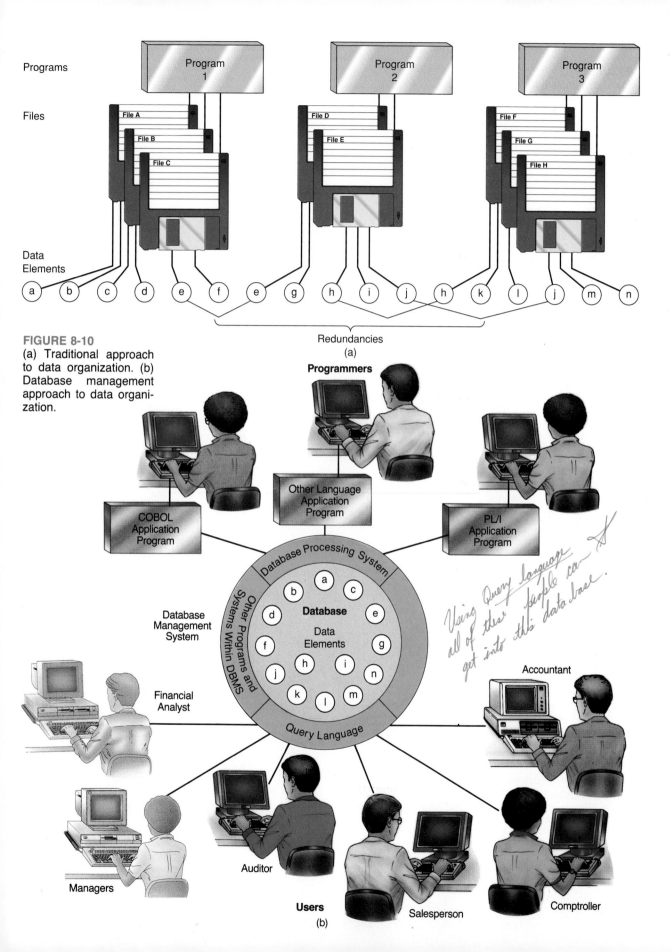

FIGURE 8-10
(a) Traditional approach to data organization. (b) Database management approach to data organization.

Programs

Files

Data Elements

Program 1
Program 2
Program 3

File A
File B
File C

File D
File E

File F
File G
File H

a b c d e f e g h i j h k l j m n

Redundancies
(a)

Programmers

COBOL Application Program

Other Language Application Program

PL/I Application Program

Database Management System

Database Processing System

Other Programs and Systems Within DBMS

Database
Data Elements

a b c d e f g h i j k l m n

Query Language

Financial Analyst

Managers

Auditor

Users

Salesperson

Comptroller

Accountant

Using Query language, all of these people can get into this data base.

(b)

FIGURE 8–11
Database implementation procedure.

Step	Description	Responsibility
1. DEFINE SCOPE OF THE DATABASE PROJECT		
	a. Identify which organizational subdivisions will be served by the database	DP steering committee
	b. Define which functions within these organizations will utilize the database	DP steering committee
	c. Identify which existing and planned applications will be converted to the database system	Data processing
	d. Prepare proposal for management and obtain go-ahead	Data processing
2. ORGANIZE DATABASE PROJECT		
	a. Pick users for design team	Top management
	b. Select database administrator (DBA)	Data processing
	c. Establish regular meetings and periodic management reporting for design team	DBA
3. SELECT DATABASE MANAGEMENT SYSTEM PRODUCTS		
	a. Document requirements in formal proposal requests	DBA
	b. Select DBMS vendor	Design team
4. DEVELOP INITIAL IMPLEMENTATION PLAN AND SCHEDULE		
	a. Identify files that will be converted	Data processing
	b. Identify programs within applications specified	Data processing
	c. Estimate programmer hours needed to modify applications programs	Data processing
	d. Estimate user clerical support needed to verify data during conversion	Design team
	e. Develop implementation schedule	Design team
5. DESIGN DATABASE		
	a. Complete detailed information requirements	Design team
	b. Identify data requirements	Design team
	c. Determine data structure and complete design specifications	DBA
	d. Review and approve design specifications	Design team
6. PERFORM TRAINING		
	a. Develop training requirements and training schedule	DBA and DP manager
	b. Train programmers in use of DML (data manipulation language)	Vendor
	c. Train DBA in DMCL (data manipulation control language) and DDL (data definition language)	Vendor
7. INSTALL AND TEST DATABASE		
	a. Code DMCL, schema and subschema	DBA
	b. Modify representative programs for DBMS test	Applications programmers
	c. Code conversion programs	Applications programmers
	d. Generate the database	DBA
	e. Test and debug	DBA and applications programmers
	f. Review and approve test results	Design team
8. DEVELOP DETAILED CONVERSION PLAN		
	a. Make individual programming assignments for each program to be modified and each file to be loaded	DP manager
	b. Schedule users to verify and correct file contents	Design team
	c. Schedule computer availability	Data processing
	d. Prepare formal written conversion schedule and obtain commitments from all parties involved	DBA
	e. Approve conversion plan	Design team
9. CONVERT EXISTING APPLICATIONS		
	a. Bring up one application at a time	Data processing
	b. Update and regenerate database as required	DBA
	c. Approve revised applications as they are converted	DP steering committee
	d. Begin using database for new applications and programs	Data processing
10. FINE-TUNE DATABASE		
	a. Monitor DBMS access statistics and visible performance, and modify database as required	DBA
	b. Regenerate database when necessary	DBA
11. PERIODICALLY REVIEW DATABASE PERFORMANCE		
	a. Restate organizational goals and information requirements	DP steering committee
	b. Evaluate success of database project	DP steering committee
	c. Begin new database projects when required	DP steering committee

DATABASE—AN APPRAISAL

Using a database and a DBMS is not without its drawbacks. Table 8-1 summarizes the advantages and the disadvantages of this approach.

TABLE 8-1
Database—Advantages and Disadvantages

ADVANTAGES	DISADVANTAGES
■ Reduced data redundancy ■ Reduced updating errors and increased consistency ■ Greater data integrity and independence from application programs ■ Improved data access to users through use of host and query languages ■ Improved data security ■ Reduced data entry, storage, and retrieval costs ■ Facilitates development of new application programs	■ Database systems are complex, difficult, time-consuming to design ■ Substantial hardware and software start-up costs ■ Damage to database affects virtually all application programs ■ Extensive conversion costs in moving from a file-based system to a database system ■ Initial training required for all programmers and users

SUMMARY AND GLOSSARY OF KEY TERMS

■ Because many files are used by a company, it is possible that the same data may appear on several of these files. This results in duplicate, or **redundant data,** and thus in the need for a **database**—a set of logically related files consolidating several smaller files, organized in such a way that data access is improved and redundancy is minimized.

■ Other reasons for establishing a database are to integrate existing data files, to share data among all users, to incorporate changes easily and quickly, to simplify the use of data files, to lower the cost of storing and retrieving data, to improve accuracy and consistency, to provide data security from unauthorized use, and to exercise central control over standards.

■ To facilitate adding to, modifying of, and retrieving of existing data within a database, a set of programs referred to as a **database management system (DBMS)** is generally required.

■ When using a DBMS, the application program utilizes special **host** or **command language** instructions to communicate requests for data to a portion of the DBMS known as the **database processing system.**

■ A **data dictionary** is a repository for information concerning the database—data definitions and other characteristics.

■ Most DBMSs also provide a **query language,** which enables a user to request and receive information from the system without the need for a specially written program.

■ The structure of data within a database can be viewed in two ways, physically and logically. The **physical data structure** is the physical arrangement of the data on the storage device (usually a disk). The **logical data structure** pertains to how the data "seems" to be arranged and the meanings of the data elements in relation to one another. This **model** is defined in terms of a **schema**—an overall conceptual view of the logical relationships between the data and the elements in the database. It includes the names of the major elements, their attributes, and the logical relationship between them.

■ The subset of the database schema required by a particular application program is a **subschema,** or **user's view.** This logical arrangement clarifies the user's view and enhances data security.

- Today databases utilize three logical data structures: hierarchical, network, and relational.
- In a **hierarchical structure,** sometimes referred to as a **tree structure,** the stored data get more detailed as one branches further and further out on the tree. Each branch, or **node,** may be subdivided into several other branches but itself may come from only one parent branch.

- A **network structure** is similar to a hierarchical structure with the exception that a branch may have more than one parent branch.
- The **relational structure** organizes data in the form of two-dimensional tables. This structure is the most complex to organize but is preferred by the majority of users.

EXERCISES

True/False

_T_ 1. A database is a set of logically related files organized to facilitate access by one or more application programs.

_T_ 2. In order to handle the access, additions, deletions, and modification of data within a database efficiently, a set of programs referred to as a database management system is necessary.

_T_ 3. When using a DBMS the application program utilizes special host or command language instructions. sort,

_T_ 4. The database processing system forms a link between the user program and the database itself.

_F_ 5. The design of DBMS is not influenced by applications programs.

_T_ 6. A schema is an overall conceptual view of the logical relationships between the data elements in a database.

_F_ 7. The physical data structure pertains to how the data "seems" to be arranged. *logical*

_F_ 8. In the hierarchical file structure, a node may have more than one parent.

_T_ 9. Integrating existing data files is a general objective when establishing a database. *DBMS*

_T_ 10. A database is accessed via a special query language.

_F_ 11. A repository of information about a database is called a DBMS. *Data dictionary*

_F_ 12. A hierarchical structure is commonly used with microcomputers.

_T_ 13. A network structure is commonly used with mainframes and minicomputers and rarely with microcomputers.

_F_ 14. dBASE III PLUS is an example of a mainframe database package.

_F_ 15. The database structure of a large database will contain rather simple relationships.

Fill-in

1. A DBMS utilizes special ___*host*___ or *command language* instructions to communicate requests for data.

2. A(n) *data dictionary* is a repository of information concerning a database.

3. A(n) *query language* enables a user to request and receive information from a DBMS.

4. There are ___*several*___ different logical database structures. *three* *heir. relational +*

5. A hierarchical structure is sometimes referred to as a(n) *tree structure* structure.

6. A hierarchical structure is generally used on *mainframes* computers.

7. A(n) _network structure_ structure permits a branch to have more than one parent branch.

8. The _relational_ structure is the most complex to organize but is preferred by DBMS users.

9. An example of a microcomputer database package is _dBase III Plus_.

10. The overall conceptual view of the logical relationship between the data elements in a database is called a(n) _schema_.

Problems

1. Define the following terms:

Data dictionary	Network structure
Database	Physical data structure
Database management system	Query language
Database processing system	Redundant data
File organization	Schema
Hierarchical structure	Subschema
Index	Tree structure
Logical data structure	

Projects

1. How might you organize a database to be used by all of the above application areas in a company? What fields would this database contain? Would a single database be feasible? Why or why not?

2. Visit the computer center in your school, or at some other location. Investigate and describe the database(s) you find there. Discuss the logical and physical structure and describe the contents of the data dictionary.

CROSSWORD PUZZLE

1. The number of records in a file
2. A structure in which a node may have more than one parent
3. Duplicate data
4. Subschema
5. What relational structures use economically
6. A single database can replace many separate _____
7. A segment of a hierarchical structure
8. A repository for information concerning the database
9. The segment at the top of a hierarchical structure
10. Another name for a database command language
11. A high-level language used to write database programs.
12. A hierarchical structure
13. A set of programs used with a database

1. Overall conceptual view of the logical relationships between data elements in a database
14. A segment of a hierarchical structure
15. A database structure that organizes the data in the form of two-dimensional tables
16. A database management system
17. Redundant data creates a need for this
18. A DBMS language
19. A consideration when designing a database management system
20. Logically related files

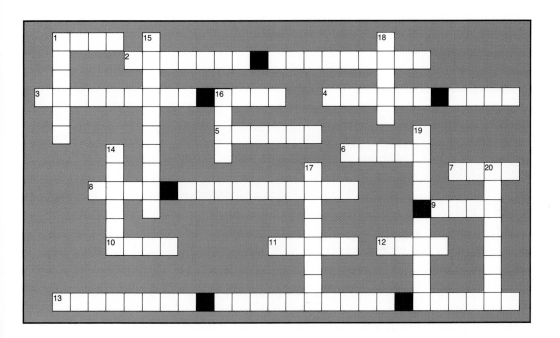

9

THE OPERATING SYSTEM
The Commander-in-Chief

Objectives

- Describe an operating system.
- Explain the functions of an operating system.
- Describe the control and service programs that constitute an operating system.
- Explain the operations of the command processor and interrupt handler.
- Describe the operation of the input/output control system.
- Compare mainframe and microcomputer operating systems.
- Boot a system.
- Name and describe some commonly used microcomputer operating systems.
- Understand the importance of a user interface.
- Understand and use the key terms presented in this chapter.

I n Chapter 2 we learned that stored programs or software are of two types: applications programs and systems programs. **Applications programs** fulfill end-user needs, allow people to do things like make calculations, print out a report, write a paper, and generate a spreadsheet. **Systems programs** perform essential support functions and consist of programs to start up the computer; read, store, and execute applications programs; store and retrieve files; and otherwise make the computer's resources available to applications programs. Foremost among systems programs is the operating system (see Fig. 9-1).

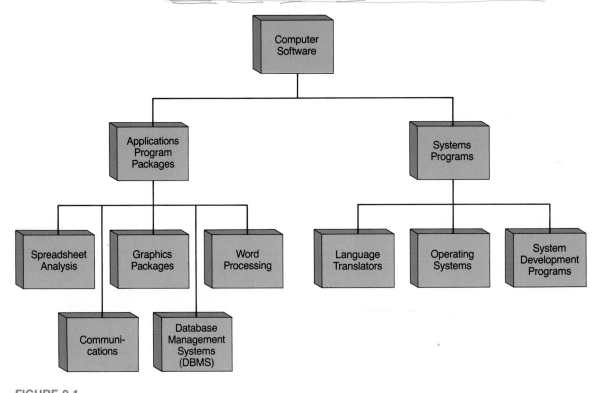

FIGURE 9-1
The software or computer programs necessary to support a computer system consist of two types: applications programs and systems programs.

WHAT IS AN OPERATING SYSTEM?

An **operating system (OS)** is a collection of systems programs that control and coordinate the overall operation of a computer system. These programs act as an interface between the hardware and the applications programs. Variously described as a "traffic cop," "supervisor," or "office manager," the OS manages the resources of the computer, namely the CPU, memory, and I/O devices. Normally transparent to the user, the operating system performs its

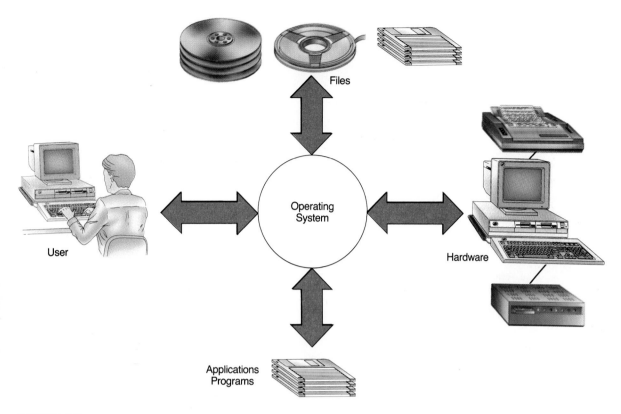

Files

Operating System

User

Hardware

Applications Programs

FIGURE 9-2
The systems programs within an operating system act as an interface among the hardware, applications programs, files, and the user.

tasks without intervention; the user is usually unaware that the OS is quietly at work assisting the user in various ways (see Fig. 9-2).

The **nucleus,** or **kernel** of an operating system is the small portion that must be *resident* in memory at all times to perform basic functions and to access other portions of the operating system. The remaining, larger portion of the operating system is maintained in secondary storage ready to be called into memory as needed. If the OS is stored on tape, it is known as a **tape operating system (TOS).** A **disk operating system (DOS)** stores the systems programs on disk (see Fig. 9-3).

THE MAKING OF AN OPERATING SYSTEM

The Ubiquitous Computer
Today, computers perform more than 100,000 calculations for every person living in the United States. The average citizen's name will be processed by a computer more than 30 times a day.

An operating system performs support functions. Before the advent of operating systems in the early 1960s, computer operators had to perform the support functions that are now done by the operating system. Operators of mainframe computer systems had to log and prioritize all jobs. It was the operator's responsibility to load the appropriate compiler and program, followed by the accompanying data files. If anything went wrong with program execution or with any of the peripheral devices, the computer operator had to locate the problem and take steps to correct it. Enormous workloads eventually made the operator's

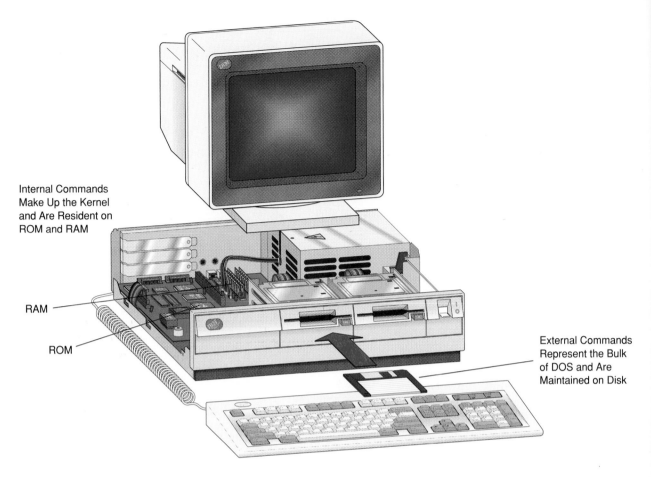

Internal Commands Make Up the Kernel and Are Resident on ROM and RAM

RAM

ROM

External Commands Represent the Bulk of DOS and Are Maintained on Disk

FIGURE 9-3
The nucleus or kernel of a disk operating system (DOS) resides in memory, while the bulk of the systems software is on disk.

task impossible. Today, operating systems have been mercifully successful in performing many of the functions previously assigned to operators; furthermore, modern operating systems perform these functions better, faster, and more economically.

Functions performed by a modern operating system include:

- Provides for human-computer interaction
- Boots, or starts the computer operation
- Schedules jobs — *Makes sure documents do not overlap*
- Controls input and output operations
- Controls program execution   *DOS tells you if keyboard is not connected*
- Manages data and file storage
- Assigns different tasks to the CPU
- Provides security and control

DOS helps to free up programmer from writing in general routines

DOS has a protect command that locks program

The OS may direct the CPU to handle interrupts and load language translators into memory. On larger computers the OS can coordinate timesharing and multiprogramming and can provide for security by thwarting unauthorized access to data and programs. For example, an operating system can control

268

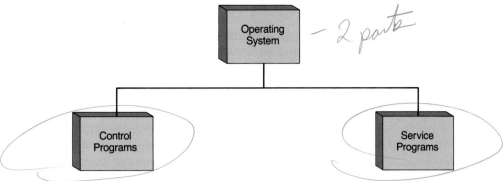

— 2 parts

FIGURE 9-4
An operating system is made up of control programs and service programs.

file access by restricting access to read-only or write-only operations. To accomplish these functions, the operating system utilizes control and service programs (see Fig. 9-4).

Control Programs

Control programs permit user-computer communication, log jobs, and oversee the overall computer operation to ensure that the various activities run smoothly and to completion. The principal control programs are shown in Figure 9-5.

Supervisor Program

The major operating system control program is commonly called the **supervisor.** *Oversees*
The supervisor handles the overall management of a computer system. It is maintained in memory and supervises the loading of other parts of the operating system from secondary storage into memory as they are needed. It also supervises the loading of application programs for execution. The supervisor also interprets user messages and responds in kind, and it keeps track of jobs run and the computer's compilation and execution times.

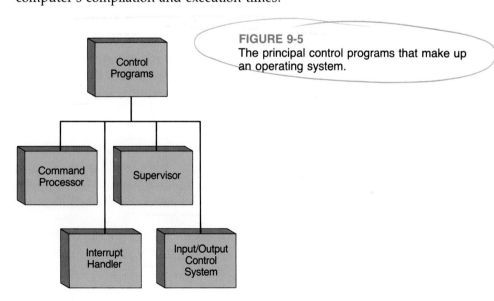

FIGURE 9-5
The principal control programs that make up an operating system.

Command Processor

An operating system is not capable of independent thought. It can only perform specific support functions, and then only when directed by the user of the computer system. The portion of the operating system that can accept, interpret, and carry out user commands is referred to as the **command processor.** The command processor consists of a number of individual program modules, each responsible for handling a single command.

Individual user commands to COPY a file, LOAD an application program, FORMAT a disk, and so on, are handled by the command processor. Commands to the operating system of a microcomputer are actually requests to execute individual command processor programs. For example, the command

COPY A:PROGRAM1 B:

directs the command processor to execute the memory-resident *copy program*, whereas the command

FORMAT B:

requests the externally stored *format program* to be executed (see Fig. 9-6).

Interrupt Handler

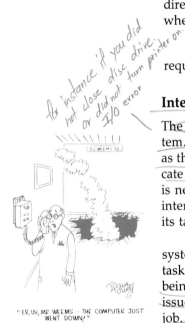

for instance if you did not close disc drive, or did not turn printer on. I/O error

"ER, UH, MR. WEEMS -- THE COMPUTER JUST WENT DOWN!"

The **interrupt handler** acknowledges and processes all interruptions to the system. One of the most common sources of interrupts is from I/O devices such as the keyboard, printer, and secondary storage. These devices must communicate with the CPU through the operating system. Thus the operating system is never idle, but must constantly be on the alert for an interrupt triggered by internal or external events, such as an I/O device indicating that it has completed its task or that an error condition may have occurred.

The function of the interrupt handler can vary greatly from a microcomputer system to a mainframe system. Most microcomputer systems handle only one task at a time. Hence, interrupts generally come from the particular device being used at that moment, or from a user-initiated activity, such as a command issued from the keyboard to load a program, execute a program, or abort a job. abort, retry, fail

The handling of interrupts, like the performance of other operating system functions, is more complex in a mainframe environment. Unlike microcomputer systems, mainframe systems must perform a number of tasks at the same time if the resources of the system are to be used efficiently. This generally requires that the CPU jump back and forth between a number of tasks or application programs being processed in the computer at the same time. For example, let's assume that the CPU is processing a high-priority job that requires the reading of data records from disk. While records are being accessed, the CPU would be idle. Thus the supervisor saves all necessary information concerning the first program, and then assigns the CPU to another program that is processed concurrently. Upon completion of the reading operation, the channel or disk controller issues an interrupt. The operating system must now respond and save what is currently being worked on, branch to the interrupt handler, and resume processing the original job. A typical mainframe system can handle dozens of programs and monitor an even greater number of peripheral devices concurrently.

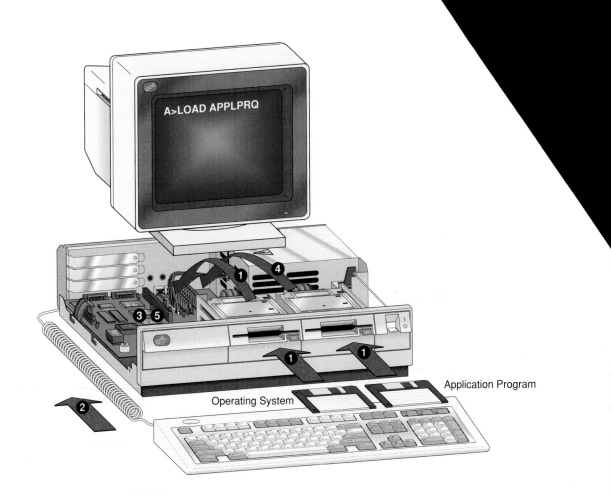

A>LOAD APPLPRQ

Application Program

Operating System

1 The operating system and application program disks are inserted and the operating system is loaded.

2 The user enters a command to LOAD the application program.

3 The LOAD command is interpreted by the command processor, which passes control to the program loading module.

4 The loading program reads the application program into memory.

5 Control is returned to the command processor, which prompts the user or directs the operating system to execute the loaded program.

FIGURE 9-6
Many individual steps must be performed by the operating system in responding to user's commands to load an application program from secondary storage.

Input/Output Control System (IOCS)

The **input/output control system (IOCS)** schedules and activates the proper I/O device as well as the storage unit. It also monitors the operation of input/ output devices. If a needed device is not available or is malfunctioning, the IOCS will substitute another device in its place. It controls and coordinates the flow of data between I/O devices, for example, from a terminal keyboard to a display screen, or to other output devices like disk drives and printers.

Because of its constant use, the IOCS control program is generally RAM-resident on mainframe computer systems. On a microcomputer system this program is generally maintained in ROM and referred to as the **BIOS** (basic input/output system). The IBM PC BIOS is stored on a set of two or four

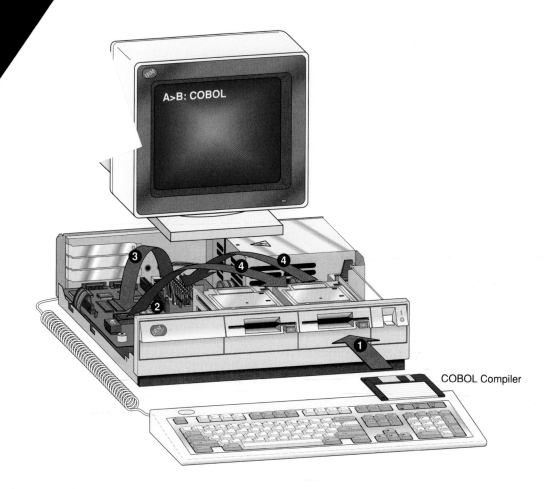

A>B: COBOL

COBOL Compiler

1 The COBOL compiler disk is inserted and a load command is entered.

2 The command processor interprets the command and executes the load program.

3 The load program assigns the job to IOCS.

4 IOCS directs the following operations:
   a. Determine the location of the COBOL compiler from the disk directory.
   b. Direct the read/write heads to the correct track on the disk.
   c. Read the compiler from disk into memory.

5 The IOCS returns control to the load program (Step 3 reversed).

6 The operating system awaits the user's next command.

FIGURE 9-7
The role of the Input/Output Control System (IOCS) in loading a COBOL program.

means you have to pay royalties to get this

proprietary PROM chips and represents an important area of difference between an IBM PC and PC compatibles or **clones.** *make their own that does similar things*

To illustrate how the IOCS might work in a microcomputer system, let us examine what takes place when a user issues the command

B:COBOL

to load the COBOL compiler from disk drive B into memory (see Fig. 9-7).

272

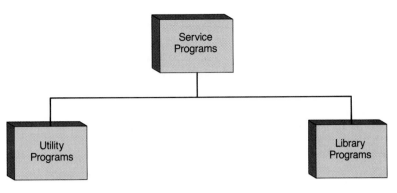

FIGURE 9-8
The principal service programs that make up an operating system.

Service Programs

Essentially, the two types of service programs, utility and library programs, perform a variety of labor-saving tasks and functions for the programmer (see Fig. 9-8). Whenever a specific task is required, the appropriate service program is accessed and executed by the operating system.

Utility Programs

DOS has utility commands

Utility programs give the user greater control over the computer system through efficient **file management.** For example, files can be easily prepared, copied, deleted, merged, sorted, and updated by using the appropriate utility program.

DOS Also has delete & copy (internal) Sort,

Library Program

The **library program** maintains a directory of frequently used software modules and their locations. These programs might consist of manufacturer-supplied or user-written routines or complete programs to compute mathematical functions, control input/output devices, maintain appointments, and so on. The library program makes these routines available when requested by the user, the operating system, or an application program. Many library programs maintain a multilevel directory where access to each level is restricted to certain individuals.

MAINFRAME OPERATING SYSTEMS

*Micros one thing happens at a time
Mainframe — Multiple computers working at same time.*

As mentioned earlier, since large computer systems can perform more functions, mainframe operating systems are larger and more complex than microcomputer systems. Large systems must be able to run several jobs concurrently. You will recall that **concurrent programming,** or **multiprogramming,** means that the computer has more than one activity in progress at any one time. In this way, two or more computer programs can be executed concurrently. While one program is being processed by the CPU, for example, another might be dumping its output to a printer (see Chapter 5).

Other functions normally performed by large operating systems include:

- Multiprocessing
- Time-sharing
- Remote-job entry (RJE)
- Virtual storage management

Mainframe operating systems, such as IBM's Multiple Virtual Storage and Virtual Machine, require the use of a complex Job Control Language to communicate with the CPU. With JCL a user identifies the function to be performed by the computer and describes its requirements to the operating system.

MICROCOMPUTER OPERATING SYSTEMS

Generally Speaking

In general microcomputer operating systems do not support all of the complex functions mentioned above, although a small but increasing number of these "small" systems can support many complex features. Small operating systems are typically **single-task,** that is, only one program can be run at a time. Accordingly, only one user is normally in command of the system at any given time.

Although microcomputer operating systems will run on many computer systems, they are usually **proprietary,** designed around a particular microprocessor or family of microprocessor chips.

As newer, faster, and more capable microprocessors are developed, existing operating systems are modified to take advantage of these features. Often the changes are so extensive that a completely new operating system is created. To make the transition as smooth as possible, new microprocessors within the same family will generally run the old operating system in **emulation mode** (using no new features) until an updated operating system can be developed.

In general, microprocessors not from the same family will require different operating systems. For example, users of Apple computers will use either the *Apple DOS* or *Pro DOS* operating systems.

Booting the Operating System

You will recall that the nucleus or kernel of the operating system must be in memory for the system to function. The remainder of the operating system resides in secondary storage until needed. But how does the kernel get into memory? It's not there when the system is turned on. A small routine stored in ROM, sometimes referred to as the **monitor,** is executed whenever the system is powered up. Whereas memory or RAM is volatile, that is, its contents are lost when power is removed, ROM (read only memory) is permanent; it does not lose its contents when power is turned off. The first function of the monitor is to check the computer's memory. Once memory is verified to be operational, the monitor accesses the first track of the **system disk** and loads a small portion of the operating system, known as the **boot,** into RAM. This program then pulls the remainder of the operating system kernel into RAM "by its bootstraps." This is known as **booting the system.** Once the operating system has been loaded into main memory, a system prompt, for example, *A>,* tells you that the system has been successfully loaded. At this point, you may enter system commands, key in a program, load or run programs, obtain a printout, or perform other functions. All the computer's resources are at your disposal (see Fig. 9-9).

DOS

With the development of the IBM PC, a new operating system was needed—one that would run with the 16-bit microprocessor used by the IBM PC. Commissioned by IBM, Bill Gates and others from Microsoft Corporation came up

274

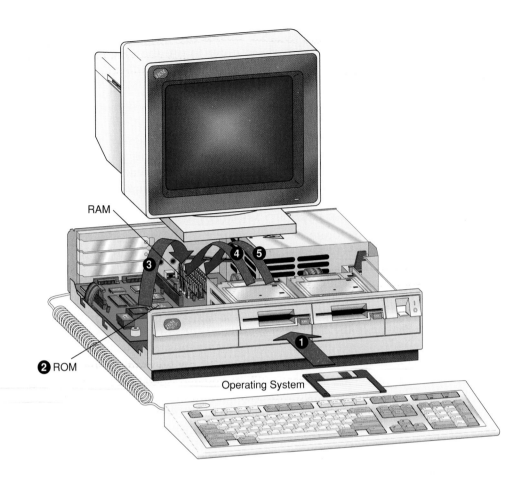

RAM

3

4 **5**

2 ROM

Operating System

1 The operating system disk is inserted and the system is turned on.

2 Control is given to the ROM-based monitor.

3 The monitor checks memory.

4 The monitor loads the boot into RAM.

5 The boot pulls the remainder of the operating system kernel into RAM.

6 The operating system awaits the user's commands.

FIGURE 9-9
Booting the operating system.

portable—meaning it could go on other computers.

with **PC DOS** (Personal Computer Disk Operating System) for the IBM PC. This was a proprietary operating system in that it used IBM's patented BIOS (Basic Input/Output System). Microsoft later developed **MS DOS** (Microsoft Disk Operating System), a portable version of PC DOS that would run on any 8086 family microprocessor. The two systems, virtually indistinguishable, have become industry standards for 16-bit machines. DOS is the most successful operating system in microcomputer history.

As new, improved microprocessors are developed, operating systems are accordingly updated to reflect the modifications and enhancements. These revised operating systems are labeled and identified by **version** number. IBM's PC DOS comes in many versions, the most recent versions being 3.3 and 4.0.

MS DOS and PC DOS are **command-driven**. A user must know what the various commands do in order to use the system. All of these programs use resident (called **internal**) commands and disk (known as **external**) commands.

How DOS Works

DOS consists of a series of programs designed to control the computer's resources and assist the user in running applications. It assists the user by performing services such as addressing and managing memory, managing files, and controlling input and output requests. Let's take a brief look at these services.

ADDRESSABILITY AND MEMORY MANAGEMENT. DOS uses a **memory manager** to locate each program it loads into RAM. The memory manager does little more than keep track of programs residing in up to 640 KB of RAM. Any additional memory management responsibilities are passed on to the application program that is being run.

FILE MANAGEMENT. DOS employs a hierarchical file system. The basic element of the system is the **file**. A file is DOS's eyes in an assembly of disk sectors having an eight character name and an optional three character extension. The **directory** contains the names of the stored files. Each disk, whether it is a floppy or hard disk, contains a root directory and may have subdirectories. Files located within subdirectories can be assessed by using a qualifier before the file name to describe the **path** to the file.

DOS's file management facility contains a series of commands that can be used to copy, rename, compare, or delete files from RAM or some external storage facility, such as a floppy disk.

INPUT AND OUTPUT CONTROL. The flow of data throughout the microcomputer system is controlled by the I/O facility of DOS. This facility, called BIOS in non-IBM computer systems as well as some IBM systems, is responsible for everything ranging from accepting data from the keyboard to storing data on disk. The IBM PS/2 Model 50Z and higher incorporate IBM's Micro Channel Architecture as its BIOS.

BOOTING UP AND RUNNING DOS. When you boot your computer system, the monitor verifies that all systems are go and then loads the DOS command processor, COMMAND.COM, and some hidden files into RAM. COMMAND.COM interprets and executes DOS file maintenance commands. Without it on your start-up, or boot disk, you cannot start DOS.

Finally, a special system configuration file (CONFIG.SYS) is read and interpreted and a DOS AUTOEXEC.BAT file is executed, if present on your boot disk. CONFIG.SYS is designed to customize your computer system to your needs, while AUTOEXEC.BAT contains a batch of commands designed to automatically execute as the system is booted. Hence the name AUTOEXEC.BAT.

Once your computer is started and DOS is resident in RAM, you are presented with the traditional **text-oriented** DOS user interface—the familiar A> prompt. From this prompt you can execute internal or external DOS commands or you can start an application. DOS offers no online help facility to which you can refer for assistance in performing any of its functions. In an ef-

276

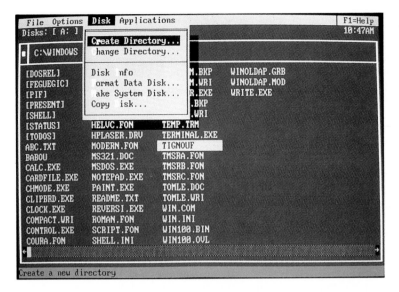

FIGURE 9-10
The DOS 4.0 Graphical User Interface (GUI).

fort to make DOS easier to use, DOS version 4.0 utilizes an **object-oriented** user interface. An object-oriented, or Graphical User Interface **(GUI)** utilizes graphic images, called **icons,** to assist the user in carrying out operating system services (see Fig. 9-10). For convenience, a **mouse** input device is used to select a service.

DOS internal commands utilize programs that are hard wired into the computer's circuitry as well as programs that are stored on disk. These programs provide DOS users with access to the DOS memory management facility. External commands, or utility programs as they are sometimes called, are general purpose file management commands. They provide the user with access to the DOS file management and memory management facilities.

When an application is started, DOS passes the task of memory management and I/O control to the application program. The application program alone must determine where information is to be stored and how the input/output devices are to be used. Thus, if an application fails or hangs up, the computer must be rebooted to put DOS back in control. Generally, there is no other way for DOS to regain control.

DOS Limitation

limited to 640k —this is a problem

1. DOS has limited addressability. That is, DOS can only address 1 megabyte of internal memory (actually 640 KB is RAM and the remainder is used by the system). Thus, DOS cannot run programs whose memory requirements exceed 640 KB. One reason for this is that the 8086 family of microprocessors do not provide DOS with any memory management help.

2. The DOS memory manager never manages memory. It passes the burden on to the application it is running. This means that the application, not DOS, owns memory. This factor severely inhibits the ability of DOS to run more than one application or program at a time, as the application currently running can use memory as it sees fit and not as the operating system directs.

3. DOS considers all addressable memory up to its 640 KB limit to be one block of memory. This space cannot be subdivided into independent segments, with each segment capable of running an application completely protected from applications running in other segments. Thus, if several small programs reside in RAM at a

given time, any one of them could cause the system to crash and terminate all other programs currently in RAM.

The 80286, 80386 and 80486 microprocessors can run in either of two modes; real or protect. In **real mode** the 80286/80386/80486 chip functions as an 8088/8086 in a 640-KB environment. In **protect mode** the 80286/80386/80486 supports the running of multiple applications, each being protected from the others. For example, an interrupt generated by an application in one protected area of RAM will not affect an application running in a different protected area of RAM.

DOS can only run the 80286/80386/80486 microprocessors in real mode. In real mode these microprocessors act like, or **emulate,** the 8088/8086 microprocessors, only they run much faster and they cannot offer protection to applications running concurrently.

4. DOS provides full I/O control to any application it runs. This means that an application will manipulate hardware without first consulting with DOS. For example, one could begin a printing process within an application, and in the middle of the printing decide to cancel the job. The DOS [Ctrl][Break] key sequence might not interrupt the printing as the application, not DOS, is controlling the printer. One would have to consult the documentation accompanying the software to determine the key sequence that must be used to stop printing. As long as only one program is running, the above scenario may not be a problem. However, when several applications are running, the direct I/O capabilities of applications run under DOS are problematic.

5. DOS does not provide for multitasking. That is, DOS does not permit two applications to run concurrently in memory, completely protected from each other. You can run a multitasking program such as **Microsoft** *Windows* in DOS. However, *Windows*, and not DOS, would have the multitasking responsibility. This difference affects the integrity of programs running concurrently under DOS.

GUI: HOW PCs AND USERS BECAME FRIENDS

There was a time when all that appeared on your PC screen when you turned it on was a lonely A or C prompt. There were no windows, boxes, arrows, garbage cans, mail trucks, or clipboards anywhere to be found. The screen was dark except for the letters and characters you typed in. An icon was something you thought you'd only find in church.

That was before the revolution.

It was a team of researchers at Xerox's Palo Alto Research Center-(PARC) in the mid-'70s that broke through. They focused on the ancient idea that icons or symbols could sometimes be used to represent information much more effectively than words. The team then developed a hardware/software package that included what is considered the first Graphical User Interface (GUI), which the team members called Xerox Star.

A few years later, in the early 1980s, when Steve Jobs and his team were working on the Macintosh at Apple Computer Inc., Jobs toured Xerox PARC and knew he had found the one thing that would set his new machine apart. A GUI would make the Macintosh the most user-friendly computer in history, slashing training time and easing the initial fears of most first-time users.

By 1987, Microsoft had decided it would bring a GUI to the most popular microcomputer operating system ever—DOS. It called its product Windows and incorporated some of the features of the original Xerox Star, which had by now become a *defacto* standard, thanks to the Mac. IBM and Microsoft also decided that the operating system for IBM's new line of PS/2 machines, called OS/2, would have a GUI as well. This would eventually become known as the Presentation Manager. Over time, the Presentation Manager would take on greater significance as the common user interface into IBM's Systems Application Architecture (SAA).

This year, the Graphical User Interface has been the hot topic, and executives are no longer embarrassed to be seen rolling a mouse or clicking a trash can to dispose of an unwanted file.

OS/2 makes IBM machines run faster. Does multitasking!

OS/2, Operating System 2, represents the latest example of systems software designed specifically to address the requirements of the microcomputer industry. Announced in 1987 as the joint development effort of IBM and Microsoft Inc., OS/2 was designed to harness the power of the Intel 80286/80386/80486 family of microprocessors. This family of microprocessors is used in the IBM PC AT, PS/2 Model 50, 60, 70 and 80, and IBM compatibles.

Why Is OS/2 Necessary?

To fully understand why OS/2 was developed, one must first understand some of the limitations of DOS. Most of the limitations of DOS stem from the way in which it uses the CPU. Regardless of whether an 80286/80386/80486 microprocessor is being used, DOS runs everything as if it were using an 8088 or 8086 microprocessor, only faster. For the last couple of years, users were satisfied to simply enjoy the increased speeds. Now, however, users are more sophisticated and want to utilize the heretofore untapped capabilities of the 80286/80386/80486 chips.

How OS/2 Works

From our previous discussion of DOS you should realize that DOS will not be able to handle your future needs or take advantage of the capabilities of the newer microprocessors. Fortunately, OS/2 should resolve these problems. Let's see how OS/2 works.

As we mentioned earlier, an operating system provides services to its users. Among the services offered by OS/2 are extended addressability, enhanced memory and file management features, complete control of input and output requests, and **multitasking** (running programs concurrently). Let's take a brief look at these services.

ADDRESSABILITY AND MEMORY MANAGEMENT. OS/2 provides significant memory management improvements over DOS. OS/2's memory management dynamically allocates and releases memory as needed, and collects fragmented memory as appropriate.

Programs run under OS/2 are not limited to 640 KB of memory, because OS/2 utilizes the capability of the 80286/80386/80486 chips to address 16 MB of RAM. Even the physical amount of RAM present poses no limit to OS/2 as its protect mode enables it to run applications requiring more memory then is physically present. This storage management technique is referred to as segment swapping.

Segment swapping allows OS/2 to run one or more programs in protect mode while exceeding the total physical memory of the system. This is similar to the virtual storage concept employed by many mainframe computer systems and, as with virtual storage, it is completely transparent to the user. However, the more physical memory the system has to run applications, the less segment swapping will be required, and the more improved the system performance will be.

Since the 80286/80386/80486 microprocessors can run in both real and protect modes, OS/2 must provide facilities for allocating memory to each mode. OS/2 does so in the following way. The lower order 640 KB, or less, of physical memory is allocated to DOS programs running in real mode. You can configure

OS/2 to allocate from 0 to 640 KB to real mode applications, and the remainder of physical memory to protect mode applications.

FILE MANAGEMENT. The OS/2 file system is very similar to that of DOS. One can expect compatibility between DOS and OS/2 with respect to the manner in which one names and locates files on various media.

OS/2 harnesses both the protect and real mode capabilities of the 80286/80386/80486 chip. Old DOS programs can only run in OS/2 real mode. DOS programs that run in OS/2 real mode behave as if they were running with an 8088/8086 microprocessor.

OS/2 designed software, on the other hand, can run only in protect mode. When using protect mode, OS/2 determines the memory requirements of the application, and then isolates that space from other applications which may also be running, thus virtually eliminating the possibility of a system crash resulting from a problem associated with a particular application program.

An interesting question arises regarding access to files in a multitasking environment. How does OS/2 handle a situation in which two different applications, running concurrently in OS/2, decide to request access to the same file? Well, OS/2's solution to this problem is to control file access. One way OS/2 accomplishes this is by providing **file sharing** and **record locking**—an ability to protect a record or portion of a file from access or alteration by other applications until released by the current application.

As with DOS, OS/2's file management facilities include commands specifically designed to provide you, or the application you are running, with the ability to copy, verify, or delete files from RAM or an external storage device.

INPUT AND OUTPUT CONTROL. Regardless of the command processor invoked, the commands executed, or the mode of execution, each computer system generally has only one keyboard, display, and printer with which to input and output data. When OS/2 is running multiple applications, these hardware devices must be managed carefully as only one application can be using a device at a given instant. OS/2 serves as controller, rather than consultant with respect to the way application software interacts with the computer hardware. This means that the application must consult with OS/2 before I/O privileges are granted. This procedure is essential to any operating system which can run multiple applications.

OS/2 accomplishes its hardware management tasks by reading or writing into buffers. When ready, OS/2 transfers the data from these buffers to the processor, display, or printer.

MULTIPROGRAMMING AND MULTITASKING. The **multiprogramming** feature of OS/2 allows a user to run several applications concurrently. For the most part, each application will appear to have the entire system unit to itself and may be designed in much the same manner as is done using DOS.

Multitasking means the sharing of the computer's resources among tasks. Each application program can create or control one or more tasks. The **foreground** application is the current user of the display, keyboard, or pointing device. A **background** application can be running or be suspended. Multitasking permits development of an application that starts one or more tasks and allows the operating system to manage the execution of these tasks.

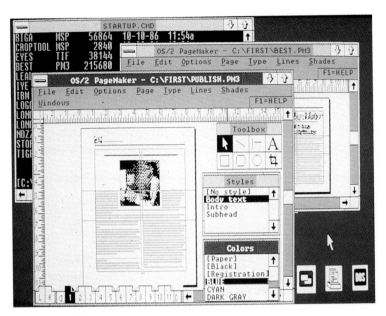

FIGURE 9-11
The OS/2 GUI utilizes windowing and icons.

BOOTING UP AND RUNNING OS/2. As with DOS, when you start your computer system using OS/2, it runs a start-up program or monitor. This program is stored in ROM and its task is to verify that all systems are go. If there are no error messages, the monitor loads the OS/2 command processor CMD.EXE and some necessary hidden files into RAM. Then a special system configuration file is read and interpreted, and the OS/2 batch file STARTUP.CMD is executed if present on the boot disk. The configuration file performs basically the same function as the DOS file CONFIG.SYS while the batch file STARTUP.CMD performs the same function as the DOS file AUTOEXEC.BAT.

Once booted, the OS/2 **Presentation Manager** appears. The Presentation Manager is the OS/2 GUI. It provides windowing and icons that make it easier for the user to select OS/2 service functions see Fig. 9-11.

Windowing allows multiple applications to be viewed by the end user at the same time. Each application can, in turn, support multiple windows, which are organized in a hierarchical parent-to-child basis. A child window is contained within its parent and lies on top of it. Windows can be scrolled, and window functions can be chosen using icon selection or a menu bar. A clipboard function enables the user or application to extract data from one window and move it to another window or from one application to another.

UNIX

Developed by AT&T's Bell Laboratories, the **UNIX** operating system was once only used on mini- and mainframe computers, but has now been adapted for microcomputers as well. UNIX is a portable, multitask, multiuser, layered operating system. The **kernel** interfaces directly with the computer's CPU and is modified to run on different CPUs and to alter hardware-related operations such as memory management.

Because UNIX is written in **C**, a high-level language, it is less hardware-dependent than operating systems written in lower-level machine language; this makes UNIX easy to transport from one system to another. Surrounding the kernel is the **shell**, which serves as a programming language and as a

Microsoft invented Windows called windowing.

IBMs version of windowing.

IBM does not still a mouse called a pointing device.

command language interpreter, reading lines typed in by the user and interpreting them as requests to execute certain programs. Around the shell are various **utilities,** such as text processing and support for the C, Ada, COBOL, and FORTRAN 77 languages (see Fig. 9-12).

The original text-oriented UNIX user interface is a shell and contains commands that have been criticized as being cryptic and thus difficult to remember. More user-friendly GUIs have been developed for use with UNIX by companies such as SUN Microsystems and NeXt Incorporated. This has led to an increased use of UNIX in business and education. Today we find business offices and educational research centers equipped with UNIX-based work stations, that is, one or more microcomputers containing a powerful microprocessor, much memory, and running under UNIX with a user-friendly GUI shell. The dollars spent on computer operating systems including mainframe, mini-, and microcomputers are phenomenal.

ZENIX

ZENIX, developed by MicroSoft, Inc., is an implementation of the UNIX operating system for microcomputers. This type of operating system is gaining rapid acceptance because of its multiprogramming capabilities, many useful utilities, and GUI.

Unix best for networks — multiuser type things.

FIGURE 9-12
A pictorial view of the UNIX layered operating system.

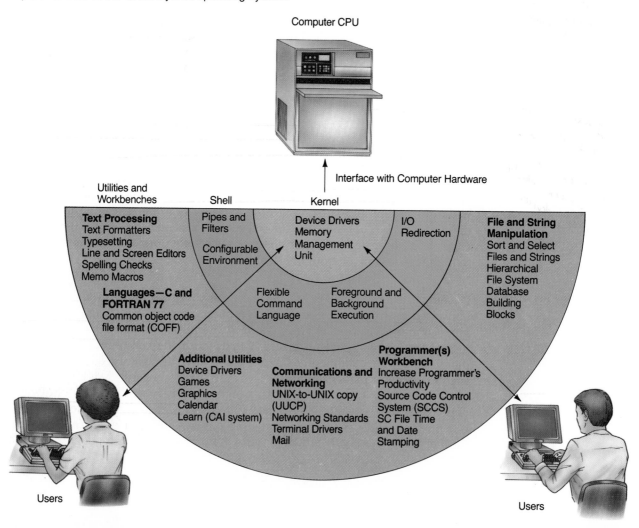

Computer CPU

Interface with Computer Hardware

Utilities and Workbenches   Shell   Kernel

Text Processing
Text Formatters
Typesetting
Line and Screen Editors
Spelling Checks
Memo Macros

Languages—C and FORTRAN 77
Common object code file format (COFF)

Pipes and Filters

Configurable Environment

Flexible Command Language

Device Drivers
Memory Management Unit

I/O Redirection

Foreground and Background Execution

File and String Manipulation
Sort and Select
Files and Strings
Hierarchical File System
Database Building Blocks

Additional Utilities
Device Drivers
Games
Graphics
Calendar
Learn (CAI system)

Communications and Networking
UNIX-to-UNIX copy (UUCP)
Networking Standards
Terminal Drivers
Mail

Programmer(s) Workbench
Increase Programmer's Productivity
Source Code Control System (SCCS)
SC File Time and Date Stamping

Users

Users

SOVIETS TRAIL IN THE COMPUTER RACE

How well is the Soviet Union coping with the computer revolution? Not only is the U.S.S.R. lagging behind the West in computers and their applications, but the gap is increasing. This is occurring despite enormous efforts by the Soviet government to meet the Western challenge in computers. Recently the Central Committee of the Communist Party of the Soviet Union issued several resolutions meant to accelerate computer development and initiate a massive effort to introduce mandatory computer education in Soviet elementary and secondary schools. Yet at the present time, the total number of personal computers in the Soviet Union is estimated by Western specialists as fewer than 10,000.

The Soviet computer campaign in education looks impressive at first glance, but its goal of having 1 million computers in the classroom by the mid-1990s seems decidedly modest when one realizes that there were more personal computers than that in American schools in 1985. And amazingly, not only is it impossible today for a Soviet private citizen to buy a personal computer in a local electronics store, but there seem to be no plans to open up the market to individuals (as opposed to institutions) in the foreseeable future.

Why are the Russians moving so slowly with personal computers? The answer is not primarily lack of technical ability (the Soviets are already producing acceptable microcomputers, such as Agat and the DVK) but political, social, and economic resistance. Soviet society is not receptive to personal computers. It is a society that has always prohibited the private possession of photocopiers and printing presses out of fear that they could be used to reproduce and circulate underground political documents; the specter of millions of personal computers and printers churning out uncontrollably large numbers of documents is truly frightening to Soviet political authorities.

But the desire to exercise censorship is only one of many reasons why personal computers are spreading slowly in Soviet society. In order to understand this resistance, one needs to compare the U.S.S.R. against factors in the United States that have used personal computers to proliferate here:

- A tradition of creating large amounts of reliable accurate data about the economy.
- Widespread education in business and technological skills, including typing and programming.
- Adequate phone lines that can be used for remote access.
- A tradition of entrepreneurship and innovation in which a person who develops a successful product can realize a profit from it.

- A decentralized economy in which new computer applications can "bubble up" from below.

The Soviet Union has major problems in every one of these areas. Because it has a tradition of prohibiting individual control over communication technologies, information is zealously guarded. It has a financial system that appears almost as if it had been designed to make personal computers unimportant for individuals: private investment is prohibited, so financial spreadsheets and access to stock market prices do not make sense.

The Soviet Union does not have an educational system that emphasizes business or "hands-on" technological skills, and typing is not widely taught in the Soviet high schools; Soviet college-level education is strong on the theoretical or mathematical side, but weak on the practical side. A "hacker culture" has been very slow to develop.

The Soviet telephone system is of such low quality that the attempts made so far to establish modern communication have had to rely on special lines on a "search" system by which only one out of 20 or 30 possible circuits is deemed good enough.

Finally, business entrepreneurship is prohibited in the Soviet Union, so hardware, software, and peripheral products exist only when the central authorities have authorized their production. Understandably, the central planning bodies are not omniscient and often fail to produce the galaxy of supporting technologies and supplies necessary for the rapid diffusion of computers.

Of course, there are many areas of the Soviet economy where computers are being used: economic planning, the military, and the space program. But most of these applications are best suited for mainframes.

The greatest weakness of the Soviet computer industry is on the lower end of the scale: individually controlled personal computers. But even when the Soviet Union produces personal computers, it places them under institutional controls. As a result, spontaneity and innovation are suppressed.

Unless the Soviet Union makes basic changes in its system of political and economic controls, it will not be able to participate fully in the personal computer revolution that is now sweeping Western countries. So far, the leaders have shown no signs of making the radical reforms that would be necessary to utilize personal computers effectively. Whether the Soviets can maintain their international status atop an already backward economy that falls increasingly behind a computer-dominated world is a profoundly troubling question for the rulers in Moscow.

Macintosh

Apple's Macintosh operating system is a *proprietary* system that incorporates an extremely user-friendly GUI. This system uses menus and icons rather than commands. Using a **mouse** input device, the user merely moves a pointer to a word or icon on the screen and presses a button on the mouse. A menu appears and more selections can be made. Thus it is not necessary to know commands. You simply have to select from a list of options that are presented at appropriate times in order to direct the computer's actions. The Macintosh operating system is slower than command-driven systems, but for many users, computing has never been so much fun.

The Macintosh was initially criticized for not being able to run DOS applications. This is one reason why it has not been accepted as a business computer. Today, a Macintosh can be purchased that will run DOS-based software, thus making it more appealing to industry. However, the graphics capabilities of the Mac, and not its ability to run DOS applications, have made it what it is today—the microcomputer specifically designed for publishing and computer assisted design.

Apples - first in schools not in business

SUMMARY AND GLOSSARY OF KEY TERMS

- **Applications programs** fulfill end-user needs, allow people to do things like make calculations, print out reports, or play games. **Systems programs** perform support functions and make the computer's **resources** available to application programs.

- An **operating system (OS)** is a collection of **systems programs** that control and coordinate the overall operation of a computer system. It acts as an interface between the hardware and the application programs. A small portion of the operating system, the **nucleus** or **kernel,** is resident in memory at all times to perform basic functions. The remainder of the operating system is stored on disk **(disk operating system, DOS)** or on tape **(tape operating system, TOS).**

- Some of the **functions** performed by an OS are: it provides human-computer interaction, boots the computer, schedules jobs, controls I/O operations, controls program execution, manages data and file storage, assigns different tasks to the CPU, and provides security and control.

- Two major categories of programs comprising a typical OS are control programs and service programs.

- **Control programs** permit user-computer communication, log jobs, and oversee the overall computer operation. Among the principal control programs, the **supervisor** controls the overall management of a computer system, is maintained in memory, and supervises the loading of other parts of the OS from secondary storage into memory; the **command processor** contains modules that handle user commands like COPY, LOAD and FORMAT; the **interrupt handler** processes all interrupts from I/O devices (a typical

mainframe system can handle dozens of programs and monitor many peripheral devices with the aid of interrupts); the **IOCS (input/output control system)** schedules and activates the proper I/O devices and monitors the operation of I/O devices.

- **Service programs** perform a variety of tasks and functions for the programmer. **Utility programs** provide **file management** tasks where files are easily prepared, copied, deleted, merged, sorted and updated; **library programs** maintain a directory of frequently used modules which can compute mathematical functions and control I/O devices.

- **Mainframe operating systems** are larger and more complex than micro systems. They provide for **concurrent programming** (two or more programs executed concurrently). Other functions performed by large operating systems: **multiprocessing, time-sharing, remote-job entry (RJE),** and **virtual storage management.**

- Microcomputer operating systems are typically **single-task**—only one program can be run at a time—and they are usually **proprietary,** i.e., designed around a particular microprocessor. New microprocessors will generally run the old OS (in the same family) in **emulation mode** (using no new features) until an updated OS can be developed.

- The **monitor** is a small program within a microcomputer OS that resides in ROM and is executed when the system is powered up; it checks memory and then accesses and loads part of the OS (known as the **boot**) residing on the **system disk.** The boot program then pulls the remainder of the operating system kernel into RAM—this is **booting the system.**

284

- **PC DOS (Personal Computer Disk Operating System)** is the proprietary operating system for the IBM PC microcomputer. **MS DOS (Microsoft Disk Operating System)** is a portable OS that runs on most other 8086 family microcomputers. These systems are **command-driven.**

- **OS/2** is designed to harness the power of the Intel 80286/80386/80486 family of microprocessors. It was developed out of a need to improve upon the limitations of DOS. OS/2 offers addressability beyond the 640-KB barrier, complete memory management, full I/O control, a **real** and **protect** mode of execution, and **multitasking.**

- The **real mode** of execution permits OS/2 to run DOS applications, while the **protect mode** is reserved for those applications designed to run under OS/2 only.

- OS/2 manages memory by employing a feature known as **segment swapping.** This feature permits OS/2 to run several programs in protect mode while exceeding the physical memory of the computer system.

- **Multitasking** means the sharing of computer resources among tasks. A task can run in the **foreground** or **background.** A task running in the foreground is the current user of the computer's facilities, while the background task can be running or suspended.

- The **UNIX** operating system developed by Bell Labs is a portable, multitask, multiuser operating system written in C. It is a layered system: the **kernel** interfaces directly with the CPU; the **shell** serves as a programming language and a command language interpreter; around the shell are various **utility programs** such as **text processors** and **support programs** for the languages C and FORTRAN.

- **ZENIX,** developed by MicroSoft, is an implementation of the UNIX operating system for *microcomputers.*

- The **Macintosh operating system,** from Apple, is a **proprietary** system that uses **menus, icons** and a **mouse.**

EXERCISES

True/False

_F_ 1. Systems programs fulfill end-user needs.

_F_ 2. DOS stands for direct operating system.

_T_ 3. A typical operating system can boot, or start the computer operating.

_T_ 4. The major operating system control program is commonly referred to as the supervisor.

_T_ 5. The command processor contains modules that handle user commands.

_F_ 6. Interrupt handling is not part of the operating system. *It is*

_F_ 7. IOCS stands for input/output command system. *control*

_T_ 8. Service programs perform tasks and functions for the programmer.

_T_ 9. Utility programs help the program through efficient file management.

_F_ 10. The library program consists of routines that cannot be accessed directly by the user.

_F_ 11. Small operating systems are generally single-task.

_T_ 12. Mainframe operating systems normally are capable of running several jobs concurrently.

_T_ 13. Concurrent programming is also referred to as multiprogramming.

_T_ 14. The large majority of microcomputer operating systems are single-task—only one program can be run at a time.

_F_ 15. Proprietary operating systems are designed to run on many computer systems.

_T_ 16. MS DOS is a portable operating system that runs on microprocessors in the Intel 8086 family.

_F_ 17. The monitor is stored in RAM. *ROM*

_F_ 18. The monitor will load a small portion of the OS, known as the shoe, into RAM. *boot*

_T_ 19. Since loading a program from disk requires that a disk be accessed, the IOCS is invoked when a load operation is requested.

#'s mean # of microchips (3) 486 best because faster

_F_ **20.** The first operating system developed for microcomputers was MS DOS.

_T_ **21.** GUIs are more user-friendly than text-oriented interfaces. *PC*

_T_ **22.** The IBM version of MS DOS is called PC DOS.

_F_ **23.** MS DOS and PC DOS are menu-driven operating systems. *command-driven*

_F_ **24.** Because UNIX is written in C, a high-level language, it is more hardware-dependent. *less*

_T_ **25.** UNIX is a layered OS consisting of a kernel, shell, and utilities.

_T_ **26.** ZENIX is an implementation of UNIX for microcomputers.

_F_ **27.** Apple's Macintosh operating system is a portable system.

_T_ **28.** Icons are small symbols on a screen that represent commands.

_T_ **29.** The Macintosh uses menus and icons.

_F_ **30.** The Macintosh is not very "user-friendly."

_F_ **31.** OS/2 can run on computer systems equipped with the Intel 8088 microprocessor.

_T_ **32.** Under DOS, the flow of data through a microcomputer system is controlled by the I/O facility.

_T_ **33.** DOS is unable to harness the protect mode of the Intel 80286 microprocessor. *p.278*

_F_ **34.** DOS applications can run in the protect mode only. *only real* / *real only*

_T_ **35.** OS/2 is capable of addressing up to 16 megabytes of memory.

_F_ **36.** No compatibility exists between OS/2 and DOS.

_T_ **37.** OS/2 serves as a controller, rather than a consultant with regard to the way applications software interacts with the computer hardware.

_T_ **38.** The sharing of computer resources among tasks is referred to as multitasking.

_T_ **39.** The OS/2 GUI is called the Presentation Manager. *true p.281 ?*

_T_ **40.** The Macintosh can now be equipped to run DOS applications.

Fill-in

1. A collection of systems programs that control and coordinate the overall operation of a computer system is known as a(n) _operating system_.

2. _Systems programs_ are programs that perform essential support functions and make the computer's resources available to application programs.

3. If an OS is stored on disk, it is known as a(n) _DOS (Disc Operating System)_

4. The two main categories of programs that comprise an operating system are _control_ and _service programs_

5. The _Supervisor_ is the major OS control program.

6. The control program that can accept, interpret, and carry out user commands is referred to as the _command processor_

7. The program that acknowledges and processes all interrupts to the system is known as the _interrupt handler_

8. The system that schedules and activates the appropriate I/O device and storage unit is the _input/output control system_

9. In a microcomputer system, the IOCS control program is referred to as the _Input/output control system_ *p.271 / not the one w/BIOS*

286   Unit 3 Applications and Systems Software

10. Basically, service programs perform a variety of tasks and functions for the _programmer_.

11. The _library program_ maintains a directory of frequently used routines and programs to compute mathematical functions, control I/O devices, and maintain appointments.

12. Language translators convert applications programs from _source language_ to _machine language_

13. Larger computer systems are typically capable of _concurrent programming_, that is, while one program is being processed by the CPU, another might be utilizing an input or output device.

14. A(n) _single-tasking_ OS is one that can run only one program at a time.

15. Microcomputer operating systems are usually _proprietary_ or designed for a specific microprocessor or family of microprocessors.

16. MS DOS is an example of a(n) _portable_ operating system because it can run on virtually any microprocessor in the Intel 8086 microprocessor family.

17. Newly developed microprocessors within the same family will generally run the old operating system in _emulation mode_, that is, using no new features.

p.284 18. A small routine, sometimes referred to as the monitor, is stored in _ROM_.

19. The _boot program_ pulls the remainder of the OS kernel into RAM "by its boot-straps."

20. DOS VERSION _4.0_ utilizes a GUI that is user-friendly.

21. The Presentation Manager is the GUI of _OS/2_.

22. An operating system used with 16-bit microprocessor computers is _MS DOS_.

23. Revised operating systems are labeled and identified by _version_ number.

24. PC DOS and MS DOS are _command_ driven operating systems.

25. UNIX is an OS written in the high-level language _C_.

26. UNIX is known as a(n) _layered_ OS consisting of a kernel, shell, and utilities.

27. _Zenix_ is an implementation of UNIX for microcomputers.

28. Macintosh is a user-friendly OS that uses _menus_ and _icons_.

29. OS/2 utilizes the _80286/80386_ _80486_ microprocessor family.

30. DOS programs run in real mode utilize the command processor _COMMAND.COM_

31. Some OS/2 commands will only run in _protect_ mode.

32. A(n) _background_ application can be running or be suspended.

33. The _multitasking_ feature of OS/2 allows a user to run several applications concurrently.

34. OS/2 accomplishes its hardware management tasks by reading or writing into _buffers_.

35. OS/2 is a natural extension of _DOS version_ 3.3

36. DOS can address up to _one megabyte_ of memory.

Projects

1. Visit a computer center in your school or some other facility. Name and classify the operating system used there and describe some of its functions.
2. Gain access to a microcomputer, boot the system with the system disk, and load and run a program of your choice. Describe as far as you can the actions of the operating system throughout this process.
3. Describe the relationship between Microsoft Windows and OS/2 Presentation Manager.
4. Bill Gates of Microsoft Corporation was instrumental in the development of MS DOS. Research Bill Gates and his many contributions in the area of computers.
5. The UNIX operating system was described in this chapter. Research and describe some of the applications for which UNIX is being used today.
6. Visit a computer store that sells the Macintosh computer. Become acquainted with this system by using some of the various menus and icons. Report your experiences.

CROSSWORD PUZZLE

Across

1. The kernel of an operating system
2. Language translators convert source language to _____ language
3. A microcomputer IOCS
4. Programs that permit user-computer communication, log jobs, and oversee the overall operation of a computer system
5. A portable version of PC DOS
6. Operating systems designed around a particular microprocessor
7. The part of an operating system that controls the overall management of the computer system
8. Not menu-driven but _____ -driven
9. Tasks in which files are prepared, copied, deleted, merged, and sorted are called _____ management tasks
10. An operating system that can be used with several microcomputer systems
11. Programs that perform support functions and make the computer's resources available
12. A program that pulls the remainder of the operating system kernel into RAM
13. Disk operating system
14. The boot of the operating system is loaded into this area when a computer is started

Down

15. Programs written to fulfill end-user needs
16. Convert applications source programs to machine language
17. Programs that provide file management tasks
18. A collection of systems programs that control and coordinate the overall operation of a computer system
19. A signal to the processor that an I/O operation is completed
20. I/O control system
21. An operating system consists of control and _____ programs
22. A small operating system routine stored in ROM and executed when the system is turned on

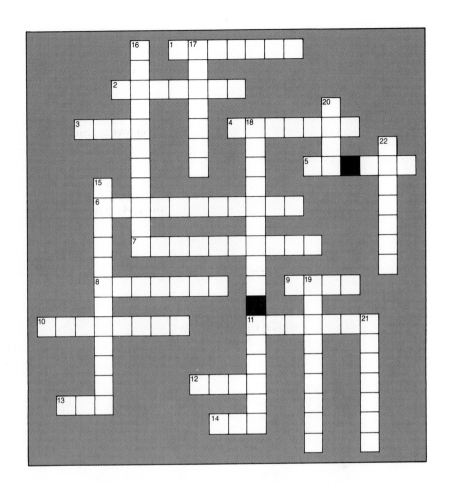

10

PROBLEM SOLVING WITH FLOWCHARTING
Designing a Solution

Objectives

- Describe a program flowchart.
- Read and understand a program flowchart.
- Describe the basic flowcharting techniques and use them in the development of program flowcharts.
- Understand and use decision tables.
- Describe top-down program design.
- Describe the types of HIPO charts.
- Identify the basic structures used in structured programming.
- Compare and contrast flowcharts with pseudocode.
- Understand and use the key terms presented in the chapter.

The accountant, business manager, and other computer users often rely on the programming department or outside consultants to solve their problems on a computer. Since these individuals must convey the nature of the problem to a programmer, it is essential that they have a basic understanding of the steps that a programmer must go through in order to produce a computerized solution to the problem.

PREPARATION FOR PROGRAMMING

You might think that a programmer simply has to look at a problem and can immediately begin to write the coded instructions that the computer must carry out to solve the problem. This is not the case. A considerable amount of preparation is necessary before a programmer actually begins to write the first instruction. The programmer must consider many areas and answer many questions about the nature of the problem. Some of these questions are as follows:

- What is to be output?
- What are the output media? *floppy disc*
- What input is needed to produce the results? *keyboard*
- Is this input already in a computer-acceptable form?

These questions are typical of some of the multitude of questions that the problem analyst must answer in preparing an application for a digital computer. The problem analyst must be able to see the problem both as a whole and as its component parts. In general, there are five steps that the problem analyst or programmer must consider in the course of developing a computerized solution to a problem:

- Analyze and define the problem.
- Devise an algorithm. *algorithm means a procedure*
- Code the program.
- Test and debug the program.
- Document and maintain the program.

Used in Bus. Comm.

In this chapter we shall consider the first two of these steps. We shall consider the remaining steps in Chapter 11.

ANALYZE AND DEFINE THE PROBLEM

The first step in the program development process is to determine what the problem is and to determine whether it can be solved by a computer. This process will generally involve an examination of current practices as well as meetings with those most closely involved with the problem.

Once defined, the problem should be carefully analyzed to ascertain whether or not writing a complete computer program is the most appropriate and efficient means of solving the problem. Often this analysis will reveal that the user's needs can be satisfied inexpensively by using one of the many available preprogrammed software packages. Some of these packages will be discussed in Chapters 12 and 13 and in the tutorials in the accompanying applications book.

Whether a software package is to be used or a complete program is to be written, we must analyze the source data, develop the procedures that will be needed to solve the problem, and determine the form of the final output. In the case of a simple payroll application, this analysis would reveal that the required input will include regular hours worked, overtime hours worked, and a disk file containing deductions, exemptions, and other data pertinent to payroll computations. It would also reveal that required outputs should include gross pay, withholding taxes, FICA deductions, accumulated tax-year withholdings and earnings, and, in addition, several detailed reports.

DEVISE AN ALGORITHM

Once the programmer understands the problem to be solved, a specific set of step-by-step procedures for the solution of the problem must be developed. These procedures are collectively referred to as an **algorithm.**

A simple algorithm would be needed to calculate total cost if both the unit cost and quantity were known. The algorithm would simply be

- Input the unit cost.
- Input the quantity.
- Multiply the unit cost by the quantity.
- Output the product or total cost.

A complex algorithm, such as the one needed to produce payroll checks and statements, would present problems to the programmer that a simple algorithm would not. There are many design aids available to assist the programmer in designing and documenting a complex algorithm. Some of the more common are:

- Flowchart
- Decision table
- HIPO charts
- Pseudocode

Let's begin by seeing how a flowchart can be used to help develop a step-by-step solution or algorithm.

FLOWCHARTING

The flowchart is a design aid used by problem analysts in the solution of computer related problems. It is a means of visually presenting the flow of data through an information processing system, the operations performed within the system, and the sequence in which they are performed. In general, two types of flowcharts are employed: the system flowchart and the program flowchart.

The **systems flowchart** visually describes the operations performed on

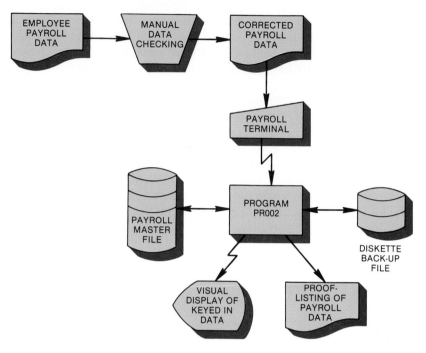

FIGURE 10-1
Simple systems flowchart.

data through all parts of a data processing system. The emphasis in a systems flowchart is on people, activities, documents, and media. It describes data sources, their form, and the stages through which they will be processed. Figure 10-1 illustrates a simple systems flowchart.

The **program flowchart,** on the other hand, is concerned with the individual steps necessary to implement a particular procedure or to solve a particular problem by computer. The program flowchart can be likened to the blueprint of a building. As a designer draws a blueprint before beginning construction on a building, so the programmer draws a flowchart before writing a computer program. Figure 10-2 illustrates a simple program flowchart.

Why Use Flowcharts?

Helps to keep people from going in circles

Flowcharts are generally useful at all stages of the problem-solving process. Initially, the system flowchart is used to describe the flow of data through the system. Thus an overall plan is devised that will utilize the available input data and produce the desired output. This flowchart can be used by programmers and nonprogrammers alike to illustrate the entire process graphically in a very concise manner. If one wishes to examine in detail how a particular process or procedure within the system flowchart is to be carried out by the computer, the program flowchart for that process or procedure could be analyzed.

A second reason for constructing a program flowchart before coding the program is that, because the flowchart is independent of any programming language, it allows the programmer to concentrate on the logical design of the program and not on the details of a programming language. Subsequently, the program flowchart can be extremely useful to the programmer as it is the basis from which the actual program code is developed. During the coding process, the programmer can concentrate his or her efforts toward expressing

294

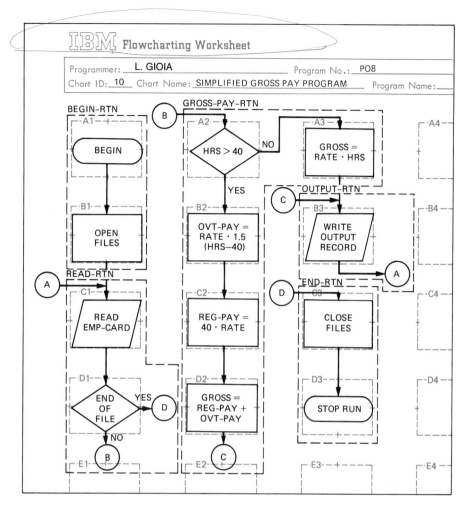

FIGURE 10-2
Simple program flowchart.

the logical steps contained in the flowchart in the appropriate programming language.

Finally, the program flowchart serves as documentation for the computer program. Often, the original programmer is unavailable when the time comes to update or modify a program. In such cases, it might be easier for the new programmer to understand the logic of the program by referring to the flowchart rather than to the actual program.

In the remainder of this chapter we will concern ourselves with program flowcharting techniques and procedures.

Flowcharting Symbols, Notes, and Flowlines

Earlier, we likened the flowchart to a blueprint. This analogy can be carried one step further. As in the case of drawing a blueprint, the flowchart must be drawn according to definite rules and utilize standard symbols adopted nationally by the **National Information Standards Organization (NISO),** formerly the **American National Standards Institute (ANSI),** and internationally by the **International Organization for Standardization (IOS).** The use of these standards

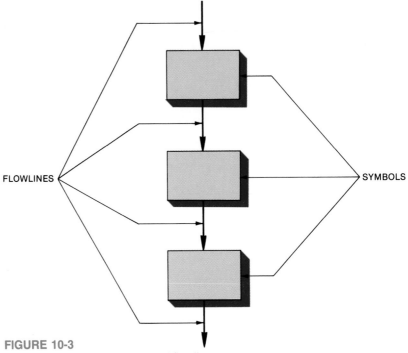

FIGURE 10-3
Standard flowchart symbols and flowlines.

is voluntary, but they have been so widely adopted that their use is recommended for all data processing personnel and others who have a need to prepare flowcharts.

To understand a flowchart, we must first understand the two basic parts of the flowchart—the flowchart symbols and the flowlines connecting these symbols (see Fig. 10-3).

Just as we read a printed page from top to bottom, we read a program flowchart in the same manner. Hence the direction of flow is from top to bottom.

Flowcharts are comprised of **flowchart symbols,** each representing a function in the program, each connected to the next in a downward direction by flowlines. Let us examine a typical flowchart, as illustrated in Figure 10-3. You will notice that the first and third symbols have the same shape and therefore represent the same function. Within a given function category, we can have several different operations. For example, within the input/output function category are such operations as reading a card, reading a tape, reading a disk, and printing a line. It is therefore necessary in a flowchart to show what specific operation is intended within a given function category. This is accomplished by means of a note within the flowchart symbol, where the symbol indicates the function and the note indicates the operation.

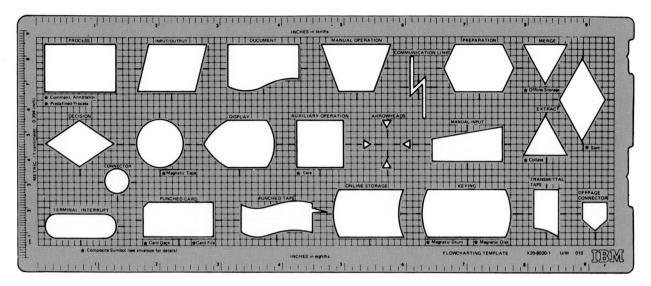

FIGURE 10-4
Program flowcharting template.

In the example, the parallelogram symbol indicates an input/output function, and the note READ EMP-NAME, HOURS-WKD, HOURLY-RATE indicates the specific operation intended by the programmer.

A **flowcharting template** is used to aid the programmer in drawing the flowchart symbols. It is a piece of transparent plastic with cutouts of various symbols. Figure 10-4 shows such a template. At this time we will discuss only the more commonly used program flowchart symbols.

Input/Output Symbol

Let us now examine in detail each of these symbols and the functions that they represent. To begin, we consider the input/output symbol:
This symbol is used whenever information is to be input to or output from the computer. The note within this symbol indicates the specific operation that is to be performed. In this case the operation is to PRINT EMP-NAME, GROSS-PAY.

Processing Symbol

The processing symbol represents another of the more commonly used flowchart symbols.

As its name implies, this symbol is used whenever data are to be manipulated or processed. The two general types of processing operations are arithmetic operations and data transfer operations.

An **arithmetic operation** could be an addition, subtraction, multiplication, division, exponentiation (raising a number to a power), or any combination of these. An example of a processing operation would be

GROSS-PAY =
HOURS-WKD*
HOURLY-RATE

This symbol and note indicate that two things are to take place. First, the values currently stored in the locations HOURS-WKD and HOURLY-RATE are to be multiplied together (the symbol * is used to represent multiplication), and second, it indicates that the result of this multiplication is to be stored in the location GROSS-PAY. It should be noted that in any processing operation the name appearing before the equal sign (=) is the name of the location into which the result of the operation is to be placed. Thus any value in the location GROSS-PAY before this multiplication is replaced by the product obtained from this multiplication.

A **data transfer operation** is, as its name implies, the transferring of an item of data. The item of data being transferred can be a constant or it can be a value previously stored in a particular location.

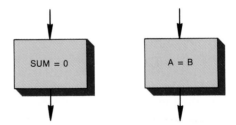

SUM = 0   A = B

In the processing operation shown at the left, the constant 0 is moved or transferred to the location named before the equal sign (SUM). Thus the value 0 is moved into the location SUM, replacing any value previously stored in SUM. In the processing operation shown at the right, the value stored in location B is transferred to and becomes the new value stored in A. Thus at the end of this data transfer operation, locations A and B contain the same value, the value that was in B prior to this operation.

Decision Symbol

The input/output and processing symbols can be used to represent many of the computer operations performed within a program. The remaining operations generally performed in a computer program are classified as logic operations and utilize a diamond-shaped symbol, which represents the logic function.

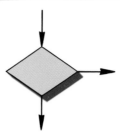

This function includes the operations required for decision making. Most common among these is determining the relationship between two data items (see Table 10-1). Is the first item greater than the second, equal to the second, or less than the second? In addition to determining the relationship between two items of data, this function symbol can be used to test for a particular condition. For example, it could be used to indicate a request for a decision from the computer concerning whether or not more data records are waiting to be read.

TABLE 10-1
Quantitative Relationships and Their
Symbolic Representations

SYMBOL	MEANING
$<$	Less than
$>$	Greater than
$\leq$	Less than or equal to
$\geq$	Greater than or equal to
$=$	Equal to
$\neq$	Not equal to

The purpose of any decision is to determine a future course of action. So it is with computers. For any decision there must be alternatives and a definite course of action for each alternative. The decision symbol is used to represent operations in which there are two possible alternatives for a given decision. To illustrate this type of operation, let us consider a hypothetical situation. Suppose we wish to determine whether the value stored in the location QUANT is equal to the value stored in another location, QUANT2. The possible results of such a decision are quite simple. If true, the two values are equal; if false, the two values are not equal. In a flowchart, this could appear as follows:

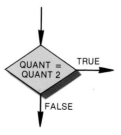

If the values stored in QUANT and QUANT2 are equal, the flow of the program would be into the decision symbol and out to the right along the flowline marked TRUE. If the values stored in QUANT and QUANT2 are not equal, the flow of the program would be into the decision symbol and out in a downward direction along the flowline marked FALSE.

The same decision could be symbolized in a slightly different way:

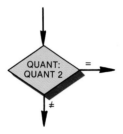

In this representation, the relationship between QUANT and QUANT2 is to be determined. If it is determined that the relationship is one of equality (QUANT = QUANT2), then the direction of flow is to the right:

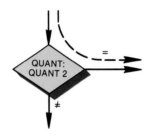

If it is determined that the relationship is one of inequality (QUANT ≠ QUANT2), then the direction of flow is downward:

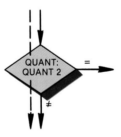

Connectors and the Terminal Symbol

The input/output, processing, and decision symbols are the primary flowchart symbols. The remaining symbols, which are shown in Figure 10-5, are equally essential, although less significant. **Connectors** are flowchart symbols that are used to connect remote portions of a flowchart with one another without using long or crossing lines and to avoid making a complex diagram into an unintelligible maze of flowlines and flowchart symbols. A common practice is to place a letter in each connector, the same letter being used at corresponding entrance and exit points. In Figure 10-6, for example, there are two connectors marked with an A. One of the connectors is an **entry connector;** the other is an **exit** or **branch connector.** For illustrative purposes, the direction of flow has been indicated by dashed lines.

300

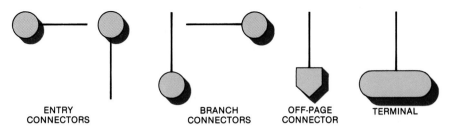

ENTRY
CONNECTORS

BRANCH
CONNECTORS

OFF-PAGE
CONNECTOR

TERMINAL

FIGURE 10-5
Connector and terminal symbols.

FIGURE 10-6
Interconnecting entry and branch connectors.

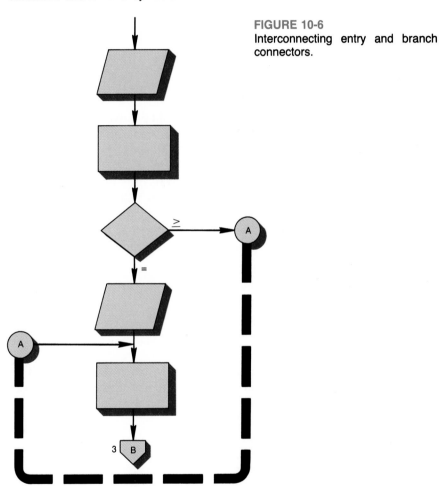

Quite often, however, the entry and branch connectors are not on the same page of the flowchart. In a case such as this, valuable time could be wasted while the flowchart reader searches through many pages attempting to locate the other half of the connector. To avoid this situation, special **off-page connectors** are used instead of the standard branch and entry connectors to indicate that the corresponding flowchart segments are contained on different pages and to indicate on what page(s) they are contained. In Figure 10-6, for example, connector B is an off-page connector, identified by its unique shape. The number 3 adjacent to the off-page connector symbol indicates that the corresponding entry off-page connector may be found on page 3 of the flowchart.

It should also be pointed out that there may be many standard or off-page branch connectors associated with one entry connector. That is, there can be many paths from which the entry connector might have come, but there can be *only one* entry connector containing a given letter within it.

The **terminal** symbol is used principally to indicate the starting and stopping of instruction execution in a program.

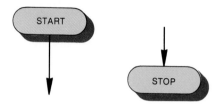

SAMPLE APPLICATION 1

Let us consider what would be involved in flowcharting a very simple problem. In this way we may verify and strengthen our understanding of the various flowchart symbols and notes.

Problem: Read two records into a computer. The first record will contain a unit price and the second will contain a quantity. Multiply these numbers, and print out the answer.

After briefly analyzing this problem you would probably reason out a plan of attack similar to the following:

1. Start the processing.
2. Read the unit price.
3. Read the quantity.
4. Multiply these numbers.
5. Print out the total cost.
6. Stop the processing.

Our next step would be to determine what kind of operation is being called for in each step and the appropriate flowchart symbol to be used. The result of this step is illustrated in Table 10-2.

TABLE 10-2
Stepwise Analysis of a Simple Program

STEP	TYPE OF OPERATION	SYMBOL
1. Start the processing	Terminal	
2. Read the unit price	Input/output	
3. Read the quantity	Input/output	
4. Multiply these numbers	Processing	
5. Print out the total cost	Input/output	
6. Stop the processing	Terminal	

Once we have the necessary flowchart symbols, we need to connect them with flowlines and insert appropriate notes. This would produce

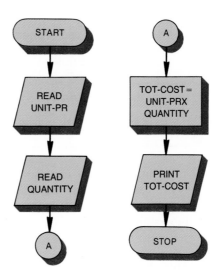

In most cases, however, it is not such a simple matter to determine a complete plan of attack as it was in this case. More often than not, the programmer cannot see a clear path to the solution and begins by attacking the problem one step at a time. Let us consider a second flowcharting problem, which is of this type.

SAMPLE APPLICATION 2

Consider the following hypothetical problem:

Problem: Read an unknown number of data records to be keyed into a terminal or read in from a file, one number or value per input record. Determine the average of these numbers and print it out.

As we have previously stated, most flowchart problems must be solved in a series of steps. Therefore, in solving this problem, we will proceed in small steps, each step refining, clarifying, and adding to the previous steps as a novice programmer might approach the problem. In this way the reader will be able to follow the thought process associated with the solution of this and other more complicated problems. As one develops more and more insight into the process of creating logical and efficient flowcharts, many of the developmental steps can be combined, if not skipped entirely.

As stated earlier, the terminal symbol is used to indicate the beginning of a flowchart. Therefore we have

The next step is not such a simple one. To determine it, we must examine our final objective and work backward toward our present position. This process,

TABLE 10-3
Flowchart Questions and Answers for Sample Application 2

QUESTION	ANSWER
What is our objective?	To develop an average of some numbers
How do I determine the average of these numbers?	Add them together and divide the sum by the number of numbers
How do I determine the value of these numbers?	Read them from a file or request the terminal operator to key them in

in its simplest form, consists of a series of questions and answers. For example, in our case these questions and answers might be those in Table 10-3.

This apparently trivial series of questions and answers leads us to our next step:

READ NUMBER

This would now give us the following cumulative flowchart:

Now we ask ourselves, Why did we read this item of data? As we see from Table 10-3, the answer is that we wished to obtain the total of the number just read and the numbers to be read subsequently. For illustrative purposes, let us call this total SUM, and the number read NUMBER. We can now begin to develop this total (SUM) by first including the number just read (NUMBER). This can be indicated with the following flowchart symbol and note:

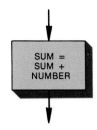

Let's examine this note carefully. To begin with, only the name of a single variable may appear at the left of the equal. This variable is the name of the location into which the result of the operation will be placed. The expression that appears at the right of the equal can be a single constant or variable (in a data transfer operation) or an arithmetic expression involving several constants and/or variables (in an arithmetic operation). In the case of a data transfer operation, the value of the constant or variable at the right of the equal is simply moved or transferred to the location specified at the left of the equal.

304

In the case of an arithmetic operation, the operation is performed on the variables and/or constants as indicated, and the result is moved or transferred to the location specified at the left of the equal. In our example, first the computer is directed to add the **present values** of SUM and NUMBER together. Because this completes the operations specified in the arithmetic expression, the result is stored in the location named to the left of the equal, in this case the location SUM. Thus the previous value stored in SUM has now been replaced by the result of the arithmetic operation. We could describe this entire operation in words as follows:

The new value of SUM is equal to the present value of SUM
plus the present value of NUMBER.

To illustrate this, let us assume that prior to this step the locations SUM and NUMBER contained the values 8 and 7, respectively. Then after this operation, SUM will contain the new value 15 and NUMBER will still contain the number 7. Thus,

$$SUM = SUM + NUMBER$$
$$15 = 8 + 7$$

In our flowcharting problem, however, we do not have a previous value for SUM, although you may have assumed it to be 0. Assuming it to be 0 is not sufficient.

Situations such as this require **initialization** and are quite common in programming. They are generally identifiable by the fact that the same variable appears on both sides of the equal sign. In our case, the variable SUM appears on both sides of the equal sign. When this occurs, it means that the value of the variable after the step will depend on the value of the variable before the step. Thus, to make certain that there is a value of the variable before the step, it must be initialized to whatever value is appropriate to the problem at hand. In our case, we should initialize SUM to 0. Incorporating this step into our cumulative flowchart will then give us the following:

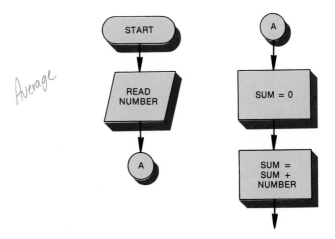

What shall we do next? To answer this we go back to our questions and answers (Table 10-3). Here we see that we wish to obtain a total of the numbers read in. Therefore we must read the next number and add this number to our total. That is, we must first read the number:

Because we no longer need the number read previously, we can store this new number in the same location, NUMBER. When a second number is stored in a location already occupied, the previous contents are replaced by the new contents. Therefore, in our case, the data name NUMBER would now contain the value of the second number read.

Proceeding to add this number to our existing subtotal SUM, we would have

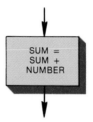

Our cumulative flowchart would appear as

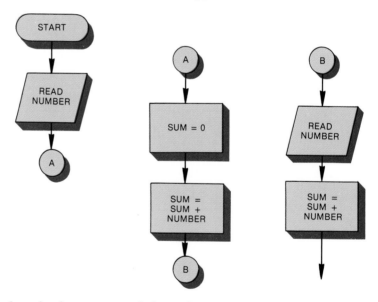

Notice that the last two symbols and notes are identical to two previously used symbols and notes. The only difference is that the previous symbols were separated by the symbol and note:

306

By simply moving this symbol and note up in our flowchart, we now have two identical flowchart sequences, one after the other.

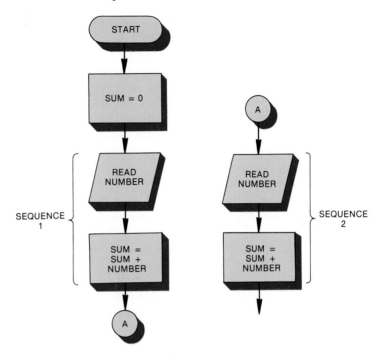

However, there is a more efficient way of indicating that a process repeats itself in a flowchart without including the flowchart of the process several times. This is done by creating a **loop,** which is a sequence of instructions that is executed repeatedly until a terminal condition prevails. In our case this loop requires the use of the CONNECTOR symbol and appears as follows.

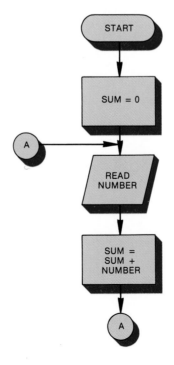

307

We must now determine a way to exit from this loop at the appropriate time. To do this, we must first determine the circumstances under which we would desire to exit from the loop. Because this loop accomplishes the reading of numbers and the accumulating of these numbers, it would be reasonable to assume that we would desire to exit from this loop *after* the last number has been read and added to SUM. But how are we going to determine whether the last number has been read? There are two commonly accepted techniques.

One way to know that the last number has been read is by a signal from the computer system that an end of data has been reached. However, this capability is not available with all computer systems or under all circumstances. In particular, if a user is keying in the data as the program requires, the computer system would not generate such a signal, as there would be no way for the system to know that there is no more input. In this case, the user would have to indicate to the program that there is no more input. This is generally accomplished by the user entering a unique data code that can be tested for in the program. Thus each time a data item is input, the program would test it to determine if it is a data item to be processed or the unique data code indicating the end of the data. This special last data record serves only to indicate an end-of-data condition and is referred to as a **trailer** record.

You must exercise caution when employing this technique. First, you must make certain that this code is truly unique. That is, you must be certain that this code could not possibly occur in the data to be processed. Second, you should test for this code immediately after the read statement. This will ensure an immediate exit from the loop and eliminate the possibility that the special code might be added to the SUM or otherwise processed as valid data.

In our case, let us assume that the number -9999999 is not possible as a valid value for NUMBER. Therefore it could be used as an end-of-data code. That is, immediately after a number is read, it would be compared to -9999999. If NUMBER is equal to -9999999, the program will branch out of the loop; otherwise, NUMBER will be processed. Incorporating this into our flowchart, we have

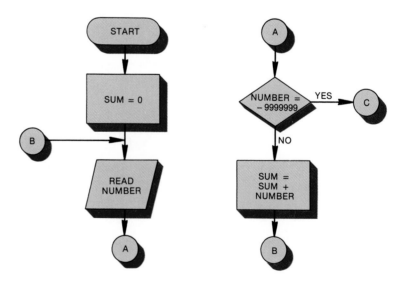

After careful examination of this flowchart, you will see that the only way the loop can be broken is if all the numbers have been read and accumulated—exactly what we wish to accomplish.

Proceeding, we must determine our next step. Again, we go back to our questions and answers (Table 10-3). Here we see that we wish to determine an average of the numbers input. Because we now have SUM, which is the total of the numbers input, we need only divide SUM by the number of numbers input. Therefore, as the number of numbers was not given, we must determine a means of obtaining this value. The simplest way to do this is to instruct the computer to *count* them as they are read. That is, we must **establish a counter** and add 1 to it each time a number is read. Let us call this counter N. Then each time a number is read, we can increment, or add 1 to, N.

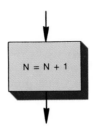

As we found it necessary in the case of SUM to assign an initial value, we must also assign an initial value to N. An appropriate initial value would be 0, because we want our counter to be set to 0 initially. In the cumulative flowchart, this would appear as follows:

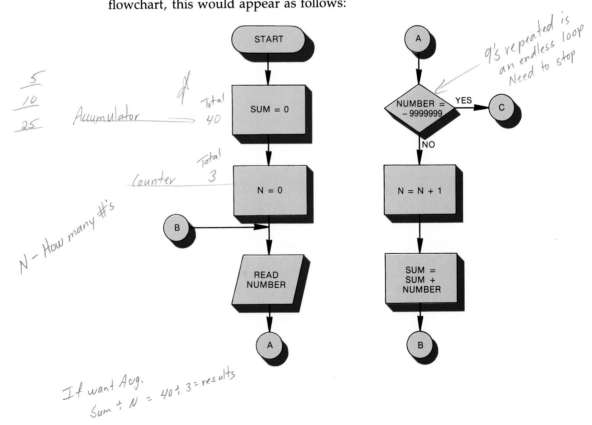

Now that we have the sum of the numbers (SUM) and the number of numbers read (N), we are able to compute the average of the numbers read. We call this quantity AVERAGE. This operation will take place after exiting from the reading loop and would appear as

It is not necessary to assign an initial value to AVERAGE because we are assigning it the value resulting from the division of SUM by N and not relying on its having or assuming it to have any specific previous value.

It now only remains for us to print out this result and terminate the program. Incorporating these steps into our cumulative flowchart, we have Figure 10-7. In the course of developing this flowchart we have encountered four major flowcharting techniques: looping, initializing, developing a sum, and developing a counter. One or more of these techniques will be used in just about every flowchart you will ever write. The importance of the flowchart as a means of documenting a program and for developing the logic of a program cannot be overemphasized.

DECISION TABLES

The **decision table** is a tool of the programmer or systems analyst and can be used either as a substitute for the flowchart or to supplement the flowchart. It affords the programmer-analyst a convenient means of recording, in tabular form, the various conditions and possible courses of action when the solution to a problem involves substantial logical decisions. The decision table separates

COMPUTERS FOR FUN AND PROFIT

Have you ever wondered how you would go about writing a video game or business program for profit? Well, you could begin by picking up a copy of *Software Writer's Market* by Kern Publications to get an idea of what people are looking for and to learn how to sell your product. If going it alone is not your cup of tea, you can sign up as an author for one of the large software or publishing houses and get a small piece of the action through royalties. The stories of people making six figures from a simple program are true, but the lucky ones are very, very few. On the average,

software authors make about $9,000 a year. To make matters worse, some writers have had a program turned down only to find that a software house improved on the idea and sold it at a tremendous profit.

Space War, the first computer game, was developed by Nolan Bushnell and a few other MIT students. Nolan redesigned the game and sold it to Bill Nutting Associates—it resurfaced as the popular arcade game *Computer Wars*. Bushnell's profit? Only $500 in royalties. But you can't keep a good man down—with his $500, Bushnell started Atari Corporation.

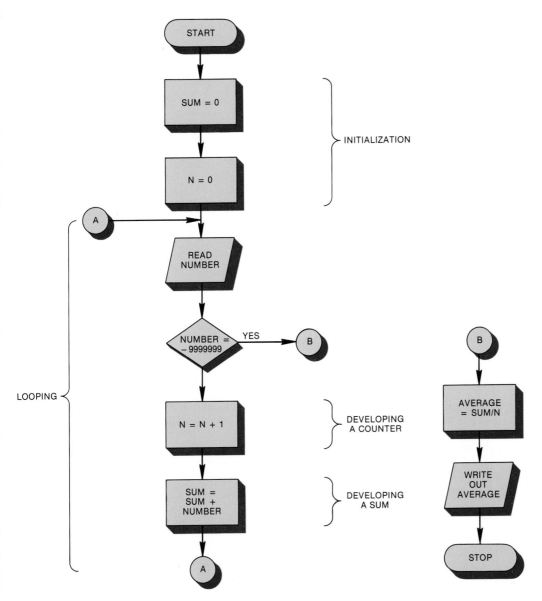

FIGURE 10-7
Completed flowchart of sample application 2 illustrating the four major flowcharting techniques.

the conditions from the courses of action and establishes a relationship between specific conditions and appropriate courses of action.

As illustrated in Figure 10-8, the decision table physically resembles a rectangle that has been divided into six parts by a series of horizontal and vertical lines. To explain the use of each of these segments, we will discuss each segment in a general way and then apply the discussion to the following problem: We wish to construct a decision table that will enumerate the conditions under which a credit sale will be accepted or rejected. The conditions are as

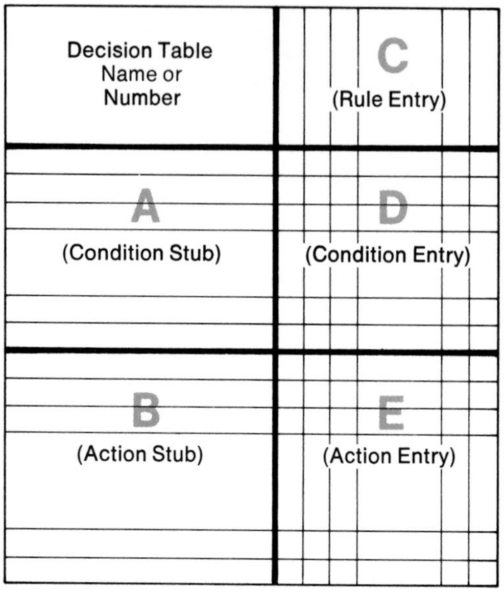

Decision Table Name or Number	C (Rule Entry)	
A (Condition Stub)	**D** (Condition Entry)	
B (Action Stub)	**E** (Action Entry)	

FIGURE 10-8
Physical layout of decision table.

follows:

1. If a customer has a charge account with the store and also has a satisfactory credit rating, allow the credit purchase.
2. If a customer has a charge account with the store but has an unsatisfactory credit rating, allow the credit purchase only if special management approval has been given.
3. Reject the credit purchase in all other cases.

Block A (condition stub) is to contain the possible conditions that exist in the problem, one condition per row with each condition being answerable with a simple *yes* (Y) or *no* (N) answer. In our sample problem, there are three separate conditions. These are concerned with the following:

1. The existence of a charge account
2. The customer's credit rating
3. Special management approval

Stating these conditions in such a way as to allow them to be answered by a simple yes or no answer and placing them in block A, we have

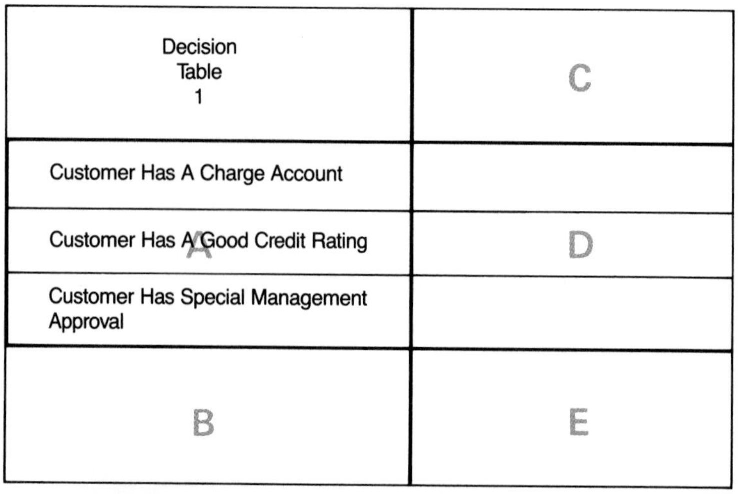

Decision Table 1	C
Customer Has A Charge Account	
Customer Has A Good Credit Rating	D
Customer Has Special Management Approval	
B	E

Block B contains the possible courses of action. In our sample problem, there are two courses of action: Allow the credit purchase *or* refuse the credit purchase.

Blocks C, D, and E are completed together. Each column contains a C, D, and E section and contains a specific combination of conditions (D) and action (E) and a name (C).

Decision Table 1	C
Customer Has A Charge Account	
Customer Has A Good Credit Rating	D
Customer Has Special Management Approval	
Accept Credit Purchase	
Refuse Credit Purchase	E

In our problem, there are four possible combinations of conditions for which action is to be taken (see Fig. 10-9).

Reading a decision table is simply a matter of reading each rule or action column to determine what combination of conditions suggests what action.

It is also possible to construct a decision table involving conditions where the response can be less than ($<$), equal to ($=$), greater than ($>$), less than or equal to ($\leq$), greater than or equal to ($\geq$), or not equal to ($\neq$) instead of a simple yes or no response. For example, suppose that we wished to determine what letter grade a student should receive for a course, given his or her numerical average in the course. A possible decision table and program flowchart are given in Figure 10-10.

TOP-DOWN PROGRAM DESIGN

For many years data processing personnel have been searching for more efficient program design techniques. For many, the methods used in writing a program were relatively unimportant; only the results were important. The programming process was considered an individual art rather than a carefully designed and structured practice. This attitude resulted in programs that were difficult to follow and often impossible to modify or update. To cope with this problem, MCAUTO[*] established a pilot task force to determine how and to what extent it could utilize some of the newer and improved programming techniques that were being developed. One of the conclusions reached by this group was that one of the new program design and coding techniques—**top-down program design**—seemed to offer the greatest potential. It has the following advantages:

[*]The McDonnell Douglas Automation Company, a division of the McDonnell Douglas Corporation.

FIGURE 10-9
Conditions and corresponding actions.

Rule	Condition	Action
1	Customer has a charge account and satisfactory credit.	Accept order
2	Customer has a charge account and unsatisfactory credit rating with special management approval for the purchases.	Accept order
3	Customer has a charge account and unsatisfactory credit rating with no special management approval for the purchase.	Reject order
4	Customer has no charge account with store.	Reject order

Placing these into our decision table, we have:

Decision Table 1	Rule 1	Rule 2	Rule 3	Rule 4
Customer has a charge account	Y	Y	Y	N
Customer has a good credit rating	Y	N	N	
Customer has special management approval		Y	N	
Accept order	X	X		
Reject order			X	X

- Improved program design
- Reduced program complexity
- Increased programmer efficiency

The top-down program design process utilizes two techniques: hierarchy plus input-process-output (HIPO) and structured programming.

Hierarchy Plus Input-Process-Output (HIPO)

HIPO, originally designed as a documentation tool, has become an invaluable aid in program design as well. The major objectives of HIPO as a design and documentation tool are as follows:

1. State the functions to be accomplished by the program.
2. Provide an overall structure or hierarchy by which the individual functions of the program or system can be understood.
3. Provide a visual description of the input to be used and the output produced by each function.

To accomplish these ends, HIPO utilizes two types of charts: a **hierarchy chart** and an **input-process-output chart.** The hierarchy chart pictorially illustrates how each program function is divided into subfunctions or modules, and the

Decision Table 3	Rule 1	Rule 2	Rule 3	Rule 4	Rule 5
GRADE: 90	≥	<			
GRADE: 80		≥	<		
GRADE: 70			≥	<	
GRADE: 60				≥	<
LETTER GRADE = 'A'	X				
LETTER GRADE = 'B'		X			
LETTER GRADE = 'C'			X		
LETTER GRADE = 'D'				X	
LETTER GRADE = 'F'					X

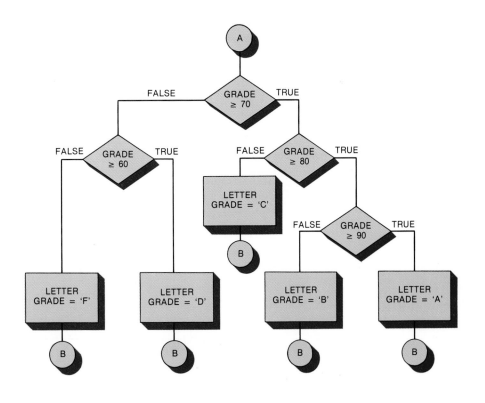

FIGURE 10-10
Decision table and flowchart for determining a student's letter grade from a numerical average.

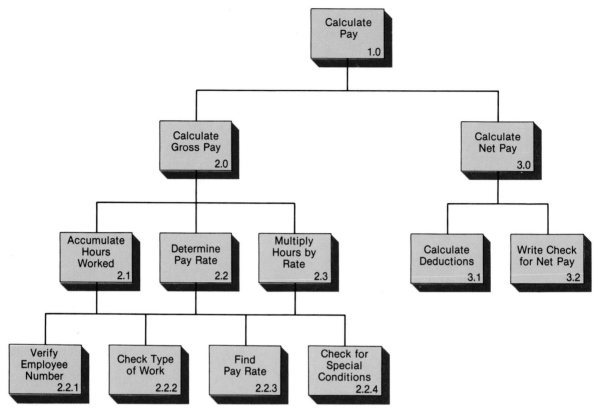

FIGURE 10-11
Example of a HIPO hierarchy chart.

FIGURE 10-12
Example of a HIPO input-process-output chart.

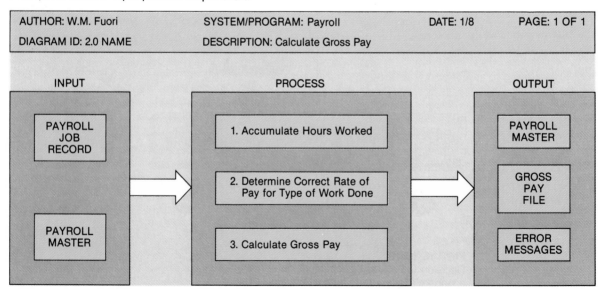

input-process-output chart expresses each module in the hierarchy in terms of its input and output considerations. Examples of these charts are shown in Figures 10-11 and 10-12.

HIPO diagrams are constantly being refined as program development continues. The initial emphasis is on ensuring that program functions are clearly understood by both the designers and users so that the resulting program will meet the needs for which it is being designed. The major functions of the program are listed at the top level and expanded to lower-level modules as more detail is required.

During this process, certain basic guidelines should be observed. All modules in the hierarchy chart should relate to one another logically, with control passing from the top module down to the next lower module, and so on. Each module in the hierarchy chart should represent only one program function and contain a single entry and a single exit. The function of each module should be specific enough so that it can be implemented with a minimum of one page or approximately 50 lines of coding. This will greatly enhance the readability of the code and simplify the testing and debugging of the module.

Once the hierarchy and input-process-output charts have been completed, the detailed program design can commence. This can be accomplished with the aid of a program flowchart or pseudocode (discussed later in this chapter).

Modules should be programmed in the same order in which they appear in the hierarchy chart. The upper-level modules should be coded and tested before the coding of the next lower level is begun. When a module is tested, some provision must be made for the fact that it will generally call or reference a module lower in the hierarchy chart, which has not yet been coded. In Figure 10-11, for example, if we were to test module 2.2 (Determine Pay Rate), it would call modules 2.2.1 through 2.2.4. As these modules would not have been coded, we would have had to replace them temporarily with "dummy" modules in order to complete the testing of module 2.2. Dummy module 2.2.3, for example, would simply return some arbitrary pay rate and control back to module 2.2.

In this manner, each level of modules is tested and debugged before the next lower level is coded. As subsequent levels are tested, the upper levels are retested until finally, when the lowest level is tested, the whole program is actually being tested.

Structured Programming

Structured programming is defined in many different ways by many people. There is general agreement, however, on its purpose and its impact.

Its purpose is to produce programs that have a definite form and are therefore more easily understood by the programmer and by anyone else who needs to read and understand them. A program written with structured programming techniques is more likely to be *correct* than was possible with previous methods.

The impact of structured programming is evident in the amount of discussion and the number of articles and books about the subject and, more important to those about to study it, in the widespread adoption of structured programming by the data processing and business communities.

A key characteristic of a structured program is that it is written using only three basic control structures: SEQUENCE, IF-THEN-ELSE, and DO-WHILE. These structures lend themselves to top-down program design, as each allows for a single entry point and a single exit. And, because control flows from the top down, structure by structure, the logic of the program can be understood easily.

The term **SEQUENCE structure** is used to describe program routines that are executed sequentially, one after the other. The following diagram illustrates a SEQUENCE structure, as routine A must be executed before routine B, and no other routine can be executed between them:

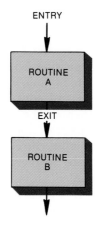

The **IF-THEN-ELSE structure** allows a program to branch to one of two routines on the basis of a condition that can be either true or false. This structure is graphically represented as follows:

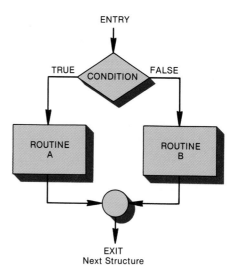

IF the condition is true, THEN routine A will be executed; ELSE routine B will be executed. Routines A and B do not necessarily have a SEQUENCE structure; they may have any of the three possible structures (SEQUENCE, IF-THEN-ELSE, or DO-WHILE). On completion of the IF-THEN-ELSE sequence, program execution will proceed to the next structure. If either the A or the B routine is not needed, the IF-THEN-ELSE structure will reduce the following:

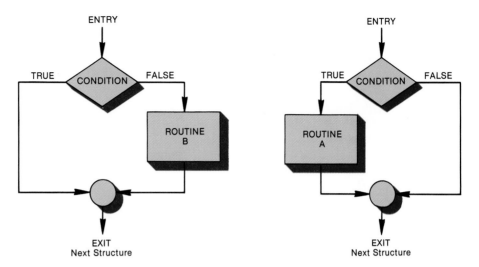

The **DO-WHILE structure** is used to describe the repetition of an action under prescribed conditions. This is commonly referred to as **looping** and is graphically illustrated as follows:

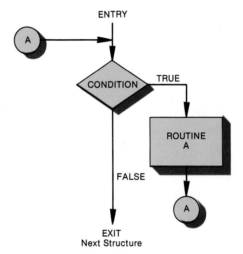

In this structure the program sequence is to DO routine A WHILE the condition is true. If the condition is false, control proceeds to the next structure. If the condition being tested is false when this structure is entered, routine A will not be executed even once. An accepted variation of this structure, referred to as the **DO-UNTIL structure,** is illustrated as follows:

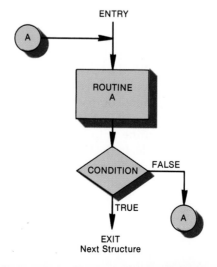

319

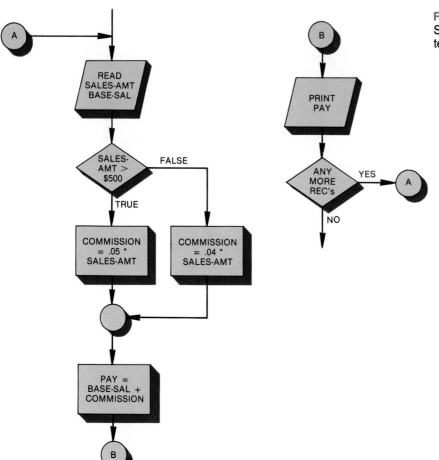

In this structure, the program sequence is to DO routine A UNTIL the condition is true. In this structure, routine A will always be processed at least once.

Figure 10-13 illustrates a segment of a structured program to determine a salesperson's pay.

In actual practice, many of these structures will be combined. Figure 10-14, for example, illustrates a sequence in which an IF-THEN-ELSE is controlled by a DO-WHILE. Figure 10-15 shows a SEQUENCE and DO-WHILE being controlled by an IF-THEN-ELSE.

Although these structures may, at first glance, appear to be somewhat limited, they can be utilized in various combinations to solve any programmable problem.

In addition to the preceding three basic structures, some analysts utilize an additional structure referred to as the **CASE structure.** This structure is not considered a basic structure since it can be formed from a series of IF structures. The principal reason for using the CASE structure is that it is often clearer and more compact than a series of IF structures.

The CASE structure is used in those situations where a different procedure or routine is to be performed, depending on the **integral value** of a specified variable. In the CASE structure illustrated below, if the specified variable contains the value 1, routine 1 will be performed, if the specified variable contains the value 2, routine 2 will be performed, and so on.

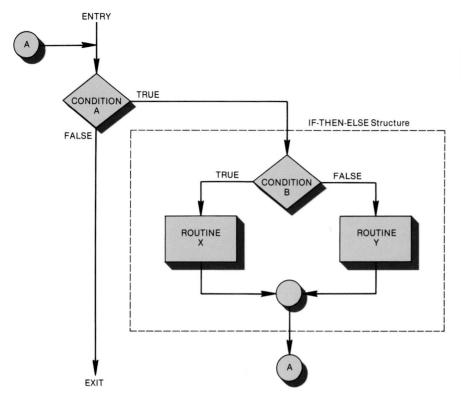

FIGURE 10-14
Example of an IF-THEN-ELSE controlled by a DO-WHILE.

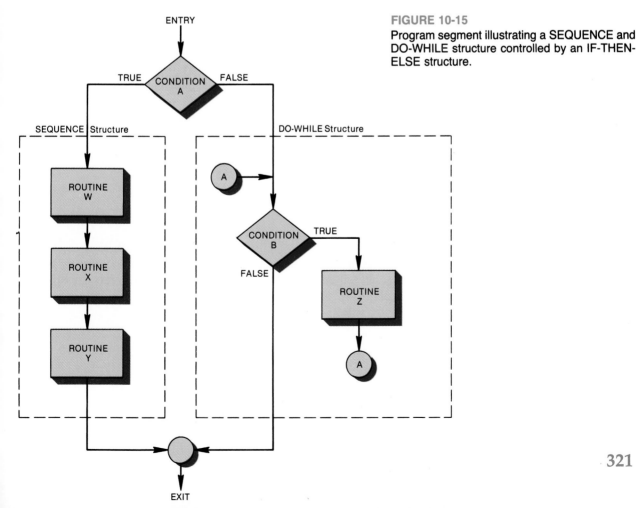

FIGURE 10-15
Program segment illustrating a SEQUENCE and DO-WHILE structure controlled by an IF-THEN-ELSE structure.

321

CASE Structure

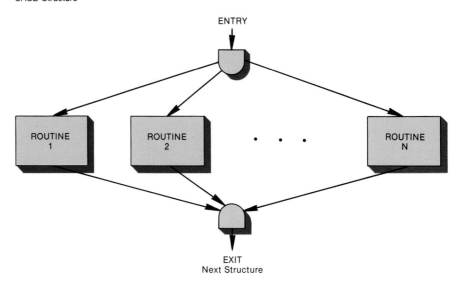

Pseudocode

Pseudocode, as its name implies, is an imitation computer code. It is used in place of symbols or a flowchart to describe the logic of a program. Pseudocode is intended to overcome the two principal disadvantages of the flowchart: The flowchart is time-consuming to create and is difficult to modify without redrawing it completely. Also, pseudocode is easier to use since it is more like English.

Pseudocode employs the basic structures utilized in structured programming (SEQUENCE, IF-THEN-ELSE, and DO-WHILE or DO-UNTIL). Figure 10-16 illustrates how these basic structures would appear in pseudocode. You will recall that these structures were used in the flowchart of a program segment to determine a salesperson's total pay based on base pay plus commission (see Fig. 10-13). The pseudocode equivalent of this flowchart would be

```
DO While there are more records
    IF sales exceed $500.00 calculate commission at 5% of sales
    ELSE calculate commission at 4% of sales
    ENDIF
    Add commission to base salary to find pay
    Write pay report
ENDDO
```

Programmers and systems analysts still disagree on whether they prefer the program flowchart or pseudocode. Both techniques are currently in use. Only the future will tell which technique, if any, will gain universal acceptance. Which do *you* prefer?

SEQUENCE Structure

FLOWCHART

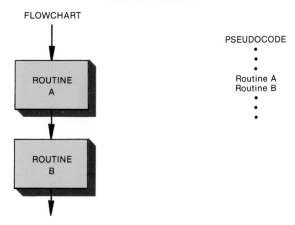

PSEUDOCODE
•
•
Routine A
Routine B
•
•
•

IF-THEN-ELSE Structure

FLOWCHART

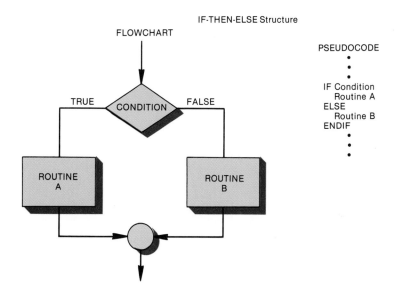

PSEUDOCODE
•
•
•
IF Condition
    Routine A
ELSE
    Routine B
ENDIF
•
•
•

DO-WHILE Structure

FLOWCHART

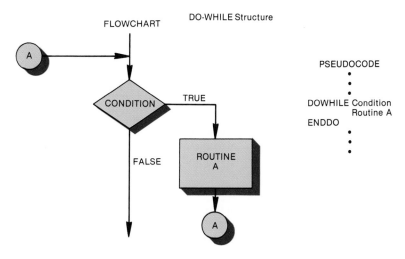

PSEUDOCODE
•
•
•
DOWHILE Condition
    Routine A
ENDDO
•
•
•

FIGURE 10-16
Basic structures shown in flowchart and pseudocode forms.

FIGURE 10-16
(*Continued*)

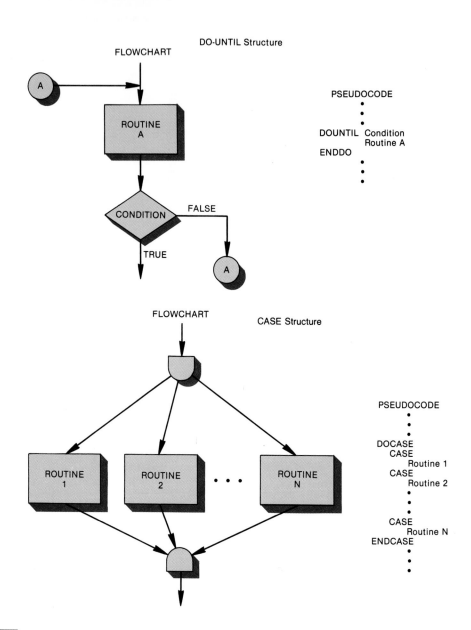

SUMMARY AND GLOSSARY OF KEY TERMS

- A program analyst must consider five steps when developing a computerized solution to a problem: **analyze and define** the problem, **devise** an algorithm, **code** the program, **test and debug** the program, and **document and maintain** the program.

- An **algorithm** is a method to solve a problem.

- A **flowchart** visually presents the flow of data through an information system and the sequence of operations performed within a system. A **systems flowchart** describes the operations performed in a data processing system, whereas a **program flowchart** is concerned

with the steps taken to solve a particular problem. In addition to graphically representing a problem, a flowchart helps the programmer in the logical design of a program and may serve as useful documentation for a system or program.

- Flowcharts are constructed using special symbols adopted by the **National Information Standards Organization (NISO)** and the **International Organization for Standardization (IOS).** Each symbol in the flowchart represents a **function.** Notes are made within each symbol to describe an **operation** taking place.

Flowlines connect each symbol and indicate the direction of flow.

- A **flowcharting template** aids in drawing flowchart symbols. The more commonly used symbols include the following:
  Processing symbol: used for **arithmetic** and **data transfer** operations.
  Decision symbol: used to show what alternative courses of action are to be taken under what conditions. Quantitative comparisons or conditions include less than ($<$), greater than ($>$), equal to ($=$), less than or equal to ($\leq$), greater than or equal to ($\geq$), and not equal to ($\neq$).
  Input/output symbol: denotes the input or output of data.
  Connectors: used to connect remote portions of a flowchart without making the diagram complicated. When used to connect flowchart segments on different pages, **off-page** connectors are used. The same letter is used within corresponding **entry** and **branch** or **exit** connectors. One entry connector may be associated with one or more exit connectors.
  Terminal symbols: used to indicate the beginning of the flowchart and points where the flowchart may end.

- The four major flowcharting techniques are **initialization**—assigning initial values to certain program variables; **looping**—performing the same sequence of instructions a number of times; **developing a counter**—counting the number of times a particular program segment or process is performed; and **developing a sum**—determining a running total of numbers as they are input or produced within a program loop.

- Most flowchart problems can be solved in a series of small steps. The more one works with flowcharts, the easier the logic and flowcharting procedures become. One must always keep in mind that there is no one solution to a particular flowcharting problem, although some solutions may be clearer and more efficient than others.

- **Decision tables** are used by programmers or systems analysts to substitute for, or supplement, flowcharts. The decision table charts conditions and possible courses of action for a problem. By reading each rule, one can determine what combination of conditions suggests what action.

- **Top-down program design** is a program design and coding technique that offers the advantages of improved program design, reduced program complexity, and increased programmer efficiency. This results in greatly reduced costs associated with the updating and modification of existing programs.

- Top-down program design utilizes two techniques: hierarchy plus input-process-output **(HIPO)** and structured programming.

- **HIPO** enumerates the program functions in hierarchical sequence and provides a visual description of the input/output produced by each function. Each program function is defined and subfunctions or modules are described. The major functions are arranged at the top level and expanded to lower levels. HIPO utilizes **hierarchy charts** and **input-process-output charts.**

- **Structured programming** gives the program a definite form. **SEQUENCE structures** describe program routines executed one after another. **IF-THEN-ELSE structures** allow a program to branch on the basis of a condition being met. A **DO-WHILE structure** describes repetition of an action while a condition is true. A **DO-UNTIL structure** repeats a routine until a condition is met. The **CASE structure** is used where different procedures are performed depending on an **integral value** of a variable.

- **Pseudocode** is an imitation computer code. It is a relatively informal way of describing logic and it is easier to construct and modify than a flowchart. It is easy to understand and is written in English-like statements.

EXERCISES

True/False

_____ 1. Variables that require initialization are generally identifiable by the fact that they appear on both sides of the equal sign in a note contained within a processing symbol.

_____ 2. The top-down design process utilizes HIPO charts and structured programming.

_____ 3. A program flowchart indicates the operations to be performed in the sequence in which they are to occur.

_____ 4. The program flowchart is an integral part of program documentation.

_____ 5. The number next to an off-page connector indicates the number of off-page connectors in the program with the same letter inside.

_____ **6.** Decision symbols should have only two exit paths.

_____ **7.** The rectangular flowchart symbol represents an input/output function.

_____ **8.** HIPO charts are used principally for program documentation.

_____ **9.** A flowcharting template aids the programmer or analyst in constructing a program flowchart.

_____ **10.** All computers signal the user when the last data item has been read by a program.

_____ **11.** A program flowchart generally contains both symbols and notes.

_____ **12.** A note is used to indicate a specific operation within a function category.

_____ **13.** A flowchart containing no notes would be impractical.

_____ **14.** Flowlines are used to connect symbols.

_____ **15.** A loop is a sequence of operations that is executed repeatedly until an exit condition is met.

_____ **16.** The function of each hierarchy module should be specific enough so that it can be implemented with approximately 50 lines of coding.

_____ **17.** The condition entry of a decision table contains the name of the decision table.

_____ **18.** Modules in a hierarchy chart should be programmed in order from the lowest level to the highest level.

_____ **19.** Structured programming concepts are not practical for the small business.

_____ **20.** Flowcharts are generally read from top to bottom.

_____ **21.** Testing of a structured program should be performed module by module beginning with the highest-level module.

_____ **22.** Programmers and analysts agree that pseudocode is superior to the program flow-chart.

_____ **23.** The DO-WHILE structure facilitates looping.

_____ **24.** Flowcharting standards are prescribed by the National Standards Bureau.

_____ **25.** Structured programming concepts encourage programmers to try new and exciting approaches to program design.

_____ **26.** A program flowchart has a similar place in programming to that of a blueprint in construction.

_____ **27.** The basic control structures should be independent and not combined where one structure might control another structure.

_____ **28.** The DO-UNTIL structure is an accepted variation of the DO-WHILE structure.

_____ **29.** The symbol = as used in a flowchart is defined as "is equal to."

_____ **30.** The two types of flowcharts are program and system flowcharts.

Matching

Match each of the symbols or decision table areas with the following names. Note that more than one symbol may be associated with a single name.

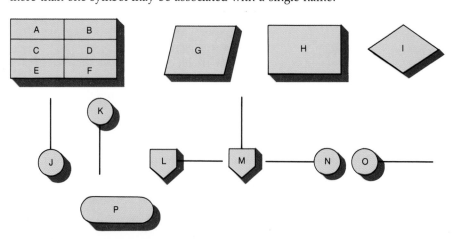

1. _____ Condition entry

2. _____ Entry connector

3. _____ Action entry

4. _____ Processing

5. _____ Action stub

6. _____ Input/output

7. _____ Decision

8. _____ Decision table name

9. _____ Off-page connector

10. _____ Terminal

11. _____ Branch connector

12. _____ Condition stub

13. _____ Rule entry

Problems

1. List the basic flowcharting symbols and name the function each represents. Describe two possible operations for each function.

2. Contrast the program flowchart with pseudocode. Which do you prefer? Explain.

3. What is the purpose of a decision table? Under what circumstances is the decision table most useful?

4. Name and describe each of the parts of the following decision table.

(a)	(d)
(b)	(e)
(c)	(f)

5. Construct a flowchart to describe the procedure you go through to determine what clothes to put out for the next day.

6. Construct a flowchart to describe the procedure you employ in studying for a test.

7. Construct a flowchart to describe how you would evaluate a used car that you are considering purchasing.

8. Draw a program flowchart to solve the following problem: Calculate gross pay from input data containing employee name, hours worked, and hourly rate. Assume that time-and-a-half is paid to any employee for those hours worked over 40 hours. Print your results.

9. Construct a decision table to determine which of the four numbers N1, N2, N3, and N4 is the smallest. If two or more of the four quantities are equal, any one of them may be selected as the smallest of the equal quantities.

10. Construct a flowchart for the problem in Problem 9.

11. Construct a flowchart for a program to determine the amount and denominations of the minimum number of coins to be given in change for a purchase of D dollars paid for with an X-dollar bill. (X is not to exceed 2 but may be less than D.)

12. Construct a flowchart to read in the current date in MM/DD/YY format (MM is the month, DD is the day of the month, and YY is the last two digits in the year) and print out this date in Julian format YYDDD (YY is the last two digits of the year and DDD is the day of the year). For example, 01/25/81 and 12/31/81 would be 81025 and 81365, respectively, in Julian format. Consideration of leap years is optional.

13. Construct a flowchart to determine the letter grade for each student in a class as follows:
    a. Read in the student's name and four examination grades.
    b. Determine the student's numerical average by averaging the student's three highest grades.
    c. Determine the letter grade appropriate for the numerical average computed in step b.
       Assume A $\geq$ 90, 90 > B $\geq$ 80, 80 > C $\geq$ 70, 70 > D $\geq$ 60, 60 > F.
    d. Print out the student's name, grades, lowest grade, average, and letter grade.
    e. Repeat steps a through d for each student until the student name END is read.
    f. Determine the average of all the students in the class and print it out.
14. Solve Problem 12 utilizing the basic control structures employed in structured programming if this was not done in Problem 12.
15. Complete a program flowchart for Problem 7 utilizing the basic control structures employed in structured programming if not done in Problem 7.
16. Solve Problem 11 using pseudocode.
17. Solve Problem 12 using pseudocode.

CROSSWORD PUZZLE

Across

1. Goes from top to bottom
2. A primary flowchart symbol
3. Preparing a routine to count the number of times through a loop
4. Describes program routines that are executed one after the other
5. Aids in meeting objectives of HIPO
6. Allows branching in structured programming
7. A top-down program design
8. Avoids longer crossing lines
9. A flowchart symbol that allows branching
10. Does a routine until a condition is true
11. Stop or start
12. HIPO, structured programming

Down

1. Aids in drawing flowcharts
5. Required when developing a sum in a loop
13. Is sometimes used in place of a flowchart
14. Aids in accomplishing HIPO objectives
15. Repeating the same process
16. Descriptions within flowchart symbols
17. Substitute or supplement to a flowchart
18. Uses three basic control structures
19. Repetition of an action while a condition is true
20. Represents a function

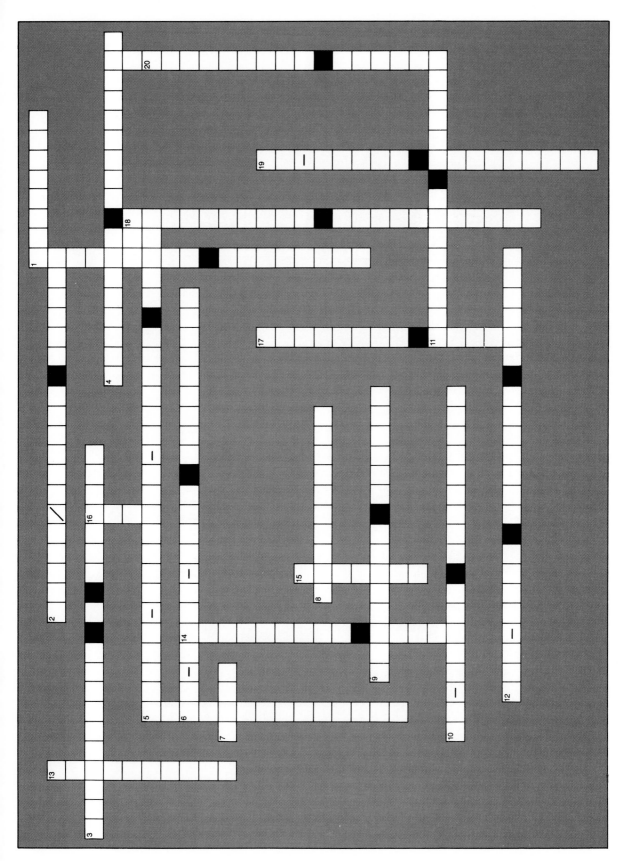

329

11

INTRODUCTION TO COMPUTER LANGUAGES AND PROGRAMMING
Implementing the Solution

Objectives

- List and describe each step in the overall programming process.
- List and describe the five types of computer instructions.
- Describe and contrast the principal types of computer languages.
- Describe the debugging process.
- Discuss the assembly and compilation processes and the purpose and results of each.
- Discuss program documentation and describe the contents of a run manual.
- Understand and use the key terms presented in this chapter.

$\boxed{I}$n Chapter 10 we learned that there are five steps that a problem analyst must consider in the course of developing a computerized solution to a problem. These steps, shown in Figure 11-1, are:

- Analyze and define the problem.
- Devise an algorithm.
- Code the program.
- Compile, test and debug the program.
- Document and maintain the program.

In the first step the problem analyst or programmer clarifies the problem, designates the available inputs and the desired outputs, and determines whether the problem can be solved by computer.

In the second step, the programmer employs top-down program design techniques to develop an algorithm to solve the problem. Design aids such as program flowcharts, decision tables, HIPO charts, and pseudocode are used to express the algorithm.

Now, let's continue our study of problem solving by examining the coding process.

CODING

After the problem has been analyzed, an algorithm developed, and a detailed program flowchart written, the programmer must code the program as detailed in the flowchart. Coding simply involves the translation or conversion of each operation in the flowchart or pseudocode into a computer-understandable language. In our study of data processing thus far, we learned that a computer program consists of a series of instructions that, when successfully carried out or executed, will accomplish the desired results. Let us now discuss the types of instructions that are available to the programmer.

Types of Instructions

Computer instructions consist of five types: input/output, control, arithmetic, logical, and specification.

1. **Input/output:** Instructions of this type direct the computer to move information to and from the computer's memory and an input or output unit.
2. **Control:** Instructions of this type control the order in which other instructions are performed. That is, they direct the computer concerning what instruction is to be executed next.
3. **Arithmetic:** These instructions direct the performance of arithmetical computations and the moving of data from one place in memory to another.
4. **Logical:** Instructions of this type enable the computer to compare items of data and proceed according to the result of the comparison as well as enabling the computer to deviate from the normal sequence of instructions in accordance with the existence or nonexistence of certain conditions.
5. **Specification:** These instructions are descriptive in purpose, and through them the programmer can inform the computer regarding such items as the types of data items used in the program, the allocation of storage, and so forth.

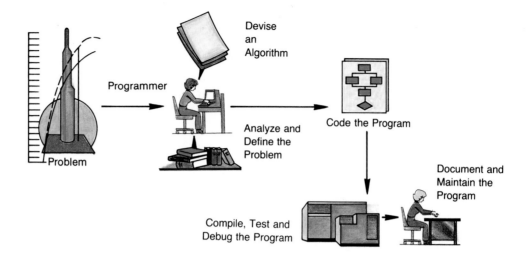

FIGURE 11-1
Direct conversion of problem to machine program.

However, we have not discussed how the programmer can communicate instructions to the computer. Many types or levels of computer languages are available to aid the programmer in communicating with the computer. Five of the more commonly used types of computer languages are the following:

- Machine language
- Symbolic language
- Procedure-oriented language
- Problem-oriented language
- Interactive programming language

Machine Language

Machine language is a series of numbers, letters of the alphabet, or special characters that are used to represent bit patterns that are recognized by the computer and cause specific operations to take place. An example of a machine-language instruction to add regular pay to overtime pay, yielding total pay, might appear as follows:

21   300   400   500

In this example, the 21 is a code that means ADD to the computer. The 300 and 400 are addresses or locations at which regular pay and overtime pay are stored. The 500 represents the storage locations for the sum, total pay.

Although machine language is ideal for the computer, programmers find it difficult and tedious to work with. Because of this fact, long and detailed programs are rarely written in machine language. Other languages that are easier to use have been devised to make the programmer's task a simpler one. However, because the computer is only capable of understanding and executing instructions written in machine language, programs written in other languages will eventually have to be translated into machine language before they can be executed. Translators for other standard languages are generally provided with the computer by the computer manufacturer. Such languages fall into four categories: symbolic languages, procedure-oriented languages, problem-oriented languages, and interactive languages.

Symbolic Language

A **symbolic language** is very closely related to machine language in that, generally, one symbolic instruction will translate into one machine-language instruction.

The advantage of such a language is in the ease with which the programmer can use the language. A symbolic instruction contains fewer symbols, and these symbols may be letters and special characters, as well as numbers. Let us consider the hypothetical machine-language instruction

21   300   400   500

The symbolic equivalent might appear as

A   RPAY   OPAY   TPAY

When this instruction is translated by a manufacturer-supplied translator, the A will be replaced by 21, the name RPAY replaced by the address 300, the name OPAY replaced by the address 400, and the name TPAY replaced by the address 500.

As you can see, the symbolic instruction is significantly easier to read and understand than the machine-language equivalent. This last factor is especially important in regard to the ease with which corrections and changes can be made. On the other hand, a certain amount of time is required to convert from symbolic to machine language, but this does not compare to the time saved by the programmer in working with a symbolic language as opposed to machine language.

The translation from symbolic to machine language is done by a computer program referred to as an **assembler.** The assembler keeps track of all memory locations and all names or symbolic tags associated with memory locations. This translation process also provides the programmer with error diagnostics to assist in detecting certain types of coding errors.

Summarizing, one could say that when the programming goal is to employ an easy-to-read, easy-to-write, and easy-to-modify language, in addition to making the most efficient use of the computer's hardware, a program should be written in a symbolic language.

However, symbolic language leaves two things to be desired: a programming language more similar to that normally used to describe the problem or procedure and a programming language that is virtually machine independent and can be used on various computers. These two properties are possessed by the procedure-oriented languages.

Procedure-Oriented Language

Assemblers and machine-oriented programming systems require a thorough understanding of the computer hardware to be used in the execution of the program by the programmer. In contrast, **procedure-oriented** programming languages for all practical purposes remove the necessity for the programmer to understand how the computer system will go about executing the program. The programmer may, instead, concentrate on expressing the procedure or logic of solving the problem. In many cases, it is not even necessary that one know what kind of computer system will be used for the execution of the program. The translation from a procedure-oriented language to machine language is done by a program referred to as a **compiler.** This name was chosen because a procedure-oriented system usually compiles many machine-language instructions from one source-language statement.

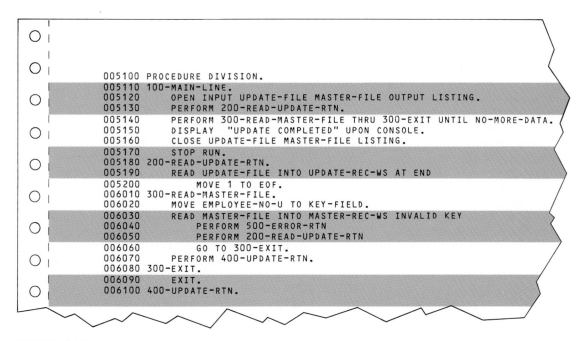

```
005100 PROCEDURE DIVISION.
005110 100-MAIN-LINE.
005120     OPEN INPUT UPDATE-FILE MASTER-FILE OUTPUT LISTING.
005130     PERFORM 200-READ-UPDATE-RTN.
005140     PERFORM 300-READ-MASTER-FILE THRU 300-EXIT UNTIL NO-MORE-DATA.
005150     DISPLAY "UPDATE COMPLETED" UPON CONSOLE.
005160     CLOSE UPDATE-FILE MASTER-FILE LISTING.
005170     STOP RUN.
005180 200-READ-UPDATE-RTN.
005190     READ UPDATE-FILE INTO UPDATE-REC-WS AT END
005200         MOVE 1 TO EOF.
006010 300-READ-MASTER-FILE.
006020     MOVE EMPLOYEE-NO-U TO KEY-FIELD.
006030     READ MASTER-FILE INTO MASTER-REC-WS INVALID KEY
006040         PERFORM 500-ERROR-RTN
006050         PERFORM 200-READ-UPDATE-RTN
006060         GO TO 300-EXIT.
006070     PERFORM 400-UPDATE-RTN.
006080 300-EXIT.
006090     EXIT.
006100 400-UPDATE-RTN.
```

FIGURE 11-2
Segment of COBOL source program listing.

Hundreds of procedure-oriented languages are currently in existence, the most popular and commonly used of these being **FORTRAN** (FORmula TRANslator), and **COBOL** (COmmon Business Oriented Language), **Pascal** (named after the mathematician Blaise Pascal), and **C** (see Fig. 11-2). The languages of FORTRAN, COBOL, C, and Pascal have become so common and so extensively used that a variation of, if not the complete version of, each of these languages is available for virtually every micro- to mainframe computer manufactured.

Table 11-1 illustrates how the assembly-language instruction

A   RPAY   OPAY   TPAY

might appear in machine language, BASIC, FORTRAN, COBOL, Pascal, or C.

TABLE 11-1
Comparison of Instructions in Different Computer Languages

COMPUTER LANGUAGE	INSTRUCTION FORMAT
Machine language	21 300 400 500
Symbolic language	A RPAY OPAY TPAY
Interactive language BASIC	10 LET T= R + O
FORTRAN	TOTPAY = REGPAY + OVTPAY
COBOL	ADD REGPAY, OVTPAY GIVING TOTPAY
Pascal	TOTALPAY: = REGPAY + OVTPAY
C	TOT_PAY: = REG_PAY + OVT_PAY

"NO, I DON'T KNOW COBOL, WHY, DOES
HE WORK HERE?"

The advantages of using procedure-oriented languages are many. Procedure-oriented languages are accompanied by extensive diagnostic routines that often make program checking far simpler than with assembly languages. Proce-

CAN COBOL LIVE FOREVER?

Until software maintenance can be eliminated, tools are needed to sustain COBOL's useful life.

The debate continues. Is COBOL dying or is there still life in the old language? While it is true that it is being replaced by fourth-generation languages in many shops, there are still millions of lines of COBOL code in use.

The major problem with these programs, however, is maintenance. Two companies have developed software packages to assist programmers in maintaining the old systems. The Analytic Sciences Corp. (TASC) in Reading, MA, calls its package *Fastbol*. Language Technology in Salem, MA, offers *Recoder*.

According to TASC, COBOL programs currently take up more than 50 percent of the maintenance effort and account for almost 60 percent of a total data processing (DP) budget. *Fastbol* is designed to solve the four major mandates to DP departments: increase productivity; enhance program quality; improve morale; and decrease application backlogs.

Fastbol is an online tool that aids in understanding COBOL programs by providing an overview and in-depth detail of interrelationships among variables. It also provides easy access to the comments and documentation written by previous programmers.

To understand a COBOL program well enough to change it, a programmer must be able to accomplish several functions. These include reviewing existing comments and the record of program changes; understanding the program's logical structure; studying the interrelationships among variables; and navigating efficiently within a program.

According to Barry Tudor, TASC's director of the Commercial Information Systems Div., "Fourth-generation languages and structured design packages are good tools for developing new systems. But when it comes to working with old code, programmers are left on their own. *Fastbol* automates the maintenance process, and thus eliminates much wasted effort."

Fastbol features a set of five commands. One function, *Logic Flow*, helps trace the path of logic, while two others, How-Set and How-Used, show variable relationships. How-Set shows the process that determines a variable's value, from input to final calculation. How-Used shows how a particular variable is used to affect the value of other variables, both directly or indirectly, through a hierarchy of variable relationships.

Other tools, *Comments* and *History*, provide access to existing documentation and allow programmers to write better documentation for successive programmers. Comments provides access to notations written within a program. History gives access to a Fastbol-maintained log of previous maintenance actions. Fastbol also incorporates a scrolling capability.

At Language Technology President Bill Engel says, "For organizations that use IBM mainframe computers and have a significant investment in old, unstructured COBOL programs, replacing or rewriting their software portfolio is not financially feasible. Software structuring is the only cost-effective solution."

dure-oriented language instructions are written in a manner very similar to that normally used to describe the problem by the scientific- or business-oriented individual (see Figs. 11-2 and 11-3). And finally, procedure-oriented languages are virtually machine-independent. That is, a computer program written for one computer installation can be used on another similar-sized computer system, even one produced by a different manufacturer, with just a few minor changes.

However, several disadvantages are associated with the use of procedure-oriented languages. The first disadvantage is the computer time lost in translating to machine language. Another disadvantage is that the machine-translated or -compiled program may not make as efficient use of the computer's resources as a program written by an experienced programmer using symbolic or machine language. Obviously, the advantages greatly outweigh the disadvantages.

As compilers are improved, an ongoing process, the advantages of their use will increase, the efficiency improve, and the disadvantages decrease.

```
C       SAMPLE FORTRAN PROGRAM
        READ (1,10) PRINC, RATE, PERPYR, NOPER
     10 FORMAT (F7.2,F4.3,F4.0,I4)
        AMT = PRINC * (1.0 + RATE / PERPYR) ** NOPER
        WRITE (3,20) PRINC, RATE, PERPYR, NOPER, AMT
     20 FORMAT (11X,'PRINCIPAL INVESTED = ',F7.2/
      -         11X,'ANNUAL RATE = ',F4.3/
      -         11X,'COMPOUNDED ',F4.0,' TIMES PER YEAR'/
      -         11X,'COMPOUNDED FOR A TOTAL OF ',I4,' PERIODS'//
      -         8X,'**********************************************'/
      -         8X,'*            AMOUNT = ',F10.2,'          *'/
      -         8X,'**********************************************')
        CALL EXIT
        END
```

FIGURE 11-3
Segment of a FORTRAN source program listing.

Problem-Oriented Language

The principal **problem-oriented language** is RPG (Report Program Generator). RPG was first introduced with second-generation computers and is still being used. It was intended for use with small computer systems for the creation of business-oriented reports requiring small to moderate amounts of mathematical calculation. Programs are written in RPG by filling out special RPG specification sheets. These sheets allow the programmer to describe the components of a program in a mechanical fashion requiring very little knowledge of the computer's hardware characteristics. Each component of the program is described on these sheets, one each for file description, input processing, calculations to be performed, and output processing.

Interactive Language

Interactive programming languages allow the programmer to communicate with the computer on a conversational basis. The programmer can simply key in the program, instruction by instruction, via a CRT or teletype terminal. After the program has been input, the computer can be directed to execute the program with a one-word command. Computer responses to the programmer's commands take place in a matter of seconds, as if the programmer and the computer were having a private conversation. In fact, possibly twenty other programmers are communicating with the computer concurrently, although no indication is given of this.

Programs written for interactive processing are generally simple and involve minimal data. Interactive programming is used to process one-time programs, transaction processing, and data inquiry.

The most common of all interactive programming languages is BASIC (Beginner's All-purpose Symbolic Instruction Code). Originally developed at Dartmouth College, BASIC was intended to be a simple language, useful for teaching programming concepts. Because of its simplicity and powerful capabilities, however, BASIC has become a popular language for use with terminals in a time-sharing environment.

In the time-sharing environment, terminal users create small to medium-sized programs and execute these directly from the terminal. BASIC, with its easily learned vocabulary and limited input/output capability, is ideally suited for this environment.

In appearance, BASIC is similar to FORTRAN, as it also uses a concise mathematical form of notation. The simplicity of the language has prompted many people to declare that BASIC is virtually the easiest programming language to learn. An example of BASIC programming is shown in Figure 11-4.

Once the programmer has determined which level of computer language and what specific language within this level is most appropriate for use in the solution of the problem, he or she is prepared to code the solution. The coding phase can be completed easily and quickly if a sufficiently detailed flowchart has previously been prepared.

TABLE 11-2
Relative Performance by Type of Languages

	HUMAN FACTORS					MACHINE FACTORS			
	Ease of Learning	Time to Write Program	Ease of Debugging	Self Docu-mentation	Ease of Maintenance	Storage Efficiency	Translation Time Prior to Execution	Execution Time	Machine Dependence
Machine Language	Worst	Worst	Worst	Poor	Worst	Best	None	Least	Very Much
Symbolic Language	Better	Better	Better	Fair	Better	Much Better	Little	Close to Least	Much
High-Level (Problem- or Procedure-Oriented)	Much Better	Much Better	Best	Excellent	Best	Better	Substantial	Little	Least
Interactive	Best	Best	Much Better	Good	Much Better	Worst	None	Very Much	Close to Least

New Languages on the Scene

Don't worry about New Lang.

Ada

Ada is a complex programming language, much like Pascal but more difficult to learn. It was developed in the late 70s for the Department of Defense to build large, reliable, and efficient military software. The goal of Ada was to provide programmers with sophisticated tools needed to create coding that would control hardware devices.

Much of the software developed by the Department of Defense is used in embedded systems, computer systems that are designed for use within other systems. At present, Ada is used to develop information systems that control weapons systems.

C

The language **C** was created by systems programmer Dennis Ritchie at Bell Laboratories in 1972. Since its conception, C has been closely associated with the UNIX operating system—the UNIX operating system was written using C. Originally written for Digital Equipment Corporation's PDP-11 minicomputer system, both C and the UNIX operating system have migrated to every type of machine, from microcomputers to the ultrasophisticated CRAY supercomputers.

21. A special form of ring LAN that uses token passing is the _token ring_ network.
22. In a LAN configuration, a central computer connects desktop computers that are known as _workstations_ .
23. LANs allow users to share programs, peripherals, and a common _data base_ .
24. Multiuser systems use a central computer for file and program storage, and most link _terminals_ rather than computers.
25. An ideal environment for a multiuser system is one in which users must constantly access a large _data base_ .
26. If a multiuser network starts to expand beyond the initial group of users, a larger _computer_ might have to be purchased.
27. The biggest advantage of a bulletin board system is its relative _low cost & ease of installation_
28. Normally, bulletin board systems do not provide _real-time_ communication.
29. Bulletin board systems are best utilized by people who have a need to communicate and share information, but do not require a great deal of _computing_ power.
30. A typical bulletin board system consists of a(n) _dedicated_ microcomputer, a hard _disk_ , bulletin board _software_ , and a dedicated _telephone line_ to send and receive messages.

Do not have to have a whole lot of power to have a data base.

Problems

1. What is a real-time system, and what are the differences between an online system and an online real-time system?
2. Ideally, what should an information system accomplish?
3. List some industries that would be well adapted for offline, online real-time processing, time sharing, and DDP.
4. Discuss the disadvantages of batch processing and of online systems.
5. What are the five major components of a real-time system?
6. Why are there not more operational management information systems?
7. What do you think are the main reasons for the rapid growth of communications networks?
8. What are the advantages and disadvantages of DDP?
9. Why is the terminal such a popular device for input?

Projects

1. Interview a manager in a local industry. Determine what level of management the person works at and find out what types of reports the person receives.
2. Research advertisements in business and computer magazines for types of commercial network packages that can be purchased.

CROSSWORD PUZZLE

Across

1. A data processing system with decentralized control
2. Interaction of humans and machines to gather and disseminate information
3. Distributed data processing
4. Reports produced at specified times
5. Needed for computer or terminals to talk to one another
6. Used to carry out I/O operations
7. An intracompany DDP network (first two words)
8. Characterized by insignificant processing delays
9. A cable used with LANs
10. Connected to a computer
11. A spider network
12. Interconnection of terminals and computers
13. Local area network
14. A serially connected computer network
15. A networking scheme using many terminals connected to a central computer

Down

5. A time-sharing mode
16. Reports that are produced when needed
17. An information system characterized by online interaction and real-time responses
18. Batch processing
19. Reporting unexpected or atypical situations
20. A service to pass and read messages (first word only)
21. Allows users to interact with a computer system to get answers to posed questions
22. A basic characteristic of a time-shared information system
23. A type of DDP network
24. A transmission medium for light waves

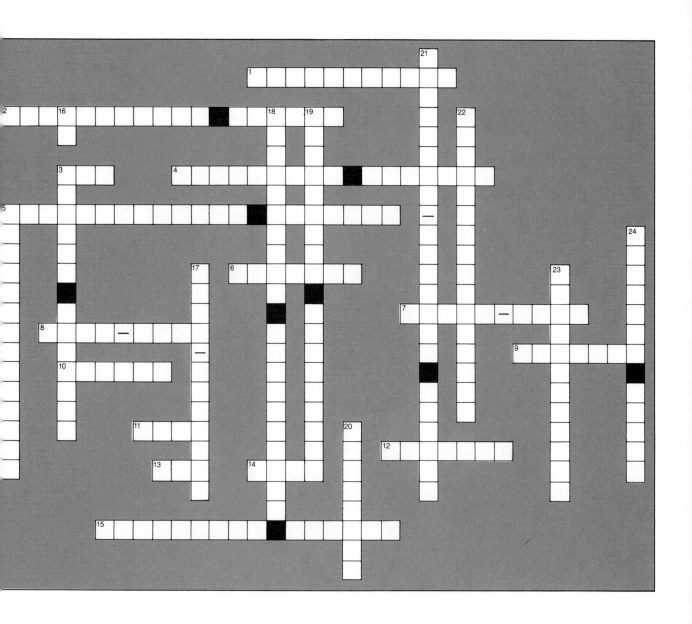

16

COMPUTER CAREERS
Where Do You Fit?

Objectives

- Understand how the computer revolution has created a need for people to fill many kinds of computer-related jobs.
- Describe the responsibilities of data processing personnel.
- Describe job opportunities that are centered around satisfying the needs of those who require computer services.
- Identify new and future trends within the computer and related fields.
- Explain how best to prepare for a job in computers.
- Describe techniques and procedures that could advance one's career.
- Understand and use the key terms presented in the chapter.

As computers continue to infiltrate virtually every area of society, the large number of occupations that already make use of computers continues to grow at a breathtaking rate. Whether your future plans include careers in music, teaching, professional sports, engineering, the arts, law, or medicine, a knowledge of computers will no doubt help you in some way. Our purpose in this chapter is to inform you of career opportunities that exist primarily within the computer industry itself. We will describe the major career options within the computer industry and provide some insight into how you can best prepare yourself to enter the field (and, once there, how to advance as rapidly as possible).

Things Look Good

If you plan to seek a career in computers, you have good chances of success. Not only is there an ever-increasing *demand* for computer professionals but there is a *shortage* of qualified people. Moreover, the U.S. Department of Labor predicts that this trend will continue at least through the next decade. There is probably no other professional area as dynamic as this one, nor one that offers so much opportunity. Basically, there are two reasons for this situation—the *computer revolution* and the fact that, until recently, there has been a shortage of adequate training programs.

The Computer Revolution

Because of the tremendous number of computers in our world, and more importantly, because of the enormous impact they are having on our lives, we are witnessing a revolution of grand proportions. In 1970, there were approximately 100,000 computers in use in the United States. Estimates for the number of personal computers alone in use by the end of the century run as high as 80 million! This happens to be the number of U.S. homes with TV sets *today*. All these computers must be designed, built, sold, delivered, installed, programmed, and repaired. This means jobs, jobs, and more jobs.

The Lag in Computer Education

A major cause of the shortage of qualified computer professionals is the lack of training. Training in computer-related subjects has been lagging behind advances in computer technology. There is a shortage of qualified teachers within our colleges' computer departments. As some professors are lured away by high-paying jobs in industry, potential instructors are attracted not to the classroom but to the business world instead. However, recently there has been a noticeable increase in computer education opportunities. Computer seminars, adult education workshops, and intensive computer programs offering certificates are springing up in most places. *Introduction to the Computer* is probably among the most popular college courses taught today.

A Winning Combination

These two factors, the great demand for people and the shortage of training programs, combine to make the job market unusually good for individuals who are well prepared. If you have the necessary education and background, you can expect to receive several job offers. Whereas most starting salaries are quite good, they are even better if you are willing to relocate to where the demand is greatest. *Source Edp*, a national recruiting firm devoted exclusively to the computing and information system fields, provided the salary survey shown in the appendix to this chapter. Because of the competition to hire experienced computer and DP people, **job hopping**—leaving one job for a more favorable one—is very common within the industry. If you enjoy traveling, a career in computers could very well afford you the freedom to move around the country and, in some cases, around the world!

A Word of Caution

Although the situation looks sunny at present, and should remain so for at least the next few years, some experts warn of a possible turn of events. If commercial software packages continue to improve in both effectiveness and ease of use, more and more applications might be handled by software houses rather than programmers. Furthermore, computer courses and training programs are beginning to turn out huge numbers of aspiring programmers in some areas. In a growing number of places, there is little demand for programmer-trainees. In these areas, would-be programmers looking for entry-level jobs are having a difficult time landing that first position. The demand continues to be for the *experienced* programmer (talk about a Catch-22!). Later in this chapter we will give you some advice on how to land that all-important first job and ways you can advance your career.

JOBS WITHIN THE COMPUTER INDUSTRY

DP operations personnel are responsible for carrying out the day-to-day processing tasks on the computer. Employees in this group work in or near the computer room and are responsible for preparing input data, operating the computer, and handling the output.

Data Entry Operator

The **data entry operator** uses key entry devices to transcribe raw data into machine-readable format. Data entry takes place principally on key-to-disk devices and microcomputers. The **remote terminal operator** also enters data but works at a remote site. Normally, a high school diploma and good typing skills are all that is necessary to obtain a job in this area.

Librarian

The **librarian** is responsible for data and programs stored on tapes, disks, microfilm, and other types of storage media. The librarian will classify, catalog, and maintain files on these items (see Fig. 16-1). This person is responsible to see that storage devices containing data and programs are secure within the library and that they are available when needed. A high school diploma and good organizational skills should be enough to obtain a position in this area.

Computer Operator

The **operator** works directly with the computer itself. Responsible for hardware-based activities, this person will prepare the equipment to run jobs, mount and remove tapes and disks, and monitor operations during the running of a job. If there is a problem with either a program or the equipment, the operator may be expected to initiate action to alleviate the problem. Jobs are available

in large as well as small installations. Because computer systems are run throughout the day and night, operators often must work night shifts. In many cases, they will work three days a week (twelve hours a day), and enjoy four-day weekends.

Because computer operators have to work with other members of the operations department, programmers, and to some degree, systems analysts, managers, and users, they should be able to communicate effectively. They must have the appropriate technical know-how and experience to keep the computer room running smoothly. Computer operators are not mere button pushers or paper handlers. It is essential that they have a conceptual understanding of what is occurring within the system as each button is pushed, each dial turned, and each switch flipped.

Although a college degree is not always necessary, a two-year degree from a community college or a certificate from a technical institute or vocational school would put an applicant at an advantage. With the current expansion of terminal networking, growth opportunities should remain high in this area.

The computer operator is the hub of the computer center. The efficient operation of this center rests in the hands of the computer operator.

INPUT FROM THE DISABLED

A greater range of employment opportunities now exists for the 36 million Americans with disabilities thanks to innovative input devices. One estimate places the market at $50 million annually and growing.

There is wireless "reflector" technology that allows the disabled to move a cursor with a nod of the head. Such a system is available from Pointer Systems Inc. of Burlington, Vt., whose FreeWheel System can be connected to eyeglasses, a hat, or a headband. The reflector bounces infrared beams from an optical camera kept in a small black box on top of the monitor.

Another device from Personnics Corp. in Maynard, Mass., allows paralyzed users to input data by puffing air into a mouth tube connected to a headset. In addition, there are Braille keyboards, Braille displays, and optical scanners for the sightless. There is also a panoply of voice recognition products, including voice synthesizers, as well as devices that respond to eye movement.

Two of the leading firms that hire the physically challenged are IT vendors. Between 5% and 7% of IBM's work force has disabilities. And the company offers a number of products geared for the handicapped developed by its Special Needs Systems group, part of the Entry Systems Division.

In addition, IBM maintains a National Support Center for Persons with Disabilities in Atlanta. Apple Computer Inc. also has a work program for the handicapped.

Another firm that has a formal program to hire the handicapped is Days Inn of America, based in Atlanta. Days Inn president Michael Levin says, "Today 30% of our reservations people are senior citizens, and 10% are people with disabilities or from our homeless program. That's something that we can be proud of."

Such hiring efforts will get a boost from the "Americans with Disabilities Act," which was recently passed by the House of Representatives and is expected to be addressed by the Senate in the near future. This legislation is a major step forward in preventing discrimination against the handicapped in both access and employment.

Programmer

Programmers are usually classified as either applications programmers or systems programmers.

Applications Programmer

The **applications programmer,** or simply, programmer, writes programs that solve specific problems (also called **applications**) for users. They will normally design, code, test, debug, document, implement, and maintain computer programs. It is estimated that 75 percent of the programmer's time is spent **maintaining**—that is, modifying or enhancing—existing programs rather than developing new ones.

Programmers who write business-oriented programs are called **commercial programmers.** When the programmers solve scientific and or engineering applications that are mathematical in nature, they are known as **scientific programmers.**

Currently, there are more jobs for applications programmers than for any other group. Most opportunities for commercial programmers exist for those with a knowledge of COBOL programming. The greatest demand will be for those who also have direct exposure to the following: large operating systems, job control language (JCL), database management, and remote processing techniques. Demand for professionals experienced in BASIC, RPG III, and Pascal will remain strong. The requirements for scientific programmers normally include a working knowledge of FORTRAN, Pascal, Assembler, or C programming languages.

It's sometimes necessary for programmers to work long and arduous hours to complete projects on schedule.

Systems Programmer

The **systems programmer** creates and maintains operating systems, monitors database programs, and so forth. The systems programmer typically will support applications programming, create new software for specific company needs, and maintain and monitor software packages. Opportunities in this area are beginning to increase in the emerging field of artificial intelligence (described in Chapter 17).

A principal function of the systems programmer is to interface the applications programs with the operating system. This requires extensive technical knowledge and experience.

Most would-be programmers have degrees from either two- or four-year colleges or certificates from technical or vocational institutes. Applicants for the systems programmer position should have at least one year of assembly language programming or a bachelor of science in computer science. Recently, some applicants for programming positions have been frustrated to find that employers are requiring a year or two of experience, as well as the necessary academic credentials. This trend is expected to continue as schools and institutes continue to feed the market with graduates eager to enter the field.

Systems Analyst

The **systems analyst** is the key person in the total computer processing cycle. This person must provide the major link between the user, management, and technical personnel (programmers, database specialists, and computer operators). After being assigned a job by someone in upper management, the analyst will often organize and head up a systems project team. This team will analyze a business system and, if necessary, design and implement a new one.

The analyst must work with the various users, who normally have little or no knowledge of computers, and with programmers, who more than likely have little or no business management skills. Some organizations have people whose functions include those of an analyst as well as those of the programmer. That person is known as a **programmer/analyst.**

The importance of this position dictates a unique blend of technical, business, and interpersonal skills. If you have a good background in computers, are personable, and can communicate well with diverse groups of people, you should be a sound candidate for this job.

Minimum requirements for the systems analyst position normally include a college degree, with courses in business, management, computer science, and information systems, as well as several years of system design experience. Like so many others, you can begin a career as a programmer and work your way up to the systems analyst position. Of course, this is only one of several possible career paths you can follow.

The analyst will spend many hours with the user clarifying and defining the system's objectives to ensure that the user's needs are met.

Database Specialist   The **database specialist** (also known as the **database administrator,** or **DBA**), creates and controls the use of an organization's database. Working with users as well as with programmers and analysts, the database specialist utilizes the facilities of the database management system, analyzes the interrelationships of data usage, and defines the physical data structures. Database specialists write procedures to insure data security, monitor database backup and recovery, and attempt to eliminate data redundancy.

Due to proliferation of DBMSs, there is a demand for persons with a knowledge of programming as well as of systems methodologies to design database-oriented applications systems. Requirements for the DBA position include a college degree covering courses in computer or information science, particularly DBMS design.

Software Engineer   The **software engineer** improves the effectiveness and efficiency of software, and designs and develops new software to drive computer systems. This person will develop firmware and sophisticated software such as graphics, CAD/CAM, and real-time monitors. The software engineer must interact with hardware engineers and application and systems programmers.

Software engineering is one of the fastest growing areas within the computer industry. There is a great demand for a variety of computer systems containing advanced technology. As this demand increases, the demand for experienced software engineers will continue to grow. The position of software engineer usually requires a degree in either computer science, engineering, or some related discipline.

Computer Engineer   **Computer engineers** design and build computer hardware. To qualify for this position, a candidate must have a degree in computer engineering in addition to having a strong background in electrical engineering and mathematics. Be-

Software engineers must be knowledgeable about a number of applications areas, as well as the hardware and software being used.

cause of the small number of qualified candidates receiving degrees in this area each year, computer hardware manufacturers recruit them vigorously. It is not uncommon for companies to provide first class transportation, food, and lodging to would-be employees.

Managers

All information systems or DP departments, whether large or small, must provide for systems analysis, programming, technical assistance, and computer operations. **Managers** are needed at all levels to oversee and integrate the activities of people and machines. An organization's corporate structure and the accompanying job titles may vary slightly from one company to another.

The technical support group designs, creates, implements, and maintains system software, such as the operating system and DBMS. The **technical support manager** controls and coordinates the activities of systems programmers, database specialists, and software engineers.

The **systems manager** is responsible for systems development and implementation. This person oversees and coordinates the efforts of the systems group as it analyzes, designs, and implements computer-based information systems.

The **programming manager** directs the efforts of programmers and programmer/analysts.

Operations within the data center or computer room must be carefully monitored. The **operations manager** directs all computer and peripheral machine operations, including data entry, data control, scheduling, and quality control.

The person responsible for planning, overseeing, and coordinating all the information resources of a corporation is often titled **director of management information systems** (other titles include **director of IS, computer systems director,** and **information systems manager**). No matter what the title, this person directs the activities of the entire DP staff, including operators, programmers, technical support personnel, and systems analysts. The director coordinates the efforts of the other DP managers and interacts with key company executives in order to establish priorities and reach corporate goals.

Although the director of information systems is primarily a manager, a good deal of computer knowledge and experience is also required. The qualifications for this position usually include a master's degree in business administration (MBA), as well as knowledge of computer hardware, software, and operating systems.

Other Opportunities

If you want to work with computers, you are certainly not limited to the career opportunities outlined above. The computer explosion has created entire industries devoted to satisfying the needs of those who need computer services, equipment, or training.

Computer Service Organizations

SERVICE BUREAUS. If you want to take advantage of a computer's power but cannot afford one, you might contract with a service bureau. Because service bureaus provide their clients with virtually every kind of computer service, they employ people from all the areas described above. Employees of service bureaus are contracted by the client company for a certain period of time or until the project is completed.

A consultant can be found to help solve computer-related problems both big and small.

TURNKEY ORGANIZATIONS. If a company does not want to design and implement its own information system, it could enlist the services of a turnkey company. A turnkey company hires people who will go to a client company and design and install an entire computerized information system—hardware and software—"from soup to nuts."

CONSULTING FIRMS. When a company requires a specialized service for a limited period of time rather than hire someone on a full-time basis, that company might seek out a **consultant** from one of the many reputable computer consulting firms. The consultant, an employee of the consulting firm, will contract with the purchasing company to provide specific services and is paid by time worked, by the project, or by some other arrangement made between the company and the consultant.

Freelance Consultant

As more and more companies turn to computers, the need for people who can provide an expertise that is otherwise unavailable continues to increase. This need has created a market for the freelance computer specialist or consultant. Unlike the consultant who is employed by a consulting firm, the **freelance consultant** is a self-employed professional who contracts with a company to provide services specified within a contract.

If you do not like staying in one place for too long and enjoy working with different types of people from various businesses, you might want to consider consulting. When you acquire the appropriate skills and experience and decide to strike out on your own, there should still be plenty of room for you.

Publishing

The publishing industry has been greatly influenced by computer technology. The phenomenon called desktop publishing has altered the traditional publishing process. This new field has given rise to many new and interesting jobs that can be accomplished in the comforts of your own home.

With the proper hardware, you can open up a typesetting business. Individuals and local businesses needing resumés, fliers, newsletters, and other documents produced at reasonable rates could become your clientele. In addition, in an effort to cut publishing costs, large corporations are currently hiring individuals able to use desktop publishing software to produce in-house publications. As a result of this trend, colleges and universities are beginning to offer training programs in this area.

Teaching

People from all walks of life are seeking formal computer training. There is a great demand for people who can provide formal training, whether it be courses offered within high schools, colleges, and universities, or seminars presented at local businesses or libraries. Anyone desiring a teaching career should earn a teaching certificate and take the necessary computer courses. College teachers are normally required to have a master's or doctorate degree in mathematics, computer science, or information management.

Today, a number of colleges and universities have followed Dartmouth's lead and require every student to purchase a microcomputer and become computer literate before graduation. As a result the demand for qualified computer teachers far exceeds the number available.

New and Future Trends

With the emergence of new technology, the very near future will see a demand for newer types of computer skills. Let's take a look at some of the trends that appear to be only in their infancy.

Microcomputers Bring New Challenges

Relatively recent uses for microcomputers—such as local area networks, micro-to-mainframe connections, and sophisticated data communications techniques—are spreading rapidly. With the drop in prices of small personal computers, it has become economically feasible for small and large businesses alike to purchase them. Data processing has become more user-oriented as fourth-generation DBMS languages continue to proliferate. Mini- and microcomputers, terminal devices, and communications networks have made decentralization more commonplace.

"SORRY, I HAVE TO GO HOME AND PRACTICE MY COMPUTER LESSONS."

Automation Opens New Possibilities

Computer-aided manufacturing (CAM), mentioned earlier, is opening exciting career opportunities within the area of industrial automation. According to one survey, these sophisticated computer-controlled devices, including robots, are actually creating more jobs than they are taking away. A recent survey of 60 leading manufacturers revealed that whereas 25,000 workers will be replaced by robots in the next decade, approximately 50,000 jobs within the robot industry will be created during that time. Computer-aided design (CAD) will also create opportunities for computerists as well as for scientists and engineers who will use the computer to aid in the design of complex industrial products.

Chrysler Corporation's designers and engineers use a CAD system to create bodies of vehicles, including the underbody and panels, steering geometry, suspension, and other systems.

GETTING STARTED IN COMPUTERS

Landing That First Job—Like It Is

Although some graduates from community colleges and technical or vocational institutes will be fortunate enough to obtain positions as programmer-trainees, most will probably land jobs within the computer operations department. After some time in the computer room, those who have some programming skills often join the ranks of programmers.

If you earn a four-year degree in data processing, information processing, or computer science, the chances are fairly good that you will find an entry-level position as a programmer, but there are no guarantees. As you will recall, the demand is for the *experienced* programmer. One way to acquire this experience

526

is to find a full- or part-time computer-related job while you are going to school. Upon graduation, you will be well prepared for that first programming position.

Before becoming a bona fide systems analyst, you can plan on first working as a programmer for at least a year or two. This period of apprenticeship does much to acclimate the would-be analyst to the overall information systems process while providing an introduction to the rigors of working "in the trenches."

Job Hunting

At long last, the day has arrived. You've completed your course of study; what can you expect as you step out into the real world, certificate, diploma, or degree in hand?

It is always a good idea to stay in touch with your school's career counselor. This person usually can offer sound advice based upon an intimate knowledge of the job situation. The counselor might be able to tell you where the jobs are, what various employers are looking for, and how much they pay. Often your school's placement office will help set up interviews. In any case, you will have at least one more hurdle to jump before you can shake hands and say "I accept"—the job interview. Before discussing the job interview, let's discuss the resumé.

The Resumé

The resumé is a written communication that clearly demonstrates your ability to produce results in an area of concern to potential employers, in a way that motivates them to meet you. Many good books are available to help the job seeker write effective resumés. We advise you to *keep it simple* and keep the reader in mind as you prepare your resumé. What is the employer looking for? *Results*, not reasons, not explanations, not hopes, not even experience or education (although these are used as predictors of your performance). How will you benefit him or her? That's the bottom line.

When prime employers, career counselors, and employment agencies were surveyed to determine what they felt were the most common repeated mistakes in the resumés they see, these were the results:

TEN MOST COMMON RESUMÉ WRITING MISTAKES

- Too long (preferred length is one page)
- Disorganized; information is scattered around the page; hard to follow
- Poorly typed and printed; hard to read; looks unprofessional
- Overwritten; long paragraphs and sentences; takes too long to say too little
- Too sparse; gives only bare essentials of dates and job titles
- Not oriented for results; doesn't show what the candidate accomplished on the job
- Too many irrelevancies; height, weight, sex, health, marital status are not needed on today's resumé
- Misspellings, typographical errors, poor grammar; the resumé should be carefully proofread before it is printed and mailed
- Tries too hard; fancy typesetting and binders; photographs and exotic paper distract from the clarity of the presentation
- Misdirected; too many resumés arrive on employers' desks unrequested, and with little or no apparent connection to the organization; cover letters would help avoid this

Interview Techniques

Let's assume you have arranged an interview with a potential employer. You now have to sell yourself in order to obtain an offer. The first impression you leave is important. Dress conservatively in business attire, not in casual or flashy clothes.

Sit, after you have been invited to, but do not slump in the chair. Sit naturally, confidently looking the interviewer in the eye. Don't fidget or fiddle with anything in your hand. Act assured, not nervous. Avoid smoking.

Be confident. Maintain a positive approach, but do not become too aggressive or offensive. Remember, the interviewer is interested in what you can do for the company and wants to know, How can this person solve our problem and fill our needs? Your conversation should always be influenced by this fact.

Be enthusiastic and ask questions. Information researched about the company in advance will help you to ask intelligent questions. Taking interviews is an art. Your ability to put your best foot forward should improve with experience.

Careering—Movin' On Up

Once you enter the computer field, there are many ways you can advance your career. Of course, promotion will depend, in part, on your ability and performance. Of equal importance is your ability to work with people, knowledge of your company's politics, and your ability to take advantage of opportunities when they come your way. Some things are out of your control. If there are no slots to move up to, advancement is virtually impossible, no matter what you do. Plain old good luck never hurt anyone's career; often, it's a matter of being in the right place at the right time.

The computer field is so volatile and dynamic right now that talk of a "typical" career path is becoming increasingly pointless. Traditionally, an operator would advance to programmer, then head programmer, to programmer/ analyst. From this position, one would either move to systems analysis or to a management spot. An ambitious and hard-working individual who obtains an advanced degree might move up to a top executive position.

Staying on the Cutting Edge

If there is a dull moment in the computer industry, it doesn't last too long. As computer technology advances, change is inevitable. Systems become outdated soon after they are installed; books become obsolete soon after they are published. With all this advancement and excitement, however, come new challenges. The computer professional can not afford to sit back and rest for too long. Keeping current by staying informed, getting involved, and upgrading skills is important in any profession, but in this field, it is an absolute necessity. For the computer pro, education is an ongoing process.

There are a variety of ways to stay current and marketable:

- College courses
- Company training programs
- Workshops and seminars
- Literature
- Conventions and exhibits
- Professional organizations

UNIVERSITIES AND INDUSTRY SCRAMBLE TO ATTRACT A SELECT BREED

Want to feel wanted? Enter a field where few degrees are awarded each year, jobs are waiting, unemployment is less than 1 percent, and salaries range up to $110,000 at universities and even more in industry.

This job-seeker's utopia is available to a select breed: doctors of computer science and engineering. Indeed, North American universities can't turn them out fast enough.

David Gries, chairman of the Cornell University Dept. of Computer Science, recently completed a survey of 102 U.S. and Canadian universities that award Ph.D.s in computer science and engineering. He found that universities scrambling to enlarge their faculties in the fastest growing science field—computing—are in stiff competition with industry and with each other.

In a recent report, *Imbalance Between Growth and Funding in Academic Computer Science*, Gries and his colleagues state that research and industrial demand for Ph.D.s is still increasing at research centers of large computer manufacturers. Newly formed institutes are hiring large numbers of Ph.D.s, the report says, as are companies such as General Motors and General Electric.

The report recommends that federal funding of computer research and teaching increase at a rate of at least 15 percent a year.

APPENDIX: PROFESSIONAL COMPENSATION

The "Going Rates" . . .

($000) PROGRAMMING:	YRS. EXP.	20TH	MEDIAN	80TH
Commercial	<2	22	27	30
	2–3	25	30	35
	4–6	29	35	40
	>6	35	41	49
Engineering/Scientific	<2	23	28	34
	2–3	27	32	37
	4–6	32	38	43
	>6	37	44	53
Microcomputer/Minicomputer	<2	22	26	31
	2–3	25	30	35
	4–6	29	35	41
	>6	34	42	50
Software Engineer	<2	24	31	39
	2–3	27	33	38
	4–6	32	38	44
	>6	39	46	56
Systems Software	<2	N/A	N/A	N/A
	2–3	28	33	38
	4–6	32	38	43
	>6	37	43	50

MANAGEMENT:				
Data Center Operations		38	50	67
Programming Development		49	58	68
Systems Development		49	57	66
Technical Services		45	56	67
MIS Director/VP		50	65	78

BUSINESS SYSTEMS:				
Consultant		38	49	60
Project Leader/Systems Analyst		38	45	54

SPECIALISTS:				
Technical Data Center Analyst	<4	30	35	40
	4–6	30	38	45
	>6	39	49	59
Database Management Analyst	<4	28	32	38
	4–6	32	38	44
	>6	41	49	57
Information Center Analyst	<4	24	28	35
	4–6	28	35	40
	>6	32	40	49
Office Automation Analyst	<4	25	30	36
	4–6	30	36	42
	>6	35	43	53

Hardware		32	45	65
Software		32	45	65
Services		38	48	65
Technical Support	<2	23	27	38
	2–3	26	31	36
	4–6	30	36	43
	>6	38	45	56
Management		49	70	92

OTHER:

Computer Operator	<2	19	22	24
	2–3	19	23	28
	4–6	22	25	31
	>6	25	30	39
Edp Auditor	<4	25	28	33
	4–6	27	32	43
	>6	38	46	56
Technical Writer	<4	24	28	34
	4–6	28	34	41
	>6	33	40	46
Telecommunications (Planning)	<4	26	31	41
	>4	37	45	56
Operations Support Technician	<4	20	24	31
	>4	25	31	38
Communications/Network Operators	<4	22	27	33
	>4	28	35	42

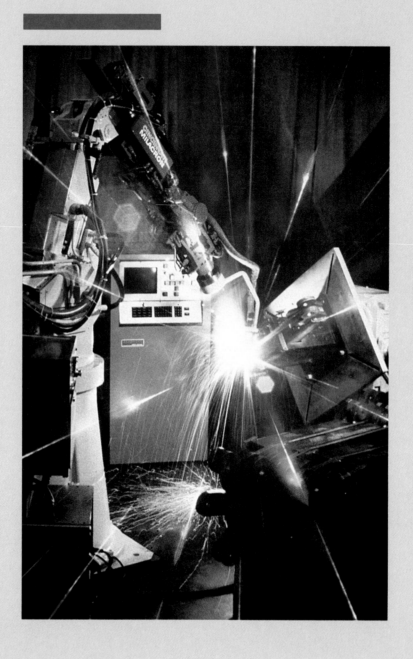

17

COMPUTERS DOWN THE ROAD
A Glimpse at What Might Be

Objectives

- Explain where we are headed in terms of computer advancement, and describe the major differences between today's hardware/software and the hardware/software technology currently being developed for future computers.

- Describe the major goals and objectives of fifth-generation computer research.

- Define the terms artificial intelligence and expert systems.

- Explain what constitutes a robot and describe how robots are presently being used and how they will be used in industry, space, and in the home.

- Describe how computer-related advances will affect the way we live and work.

- Discuss how computers are going to affect our homes and our work environment, change the nature of education, affect crime and crime detection, cause more and more techno-stress, and provide help for the disabled.

- Discuss the various socioeconomic trends that will, in all probability, materialize as a result of computer advancements.

- Understand and use key terms presented in the chapter.

These are exciting times. Electronic technology is advancing so rapidly that what we imagine and fantasize about at night might well be a reality by morning.

Throughout this book, we have talked about the impact that computers are making in our world as we move from an industrial to an information society. Changes are unfolding so quickly that there is often little or no time to react. This can make coping with change difficult. Having at least some notion of what might lie ahead will help you to adjust to a high-tech society and enable you to better chart your future as you consider various career paths.

Join us now as we take a look into tomorrow. Based on what has happened in the past and on what is happening now, we will attempt to project or extend events into the future. In most cases, we can only speculate and say that certain future events have a reasonable possibility of occurring. In any event, one thing is certain—the computer offers awesome possibilities. And just as we must understand, respect, and monitor the misuse of nuclear energy, so must we keep vigil as the computer grows in power and expands its influence over more and more areas of our lives.

THE COMPUTER OF THE FUTURE

As we mentioned earlier, the first generation of computers was housed in large rooms or gymnasiums and were powered by vacuum tubes. Typically, two or more people were assigned the job of running around and through the system with shopping carts containing tubes. As soon as one vacuum tube burned out, it was replaced by another. Often, the calculations on these early computers were repeated three or more times because a tube might burn out in the middle of a calculation. It took a majority vote to accept an answer as valid. (We've come a long way, baby!)

Since the early history of computers, the trend has been toward more capability for less money. We can safely project that future computers will be cheaper, smaller, and capable of doing more.

Hardware

Memory

About ten years ago, memory cost about $25 per kilobyte. Today, memory can be purchased for less than 10 cents per kilobyte. Not only has the price come down, but memory is now more reliable.

THE MICROCHIP. With the demand for smaller, faster, more sophisticated computers, companies are jamming ever more parts onto silicon chips. The process of shrinking electronic circuits into ever smaller areas—called **very large scale integration,** or **VLSI**—is at the heart of the current revolution in computers. The design and manufacturing techniques used in this process are so complex that computers are needed to design these **micro-** or **superchips.** A single microchip can presently carry the computing power of a third-generation mainframe computer.

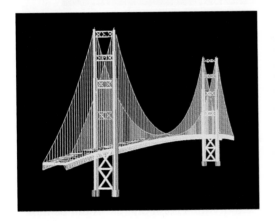

No area of human endeavor can remain unaffected by the advance of computer technology.

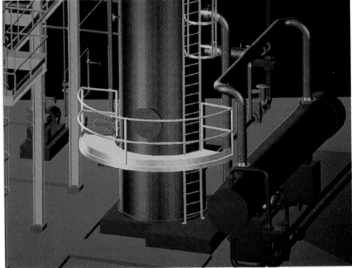

A complete microcomputer on a chip.

The next generation of computers will require chips that are more complex and capable of faster operating speeds than are available today. Based on what is happening now, there's no reason to suppose that the new technology won't be forthcoming. We can be fairly certain that very soon the average personal computer will contain 16 to 32 megabytes of memory at a cost less than what it is now. How's that for a bargain?

BIOCHIPS. Some researchers have designed diode-like switches that consist of long chains of carbon atoms. Because individual components would be molecule-sized, they could be packed to densities beyond the dreams of silicon designers.

Existing optical memory systems—laser disks—are limited in the amount of stored data by the size of the area that can be marked by a laser, the so-called "laser spot." In the space of a single laser spot, a biochip would be able to store 10,000 bits of information.

Mass Storage

Most experts agree that although you will soon be able to afford disks capable of storing millions of bytes of information, magnetic disks will *not* remain the mass storage medium of choice; instead, they will eventually be replaced by optical disks.

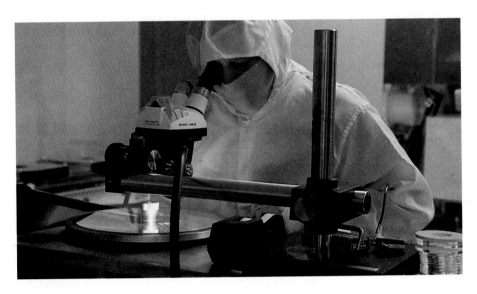

FIGURE 17-1
Manufacture of a videodisk.

OPTICAL DISKS. From all indications, the mass storage device that holds the most promise for the future is the **optical disk** (also known as the **videodisk**). Optical disks (see Fig. 17-1) are presently being used as a medium to record films, pictures, and other visual data, but their ability to store tremendous amounts of information has caught the eye of the computer industry. One computer manufacturer, NeXt Inc., supplies an optical disk as a secondary storage device for its NeXt STEP computer (see Fig. 17-2).

Data are recorded on optical disks through the use of high-intensity laser beams that burn tiny holes, or pits, into a disk's surface. Because pits can be placed closer together than can magnetic spots, data can be packed together more tightly on optical disks than they can on magnetic disks.

A serious limitation of current optical disk systems is that recorded data cannot be easily erased, nor can these systems be used to rerecord data. Consequently, optical disks are presently used for long-term storage of information that does not have to be changed often, like hugh catalogs or various types of

FIGURE 17-2
NeXt STEP computer system.

archival information. One optical disk can store nearly 100,000 average-sized books! A revolutionary **thermo-magneto-optical disk** is being tested that employs a **current optical storage** technique. It combines state-of-the-art magnetic and optical technologies to produce a rerecordable medium. Data are recorded by heating the surface with a laser while applying a magnetic field. Data are erased by heating the surface without applying a magnetic field. Several companies have produced versions of erasable optical disks that utilize this technology. Only the future will tell how practical this method is.

Also being pursued is a crystalline solution to this problem that uses a **crystalline-amorphous,** or **phase change,** technology. These disks are produced with each bit in crystalline form. Information is recorded by using a high-powered laser to heat a small area to just above the melting point. When cooled, the area is no longer crystalline, and reflects a low-powered laser's light differently than the surrounding unaltered crystalline structure. Data is erased by heating the area to just under the melting point. This returns the surface to its original crystalline form. Once the old data has been erased, new data may be recorded. The major drawback of this technology is that the number of erase-rewrite cycles is limited to a few thousand.

FLOPPY AND HARD DISKS. A number of innovations are being tested that will greatly increase the storage capacity of both hard and floppy disk drives. IBM, NEC, and other companies are developing $3\frac{1}{2}$-inch floppy disks with storage capacities ranging from 2.9 megabytes to over 20 megabytes, with even larger capacity devices on the horizon. The tradeoff, however, is that these higher capacity floppy drives are significantly slower than a hard disk with the same capacity. Some predict that floppy disks employing these technologies will virtually replace the hard disk in the laptop computer market.

Superconductivity

In Holland in 1911, physicist Kamerlingh Onnes discovered that when metals are cooled to temperatures that approach absolute zero ($-459.67°F$ or $-273.15°C$), all molecular motion stops and the metal offers no resistance to the flow of electricity; hence much more current can travel through a wire than previously possible. He referred to this phenomenon as **superconductivity.** Since that time, physicists have applied his theories.

Brian Josephson of the University of Cambridge, another pioneer in the field of superconductivity, helped develop what is now called the **Josephson junction**—a super high-speed electronic switch made up of two supercooled metals separated by an oxide insulator. The electrons passing through the junction can move at speeds that are a hundred times faster than those passing through the conventional semiconductor circuits used today. However, reducing the temperature of the metals to within a few degrees of absolute zero requires that they be submersed in a bath of liquid helium—a process that is extremely expensive, making it impractical for all but some very special applications.

But, in 1987, IBM announced a major breakthrough, a ceramic substance made up of barium, yttrium, and copper oxide that provides superconductivity at minus 288°F, approximately 172° above absolute zero. A substance can be lowered to this temperature by placing it in a bath of liquid nitrogen at a cost reduction of a whopping 98 percent over the liquid helium bath needed previously. At this temperature a wire made out of this ceramic substance can carry 1000 times more current than a normal copper wire.

Scientists are now producing even higher temperature superconducive materials in their search for the ultimate superconductor—one that will exhibit superconductive properties at or near room temperature. Imagine, a entire computer system could be hundreds of times faster than existing computers and operated for a year by a few ordinary flashlight batteries. The potential is awesome.

Software

It is not difficult to project future trends concerning software; software is going to get cheaper, more versatile, and easier to use. Data communications advances will make it easier for you to communicate from computer to computer. There will be a proliferation of various kinds of applications programs that will be easier to use, making computers accessible to more people. But perhaps the most dramatic break from traditional computers will be the development of computers that can listen to questions, provide expert opinions, and speak.

Talking Computers

Voice recognition and audio response systems were mentioned earlier in the text. There appears to be a difference of opinion concerning whether or not this technology will really take hold in the near future.

AUDIO RESPONSE. Machines that can "speak" convert stored digital data into sounds that form prerecorded words. A major limitation of this technology is that the number of words or messages a typical system can produce is quite small. Most systems have a built-in vocabulary of less than 100 or 200 words and a very limited ability to combine words dynamically to form sentences.

Perhaps you've encountered a talking computer in your travels. Technology has already produced talking vending machines and elevators, and cars, clocks, and calculators can tell you what's on their "minds." Airline terminals use voice response systems to inform people about flight arrivals and departures.

VOICE RECOGNITION. Wouldn't it be great if we could just talk to a computer and have it jump (at the speed of light no less) into action? The computer might well replace the dog as a person's best friend. Currently, however, teaching a computer to "speak" is not as difficult as getting it to "listen."

Voice recognition devices gather sound waves, remove unwanted noises, and compare the incoming signal against a pattern (**template**) stored in memory. If the incoming sound closely approximates the template, the word is recognized. If the sound is not similar enough to any stored template, then the system fails to recognize it, or if the sound is distorted it may cause the system to correlate the word with the wrong template.

Voice recognition has progressed more slowly than audio-response technology for a number of reasons. One of the main problems has to do with the current limitations imposed on the size of internal memory. Speech recognition systems require an enormous amount of memory to store the vocabulary necessary to recognize conversation. Another problem is **speaker-dependency;** the system recognizes only the voice of the person with whom it has been trained. In addition to these problems, voice-recognition devices are constrained in that

Research teams study speech waveforms in developing new systems for speech recognition and speech synthesis.

words must be spoken *individually*, instead of in a normal stream. The recognizer uses the periods of dead air to determine when one word stops and another starts; without the silences, it would be lost. While adequate for dictating short command words or phrases, such discrete-utterance units are generally considered unsuitable for voice-activated devices.

Some feel progress will be slow to come in the area of voice recognition. However, larger memories will permit the storage of larger vocabularies; this should help solve part of the problem. Also, as software development related to artificial intelligence (a topic we will discuss shortly) makes headway, the necessary software for reliable voice recognition devices should be forthcoming.

Just recently, voice-processing software has become cheaper and far more reliable. A medical communications company has developed a system that can understand 25,000 discretely spoken words, or about 60 percent of the average person's vocabulary.

As computing power and memory become cheaper, it will become cost-effective to make voice recognition systems that are more versatile than today's breed. The consensus in the field, however, is that the large-vocabulary, speaker-independent, continuous-speech recognizer will not appear until the mid-1990s.

Fifth-Generation Computers

The fifth generation! It's hard to believe that computers have been with us for only thirty years. How many of you remember the first four generations? Here's a quick review.

- **First-generation** computers used vacuum tubes as switches and vacuum tubes and magnetic cores for storage. They were big, hot, expensive, unreliable, and very difficult to use.

- **Second-generation** computers used transistors as switches; they were smaller, faster, more reliable, and easier to use than their predecessors.
- **Third-generation** computers utilized integrated circuits (ICs)—thousands of small circuits etched onto a small silicon chip. They were still faster, smaller, and more reliable than previous models.
- **Fourth-generation** computers are characterized by the microminiaturization of integrated circuits composed of silicon chips that contain tens of thousands of circuits. These circuits, microscopic in nature, have become known as very large-scale integrated circuits (VLSI).
- **Fifth-generation** machines will use microchips—the more advanced forms of VLSI chips described earlier. But, more importantly, they will be *qualitatively* different, having new forms of computer architecture. Rather than having one or even several CPUs working simultaneously in parallel (multiprocessing), these giants are envisioned to have more than *1 million* processors linked together working in parallel!

Japan and, to a lesser degree, the United States and other countries, have invested time and money in the development of fifth-generation computers. The first of the new breed of computers will probably perform upwards of 70 times more calculations each second, and have approximately 3,000 times the internal memory of **supercomputers**—the largest computers currently in use. Presently, there are less than 100 of these supercomputers—all of them American. The VLSI circuitry is so fast and dense in these machines that a freon gas coolant is pumped through the circuitry to prevent it from melting.

Japan's Mission

Japanese Style Ever fashion-conscious, the Japanese have come up with the world's first software for hair salons. Customers have their photographs fed into a pasa-kon, or personal computer, so they can see how they would look in the different hair styles that are simulated on-screen.

A formal program to build the world's most advanced computer was begun in 1982 when Japan's Ministry of International Trade and Industry announced an unprecedented $300 million fifth-generation computer project. This ministry sponsored a conference that was composed of Japan's largest electronics firms to form the Institute for New Generation Computer Technology (ICOT). A national ten-year plan was devised to research and develop a new computer family that would be radically different from the present crop of supercomputers. In fact, the fifth generation is to be unlike any computer ever built. They are to be capable of reasoning their way through massive amounts of knowledge and data. They are expected to be able to learn, associate, make inferences, make decisions, and otherwise behave in ways usually considered the exclusive province of human reason.

Beyond von Neumann

You may recall that a man named John von Neumann developed the stored-program computer. To date, all computers use von Neumann architecture in which a CPU executes one instruction at a time, stores the results in memory, and then proceeds to execute the next instruction. The speed of a computer is measured in how many operations it can perform in one second. This measurement has become known as a **megaflop**. Today's larger mainframes can run at about 2 megaflops—about the limit of the one-step-at-a-time von Neumann machines.

To compute at speeds that are much higher than 1 or 2 megaflops, a technique known as **parallel processing** was developed. Essentially, this technique involves the use of multiple processor chips to divide the work under the control of a central processor. The processors solve portions of a job simultaneously by working in parallel. The result is a very fast machine. Supercomputers such as those produced by the CRAY Corporation use parallel processing (see Fig. 17-3). These machines can execute instructions at more than 20 megaflops, and for mathematical calculations, speeds of 100 megaflops or more are possible.

Well, what does all of this talk about megaflops and parallel processing have to do with the fifth-generation computers? Just this: Japan plans to use a different architectural scheme for its new generation of computers. It will be based on parallel-type processing but will be somewhat different and is expected to go well beyond that concept. In the near future ICOT will develop an all-new prototype to be called the **parallel inferential machine,** which will have at least 100 *billion* bytes of memory.

ARTIFICIAL INTELLIGENCE

Up to this point, we have only alluded to a concept and technology known as **artificial intelligence (AI).** As the Japanese see it, artificial intelligence will form the bedrock upon which their new computers will stand. The next generation will see a shift from mere data processing, which is the way current computers function, to an *intelligent* processing of knowledge. The new computers

FIGURE 17-3
(a) A CRAY supercomputer, one of the world's most powerful computer systems, containing four separate processing units. (b) Seymour Cray and J. Rollwagen with a CRAY supercomputer memory module.

a

b

542

will be designed to run programs capable of performing tasks at a level comparable to human experts.

It is difficult to define AI. Perhaps it would be best to provide you with a demonstration of artificial intelligence at work. Margot Flowers, a scientist, sits down and begins a conversation with her friend Abdul. The subject? Mideast politics.

Margot: Who started the 1967 war?
Abdul: The Arabs did, by blockading the Strait of Tiran.
Margot: But Israel attacked first.
Abdul: According to international law, blockades are acts of war.
Margot: Were we supposed to let you import American arms through the strait?
Abdul: Israel was not importing arms through the strait. The reason for the blockade was to keep Israel from importing oil from Iran.

In your opinion, who won the argument? Actually, Margot Flowers is one of three scientists who created *Abdul*, a computer program that understands the spoken word, can scan data stored in its memory, and can reason out answers to questions.

Artificial intelligence has been defined as behavior by a machine that, if exhibited by a human, would be called intelligent. Seeing the Abdul program in action should give you some feeling for what an AI program can do. In part, it exhibits the characteristics we associate with intelligence in humans—reasoning, learning, solving problems, and understanding language. Since its inception in the mid-1950s, AI enthusiasts have been concerned with the simulation of human skills and human personality through computer programs.

Unlike conventional computer programs, AI programs deal with knowledge, not with numbers, and with logical operations more than arithmetic ones. Huge memory banks are needed to store the vast amounts of knowledge needed for these programs.

The field of AI was started in 1956 by John McCarthy, who coined the term artificial intelligence. In 1958, he created LISP, the programming language used to write AI programs.

Expert Systems

A class of commercial products is emerging from **knowledge engineering,** which is a branch of AI research devoted to building systems that automate human expertise. **Expert,** or **knowledge-based, systems** actually draw conclusions from the computer-stored knowledge obtained from human specialists and experts. Since their conception over 10 years ago, expert systems have developed an ability to solve problems that previously required human intelligence.

Expert systems are said to possess the following attributes. They

- cover a specific domain of expertise
- contain a **knowledge base,** that is, a database of facts and rules for dealing with those facts
- can be used to reason with uncertain data
- can reveal the results of that reasoning in an understandable way

Many of the latest expert systems can grow incrementally and deliver advice as well as facts and figures. The purpose of these systems is to capture the expertise of key people within an organization or field of study and make it available to the user of the program. Whenever one of these systems is queried, it attempts to respond to the user's questions by searching through the rules and facts in its knowledge base. A few years ago, expert systems developed to the point where they began to move out of the laboratory and into the factory, office, and home.

How They Work

Unlike the standard database which contains only data, the knowledge base contains facts in relationships and contexts. These facts are associated with the rules that control those facts.

With the larger expert systems, the knowledge is separate from the control strategy or inference engine. That is, the rules that use the facts to reason or draw conclusions concerning the problem under consideration.

Shells

The expert system software that has been stripped of its knowledge leaves only a **shell:**—the control strategy, rules, and reasoning mechanisms that interpret and draw conclusions from the knowledge.

In the past three years, dozens of companies have developed and marketed these shells, or development tools, to speed the production of the full-blown expert systems. All a company need do is pick the brains of their resident experts and encode this knowledge in the language understood by the shell supplied by a vendor. A typical brochure boasts: "you supply the knowledge, we supply the intelligence."

Ironically, gathering and encoding the knowledge needed to solve a specific problem is the most difficult and time-consuming part of building an expert system. The shells are purchased to expedite the construction and testing of knowledge bases. Full-blown program shells designed for Digital Equipment Corporation's VAX minicomputers sell for over $50,000, while microcomputer-based products cost in the neighborhood of $500 to $1500. By giving users a framework upon which to build expert system applications, these preprogrammed shells are simplifying the programming process and cutting development times from years to months.

Expert Systems in Action

One of the first expert systems, developed by Stanford University in the mid '70s, was **MYCIN,** a medical system designed to diagnose blood infections. This classic system contains 475 rules in its knowledge base. Later, a shell was developed for MYCIN called **Essential MYCIN** (EMYCIN), to aid in the creation of other automated medical experts. When drilling a new oil well, oil companies must select the best drilling lubricant. **Mudman** is an expert system that can do just that.

Consultants and medical experts helped provide the large quantities of real-world knowledge needed to develop the medically oriented expert system **Internist/Caduces**. Developed at the University of Pittsburgh as a diagnostic aid in internal medicine, its knowledge base includes facts on more than 500 diseases and 3,500 symptoms of disease. The physician enters the patient's history and lab test results into the computer, and the program uses its knowledge base to come up with possible diagnoses.

Caduces acts as a consultant, asking the physician questions and providing explanations, such as, "Orange skin and upset stomach could indicate an excessive consumption of carotene; suggest patient discontinues eating carrots and tomatoes."

Computer Science Corporation's largest AI applications are expert systems designed to further the goals of the Strategic Defense Initiative. One such expert system program transfers data flow diagrams into structured, top-down program design. Expert programs that can generate program source code from the program designs are already on the drawing boards.

In general, knowledge-based systems are limited to highly specialized application areas, such as science, medicine, business, and industry. Human experts are always in short supply. They get sick, die, or leave the company. In those areas where large amounts of knowledge are held by a few human experts, a loyal, immortal, tireless "expert" can increase company productivity.

Some Problems

In reality, expert systems cannot perform at the level of human experts. When solving problems humans rely on their experience, intuition, and insight. No systems yet devised can match the wisdom of the wise. Actually, it is not expertise but competence that these knowledge-based systems can achieve, that is, competence in performing a clearly defined, narrowly scoped problem for which they are specifically designed.

Other problems facing expert systems development involve the physical constraints caused by today's computers—namely, speed and memory size. However, as computer technology advances, these constraints will diminish.

Knowledge-based systems are also limited by the number of rules they contain. Most expert system programs are comprised of several hundred to several thousand IF . . . THEN rules. A program consisting of more than 10,000 rules would be too slow to arrive at a conclusion in a timely manner on a conventional mini- or microcomputer.

Before a mass market can open up for expert systems, vendors of expert system development tools will have to remove a few bugs from their products. Although most vendors claim their programs are easy to learn and implement, most users require extensive training from suppliers and assistance from knowledge consultants.

The most difficult way to build an expert system is from scratch. Instead of buying some and building the rest, some AI users will opt to build a tailor-made system from the ground up.

AI Languages

Anyone desiring to build their own expert system from the ground up would probably be led to the most popular AI languages used today—LISP and PROLOG.

LISP

LISP (LISt Processing) is not a new language. It is over 25 years old, but is still the most widely used language for building expert systems. Although there are many dialects of the language, a standard called Common LISP has been developed, largely through the efforts of the U.S. Defense Department.

LISP differs substantially from other high-level languages such as COBOL, FORTRAN, or Pascal and is not a particularly easy language to learn. Although these and other languages can be used, LISP is particularly suited for expert system development because it has the ability to create and analyze text information with relative ease. That is, it can expeditiously handle large strings of words. It contains instructions for adding and deleting words and controls program branching based on the content of those words. LISP also has the ability to use **logical inference** techniques, that is, the searching and analyzing of large, nonnumeric knowledge bases to come up with conclusions.

LISP is known as an **extensible** language because it can be expanded. New commands written as subroutines can be added to the original list of commands as if they were part of the original language.

PROLOG

PROLOG (PROgramming in LOGic), invented in 1970 by Alain Colmerauer in France, was designed specifically for expert systems and has become the language of choice for Japan's "Fifth Generation" project. PROLOG contains direct mechanisms for implementing an inference engine as well as developing search techniques. The rapidly growing popularity of PROLOG has led some AI experts to believe that this language will replace LISP as the principal language of AI. PROLOG's basic terms express logical relationships among objects, and not just equations as most languages do.

What We Can Expect

The creation of HAL 9000 isn't right around the corner, but AI technology is currently performing useful work that could not have been done a few years ago. With the continued development of faster computers and better software, more and more applications that exhibit some degree of artificial intelligence will be forthcoming.

ROBOTICS

The robots are coming! Actually, robots have been with us for some time now. Down through time from the Golden Age of Greece to the present, people have written about and have been fascinated by the concept of artificial life (shades of Frankenstein!). In the 1973 edition of the Oxford English Dictionary, the entry for "robot" reads:

> **Robot** (ro-bot) 1923 (—Czech, f. *robota* compulsory service) One of the mechanical men and women in the play *R.U.R.* (*Rossum's Universal Robots*) by Karel Čapek; hence, a living being that acts automatically (without volition). b. A machine devised to function in place of a living agent; one who acts automatically or with a minimum of external impulse.

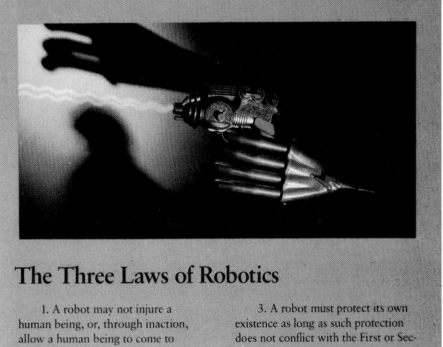

The Three Laws of Robotics

1. A robot may not injure a human being, or, through inaction, allow a human being to come to harm.

2. A robot must obey orders given it by human beings except where such orders would conflict with the First Law.

3. A robot must protect its own existence as long as such protection does not conflict with the First or Second Law.

—from *I, Robot*, by Isaac Asimov (Gnome Press, 1950; Doubleday, New York, 1977)

The three laws of robotics. Variations of these laws have appeared in science fiction books and films for many years. Now they are nonfiction!

Karel Čapek first coined the word **robot** in his classic play *R.U.R.* In the story, a corporation called Rossum's Universal Robots (R.U.R.) creates humanlike creatures to serve the human race. The creators of these robots, or workers, manage to develop their products to the point where the machines eventually revolt against their masters and proceed to take over the world. And to add insult to injury, with humanity practically extinct, and the robots due to wear out in a few years, two robots are created, a male and a female, that are different from all the rest—they have the power to recreate themselves.

What Is a Robot?

What makes a machine a robot? The Robot Institute of America (RIA) defines a robot this way: "A robot is a *reprogrammable* multifunctional manipulator designed to move material, parts, tools, or specialized devices through variable programmed motions for the performance of a *variety* of tasks."

Robotics is closely related to **cybernetics**—the use of computers and automatic machinery to control complex mechanical operations.

To get a better idea of what place robots will play in your future, let's take a look at some of the major categories of computer-programmable robots and see how they are being used today and what they will be doing tomorrow.

RB Robot is one of the more popular and useful mobile robots.

Industrial Robots— The Steel-Collar Workers

There are about 15,000 robots in use in American industry today costing about $30,000 to $100,000 each. Fifty to sixty percent of them are used in the automotive industry. Stiff competition in the field of industrial robotics is coming primarily from Japan.

One of the reasons Japan produces so many robots is because of an extensive industrial labor shortage there, especially in the automotive industry. Motivated by a desire to increase productivity and become preeminent in the field, the Japanese are making advances in robotics at an unprecedented rate.

Automatons provide their human supervisors with numerous benefits. Robots are fearless, they can be used to perform difficult or dangerous tasks, and they do it without complaining (see Fig. 17-4) "Herman," a remote-controlled mobile manipulator, was on standby alert during the 1979 accident at the Three Mile Island nuclear plant ready to venture into areas of high radioactivity.

FIGURE 17-4
Robots can do things humans cannot. A robot's access arm can be programmed to grasp and hold objects that are literally "too hot to handle" for mere humans.

ROBOTS ON THE MOVE

The use of industrial robots is increasing. Whereas a conventional machine is designed to perform a particular function, an industrial robot is designed to perform complex motions that often depend on judgments. These robots are not at all like fictional robots. Basically, they consist of an articulated arm with wrist and fingers. The arm is computer controlled and programmed to perform tasks. If you put two arms together, you effectively have a pair of hands.

Underwater robots are being developed for use in oil exploration, off-shore mineral exploration, placing explosive charges, mine warfare, and in underwater rescues and repairs. Such robots can travel down to 5000 meters, while a diver is limited to 350 meters. In Australia, an underwater robot called TREC (an acronym for "tethered remote camera") is used to assess artificial reefs and their attraction to fish. This helps marine biolgists find out why there is little marine life in some parts of the ocean.

In Japan, a computerized supermarket not only uses robots, but also sells them. A central computer within the store controls such functions as lighting, air conditioners, freezers, store security, and the kitchen's sterilization system. It also keeps a running inventory of goods in the store to facilitate reordering. When goods arrive, an unmanned transportation and storage system unloads the goods, transfers them to carts, and arranges the carts in an unstaffed warehouse. When the store is closed, the carts are moved to the store and put in front of the appropriate shelves ready for final distributions by store workers. The most expensive component of this computerized store is the automated warehouse and transportation system—and one of these was sold in the first five months of the store's operation. Other sales generated include parking robots, automated meat slicers, and food-sorting devices.

You can send robots into coal mines, to the bottom of the ocean, and even into outer space. In many places within our nation's factories, people have been maimed or killed doing routine but dangerous jobs. If a robot happens to leave an arm somewhere, there's no harm done; another one can be attached.

Robots can perform the most boring and tedious tasks and never get tired or frustrated. Many jobs that require extreme precision can be performed with more accuracy by robots than by humans. When robots become too worn or obsolete, they can be let go—without a pension.

The Displaced Worker

Each robot on an assembly line replaces, on the average, two people. Only a single human overseer is needed for every four or five machines. Replacing people with machines is obviously a hot issue and will become even hotter as the robot invasion intensifies. According to management, there is little or no problem concerning job security. Robots enter the work force gradually, at the normal attrition rate. The attrition rate in metalworking in the United States is about 6 percent a year; this figure includes job hopping, pregnancy, retirements, and resignations. Robots are placed, says management, in jobs that are vacant, in jobs that are left by those who retire, or in jobs that are so miserable nobody wants them.

Some say that robotics and automation will actually create more jobs than they will eliminate. "Automated" labor offers potential benefits to workers, including more interesting jobs and more responsibility. However, some experts foresee a time when those workers who cannot or will not learn required skills will have a rough time finding a place in the automated factory. In any event, predictions are that there will be more than 150,000 industrial robots in use by 1995. We are truly entering the "age of robotics."

Homesteading, Robot Style
Scientists believe that sometime in the 21st century, a seed community of robots armed with a starter kit of manufacturing equipment could construct an autonomous facility for research and processing of mineral resources on the moon. The facility would be constructed out of lunar materials and be operated with minimal human supervision. This technology could then eventually be employed on the planet Mars.

This ambitious plan stems in part from a welter of proposals for so-called self-replicating systems, automata that can build their own offspring, which can in turn duplicate themselves. In the first phase of the lunar development, this method would be used to create a large force of robot prospectors, miners, and factory workers.

What's Down the Road?

Most factory robots are still sightless and lack a sense of touch—they're blind grabbers, reaching mindlessly toward where a part should be. A new generation of robots is leaving the laboratory and entering the factory. This new breed of robot will be cheaper and smarter than their predecessors. They will be more intelligent, and their senses of vision, touch, and, sometimes, hearing, will enable them to work in more sensitive areas.

Recently, Japan's Hitachi Corporation has developed an experimental robot manipulator, modeled on the human hand, that can manipulate objects with far greater dexterity than the pincerlike grippers currently used on industrial robots (see Fig. 17-5). Some claim that it is actually as nimble as the human hand. One drawback inherent in any manipulator is that while the brain uses sensations to guide the movements of the body, machines presently cannot. Only when a robotic hand can sense the results of its actions can it begin to mimic human abilities.

Don't look for robotic diamond cutters in the very near future.

FIGURE 17-5
The new gripper gets its dexterity from its similarity to the human hand. Its wrist and three fingers correspond to the human index finger, middle finger, and thumb. Each finger has four joints, enabling the hand to grasp objects firmly (it can lift up to 2 kg, or 4.4 lbs).

Personal Robots

A few short years ago we saw the first few industrial computers trickle into several factories across the land. Today, we are witnessing a parallel phenomenon—personal robots are now rolling and squeaking their way into our homes (see Fig. 17-6).

The 1990s could be the decade during which the household robot becomes more practical. The new home might soon become an electronic complex. Because each home has a different floor plan and arrangement of furniture, robots will be customized to that particular home through programming. In order for a household robot to negotiate through the average room, it must have an internal map of the furniture placement and permissible pathways. In order for a robot to perform various chores, it needs to be programmed and given an appropriate internal map so it won't mistake your best china for a nail as it attempts to use a hammer.

b

a

FIGURE 17-6
(a) *Hero* can entertain and serve you. Once you've programmed *TOPO*, you can command him with a simple computer instruction or joystick movement. (b) *Hero-1*, in kit form, provides an excellent educational experience. Once assembled, it can listen, move around, and talk.

But What Do They Do?

Today's personal robots move, talk, can determine distances, sense light, heat, and motion, grip objects, and more. With the proper programming, a robot could engage in simple dialog, and at the switch of a program, it could play chess with you. (If you're a bad player, you could even program it so it will give you a good game and ultimately lose.) A robot might also help with the shopping by walking to the store with you and then carrying the bundles home.

The *EZ Mower* was recently awarded the "most useful" award by the First International Personal Robot Congress. This robot is a remote-controlled automatic lawn mower that can actually cut your lawn.

Hero-1 (Heath Education Robot), made by Heathkit, is the world's first mass-produced personal robot. At its "coming-out" press conference, it introduced itself by saying, "Good morning. I am Hero-1. I can walk. I can talk. I can see. I can hear." It is 20 inches tall, weighs 40 pounds, can lift up to 1 pound with its single arm, and is built around a 16-bit microprocessor. You can have Hero-1 for under $1,000 in kit form.

Although personal robots are in their infancy and possess only limited functions, they definitely have the potential to become as versatile and useful as the personal computer.

Robots in Space

The history of space travel is essentially the history of space robotics. Through a combination of human ingenuity and computer technology, roboticized spacecraft have enabled Earth's population to experience the wonders of the solar system secondhand (see Fig. 17-7).

On the morning of July 20th, 1976, *Viking*, the first terrestrial visitor (we *think* it was the first!) to another planet, set foot—that is, set a metal leg—on Mars. The Viking lander was, in every sense of the word, a robot. The Viking's actions were directed from Earth by remote control to scoop up soil samples and deposit them in the craft where experiments were carried out (again, by remote control).

The *Rover*, a remote-controlled four-wheeled vehicle, is under construction and is scheduled to land on Mars before the end of this century. It will roll about the alien planet and send back information via satellites that will be placed in orbit above Mars.

Robots can be used to assemble solar power stations, which could then send energy through the atmosphere to an earth power station.

Many scientists and futurists believe that humanity's future is in space, and that robots will be the key to making that dream a reality. The space shuttle's robot arm has already demonstrated a great variety of applications. As advances are made in the field of artificial intelligence, the "brain" that brings life to a robot will become more humanlike. The future should be quite interesting.

a

b

c

FIGURE 17-7
(a) The launching of the space shuttle opened a new frontier for exploration and eventual habitation. (b) The Remote Manipulator System (RMS), a robot counterpart of the human arm, has shoulder, elbow, and wrist joints, plus a series of electronic motors that function as "muscles." (c) Future space stations such as this will be completely computer controlled.

ISSUES AND CONCERNS

How will the changes we have discussed affect your immediate future? Very likely, some or all the changes we've mentioned will appear in your lifetime. How well will you cope with the social demands of a high-tech environment?

Instead of simply summarizing the material presented in this chapter, we felt it would be more useful if we listed some of the growing trends and some of the issues that are being raised due to computer-related advances.

Trends and Issues

Education

The trend toward more computer literacy will increase. A basic understanding of computers will be required for graduation from high school *and* college. Many institutions are demanding that their students purchase personal computers. All branches of academia are undergoing a transfusion fueled by computer technology. The computer education field has already become big business. Programs ranging from formal college-level instruction to informal sessions in computer stores and local libraries through user groups will broaden and spread to all parts of the country.

Computer camps offered to children and adults alike will continue to grow in popularity. Most offer camp activities as well as computer programming courses; advanced students will learn more complex computer subjects.

In the future, college-bound students will be required to be proficient in the use of computers.

Today, most camps offer hiking, fishing, boating, and so on. Some camps, like the one shown, even offer computer activities.

The Education Utility

Recently, Hall High School in Illinois became the first school in the country to team up with NASA to receive satellite-transmitted pictures of Saturn during the *Voyager 2* mission. For several years now, Hall High has pointed its radar disk at the NASA satellite to downlink and monitor flights of the space shuttle. As a result of the space-related activities of Hall High, a national organization called Classroom Earth has since evolved to promote direct satellite transmission to elementary and secondary schools nationwide.

Perhaps the most ambitious plan to integrate microcomputers throughout our national school system is the telecommunications solution proposed by the **Education Utility** (Fig. 17-8). Jack Taub, the creator of this mammoth proposal, sees the Education Utility as just that, a utility as basic as the electricity or gas that flows through our other utility lines. The Utility seeks to use computer and video technologies as it delivers a wide variety of instructional materials to the teacher in the classroom through telecommunications technology. The four basic components of the utility are:

1. A **repository** of software and a *database* containing information from textbooks, journals, magazines, encyclopedias, and other instructional materials stored at the computer center in Virginia.
2. A **distribution system,** or **network,** to send materials though telecommunications carriers to state switching centers or directly to the school site.
3. A **computer/controller** at the school where the materials are temporarily stored for use by teachers, administrators, and students.
4. **Computers** and other equipment in the classroom that can then access materials directly from the school's computer/controller.

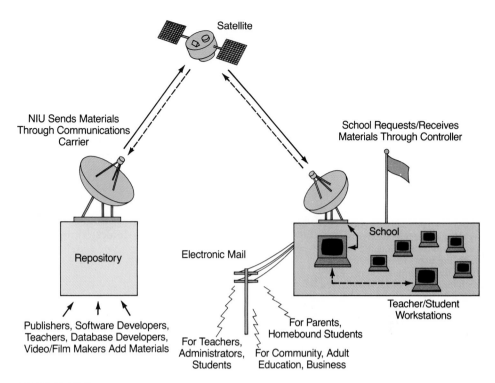

FIGURE 17-8

The *Education Utility*, based in Leesburg, Virginia.

The most important aspect of the Education Utility lies in its capacity to store and instantly make available, through data communications, a wide assortment of instructional and management materials. These materials are held in the Utility's repository, and when the school requests something, it is transmitted via satellite to the school's transmission disk. Each student's desktop computer could conceivably run a different program at the same time.

The Utility will also include an electronic mail system whereby teachers' homebound students and others will be able to communicate with each other and, as the system expands, with people in other countries, sharing information and ideas.

The Home

Homes will continue to become more automated. They will contain a central computer that will regulate various systems, such as lights, heat, air conditioning, and security control. Lights could be switched on automatically when the natural light level drops. They could be switched off and the room temperature adjusted if no one was in the room for a predetermined period of time (this would be detected by sensors in its "eye"). The computer could also control all of the locks in the house and decide whether to let someone in by comparing his or her voice to a standard reference tape.

We are unlikely to find anything like the robot butlers and servants depicted in science fiction stories. What we will see is robots behaving like household pets or companions. Robots offer at least one advantage over pets—while you can pet a dog, you can't have a conversation with it.

Computer Crime

With the proliferation of computers will come an increase in computer crime. Types of computer crimes include theft of money, data, hardware and software, as well as the destruction of data and software. Until now, the computer industry has been extremely vulnerable to the would-be criminal who can do much mischief in the comfort of his or her own room.

The FBI presently leads the fight against computer crime in the United States but is seriously hampered by the lack of federal laws that specifically prohibit this kind of crime, and is hamstrung by the fact that up to three-quarters of the computer mischief is done by juveniles, who can't be prosecuted to the full extent of the law. To help solve the problem computer training programs have been instituted, and known **hackers,** or computer buffs, have been hired to help prevent and detect computer crime (often perpetrated by other hackers).

The Office

Human safety and comfort within the work environment, known as **ergonomics,** is, and will continue to be, an issue of the computer age (see Fig. 17-9). Systems must be designed with the physical and psychological well-being of people in mind. Will the environment be noisy? Will people hurt their eyes from the screen's glare? Will the user be required to sit at a terminal for too long a period of time? All these questions must be addressed and resolved. As computer applications are used more and more, these questions will become increasingly important.

Two Tips on Computer Safety
In general, because of the possible danger of radiation, it's a good idea to sit as far away from your computer screen as comfort allows. Children using television screens should be especially careful, as some older television sets serving as monitors could be exposing users to nearly nine times the maximum recommended dosage of radiation.

Also, it's a good idea to take a break from your computer by stretching and taking a little walk every 30 minutes or so. You can also exercise your eyes by focusing on objects at different distances from you; this prevents the weakening of eye muscles that can result if you focus on the computer screen surface for long periods.

SLOUCHING TOWARD ERGONOMICS

Let's imagine that a major TV network (miraculously able to get security clearance) has decided to make your data processing installation or information center the focus of a documentary on modern working conditions.

Would you jump at the chance for notoriety, confident your company would be presented on film as a paragon of ergonomic virtue? Or would you decline the chance to be immortalized, suspecting that the cinematographer would use your people to portray the utmost in physical discomfort computer users can endure?

Most electronic office environments probalby fall somewhere between the two extremes. Yet if you look around and see many makeshift alterations—cardboard tents around VDT screens, keyboards balanced on desk drawers, books and manuals propped under VDTs to set them at an angle, bulbs removed from overhead fluorescent lamps, pillows propped behind people's backs—then you've got cause for concern.

T. J. Springer, a St. Charles, IL, consultant in ergonomics, told me, "People who change their work environments with Rube Goldberg-like contraptions are doing so because there's a problem." And while management may not like looking at all this creative retrofitting, "they had better pay attention to what these people are doing."

Part of the problem of worker discomfort traces back to architects' and office designers' lack of awareness of human needs. "I've actually heard them say, 'if we could keep people out, we'd have a good design,'" said Springer.

Also, traditional offices were meant to support people working with paper. "That's one reason why so many offices are overlit: about 150 foot candles, the recommended level for drafting work," asserted T. J. Springer, a St. Charles, IL, consultant. But modern display media are not like paper. "The image isn't constant, there is a dark background, and there is flicker," he pointed out. And in order to see the screen well, people are forced to adjust themselves to the position of the machine, often with ill effect.

For example, place a video terminal with its back to a bright window. Each day its user's eyes will have to make hundreds of thousands of adjustments between the dark screen and the light surrounding it. The human eye is strong, but so many adjustments between light and dark are an unnatural strain that can cause irritation and blurred vision, Springer said.

A different problem arises for users who wear bifocals. They might find it impossible to view a nonadjustable screen unless they keep their heads and necks bent at uncomfortable angles.

Also, because video terminal users perform more tasks from a seated position, they need chairs that allow them to lean far back without toppling over. A chair that keeps one in a rigid position may cause blood to pool in legs and feet leading to numbness. It could also hasten back problems by putting pressure on spinal discs. (I was surprised to learn from Springer that the supine slouch so popular with many programmers is a good posture to keep while computing. This "driving position" is much less likely to cause muscle fatigue or spinal disc pressure, he claims.)

But what if you're aware of these problems yet don't have the budget to purchase ergonomic equipment—and management isn't sympathetic because, after all, the work still gets done?

Sometimes doing little things—like adjusting chair heights ("almost all office chairs are adjustable but not by users," noted Springer) or turning down the brightness and contrast on a terminal screen—can make a difference. And do what you must to cut down on glare from lights and windows, he suggested.

Most important, ask your staff what *they* think needs to be done. "Often they have suggestions that can be effective but don't cost a lot," he said. And using their ideas usually guarantees acceptance.

And while it's difficult to please everyone, Springer believes management must take steps to fit the environment to the worker, and not keep forcing the worker to try to fit the environment.

Technostress

"A modern disease of adaption caused by the inability to cope with computer technologies in a healthy manner"—this is author and psychotherapist Craig Brod's definition of **technostress**. Brod is certainly not alone in his belief that office automation is causing a good deal of psychological and physical stress to office workers; left unchecked, many believe the situation will worsen in the future.

Research has shown that a symptom of technostress developed by people who work with computers a good part of each day is that they begin to overidentify with computers, resulting in the loss of empathy toward others and a diminished desire for social interaction. Another symptom of technostress is resistance or fear of computer technology. These fears often manifest as irritability, nightmares, and the resistance to or rejection of computers.

Very often, an antidote for the stress and frustration caused by computers is to get to know them better. That is, computer literacy courses should help people overcome the fear that is often caused by computer ignorance. On a corporate level, a business can humanize its electronic workplace by implementing a policy that takes the workers into account. In the future, users of automated equipment will need improved training, and management will have to avoid having unrealistic goals or expectations.

Help for the Disabled

If things continue the way they have been, people who are disabled will continue to benefit greatly through the use of computer-related equipment. Because computer access can be facilitated by modifications to the hardware and software,

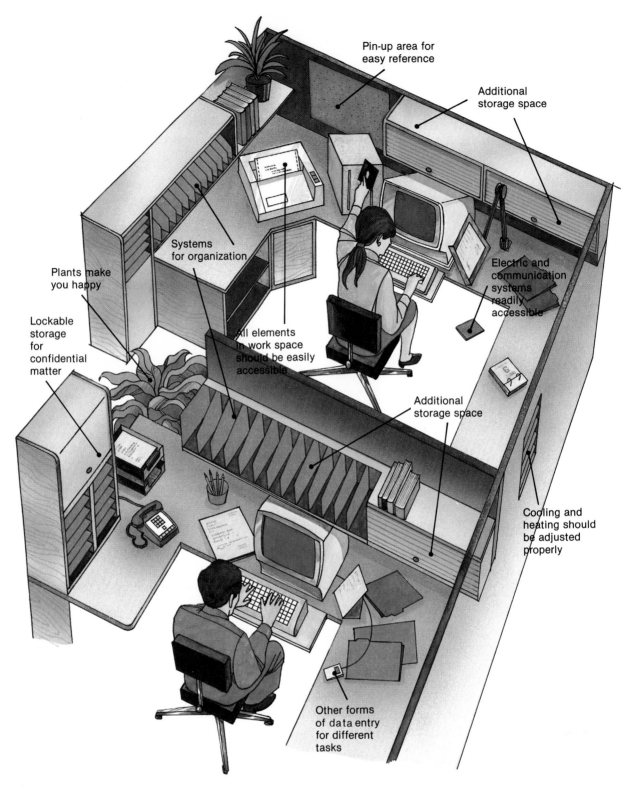

Pin-up area for easy reference

Additional storage space

Systems for organization

Plants make you happy

Electric and communication systems readily accessible

Lockable storage for confidential matter

All elements in work space should be easily accessible

Additional storage space

Cooling and heating should be adjusted properly

Other forms of data entry for different tasks

FIGURE 17-9
Today, managers must consider ergonomics—the comfort and well-being of employees who work with various kinds of equipment.

many physical disabilities are being circumvented. For example, a special pointing device worn on the head can be used with an electronic voice synthesizer to allow the user to speak. To produce sounds, the user touches the appropriate key on the keyboard by using the head pointer. People who are disabled with cerebral palsy, for example, who can't use their hands or feet and can't speak intelligently, could use this system to communicate to others and perform other computer-related activities.

The Disabled Interest Group/Special Interest Group (DIG/SIG) is a computer users' group from San Diego that finds ways for computers to help the disabled help themselves. People with technical know-how assist by revamping switches and attaching devices to compensate for a disabled person's inability to handle these items. Others help by introducing aids and special devices for using a computer.

Some companies are introducing worker programs and opportunities for handicapped people. Other companies are encouraging the employment of home-bound handicapped workers, allowing them to receive full company benefits even though they do not work at the company's main office. Yes, in many ways, the computer represents hope.

In Conclusion

Whereas some experts believe that computers hold the key to great progress for the human race, others feel that computers will eventually lead to depersonalization, unemployment, an invasion of our privacy, and the nuclear destruction of our planet. While some are moving with the flow and striving to acquire computer knowledge and skills, others are laying back and hoping computer technology will not disrupt their lives too much.

As with any powerful scientific advancement, the computer can be a curse or a blessing. Historically, humans have never reached a new level of technological advancement and deemed it too dangerous to use. Despite its destructive capabilities, there is little chance that we will ever ban the use of nuclear energy; similarly, it looks as though computers are here to stay. But is it the computer we should fear? Or is it the nature of those who would harness its power for good or evil? As always, it is not the *tool* but the *tool user* that must be monitored.

One of the goals of artificial intelligence research is to help us determine how we think, why we interpret as we do, and ultimately, who we are. We humans have been perplexed by our existence since earliest history. By providing us with a clearer understanding of the human mental process, perhaps AI research may eventually lead us to a better understanding of self. As was once said many years ago, "The answer lies within."

A

COMPUTER NUMBER SYSTEMS AND DATA REPRESENTATIONS
How the Computer Does It

You now know that computers deal extensively with numbers and numerical quantities. You also know that, internally, computers operate on numbers and numerical quantities that are represented in a form other than the traditional decimal number system. You are now ready to study number systems and data representations.

WHAT IS A NUMBER SYSTEM?

Before we can discuss the various number systems used with computer systems, we must first answer the question: What is a number system?

Briefly stated, a **number system** is a method for representing physical quantities. This very simple method is based on and dependent on a fixed set of weights. To understand this concept, let us consider the hypothetical example of a butcher who sells meat by the pound, employing a simple balance scale (see Fig. A-1). Let us further assume that the butcher has available 27 weights, 9 each of 1 pound, 10 pounds, and 100 pounds. Given the above, how could the butcher weigh out 208 pounds of beef?

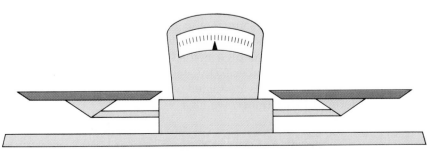

FIGURE A-1
Simple balance scale.

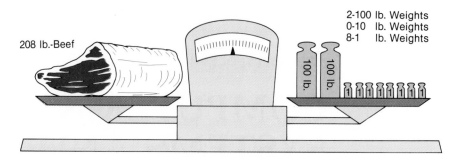

FIGURE A-2
Weighing out 208 pounds on a simple balance scale.

First, he could select a combination of available weights that together would equal 208 pounds. This could be accomplished, as shown in Fig. A-2, with 2 100-pound weights, no 10-pound weights, and 8 1-pound weights.

$$2 \text{ 100-lb} + 0 \text{ 10-lb} + 8 \text{ 1-lb}$$

The butcher might then write down the combination as

$$2\text{–}0\text{–}8$$

for the sake of brevity, realizing that each of these digits represents the quantity of weights used in decreasing order of value. That is, the 2 refers to the number of 100-pound weights, the 0 refers to the number of 10-pound weights, and the 8 refers to the number of 1-pound weights. As the butcher becomes more familiar with the system, he may even denote the same total as 208, omitting the dashes.

We recognize this to be the decimal notation for 208. We also know it to be

$$(2 \times 100) + (0 \times 10) + (8 \times 1)$$

which we shall refer to as the **expanded form** of the number. Therefore we have the relationship that

$$208 = (2 \times 100) + (0 \times 10) + (8 \times 1)$$

In a similar manner, any decimal number could be represented by a combination of weights, related in that the smallest weight is one (1) and successive weights are found by multiplying 10 times the previous weight. That is

$$1, 10 \times 1, 10 \times (10 \times 1), 10 \times (10 \times (10 \times 1)), \text{ etc.}$$

or

$$1, 10, 100, 1{,}000, \text{ etc.}$$

Because "deca" means ten, and the weights in the system result from multiplication by 10, this system became known as the **base 10** or **decimal** number system. This kind of a system is also termed a **positional** or **place-value number system** in that the actual value of a specific digit in a number is determined by (1) the place that the digit holds in the number and (2) by the value of the digit itself. In the number 30303, for example, there are three 3s, each with a different value, as each is associated with a different weight. Writing out the expanded form of this number, we have

$$30303 = (3 \times 10{,}000) + (0 \times 1{,}000) + (3 \times 100) + (0 \times 10) + (3 \times 1)$$

It is now more easily seen that the position of the first 3 gives it a total value of 30,000, whereas the position of the second 3 gives it a total value of 300, and similarly the position of the third 3 gives a total value of 3. We can now more clearly understand our number system and why it is called a positional or place-value number system and why it is given the name the "decimal number system." It should also be clear that the decimal number system has two distinct features: (1) the digits 0, 1, 2, 3, 4, 5, 6, 7, 8, and 9, and (2) weights that are derived from multiplying by 10.

THE BINARY NUMBER SYSTEM

Concepts

Let us now consider a place-value number system with only the two digits 0 and 1 and with a set of weights that are derived from multiplications by 2. This number system is referred to as the **base 2** or **binary** number system. To avoid any possible confusion as to whether a number is expressed in the binary number system or the decimal number system, a special notation is employed. A subscript 2 is inserted just after, and slightly below, the right-most digit in any binary number. Decimal numbers are written as usual, without a subscript to indicate the base. Employing this convention, the binary number 101011 would then be written

$$101011_2$$

Binary-to-Decimal Conversions

In order to convert from one number system to another, we must be familiar with the weights employed in each number system. In the binary number system the weights would be explicitly determined as follows:

...	2×16	2×8	2×4	2×2	2×1	1
...	32	16	8	4	2	1

Utilizing these weights and our knowledge of the expanded form of a number, we could represent the binary number 1101_2 as

$$1101_2 = (1 \times 8) + (1 \times 4) + (0 \times 2) + (1 \times 1)$$

A few simple calculations would reveal that this evaluates to be equal to the decimal number 13. What we have done is to determine the decimal equivalent of a binary number. Thus the process to convert a binary number to its decimal equivalent is straightforward and involves two simple steps: (1) Write out the expanded form of the binary number, and (2) perform the indicated arithmetic operations.

Just to be certain that you understand the process, determine the decimal equivalent of the binary number 101011.

Step 1: $101011_2 = (1 \times 32) + (0 \times 16) + (1 \times 8) + (0 \times 4) + (1 \times 2) + (1 \times 1)$

Step 2: $\qquad = \quad 32 \quad + \quad 0 \quad + \quad 8 \quad + \quad 0 \quad + \quad 2 \quad + \quad 1 \quad = 43$

Some examples of equivalent numbers in the binary and decimal number systems are shown in Table A-1.

TABLE A-1
Binary Equivalents of Decimal Numbers

100	10	1	64	32	16	8	4	2	1
DECIMAL VALUE			VALUE IN BINARY NUMBER SYSTEM						
100	10	1	64	32	16	8	4	2	1
		1							1
		2						1	0
		3						1	1
		4					1	0	0
		5					1	0	1
		6					1	1	0
		7					1	1	1
		8				1	0	0	0
		9				1	0	0	1
	1	0				1	0	1	0
	1	1				1	0	1	1
	1	2				1	1	0	0
	1	3				1	1	0	1
	1	4				1	1	1	0
	1	5				1	1	1	1
	1	6			1	0	0	0	0
	1	7			1	0	0	0	1
	1	8			1	0	0	1	0
	1	9			1	0	0	1	1
	2	0			1	0	1	0	0
	2	1			1	0	1	0	1
	2	2			1	0	1	1	0
	2	3			1	0	1	1	1
	2	4			1	1	0	0	0
	2	5			1	1	0	0	1
	2	6			1	1	0	1	0
	2	7			1	1	0	1	1
	2	8			1	1	1	0	0
	2	9			1	1	1	0	1
	3	0			1	1	1	1	0
	3	1			1	1	1	1	1
	3	2		1	0	0	0	0	0
	3	3		1	0	0	0	0	1
	3	4		1	0	0	0	1	0
	3	5		1	0	0	0	1	1
	3	6		1	0	0	1	0	0
	3	7		1	0	0	1	0	1
	3	8		1	0	0	1	1	0
	3	9		1	0	0	1	1	1
	4	0		1	0	1	0	0	0

Decimal-to-Binary Conversions

It is equally important for us to understand how to convert a decimal number into binary—the form in which numbers are stored in the memory of a computer. The fastest and simplest method of accomplishing this involves a division process referred to as the **division algorithm.**

The process consists of dividing the decimal number by 2 repeatedly until a quotient of zero is obtained and recording the remainders from the last to the first. Let us illustrate this algorithm by converting the decimal number 43 to binary.

$$\begin{array}{r} 21 \\ 2\,\overline{)\,43} \end{array}$$ Remainder 1   last binary digit

$$
\begin{array}{r}
10 \\
2\overline{)21}
\end{array} \quad \text{Remainder 1}
$$

$$
\begin{array}{r}
5 \\
2\overline{)10}
\end{array} \quad \text{Remainder 0}
$$

$$
\begin{array}{r}
2 \\
2\overline{)5}
\end{array} \quad \text{Remainder 1}
$$

$$
\begin{array}{r}
1 \\
2\overline{)2}
\end{array} \quad \text{Remainder 0}
$$

$$
\begin{array}{r}
0 \\
2\overline{)1}
\end{array} \quad \text{Remainder 1} \quad \text{first binary digit}
$$

Thus the binary equivalent of 43 is 101011_2. Expressing this process more compactly:

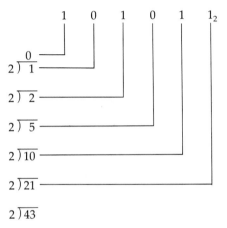

It should be clear that we can represent any number using either the decimal or binary number system, just as we can have the same value of money in two different currencies. And, as we would need to understand the French monetary system to do business in France, so must we have a working knowledge of the binary number system to do business with an individual who calculates in binary.

You may ask, who calculates in binary? The answer is, simply, not a person but a thing—a computer. Computers, in general, operate in binary, and to understand the workings of a computer one must understand the binary number system. As was illustrated above, a number expressed in the binary number system can also be expressed in the decimal system. Similarly, there is a correspondence between the numbers in any one number system and the numbers in any other number system. Therefore, as long as the basic rules of arithmetic are observed, the result of any calculation or series of calculations will lead to equivalent results.

Why Not Base 10?

We know that the result of any calculation is independent of the number system employed, as long as the basic laws of arithmetic are observed. Therefore a computer should utilize the number system that is most convenient and that can be made to operate most rapidly and efficiently.

Naturally, the decimal number system is the most convenient for us because we are most familiar with this system. In the previous illustration, we demonstrated that $101011_2 = 43$. It would appear that the decimal system is also more efficient, as only two decimal digits are required to represent the quantity in the decimal system, while six bits or binary digits are required to represent the quantity in the binary number system.

Why, then, with these advantages of the decimal system, do computers utilize the binary number system? The answer is a simple one. Designers and engineers can design or develop computers that are faster and much less expensive utilizing the binary number system than if they were to utilize the decimal system in an otherwise comparable computer. Computer designers have also realized that utilizing the binary system results in a computer that is significantly more reliable (many fewer components) and significantly smaller.

We have learned of magnetic bubble memory devices that can store 1 million bits on a chip the size of a quarter. We have also learned of the CRAY X-MP supercomputer system, capable of performing more than 100 million operations per second on quantities stored in the binary system. Certainly there can be little doubt that the use of the binary number system is both extremely fast and extremely efficient.

THE HEXADECIMAL NUMBER SYSTEM

In addition to utilizing the binary number system, many computers also make use of another number system, the **base 16** or **hexadecimal** number system. A unique relationship between the binary number system and the hexadecimal number system makes this system suitable for use in computers. This relationship will become apparent later.

In dealing with the hexadecimal number system, a new problem arises. We know that there should be sixteen digits, but we are only familiar with the ten digits 0, 1, 2, 3, 4, 5, 6, 7, 8, and 9. Therefore we must create six additional symbols to represent the six additional hexadecimal digits. Traditionally, the symbols chosen and their representations are A, B, C, D, E, and F where A = 10, B = 11, C = 12, D = 13, E = 14, and F = 15. The 16 hexadecimal digits, then, are:

$$0, 1, 2, 3, 4, 5, 6, 7, 8, 9, A, B, C, D, E, \text{ and } F$$

Hexadecimal-to-Decimal Conversions

In the hexadecimal number system, the weights are based on multiples or powers of 16. The hexadecimal weights are determined as follows:

...	16×256	16×16	16×1	1
...	4096	256	16	1

Employing these weights and the expanded form, we could express the hexadecimal number $3B_{16}$ as follows:

$$3B_{16} = (3 \times 16) + (B \times 1)$$

Because the hexadecimal digit B is equal to 11, we have

$$3B_{16} = (3 \times 16) + (11 \times 1)$$
$$= \quad 48 \quad + \quad 11$$
$$= \quad\quad 59$$

To verify your understanding, consider a second example. Determine the decimal equivalent of the hexadecimal number $15A_{16}$:

$$15A_{16} = (1 \times 256) + (5 \times 16) + (A \times 1)$$
$$= (1 \times 256) + (5 \times 16) + (10 \times 1)$$
$$= \quad 256 \quad + \quad 80 \quad + \quad 10$$
$$= \quad\quad\quad\quad 346$$

Decimal-to-Hexadecimal Conversions

As it was important for us to develop a capability to convert decimal numbers to binary, it is equally important that we be able to convert decimal numbers to hexadecimal, for reasons we will discuss later. And, as we used the division algorithm with conversions to binary, we shall also use this algorithm with conversions to hexadecimal. The only difference with conversions to hexadecimal is that you divide by 16 instead of 2, otherwise, the procedure is identical (see Table A-2). To illustrate this, let us convert the decimal number 346 to

TABLE A-2
Hexadecimal Equivalents of Decimal Numbers

DECIMAL VALUE			HEXADECIMAL VALUE		
100	10	1	256	16	1
		1			1
		2			2
		3			3
		4			4
		5			5
		6			6
		7			7
		8			8
		9			9
	1	0			A
	1	1			B
	1	2			C
	1	3			D
	1	4			E
	1	5			F
	1	6		1	0
	1	7		1	1
	1	8		1	2
	1	9		1	3
	2	0		1	4
	2	1		1	5
	2	2		1	6
	2	3		1	7
	2	4		1	8
	2	5		1	9
	2	6		1	A
	2	7		1	B
	2	8		1	C
	2	9		1	D
	3	0		1	E
	3	1		1	F
	3	2		2	0
	3	3		2	1
	3	4		2	2
	3	5		2	3

hexadecimal. This would be accomplished as follows:

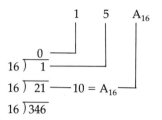

A Unique Relationship

If we were to convert this same number to binary, we would arrive at 101011010_2. Verification of this fact is left to the reader as an exercise. Examining these two representations for the decimal number 346, we see a very interesting and unique relationship. That is

1	5	A	(hexadecimal equivalent of 346)
0001	0101	1010	(binary equivalent of 346)

Starting from the units or low-order side of each number, you'll notice that a group of four binary digits is equal in value to one hexadecimal digit. That is

$$1010 = (1 \times 8) + (0 \times 4) + (1 \times 2) + (0 \times 1) = 10 = A_{16}$$
$$0101 = (0 \times 8) + (1 \times 4) + (0 \times 2) + (1 \times 1) = 5_{16}$$
$$0001 = (0 \times 8) + (0 \times 4) + (0 \times 2) + (1 \times 1) = 1_{16}$$

In general, conversions from one system to another are not this simple. The exception in this case is due to the fact that there is a whole power relationship between these bases, that is

$$2^4 = 2 \times 2 \times 2 \times 2 = 16^1$$

Simple and rapid conversions, such as the one illustrated, will exist between numbers when the bases in which the numbers are represented have such a whole power relationship. Moreover, the relationship between the number of digits in one system that corresponds to one digit in the other system will exactly match the relationship between their exponents in the power relationship. That is, since four 2s must be multiplied together to produce one 16, four binary digits will be required to equal one hexadecimal digit. A complete list of all binary to hexadecimal digits is shown in Table A-3.

Let us consider two more conversions.

1. $1011010111011001_2 = ?$ (hexadecimal equivalent)

1011	0101	1101	1001	(binary number)
B(11)	5	D(13)	9	(hexadecimal equivalent)

Therefore, $1011010111011001_2 = B5D9_{16}$

2. $13A4F_{16} = ?$ (binary equivalent)

1	3	A(10)	4	F(15)	(hexadecimal equivalent)
0001	0011	1010	0100	1111	(binary equivalent)

Eliminating leading zeros, we have

$$13A4F_{16} = 10011101001001111_2$$

TABLE A-3
Binary-to-Hexadecimal Conversions

BINARY DIGITS	HEXADECIMAL DIGITS
0000	0
0001	1
0010	2
0011	3
0100	4
0101	5
0110	6
0111	7
1000	8
1001	9
1010	A
1011	B
1100	C
1101	D
1110	E
1111	F

DATA REPRESENTATIONS

Several binary coding schemes are employed in modern computer systems to represent both numeric and nonnumeric data. Foremost among these schemes are the BCD, EBCDIC, and ASCII coding schemes.

Let's examine these coding schemes in greater detail.

BCD

The **BCD,** or **Binary Coded Decimal,** coding scheme is one of the simplest of all computer coding schemes. The BCD scheme utilizes a zone/decimal structure as is generally used to encode data onto magnetic tape. That is, data are represented in the BCD scheme on a character-by-character basis with each character consisting of a zone portion and a decimal or numeric portion. All BCD characters are subdivided into four groups, each group being uniquely identified by a combination of two zone bits. With respect to letters of the alphabet and digits, the four zones and what they represent are as follows:

BCD ZONE BITS	LETTERS OR DIGITS REPRESENTED
11	Letters A through I
10	Letters J through R
01	Letters S through Z
00	Digits 0 through 9

To distinguish the individual letters or digits from one another in a given group, each is uniquely assigned a decimal or numeric code represented by a combination of four bits, as follows:

BCD DECIMAL OR NUMERIC CODE	LETTERS OR DIGITS REPRESENTED
0000	0 (zero)
0001	A, J, or 1
0010	B, K, S, or 2
0011	C, L, T, or 3
0100	D, M, U, or 4
0101	E, N, V, or 5
0110	F, O, W, or 6
0111	G, P, X, or 7
1000	H, Q, Y, or 8
1001	I, R, Z, or 9

Thus, the character A would be represented in the BCD coding scheme as

$$11\ 0001$$

Note that the zone bits always appear first and are followed by the bits representing the numeric or decimal portion of the character. For ease of reference, each of the bits in a BCD character representation is assigned a name. The BCD zone bits are referred to as **B** and **A** from left to right, and the numeric or decimal bits are referred to as **8, 4, 2,** and **1** from left to right. Thus, any character can be represented in BCD by an appropriate combination of B, A, 8, 4, 2, and 1 bits. Employing these names, the character A described above as 11 0001, would appear as

$$BA1 \quad or \quad BA\ 1$$

To reinforce your understanding of the above, verify the BCD representations for the characters M7Z given below.

CHARACTER	BIT CODE	NAMED BITS
M	10 0100	B4 or B 4
7	00 0111	421
Z	01 1001	A81 or A8 1

In addition to the six bits required to represent a character in BCD, one additional bit is provided by the computer and is called the **C** bit (**parity** or **check bit**). Its only purpose is for internal checking by the computer. It is possible, although very unlikely, that the computer could introduce a coding discrepancy while attempting to read, write, or process a character. To prevent such an occurrence going unnoticed, a check or C bit is assigned to each character within the machine *before* any process or transmission of data in such a way as to make the total number of 1 bits in the character equal to an even or an odd number, depending on the manufacturer's specifications for the machine.

For simplicity we will limit our discussion to machines in which the total number of 1 bits in each character is odd. The practice of maintaining an odd number of 1 bits at all times is called **odd parity.** To clarify this principle further, let us consider the BCD representation of the decimal digit 6:

Bit names	C	B	A	8	4	2	1
BCD code	?	0	0	0	1	1	0

You will notice that there are two 1 bits or an even number of 1 bits in this representation. The computer would, therefore, assign a 1 to the C bit, making the total number of 1 bits odd, and produce the following BCD representation for the digit 6:

Bit names	C	B	A	8	4	2	1	
BCD CODE	1	0	0	0	1	1	0	(odd parity)

To see how maintaining an odd parity with each character in a computer allows the computer to detect when a single bit has been lost or gained accidentally, let us consider two cases.

CASE 1: Let us assume that somehow the computer misread the character 6 as follows:

C	B	A	8	4	2	1	
1	0	0	0	1	0	0	(a 1 bit was lost)

This condition would be immediately sensed by the computer's control unit because the parity check would result in an even total.

CASE 2: Let us assume that the BCD code for the character 6 was misread as follows:

C	B	A	8	4	2	1	
1	0	0	0	1	1	1	(a 1 bit was added)

As in Case 1, this condition would be easily detected by the parity check error and reported to the computer operator.

Therefore, by adding one additional bit, the C bit, to the bit configuration of each character, the computer is able to determine, quickly and easily, whether or not a 1 bit has been gained or lost.

However, if two 1 bits are lost, or two 1 bits are gained, or if one 1 bit is gained and one 1 bit is lost, for example, the computer would be incapable of detecting this situation. The reason for this is simply that the parity would have remained odd. But computer designers have determined that the likelihood of an error occurring in more than one bit of a character at the same time is so small that the additional complex design that would be required to detect such a condition is not practical.

A complete list of the 7-bit BCD codes is given in Fig. A-3.

Standard binary coded decimal (BCD) code.

NUMERIC CHARACTERS		ALPHABETIC CHARACTERS		SPECIAL CHARACTERS		
CHARACTER	CODE	CHARACTER	CODE	CHARACTER		CODE
0	C 8 2	A	BA 1			C
				BLANK		
1	1	B	BA 2	.		BA8 21
2	2	C	CBA 21	□		CBA84
3	C 21	D	BA 4	(	Left parenthesis (special character)	BA84 1
4	4	E	CBA 4 1	<	Less than (special character)	BA842
5	C 4 1	F	CBA 42	‡	Group mark	CBA8421
6	C 42	G	BA 421	&		CBA
7	421	H	BA8	$		CB 8 21
8	8	I	CBA8 1	"		B 84
9	C 8 1	‡ (Minus zero)	B 8 2	)	Right parenthesis (special char.)	CB 84 1
		J	CB 1	;	Semicolon (special character)	CB 842
		K	CB 2	¬	Delta (made change)	B 8421
		L	B 21	-		B
		M	CB 4	/		C A 1
		N	B 4 1	'		C A8 21
		O	B 42	%		A84
		P	CB 421	=	Word separator	C A84 1
		Q	CB 8	'	Apostrophe (special character)	C A842
		R	B 8 1	"	Tape segment mark	A8421
		‡ Record mark	A8 2	¢	Cent (special character note 2)	A
		S	C A 2	#		8 21
		T	A 21	@		C 84
		U	C A 4	:	Colon (special character)	84 1
		V	A 4 1	>	Greater than (special character)	842
		W	A 42	√	Tape mark	C 8421
		X	C A 42	?	(Plus zero)	CBA8 2
		Y	A8			
		Z	A8 1			

A careful examination of the possible BCD character representations will show that there are a total of 64 BCD characters. Many computer applications require additional characters, for example, the lowercase letters of the alphabet. For this and other reasons, IBM devised and introduced a coding scheme consisting of 256 characters. Some of these character representations are shown in Fig. A-4.

EBCDIC

The **EBCDIC,** or **Extended Binary Coded Decimal Interchange Code,** is similar to the BCD code in that it is a character or zoned-decimal scheme. As a matter of fact, the EBCDIC representation for the numeric portion of most characters is identical to the BCD representation for the same characters. They differ with respect to their zone representations. A comparison of BCD and EBCDIC zone representations is given in Table A-4.

FIGURE A-4
A comparison of ASCII and EBCDIC 8-bit codes.

CHARACTER	EBCDIC BIT REPRESENTATION		HEX NOTATION	ASCII BIT REPRESENTATION	
0	1111	0000	F0	0101	0000
1	1111	0001	F1	0101	0001
2	1111	0010	F2	0101	0010
3	1111	0011	F3	0101	0011
4	1111	0100	F4	0101	0100
5	1111	0101	F5	0101	0101
6	1111	0110	F6	0101	0110
7	1111	0111	F7	0101	0111
8	1111	1000	F8	0101	1000
9	1111	1001	F9	0101	1001
A	1100	0001	C1	1010	0001
B	1100	0010	C2	1010	0010
C	1100	0011	C3	1010	0011
D	1100	0100	C4	1010	0100
E	1100	0101	C5	1010	0101
F	1100	0110	C6	1010	0110
G	1100	0111	C7	1010	0111
H	1100	1000	C8	1010	1000
I	1100	1001	C9	1010	1001
J	1101	0001	D1	1010	1010
K	1101	0010	D2	1010	1011
L	1101	0011	D3	1010	1100
M	1101	0100	D4	1010	1101
N	1101	0101	D5	1010	1110
O	1101	0110	D6	1010	1111
P	1101	0111	D7	1011	0000
Q	1101	1000	D8	1011	0001
R	1101	1001	D9	1011	0010
S	1110	0010	E2	1011	0011
T	1110	0011	E3	1011	0100
U	1110	0100	E4	1011	0101
V	1110	0101	E5	1011	0110
W	1110	0110	E6	1011	0111
X	1110	0111	E7	1011	1000
Y	1110	1000	E8	1011	1001
Z	1110	1001	E9	1011	1010

TABLE A-4
Zone-bit Combinations

BCD	EBCDIC
11	1100
10	1101
01	1110
00	1111

To reinforce your understanding of EBCDIC, consider the representation of the three characters M7Z.

CHARACTER	ZONE BITS	NUMERIC BITS
M	1101	0100
7	1111	0111
Z	1110	1001

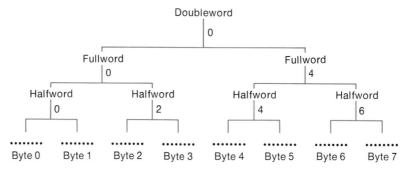

FIGURE A-5
Relationship of byte, halfword, fullword, and doubleword.

Each of the above characters was represented in EBCDIC in eight bits as are all EBCDIC characters. This unit of 8 bits is referred to as a **byte.** Two bytes is referred to as a **halfword,** 4 bytes as a **word** or **fullword,** and 8 bytes as a **doubleword** (Fig. A-5). Typically, the sizes of computer memories are specified in bytes or words.

When it becomes necessary for a programmer to verify that an item of data has been correctly stored, the programmer can call for a **dump,** or a printout of a specific area of the computer's memory. When this request occurs, the computer dumps its memory in a shorthand form of EBCDIC referred to as **hex notation.** The hex notation of the digits and letters of the alphabet are shown in Fig. A-4. In hex notation, the first four bits of each byte are converted to one hexadecimal character and the second four bits of the byte are converted to a second hexadecimal character. Thus each character will appear as two hexadecimal characters in hex notation.

As with BCD character representations, EBCDIC characters also employ parity bits to detect gained or lost bits during the transmission or processing of data.

ASCII and ASCII-8

Because EBCDIC was not universally accepted by computer manufacturers, the American National Standards Institute sponsored the development of an 8-bit code known as **ASCII-8 (American Standard Code for Information Interchange).** This code was developed by a number of computer manufacturers and was intended to provide a computer user with a coding scheme that would be acceptable on virtually all makes and models of computers. The 8-bit ASCII-8 code is shown in Fig. A-4.

Many microcomputer systems employ a 7-bit ASCII code for internal storage of data and for intracomputer transmissions. Some of these character representations only have meaning for screen displays, others represent characters that cannot be printed or displayed but can be used in system commands, and still others have a more universal meaning. Some of these character representations and their typical displays are shown in Fig. A-6.

FIGURE A-6
7-bit ASCII representations and displays.

7-BIT CODE	DECIMAL VALUE	GRAPHICAL DISPLAY	7-BIT CODE	DECIMAL VALUE	GRAPHICAL DISPLAY
0000000	00	(null)	1000000	64	@
0000001	01	☺	1000001	65	A
0000010	02	●	1000010	66	B
0000011	03	♥	1000011	67	C
0000100	04	♦	1000100	68	D
0000101	05	♣	1000101	69	E
0000110	06	♠	1000110	70	F
0000111	07	(beep)	1000111	71	G
0001000	08	■	1001000	72	H
0001001	09	(tab)	1001001	73	I
0001010	10	(line feed)	1001010	74	J
0001011	11	(home)	10010011	75	K
0001100	12	(form feed)	1001100	76	L
0001101	13	(carriage return)	1001101	77	M
0001110	14	♪	1001110	78	N
0001111	15	☀	1001111	79	O
0010000	16	►	1010000	80	P
0010001	17	◄	1010001	81	Q
0010010	18	↕	1010010	82	R
0010011	19	‼	1010011	83	S
0010100	20	¶	1010100	84	T
0010101	21	§	1010101	85	U
0010110	22		1010110	86	V
0010111	23	↨	1010111	87	W
0011000	24	↑	1011000	88	X
0011001	25	↓	1011001	89	Y
0011010	26	→	1011010	90	Z
0011011	27	←	1011011	91	[
0011100	28	(cursor right)	1011100	92	\
0011101	29	(cursor left)	1011101	93	]
0011110	30	(cursor up)	1011110	94	∧
0011111	31	(cursor down)	1011111	95	—
0100000	32	(space)	1100000	96	`
0100001	33	!	1100001	97	a
0100010	34	"	1100010	98	b
0100011	35	#	1100011	99	c
0100100	36	$	1100100	100	d
0100101	37	%	1100101	101	e
0100110	38	&	1100110	102	f
0100111	36	'	1100111	103	g
0101000	40	(	1101000	104	h
0101001	41	)	1101001	105	i
0101010	42	*	1101010	106	j
0101011	43	+	1101011	107	k
0101100	44	'	1101100	108	l
0101101	45	-	1101101	109	m
0101110	46	.	1101110	110	n
0101111	47	/	1101111	111	o
0110000	48	0	1110000	112	p
0110001	49	1	1110001	113	q
0110010	50	2	1110010	114	r
0110011	51	3	1110011	115	s
0110100	52	4	1110100	116	t
0110101	53	5	1110101	117	u
0110110	54	6	1110110	118	v
0110111	55	7	1110111	119	w
0111000	56	8	1111000	120	x
0111001	57	9	1111001	121	y
0111010	58	:	1111010	122	z
0111011	59	;	1111011	123	{
0111100	60	<	1111100	124	¦
0111110	61	=	1111101	125	}
0111110	62	>	1111110	126	~
0111111	63	?	1111111	127	⌂

B

GLOSSARY*

Access Time 1. The time interval between the instant at which data are called for from a storage device and the instant delivery begins. 2. The time interval between the instant at which data are requested to be stored and the instant at which storage is started.

Accumulator A storage location that maintains a running total of values during the **processing** of a **program.**

Acoustic Coupler A cradle-like device that permits **data communications** over standard telephone lines.

ADA A complex programming language developed for the Department of Defense.

Adder 1. A device whose output is a representation of the sum of the quantities represented by its inputs. 2. See **half-adder.**

Address 1. An identification, as represented by a name, label, or number, for a **register,** location in **storage,** or any other **data** source or destination such as the location of a station in a communications network. 2. Loosely, any part of an **instruction** that specifies the location of an **operand** for the instruction.

Address Register A register in which an **address** is stored.

Algorithm A prescribed set of well-defined rules or **processes** for the solution of a problem in a finite number of steps, e.g., a full statement of an arithmetic proce-

*Boldfaced terms are defined in this glossary.

dure for evaluating SIN x to a stated precision. Contrast with **heuristic.**

Alphabetic Code Characters consisting of only letters and associated special characters.

Alphanumeric Pertaining to a character set that contains letters, digits, and usually other characters such as punctuation marks. Synonymous with alphameric.

ALU See **arithmetic logic unit.**

Analog 1. Pertaining to representation by means of continuously variable physical quantities. 2. Contrast with **digital.** 3. See **analog network.**

Analog Computer 1. A computer using mainly analog representation of data. 2. A computer that operates on analog data by performing physical processes on these data. Contrast with **digital computer.**

Analog Network The expression and solution of mathematical relationships between variables using a circuit or circuits to represent these variables.

Applications software Programs designed for specific user applications. Includes programs which make up typical business systems, commercially available software packages, and so on. Contrast with **systems software.**

Arithmetic Logic Unit (ALU) A computational subsystem that performs the mathematical and logical operations of a digital computer. A basic element of a central processing unit.

Arithmetic Operation Any of the fundamental operations of arithmetic, for example, the binary operations of addition, subtraction, multiplication, and division, and the unary operations of negation and absolute value.

Arithmetic Unit The unit of a computing system that contains the circuits that perform arithmetic **operations.**

Artificial Intelligence (AI) Behavior by a machine that, if exhibited by humans, would be called intelligent.

Ascender The top of the highest letter of a **font.**

ASCII (American National Standard Code for Information Interchange) 1. The standard **code,** using a coded **character set** consisting of 7-bit coded characters (8 bits including **parity check**), used for information interchange among **data processing systems,** communications systems, and associated equipment. Synonymous with USASCII. 2. An 8-bit coded character set, commonly referred to as ASCII-8.

Assembler A computer program that assembles, i.e, translates **assembly language** programs into **machine code.**

Assembly Language A **symbolic language** which employs abbreviations or mnemonic codes in its instructions.

Asynchronous Computer A computer in which each event or the performance of each operation starts as a result of a signal generated by the completion of the previous event or operation, or by the availability of the parts of the computer required for the next event or operation. Contrast with **synchronous computer.**

Asynchronous Transmission **Character**-by-**character** transmission where each **character** is marked by a start **bit** and a stop **bit.**

Audio Response A process that converts computer output to speech.

Audit Trail The means used to facilitate tracing a transaction from its source through all **processing** to the final **output.**

Auxiliary Storage See **secondary storage.**

Backup Alternative procedures, equipment, or **systems** used to restore service in the event of a system malfunction or loss of data. Also, a duplicate copy of a data file or files saved on some secondary storage medium.

Basic (Beginner's all-purpose symbolic instruction code). A high-level **interactive programming language** that is relatively easy to learn and use.

Batch Processing 1. Pertaining to the technique of executing a set of **computer programs** such that each is completed before the next program of the set is started. 2. Pertaining to the sequential input of computer programs or data. 3. Loosely, the execution of computer programs serially.

Baud The number of signal changes per second. To be distinguished from bits per second. Each signal change can be used to carry one or more bits of information. A term used to rate the speed of a communication line or device.

BCD See **Binary-coded decimal notation.**

Binary 1. Pertaining to a characteristic or property involving a selection, choice, or condition in which there are two possibilities. 2. Pertaining to the **number representation system** with a **radix** of two.

Binary-Coded Decimal Notation (BCD) **Positional notation** in which the individual **decimal digits** expressing a number in **decimal** notation are each represented by a **binary** numeral, e.g., the number 23 is represented by 0010 0011 in the 8–4–2–1 type of binary-coded decimal notation and by 10111 in **binary** notation.

Binary Digit In **binary** notation, either of the characters 0 or 1.

Binary Number Loosely, a binary numeral.

Binary to Decimal Conversion Conversion of a binary number to the equivalent decimal number, that is, a base two number to a base ten number.

Bit A binary digit.

Bit Map A series of dots arranged to form an image.

Blank Containing no recorded characters.

Block 1. A set of things, such as **words, characters,** or **digits,** handled as a unit. 2. A collection of contiguous **records** recorded as a unit. Blocks are separated by **block gaps** and each block may contain one or more records.

Block Diagram Another name for a program **flowchart.**

Block Gap An area on a data medium used to indicate the end of a **block** or **record.**

Blocking Combining two or more records into one block.

Boot 1. To start up a computer system. Uses a **bootstrap** program. 2. A small portion of an **operating system** that pulls the remainder of the operating system **kernel** into **memory.**

Bootstrap Used for starting the computer, this program usually clears memory, sets up I/O devices, and loads the **operating system** from auxiliary storage or **ROM.**

Branch 1. A set of instructions that are executed between two successive decision instructions. 2. To select a branch as in (1). 3. A direct path joining two nodes of a **network** or graph. 4. Loosely, a conditional jump.

Bubble Memory A memory device in which data is represented by magnetized spots (or bubbles) that reside on a thin film of semiconductor material.

Buffer Storage used to compensate for a difference in rate of flow of **data,** or time of occurrence of events, when transmitting data from one device to another.

Bug A mistake or malfunction in a program or a computer system.

Bulletin Board A **data communications** network that provides a means by which its users can exchange messages.

Bus An electronic pathway used to transfer data and electric signals. In a bus **network,** computers plug into a single cable that runs from one workstation to another.

Business Data Processing 1. Use of automatic data processing in accounting or management. 2. Data processing for business purposes, e.g., recording and summarizing the financial transactions of a business. 3. Synonymous with administrative data processing.

Byte 1. Four **bits.** 2. A sequence of adjacent **binary digits** operated upon as a unit and usually shorter than a computer **word.**

Cache Memory A module created by **software** to permit the **storage** of frequently accessed **data** in **RAM** rather than in **secondary storage.**

Canned Software See **applications software.**

Cathode Ray Tube (CRT) Display 1. An **output** device that presents data in visual form by means of controlled electron beams. 2. The data display produced by the device as in (1).

Central Processing Unit (CPU) A unit of a **computer** that includes the circuits controlling the interpretation and execution of **instructions.** See also **mainframe.**

Chain Printer A printer in which the type slugs are carried by the links of a revolving chain.

Channel 1. A path along which signals can be sent, e.g., **data** channel, **output** channel. 2. The portion of a **storage** medium that is accessible to a given reading or writing station, e.g., track, bank. 3. In communication, a means of one-way transmission. Several channels may share common equipment. For example, in frequency multiplexing carrier systems, each channel uses a particular frequency band that is reserved for it. 4. See **input channel, output channel.**

Character A letter, digit, or other symbol that is used as part of the organization, control, or representation of **data.** A character is often in the form of a spatial arrangement of adjacent or connected strokes.

Character Printer A device that prints a single **character** at a time. Contrast with **line printer.**

Character Recognition The identification of graphic, phonic, or other **characters** by automatic means. See **magnetic-ink character recognition, optical character recognition.**

Character Set A set of unique representations called **characters,** e.g., the 26 letters of the English alphabet, 0 and 1 of the Boolean alphabet, the set of signals in the Morse code alphabet, the characters of the ASCII/ASCII-8 alphabet.

Check Bit See **parity bit.**

Chip A thin silicon wafer containing a large-scale **integrated circuit.**

Clock 1. A device that generates periodic signals used for synchronization. 2. A device that measures and indicates time. 3. A **register** whose content changes at regular intervals in such a way as to measure time.

Clone A generic version of a name-brand component or computer.

Coaxial Cable Cables used in place of standard electrical wires for high-quality data transmission.

COBOL (Common Business Oriented Language) A **business data processing** language.

Code A set of unambiguous rules specifying the way in which **data** may be represented, for example, the set of correspondences in the standard code for information interchange.

Collating Sequence An ordering assigned to a set of items, such that any two sets in that assigned order can be collated.

COM See **computer output microfilm device.**

Communications Transmission of intelligence between points of origin and reception without alteration of sequence or structure of the information content.

Communications Link The physical means of connecting one location to another for the purpose of transmitting and receiving data.

Communications System A system capable of relaying **communications** signals over long distances.

Compact Disk A high-capacity metal **disk** on which billions of **bits** can be stored. Sometimes referred to as *compact disk read-only memory* (*CD ROM*).

Compile To prepare a machine-language program from a computer program written in another programming language by making use of the overall logic structure of the program, or generating more than one machine instruction for each symbolic statement, or both.

Compiler A program that compiles.

Computer 1. A **data** processor that can perform substantial computation, including numerous arithmetic or logic operations, without intervention by a human **operator** during the **run.** 2. A device capable of solving problems by accepting data, performing described operations on the data, and supplying the results of these operations. Various types of computers are calculators, digital computers, and analog computers.

Computer-Aided-Design/Computer-Aided Manufacturing (CAD/CAM) A process involving computers in the design and manufacture of products.

Computer-Aided Software Engineering (CASE) Software designed to automate the design and implementation of business systems totally.

Computer-Assisted Instruction (CAI) The use of computer systems to assist in the instruction of students.

Computer Instruction A **machine instruction** for a specific **computer.**

Computer Literacy A basic knowledge of computers and how to use them.

Computer Output Microfilm (COM) Device A peripheral device capable of recording computer output on photosensitive film (microfilm or microfiche) in microscopic form.

Computerphobia A fear of computers.

Computer Program A series of **instructions** or **statements,** in a form acceptable to a **computer,** prepared in order to achieve a certain result.

Concentrator A device that supervises **communications** traffic in a **data communications** environment, integrates the messages of several low-speed devices, and transmits them along a single high-speed data path.

Concurrent Pertaining to the occurrence of two or more events or activities within the same specified interval of time. Contrast with **consecutive, sequential, simultaneous.**

Connectivity The ability to link or network two or more independent computer **systems.**

Connector 1. On a **flowchart,** the means of representing the convergence of more than one **flowline** into one, or the divergence of one flowline into more than one. It may also represent a break in a single flowline for continuation in another area. 2. A means of representing on a **flowchart** a break in a line of flow.

Consecutive Pertaining to the occurrence of two **sequential** events without the intervention of any other such event. Contrast with **concurrent, sequential, simultaneous.**

Console That part of a **computer** used for communication between the **operator** or maintenance engineer and the computer.

Constant A fixed or invariable value or data item.

Contention A technique for maintaining the smooth flow of **data** in a **communications system.** Each terminal must "listen" to determine if another terminal is transmitting; if so, it must wait.

Controller A device that supervises **communications** traffic in a **data communications** environment, freeing the **computer** to perform processing tasks.

Control Unit In a **digital computer,** those parts that effect the retrieval of **instructions** in proper sequence, the interpretation of each instruction, and the application of the proper signals to the arithmetic unit and other parts in accordance with this interpretation.

Conversational The mode of interaction where the computer responds instantaneously to the user's requests.

Conversion The process of converting from one business system to a newly devised one.

Coprocessor A special microcomputer chip or circuit designed to perform one or more special tasks.

CPS "Characters per second" or "cycles per second," depending on context.

CPU See **Central processing unit.**

CRT Display See **Cathode ray tube display.**

Cursor A position indicator used in a display on a video terminal to indicate a character to be corrected or a position in which data is to be entered.

Cyberphobia A fear of computers.

Cycle 1. An interval of space or time in which one set of events or phenomena is completed. 2. Any set of **operations** that is repeated regularly in the same sequence. The operations may be subject to variations on each repetition.

Cylinder The corresponding tracks on each surface of a disk pack. The tracks within a cylinder are accessible with one positioning of the access arm.

Daisy-Wheel Printer An impact printer that prints one character at a time by using a printing mechanism consisting of a spoked wheel with characters located at the end. These printers can produce **letter-quality** output.

Data 1. A representation of facts, concepts, or **instructions** in a formalized manner suitable for communications, interpretation, or processing by humans or automatic means. 2. Any representations such as **characters** or **analog** quantities to which meaning is or might be assigned. 3. See also **input data, numeric data.**

Data Bank A place where data is stored; a **database.**

Database A set of logically related **files** organized in such a way that **data** access is improved and redundancy or duplication is minimized.

Database Administration (DBA) The person in charge of defining and managing the contents of a database.

Database Management System (DBMS) A set of programs designed to provide users with a **database** that may be accessed by various departments in a corporation.

Data Communications An environment in which data produced by a terminal or a computer are transported using some form of communications medium, such as phone lines, microwave or satellite systems, or fiber-optic channels.

Data Dictionary A repository for information about a **database.**

Data-Entry Device A device used to convert raw **data** from a source document into machine-readable form.

Data Item The name for an individual member of a set of **data** denoted by a data element. For example, the data item "Tuesday" is a member of the set denoted by the data element "weekday."

Data Medium 1. The material in or on which a specific physical variable may represent **data.** 2. The physical quantity which may be varied to represent data.

Data Name An identifier that names unambiguously an item of **data.**

Data Processing The execution of a systematic sequence of **operations** performed upon **data.** Synonymous with **information processing.**

Data Processing Cycle The combined functions of input, processing, and output.

Data Processing System A network of components capable of accepting information, processing it according to a plan, and producing the desired results.

Data Set 1. The major unit of **data storage** and retrieval in the **operating system,** consisting of a collection of **data** in one of several prescribed arrangements and described by control information to which the system has access. 2. A device which performs the modulation/demodulation and control functions necessary to provide compatibility between business machines and communications facilities.

Debug To detect, locate, and remove mistakes from a computer **program;** or malfunctions from a computer **system.** Synonymous with troubleshoot.

Decimal 1. Pertaining to a characteristic or property involving a selection, choice, or condition in which there are ten possibilities. 2. Pertaining to the **number representation system** with a **radix** of ten. 3. See **binary-coded decimal notation.**

Decimal Digit In **decimal** notation, one of the **characters** 0 through 9.

Decision Support System (DSS) A computer **information system** that assists managers in decision making.

Normally, decision support systems use **interactive** terminals, cross departmental lines, and are **user-friendly.**

Decision Table A **table** of all contingencies that are to be considered in the description of a problem, together with the actions to be taken. Decision tables are sometimes used in place of **flowcharts** for problem description and documentation.

Decode To apply a set of unambiguous rules specifying the way in which **data** may be restored to a previous representation, i.e., to reverse some previous **encoding.**

Dedicated Computer A computer designed for one specific task.

Demodulation The process of transforming **analog** data into **digital** data.

Density The number of **bits** stored within a unit of length of recording medium.

Descender The bottom of the lowest letter of a **font.**

Desktop Publishing A computer application that uses a **microcomputer** and a laser **printer** to produce printed documents containing both text and graphics of near typeset quality.

Digit A symbol that represents one of the nonnegative integers smaller than the **radix.** For example, in **decimal** notation, a digit is one of the **characters** from 0 to 9. Synonymous with **numeric character.**

Digital 1. Pertaining to **data** in the form of **digits.** 2. Contrast with **analog.**

Digital Computer 1. A **computer** in which discrete representation of **data** is mainly used. 2. A **computer** that operates on discrete **data** by performing arithmetic and logic processes on these data. Contrast with **analog computer.**

Digitizer An **input** device, usually a flat tablet, which converts line drawings and pictures to **digital** form. The designs are traced on the tablet and are automatically entered into the computer's **memory** for display on a **CRT.**

Direct Access 1. Pertaining to the process of obtaining **data** from, or placing data into, **storage** where the time required for such access is independent of the location of the data most recently obtained or placed in storage. 2. Synonymous with **random access** (1). A **storage** device in which the **access time** is effectively independent of the location of the data for display on a CRT.

Direct Access Storage Device (DASD) A device capable of **direct access.**

Disk See **magnetic disk.**

Diskette See **floppy disk.**

Distributed Data Processing (DDP) System A system

which gives control to users and decentralizes the computer system. Some DDP systems utilize a **host computer** while others do not. The general configurations of DDP systems are the star, ring, hierarchical, and fully distributed networks. **Data communications** can occur between the host and satellite sites or directly between satellite sites providing for a company-wide communications and processing system.

Division All characters with a similar design, but that come in many different styles and sizes.

Documentation Narrative and diagrams that explain the development and operation of a **program** or **system.**

DOS Disk operating system.

Dot Matrix Printer An **impact printer** that prints each character by using a series of pins that form dots as they are extended and strike the page.

Download The transmission of information from a central **computer** to a **terminal.**

Downtime The time interval during which a device is not functioning.

Drum See **magnetic drum.**

Dumb Terminal A terminal with little memory and capable only of the simplest of input and output operations.

Dump To copy the contents of all or part of internal **storage.** To dump, or print, a portion of **memory** to the **printer,** for example.

EBCDIC (Extended Binary Coded Decimal Interchange Code) A type of data representation and coding system based on the use of an 8-**bit byte.**

Edit To modify the form or **format** of **data,** e.g., to insert or delete **characters** such as dollar signs or decimal points.

EDP Electronic data processing.

EDSAC (Electronic Delay Storage Automatic Calculator) The first **stored-program computer,** completed in 1949.

Electronic Bulletin Board An electronic switching system where messages are posted and received through a computer.

Electronic Funds Transfer (EFT) A "cashless" method of paying for goods or services via a computer.

Electronic Mail A **data communications** service that permits the transmission of letters, memos, and other documents from one **terminal** or **computer** to another. Messages may be sent, stored, and retrieved when requested.

Electronic Message Service See **bulletin board.**

Electronic Spreadsheet A **software** package capable of

producing a grid or matrix so that **data** may easily be analyzed and manipulated.

Emulate To imitate one **system** with another such that the imitating system accepts the same **data,** executes the same **programs,** and achieves the same results as the imitated system. Contrast with **simulate.**

Encode To convert data to a coded form.

Encryption Scrambling or protecting **data** from being accessed by an unauthorized **user.**

ENIAC (Electronic Numerical Integrator and Calculator) The first operational electronic **digital computer,** developed in 1946.

EPROM (Erasable Programmable Read Only Memory) A special **PROM** that can be erased under high-intensity ultraviolet light and reprogrammed.

Ergonomics The science of finding ways to improve the work environment by making it safer and more comfortable for employees.

Error Message An indication that an error has been detected.

Exception Report A special report for management that indicates business conditions that are considered outside the normal range.

Execute To carry out an **instruction** or perform a **routine.**

Expert Systems A knowledge base designed to build systems and automate human expertise.

External Storage A **storage** device outside the **computer** which can store information in a form acceptable to the computer, for example, **disks** and **tapes.**

Facsimile (FAX) Machine A device that can copy and transmit pictures, diagrams, and other graphic material to a remote site.

Ferrite An iron compound frequently used in the construction of magnetic cores.

Fiber Optics The transmission of **digital** data in the form of light impulses via hairlike transparent fibers.

Field In a **record,** a specified area used for a particular category of **data,** e.g., a specific part of a **disk** record used to represent a wage rate, a set of **bit** locations in a computer **word** used to express the **address** of the **operand.**

File A collection of related **records** treated as a unit. For example, one line of an invoice may form an item, a complete invoice may form a **record,** the complete set of such records may form a **file,** the collection of inventory control files may form a **library,** and the libraries used by an organization are known as its **database.**

Firmware Instructions or data stored in a fixed or "firm" way, usually on a **ROM, PROM,** or **EPROM** as opposed to instructions or data stored in the **RAM** memory. Contrast with **software** and **hardware.**

First-Generation Computer A computer utilizing vacuum tube components.

Floppy Disk A flexible oxide-coated mylar disk (diskette) that is stored in a protective envelope. Floppy disks provide low-cost direct-access storage for **mini-** and **microcomputer** systems.

Flowchart A graphical representation for the definition, analysis, or solution of a problem, in which symbols are used to represent **operations, data,** flow, equipment, etc. Contrast with **block diagram.**

Flowchart Symbol A symbol used to represent **operations, data,** flow, or equipment on a **flowchart.**

Flowline On a **flowchart,** a line representing a connecting path between **flowchart symbols,** e.g., a line to indicate a transfer of data or control.

Font All characters with one design, style, and size.

Format The arrangement of **data.**

FORTRAN (FORmula TRANslating system) A **language,** primarily used to express **computer programs,** that makes extensive use of arithmetic formulas.

Front-End Processor A **CPU** located at the front end of a **mainframe** computer in a **communications system.** Assists the main **computer** by performing certain data editing, scheduling, and processing tasks.

General-Purpose Computer A **computer** designed to handle a wide variety of problems.

Gigabyte One billion **bytes.**

Graphic User Interface (GUI) An object-oriented user interface that utilizes images called **icons** to assist the user in carrying out operating system commands.

Greeking The process of converting text to place holders.

Half-Adder A combination logic element having two **outputs,** S and C, and two **inputs,** A and B, such that the outputs are related to the inputs according to the table below. S denotes "Sum without Carry," C denotes "Carry." Two half-adders may be used for performing **binary** addition.

INPUT		OUTPUT	
A	B	C	S
0	0	0	0
0	1	0	1
1	0	0	1
1	1	1	0

Halfword A contiguous sequence of **bits** or **characters** which comprises half a computer **word** and is capable of being addressed as a unit.

Handshaking The preestablished rules for exchanging data between one **modem** and another over a **communications** line.

Hard Copy The **output** produced by a printer.

Hardware Physical equipment, as opposed to the **computer program** or method of use, e.g., mechanical, magnetic, electrical, or electronic devices. Contrast with **software.**

Heuristic Pertaining to exploratory methods of problem solving in which solutions are discovered by evaluation of the progress made toward the final result. Contrast with **algorithm.**

Hexadecimal See **sexadecimal.**

Hierarchy Plus Input-Processing-Output (HIPO) A design and documentation tool used to 1. State the functions to be accomplished by the **program** (or **system**). 2. Provide an overall structure or hierarchy by which the individual functions of the **program** (or **system**) can be understood. 3. Provide a visual description of the **input** to be used and the **output** produced by each function.

High-Level Programming Language A language that is closer to English than other types of languages; used by most computer programmers. **FORTRAN, COBOL,** and **BASIC** are all high-level languages.

HIPO See **hierarchy plus input-processing-output.**

Hollerith Pertaining to a particular type of **code** or punched card utilizing 12 rows per column and usually 80 columns per card.

Host Computer The central or controlling computer in a multiple-computer **network** or **distributed data processing system.**

Hybrid Computer A **computer** for **data processing** using both **analog** representation and discrete representation of **data.**

ICON A graphic image used with graphic user interfaces.

Idle Time That part of available time during which the **hardware** is not being used.

Image Processing A process that digitizes and stores computer-processed images. These stored images can then be used in **pattern recognition.**

Impact Printer A printing device that imprints by momentary pressure of raised type against paper, using inked ribbon as a color medium.

Index An ordered reference list of the contents of a **file** or document together with **keys** or reference notations

582

for identification or location of those contents.

Indexed A means of organizing **data** on a **direct-access storage device.** An **index** is established to show where the data records are stored. Any desired data record can thus be accessed from the device by consulting the index(es). Data records can also be accessed sequentially.

Index Register A **register** whose content may be added to or subtracted from the **operand** address prior to or during the execution of a **computer instruction.**

Information The meaning that a human assigns to data by means of the known conventions used in their representation.

Information Processing The execution of a systematic sequence of **operations** performed on **data.** Synonymous with **data processing.**

Information Retrieval The methods and procedures for recovering specific information from stored **data.**

Information System The interaction between a person and a machine which, under the person's control, gathers **data** and disseminates **information.**

Input 1. Pertaining to a device, process, or **channel** involved in the insertion of **data** or states, or to the data or states involved. 2. One, or a sequence of, input states. 3. Same as **input device.** 4. Same as **input channel.** 5. Same as input process. 6. Same as **input data.**

Input Channel A **channel** for impressing a state on a device or logic element. Synonymous with **input** (4).

Input Data Data to be processed. Synonymous with **input** (6).

Input Device The device or collective set of devices used for conveying **data** into another device. Synonymous with **input** (3).

Input/Output (I/O) Pertaining to either **input** or **output,** or both.

Instruction A **statement** that specifies an **operation** and the values or locations of its **operands.** A series of ordered instructions comprise a **computer program.**

Instruction Register A **register** that stores an **instruction** for execution.

Integrated Circuit (IC) Interconnected circuit elements etched into a silicon **chip.**

Interactive Pertains to an application in which each entry elicits a response, as in an airline reservation system.

Interactive Programming Language A **programming language** which facilitates communication between **user** and **computer** on a conversational basis.

Interblock Gap A space on a **storage** medium used to separate groups of **records** or **blocks.**

Interface A shared boundary. An interface might be a **hardware** component to link two devices or it might be a portion of **storage** or **registers** accessed by two or more **computer programs.**

Interpreter A **computer program** that translates and executes each **source language** statement before translating and executing the next one.

Interrecord Gap See **record gap.**

I/O See **input/output.**

Job A specified group of tasks prescribed as a unit of work for a **computer.** By extension, a job usually includes one or more **computer programs,** linkages, **files,** and **instructions** to the **operating system.**

Job Control Statement A **statement** in a **job** that is used in identifying the job or describing its requirements to the **operating system.**

Joystick A small hand-held **input device** used to control **cursor** movement.

K An abbreviation for the prefix *kilo,* meaning 1,000 in decimal notation. 2. Loosely, when referring to **storage** capacity, two to the tenth power, 1,024 in **decimal** notation.

Kernel Small portion of an **operating system** that resides in **memory** at all times.

Kerning The adjusting of the amount of space between pairs of letters to make them look better on the page.

Key One or more **characters** within an item of **data** that are used to identify it or control its use.

Label A spreadsheet entry composed of any type of character.

Language A set of representations, conventions, and rules used to convey information.

Letter-Quality Of the quality produced by a typical electric typewriter.

Library 1. A collection of organized **information** used for study and reference. 2. A collection of related **files.** For example, one line of an invoice may form an item, a complete invoice may form a **file,** the collection of inventory control files may form a **library,** and the libraries used by an organization are known as its **data bank.**

Light Pen A penlike device used to write or sketch directly on the surface of a **CRT** an image which is then input to the **computer.**

Line Printer A device that prints all **characters** of a line as a unit. Contrast with **character printer.**

Literal A symbol or quantity in a source program that is itself **data,** rather than a reference to **data.**

Load In programming, to enter **data** into **storage** or working **registers.**

Local Area Network (LAN) A **network** that shares **data** and resources among several **computers** in fairly close proximity.

Logical Record A collection of items independent of their physical environment. Portions of the same logical **record** may be located in different **physical records.**

Loop A sequence of **instructions** that is executed repeatedly until a terminal condition prevails.

LSI (Large-Scale Integrated circuit). Thousands of integrated circuits on a chip.

Machine Code Instructions in a form a **computer** can execute directly.

Machine-Independent Pertaining to procedures or **programs** created without regard for the actual devices which will be used to process them.

Machine Instruction An **instruction** that a machine can recognize and execute.

Machine Language A **language** that is used directly by a machine.

Macro A series of applications software commands than can be carried out by pressing one or two keyboard keys.

Magnetic Core A donut-shaped magnetic material used as **memory** within early computer systems.

Magnetic Disk A flat circular plate with a magnetic surface on which **data** can be stored by selective magnetization of portions of the flat surface.

Magnetic Drum A right circular cylinder with a magnetic surface on which **data** can be stored by selective magnetization of portions of the curved surface.

Magnetic Ink An ink that contains particles of a magnetic substance whose presence can be detected by magnetic sensors.

Magnetic-Ink Character Recognition (MICR) The machine recognition of characters printed with **magnetic ink.** Contrast with **optical character recognition.**

Magnetic Tape A tape with a magnetic surface on which **data** can be stored by a selective polarization of portions of the surface.

Mainframe A large-scale computer system typically supported by large metal frames. Generally faster, larger, and more powerful than a **minicomputer.** The largest mainframe computers are sometimes called **supercomputers.**

Main Storage The general-purpose **storage** of a **computer.** Usually, main storage can be accessed directly by the operating registers. Contrast with **secondary storage.**

Management Information System (MIS) 1. Management performed with the aid of automatic **data processing.** 2. An **information system** designed to aid in the performance of management functions.

Mark-Sense To mark a position on a paper or cardboard form with an electrically conductive pencil, for later conversion to a machine-readable form.

Mass Storage (Online) The storage of a large amount of data which are also readily accessible to the **central processing unit** of a **computer.**

Mass Storage Device A device with a large **storage** capacity, e.g., **magnetic disk, magnetic drum.**

Master File A **file** that is either relatively permanent or that is treated as an authority in a particular **job.**

Matrix A mathematical term for an array or **table.**

Medium The material, or configuration thereof, on which data are recorded, e.g., paper tape, magnetic tape. Synonymous with **data medium.**

Megabyte One million **bytes** of memory.

Megahertz (MHz) A frequency equal to one million pulses or cycles per second.

Memory The main **storage** unit in a **computer** system. Also referred to as **primary storage.**

MICR See **magnetic-ink character recognition.**

Microcomputer A small but complete computer system, consisting of hardware and software, whose main processing part is a microprocessor.

Microfiche A sheet of photosensitive film about 4 inches by 6 inches on which the images of computer **output** may be recorded. A single sheet of microfiche is capable of recording more than 250 pages of computer **output.**

Microprocessor (MPU) 1. A simple **computer** on a **chip.** 2. The **central processing unit** of a **microcomputer.** 3. An **integrated circuit** that can perform a variety of **operations** in accordance with a set of **instructions.**

Microsecond One-millionth of a second.

Microwave High-frequency radio signals used to transmit **data** at high speed.

Millisecond One-thousandth of a second.

Minicomputer A **digital computer** that is characterized by higher performance, more versatility, and a wide selection of available **programming languages, operating systems,** and **applications software** than a microcomputer.

Minisupercomputer A type of **supercomputer** that is less expensive and possesses half the power of a **supercomputer.**

MODEM (MOdulator-DEModulator) A device that

modulates (converts data to a form that can be transmitted over communications lines) and demodulates (converts modulated data to a computer-acceptable form).

Monitor A **CRT** display device.

Monolithic Integrated Circuit A class of **integrated circuits** wherein the substrate or base to which components are attached is an active material, such as the semiconductor silicon.

Motherboard A circuit board in a **microcomputer** that contains the **microprocessor, ROM, RAM,** and other associated circuitry.

Mouse A hand-held device used to control the movement of a **cursor.**

Multiplex To interleave or simultaneously transmit two or more messages on a single **channel.**

Multiplexor A device used in a **data communications** environment to permit the **input** from several **channels** to share a single **channel.**

Multipoint Line A **communications** line that connects several **terminals** to a **computer** via a single **channel.**

Multiprocessing 1. Pertaining to the simultaneous execution of two or more **computer programs** or sequences of **instructions** by a **computer** or **computer network.** 2. Loosely, **parallel processing.**

Multiprogramming Pertaining to the **concurrent** execution of two or more **programs** by a **computer.**

Nanosecond One-billionth of a second.

National Information Standards Organization (NISO) Formerly American National Standard Institute (ANSI).

Natural Language A computer **language** that allows a user to communicate with a **computer** by using simple English questions and statements.

Network A system of interconnected **computers** and **terminals** that communicates with each other.

Network, Spider See **network, star.**

Network, Star A **network** in which all **communications** must be routed through the **host** or central **computer** before being routed to the appropriate satellite processing system.

Nonvolatile Storage Memory that does not lose its contents when the power is turned off.

Number Representation System An agreed-upon set of symbols and rules for number representation.

Numeric Character Same as **digit.**

Numeric Data Data represented by numeric **characters** and some special **characters.**

Object Code **Output** from a **compiler** or **assembler** which is itself executable **machine code** or is suitable for processing to produce executable **machine code.**

Object Language Same as **machine language.**

Object Program A fully **compiled** or assembled **program** that is ready to be **loaded** into the **computer.** Synonymous with *target program.* Contrast with **source program.**

OCR See **optical character recognition.**

Octal 1. Pertaining to a characteristic or property involving a selection, choice, or condition in which there are eight possibilities. 2. Pertaining to the **number representation system** with a **radix** of eight.

Offline Pertaining to equipment or devices not under control of the **central processing unit.**

Offline Storage **Storage** not under control of the **central processing unit.**

Online 1. Pertaining to equipment or devices under control of the **central processing unit.** 2. Pertaining to **user's** ability to interact with a **computer.**

Operand That which is operated upon. Usually identified by an **address** part of an **instruction.**

Operating System (OS) **Software** which controls the execution of **computer programs** and which may provide scheduling **debugging, input/output** control, accounting, **compilation** storage assignment, **data** management, and related services.

Operation 1. The act specified by a single **computer instruction.** 2. A **program** step undertaken or executed by a **computer,** e.g., addition, multiplication, extraction, comparison, shift, transfer. The operation is usually specified by the **operator** part of an instruction. 3. The event of specific action performed by a logic element.

Operation Code A **code** that represents specific operations. Synonymous with *instruction code.*

Operator A person who operates a **computer.**

Optical Character Recognition (OCR) The machine identification of printed **characters** through use of light-sensitive devices. Contrast with **magnetic-ink character recognition.**

Optical Disk Also known as *videodisk*; a large-capacity **storage** medium used mostly for visual information.

Optical Fibers Hairlike transparent fibers used to transmit **digital** data in the form of light impulses.

Optical Scanner 1. A device that scans optically and usually generates an **analog** or **digital** signal. 2. A device that optically scans printed or written **data** and generates their **digital** representations.

OS See **operating system.**

Output 1. Pertaining to a device, **process,** or **channel** involved in an **output process.**

Output Channel A **channel** for conveying **data** from a device or logic element.

Output Process A procedure used to convert **data** to a form that can be **output.**

Overflow 1. That portion of the result of an **operation** that exceeds the capacity of the intended unit of **storage.** 2. Pertaining to the generation of **overflow** as in (1). 3. Contrast with **underflow.**

Page Composition Software Software dedicated to the design and layout of copy.

Page Description Language A program designed to control the way laser printers form characters.

Parallel 1. Pertaining to the **concurrent** or **simultaneous** occurrence of two or more related activities in multiple devices or **channels.** 2. Pertaining to the simultaneity of two or more **processes.** 3. Pertaining to the **simultaneous** processing of the individual parts of a whole, such as the **bits** of a **character** and the **characters** of a **word,** using separate facilities for the various parts. 4. Contrast with **serial.**

Parallel Operation Pertaining to the **concurrent** or **simultaneous** execution of two or more **operations** in devices such as multiple arithmetic or logic units. Contrast with **serial** operation.

Parallel Processing Pertaining to the **concurrent** or **simultaneous** execution of two or more **processes** in multiple devices such as **channels** or processing units. Contrast with **multiprocessing, serial processing.**

Parallel Transmission In **telecommunications,** the **simultaneous** transmission of a certain number of signal elements constituting the same telegraph or **data** signal. For example, use of a **code** according to which each signal is characterized by a combination of three out of twelve frequencies simultaneously transmitted over the **channel.** Contrast with **serial transmission.**

Parity Bit A **check bit** appended to an array of **binary digits** to make the sum of all the **binary digits,** including the **check bit,** always odd or always even.

Parity Check A check that tests whether the number of 1s (or 0s) in an array of **binary digits** is odd or even. Synonymous with odd-even check.

Pattern Recognition A process used to identify objects using a camera, a **digitizer,** and a **computer.**

Peripheral Equipment In a **data processing system,** any unit of equipment, distinct from the **central processing unit,** which may provide the system with outside **communications.**

Physical Record A **record** from the standpoint of the manner or form in which it is stored, retrieved, and moved—that is, one that is defined in terms of physical qualities.

Pica A unit of measure used with type. It is equivalent to $\frac{1}{6}$ of an inch, or 12 **points.**

PL/I (Programming Language/I) A high-level **programming language.**

Point A unit of measure used with type. It is equivalent to $\frac{1}{72}$ of an inch.

Point-of-Sale A computerized system used in stores to update sales and inventory data and check the validity of credit cards; transactions are entered at the point where sales take place.

Point-to-Point Line A **communications** line that connects one **terminal** directly with the central **computer.**

Polling A technique for maintaining the smooth flow of data in a **communications system.** Each **terminal,** in turn, is "asked" if it has **data** to send.

Positional Notation A method for writing numbers where the value of a **digit** in a number is determined by the **digit** and its position relative to the decimal point.

Postscript A **page description language** that is an example of a control program to create outline fonts.

Predefined Process A **process** that is identified only by name and is defined elsewhere.

Primary Storage The **main storage** or **RAM.**

Printer See **chain printer, character printer, line printer.**

Printer Command Language A **page description language** that is an example of a printer control program. It is designed to create **bit-map** fonts.

Problem-Oriented Language A **programming language** designed for the convenient expression of a given class of problems.

Procedure-Oriented Language A **programming language** designed for the convenient expression of procedures used in the solution of a wide class of problems.

Process A systematic sequence of **operations** to produce a specified result. See **input** process, **output process, predefined process.**

Processor 1. In **hardware,** the **CPU** or **MPU.** 2. In **software,** a **computer program** that includes the compiling, assembling, translating, and related functions for a specific **programming language** (e.g., **COBOL** processor, **FORTRAN** processor). 3. See data processor.

Program 1. A series of actions proposed in order to achieve a certain result. 2. Loosely, a **routine.** 3. To design, write, and test a program as in (1). 4. Loosely, to write a **routine.** 5. See **computer** program, object program, source program.

Programmer A person mainly involved in designing, writing, and testing **computer programs.**

Programming The design, writing, and testing of a **program.**

Programming Language A language used to prepare **computer programs.**

PROM (Programmable Read Only Memory) A **memory** that is programmed by a special electronic programming device. Once programmed, it functions as **ROM.**

Protected Mode In a multitasking or **multiprogramming** environment, **memory** assigned to one task or **program** is protected from invasion by any other task or **program** executing concurrently.

Protocol A set of rules governing the transmission of **information** over a data communications **channel.**

Pseudocode An imitation computer **code.** It is used in place of symbols or a **flowchart** to describe the logic of a **program.** It employs the basic structures utilized in **structured programming.**

Punch A perforation, as in a **punched card** or **tape.**

Punched Card A card **punched** with a pattern of holes to represent **data.**

Punched Tape A paper tape on which a pattern of holes or cuts is used to represent **data.**

Queue 1. A waiting line formed by items in a **system** waiting for service; for example, **programs** arranged sequentially to be processed or messages to be transmitted in a message switching system.   2. To arrange in, or form, a **queue.**

Radix The base of a number system.

RAM (Random-Access Memory) Data can be written into and read out of **RAM** and can be changed at any time by a new write operation. RAM is the main **memory** of a **microcomputer.**

Random Access 1. Same as **direct access.**   2. In **COBOL,** an access mode in which specific **logical records** are obtained from or placed into a **mass storage** file in a nonsequential manner.

Real Time 1. Pertaining to the actual time during which a physical **process** transpires.   2. Pertaining to the performance of a computation during the actual time that the related physical **process** transpires, in order that the results of the computation are made available after a delay that is considered "insignificant."

Record 1. A collection of related items of **data,** treated as a unit. For example, one line of an invoice may form a **record;** a complete set of such records may form a **file.**   2. See **logical record.**

Record Gap An area on a **data medium** used to indicate the end of a **block** or **record.** Synonymous with **inter-record gap.**

Record Layout The arrangement and structure of **fields** of **data** in a **record,** including the sequence and size of each. By extension, a **record layout** might be the description of the above.

Reduced Instruction Set Computing (RISC) A technique that utilizes small groups of **instructions** to reduce processing time.

Redundant Data The same **data** appearing in different data files.

Reel A mounting for a roll of tape.

Register A device capable of storing a specified amount of **data,** such as one **word.**

RGB A **monitor** that uses separate red, blue, and green electron guns to produce colors.

Ring Network A **network** consisting of several computer **systems** interconnected by a single **communications link** with no one **system** acting as **host computer. Communications** can take place directly between any of the satellite **systems.**

Robotics The area of science dealing with the design and use of robots.

ROM (Read Only Memory) Nonerasable, permanently programmed **memory.** Programs stored in **ROM** are sometimes referred to as **firmware.**

Roundoff To delete the least **significant digit** or **digits** of a numeral, and to adjust the part retained in accordance with some rule.

Routine An ordered set of **instructions** (usually within a **computer program**) that may have some general or frequent use.

RPG (Report Program Generator) A high-level **computer programming language.**

RS-232-C A **serial** interface commonly used with **microcomputers.**

Run A single, continuous performance, or execution of a **computer program** or **routine.**

Schema An overall conceptual view of the logical relationship between the **data** elements in a **database.**

Secondary Storage A **storage device** in addition to the **main storage** of a **computer;** e.g., **magnetic tape, disk,** or **drum. Secondary storage** usually holds much larger amounts of **data,** but has slower access times than **primary storage.**

Second-Generation Computer A **computer** utilizing solid-state components.

Selector A device for directing electrical input pulses onto one of two output lines, depending on the presence or absence of a predetermined accompanying control pulse.

Sequential Pertaining to the occurrence of events in time sequence, with little or no simultaneity or overlap of events. Contrast with **concurrent, consecutive, simultaneous.**

Sequential Computer A **computer** in which events occur in time sequence, with little or no simultaneity or overlap of events.

Serial 1. Pertaining to the **sequential** or **consecutive** occurrence of two or more related activities in a single device or **channel.** 2. Pertaining to the sequencing of two or more **processes.** 3. Pertaining to the **sequential** processing of the individual parts of a whole, such as the **bits** of a **character** or the **characters** of a **word,** using the same facilities for successive parts. 4. Contrast with **parallel.**

Serial Access 1. Pertaining to the **sequential** or **consecutive** transmission of **data** to or from **storage.** 2. Pertaining to the **process** of obtaining **data** from or placing **data** into **storage,** where the **access time** is dependent upon the **location** of the **data** most recently obtained or placed in **storage.** Contrast with **direct access.**

Serial Computer 1. A **computer** with a single **arithmetic logic unit.** 2. A **computer,** some specified characteristic of which is **serial,** e.g., a **computer** that manipulates all **bits** of a word **serially.** Contrast with **parallel** computer.

Serial Processing Pertaining to the **sequential** or **consecutive** execution of two or more **processes** in a single device such as a **channel** or processing unit. Contrast with **parallel processing.**

Serial Transfer A transfer of **data** in which elements are transferred in succession over a single line.

Serial Transmission In **telecommunications,** transmission at successive intervals of signal elements constituting the same telegraph or **data** signal. The **sequential** elements may be transmitted with or without interruption, provided that they are not transmitted **simultaneously.** For example, telegraph transmission by a time-divided **channel.** Contrast with **parallel transmission.**

Serif Cross strokes found at the top and bottom of **characters.**

Sexadecimal 1. Pertaining to a characteristic or property involving a selection, choice, or condition in which there are sixteen possibilities. 2. Pertaining to the **number representation system** with a **radix** of sixteen. 3. Synonymous with **hexadecimal.**

Significant Digit A **digit** that is needed for a certain purpose, particularly one that must be kept to preserve a specific accuracy or precision.

Simplex Transmission A mode of **data** transmission in which a message can be sent along a **channel** in one direction only.

Simulate 1. To represent certain features of the behavior of a physical or abstract **system** by the behavior of another **system.** 2. To represent the functioning of a device, **system,** or **computer program** by another, e.g., to represent the functioning of one **computer** by another, to represent the behavior of a physical **system** by the execution of a **computer program,** to represent a biological **system** by a mathematical model. 3. Contrast with **emulate.**

Simultaneous Pertaining to the occurrence of two or more events at the same instant of time. Contrast with **concurrent, consecutive, sequential.**

Simultaneous Transmission Transmission of control **characters** or **data** in one direction while **information** is being received in the other direction.

Software A set of **programs,** procedures, rules, and possibly associated **documentation** concerned with the operation of a **data processing system.** For example, **compilers, library** routines, manuals, circuit diagrams, and **computer programs.**

Sort 1. To arrange items into sequence according to some definite rules.

Source Language The **language** from which a **statement** is translated.

Source Program A **computer program** written in a **source language.** Contrast with **object program.**

Space 1. A site intended for the **storage** of **data,** e.g., a site on a printed page or a location in a **storage medium.** 2. A basic unit of area, usually the size of a single **character.** 3. One or more space, or blank **characters.** 4. To advance the reading or display position according to a prescribed **format,** e.g., to advance the printing or display position horizontally to the right or vertically down.

Special Character A graphic **character** that is neither a letter, nor a **digit,** nor a space **character.**

Special-Purpose Computer A **computer** designed to handle a restricted class of problems.

Speech Recognition A process that converts spoken commands or **data** to a computer-acceptable form.

Spooling A technique in which **output** is transmitted to a high-speed device such as a **disk** or **tape** so that it can be **output** to a slow-speed device at a later time; also involves the reverse procedure **(input).**

Statement 1. In computer **programming,** a meaningful expression or generalized **instruction** in a **source program.** 2. See **job control statement.**

Storage 1. Pertaining to a device into which **data** can be entered, in which they can be held, and from which they can be retrieved at a later time. 2. Loosely, any device that can store **data.**

Storage Capacity The amount of **data** that can be contained in a **storage device.**

Storage Device A device into which **data** can be inserted, in which they can be retained, and from which they can be retrieved.

Stored Program A set of internally stored **instructions** that guide the **computer,** step by step, through a **process.**

Stored-Program Computer A **computer,** controlled by internally stored **instructions,** that can synthesize, store, and in some cases alter **instructions** as though they were **data,** and that can subsequently execute these **instructions.**

Structured Programming A technique for designing and writing **computer programs** which have a definite form and are therefore more easily understood by the **programmer** and anyone else who needs to read and understand them.

Structured Walkthrough A **programming** practice in which several members of a **programming** team review and critique the design of a colleague's **computer program.**

Style A variation of a **font.**

Subschema A subset of a database **schema** required by an application **program.** Sometimes referred to as a *user's view.*

Supercomputer The largest, fastest, and most powerful of the **mainframe** computer systems.

Supervisor A **routine** or routines executed in response to a requirement for altering or interrupting the flow of operation through the **central processing unit,** or for performance of **input/output** operations, and, therefore, the medium through which the use of resources is coordinated and the flow of operations through the **central processing unit** is maintained. Hence, a control routine executed in supervisor state. Part of an **operating system.**

Symbolic Address An **address** expressed as a name or in symbols convenient to the **computer programmer.**

Symbolic Code **Coding** that uses **machine instructions** with abbreviations or mnemonic operation codes and **symbolic addresses.**

Symbolic Language A **programming language** that employs **symbolic coding.** Commonly referred to as **assembly language.**

Synchronous Computer A **computer** in which each event, or the performance of any basic **operation,** is constrained to start on, and usually to keep in step with, signals from a clock. Contrast with **asynchronous computer.**

Synchronous Transmission The transmission of **blocks** of **characters** framed or marked by one or more synchronizing **bytes.**

Syntax 1. The structure of expressions in a **language.** 2. The rules governing the structure of a **language.**

System 1. An assembly of methods, procedures, or techniques united by regulated interaction for forming an organized whole. 2. An organized collection of humans, machines, and methods required to accomplish a set of specific functions.

Systems Analysis The steps taken to examine an existing computer **system** and to determine whether a new **system** should be installed; the steps taken to design and implement a new **system.**

Systems Flowchart A **system's** operations and procedures shown in pictorial form.

System Software **Software** designed to facilitate the use of a computer **system.** Includes **utility programs, operating systems,** and so on.

Table A collection or arrangement of **data** in fixed form for ready reference, frequently as stored in consecutive **storage** locations or written in the form of a grid consisting of rows and columns.

Tape Unit A device containing a tape drive, together with reading and writing heads and associated controls. Synonymous with *tape deck, tape station.*

Telecommunications Pertaining to the transmission of signals over long distances, such as by telegraph, radio, or television.

Telecommuting The process by which workers can perform their jobs within a **data communications** environment.

Teleconference A conference that uses **data communications** permitting a group at one location to hear another group. Contrast with **videoconference.**

Teleprocessing A form of information handling in which a **data processing system** utilizes **communications** facilities. (Originally an IBM trademark.)

Terabyte One trillion **bytes.**

Terminal A point in a **system** or communications **network** at which **data** can either enter or leave.

Third-Generation Computer A **computer** utilizing **LSI** components.

Throughput A measure of **system** efficiency; the rate at which work can be handled by a **system.**

Time Sharing Participation in available **computer** time by multiple **users,** via **terminals.** Characteristically, the response time is such that the **computer** seems dedicated to each **user.**

Token Electronic signal or string of **bits** that circulates around a **ring network**. A **terminal** in the ring must "grasp" the **token** (change its **bit** string) to transmit and free the **token** (restore the original **bit** string) to free the **network** for use by another **terminal.**

Token Ring Network A form of **ring network** that uses **token** passing to control traffic within the **network.**

Toner Dry ink particles used with laser **printers.**

Top-Down Program Design A technique for designing a **program** (or **system**) according to its major functions and breaking these functions down into small subfunctions.

Transistor A small solid-state, semiconducting **device,** ordinarily using germanium, that performs nearly all the functions of an electronic tube, especially amplification.

Translator 1. A **device** that converts information from one system of representation into equivalent information in another system of representation. In telephone equipment, it is the device that converts dialed **digits** into call-routine information. 2. A **routine** for changing information from one representation or **language** to another.

Turnaround Time 1. The elapsed time between submission of a **job** to a computer center and the return of results. 2. The actual time required to reverse the direction of transmission from send to receive or vice versa when using a half-duplex circuit. For most **communications** facilities, there will be time required by line propagation and line effects, modem timing, and machine reaction. A typical time on a half-duplex telephone connection is 200 milliseconds.

Typeface All characters of a **division** of type that have a single design and come in many styles and sizes.

Underflow A condition that occurs when the result of a computation is smaller than the smallest non-zero number that can be stored.

Undo A feature of software that is designed to undo a previous action.

Unit Record Historically, a **punched card** containing one complete record.

UNIVAC I (UNIVersal Automatic Computer) The first commercially available **computer.**

Universal Product Code (UPC) The bar code placed on the packages of most supermarket items.

Update To modify a master **file** with current information according to a specified procedure.

Upload Send information from a **terminal** to a central **computer.**

User Anyone utilizing the services of a **computing system.**

User-Friendly A term used to describe a computer **program** or **system** that is relatively easy to learn and use.

Utility Program A service program that performs common data-processing tasks, such as **sorting,** merging, and **I/O** tasks.

Value A spreadsheet entry that is a number of a mathematical formula.

Value-Added Network A **communications** service that offers something extra to its users.

Variable A quantity that can assume any of a given set of values.

Videoconference A conference that uses **data communications,** permitting a group of people at one location to see and hear another group on a video screen.

Virtual Storage A **storage** technique used to extend memory by using **secondary storage** devices to store portions of programs not in use.

Virus A **program** designed to destroy **programs** and **data** stored in a **computer.**

VLSI (Very Large-Scale Integrated circuit) Can be an entire **microcomputer** on a single **chip.**

Volatile Storage Storage that loses its contents as soon as the power is turned off.

Winchester Disk A rigid **disk** in a sealed container used primarily with **microcomputers;** provides a high degree of reliability and has a large **storage** capacity.

Windowing The ability to view and magnify desired areas on a display screen.

Word A **character** string or a **bit** string considered as an entity.

Word Length A measure of the size of a **word,** usually specified in units such as **characters** or **binary digits.**

Wordwrap A word processing feature that causes text typed at the end of a line to wrap around to the beginning of the next line.

Worksheet A high-end microcomputer.

Workstation A **terminal** in a computer **network.**

Worm A program that attacks a **microcomputer's** operating system.

Write Once Read Many (WORM) An **optical** system designed to write **data** once and read it many times.

C

ANSWERS TO SELECTED EXERCISES

CHAPTER 1

TRUE/FALSE (Page references are given throughout with all "false" answers.)

2. T	**4.** T	**6.** F (11)	**8.** F (17)
10. F (21)	**12.** T	**14.** F (16)	**16.** F (17)
18. T			

FILL-IN

2. voltages
4. overuse
6. computer crime

CHAPTER 2

TRUE/FALSE

2. T	**4.** F (46)	**6.** F (39)	**8.** F (42)
10. T	**12.** F (50)	**14.** F (49)	**16.** F (54)
18. T	**20.** T		

CHAPTER 3

TRUE/FALSE

2. T	**4.** T	**6.** T	**8.** F (78)
10. T	**12.** T	**14.** T	**16.** T
18. T	**20.** T	**22.** T	**24.** T

FILL-IN

2. computer output microfilm

6. daisy wheel

10. printed; computer-acceptable

14. 250

4. cathode ray tube

8. automobile; aerospace

12. optical character recognition

CHAPTER 4

TRUE/FALSE

2. F (115)	**4.** F(127)	**6.** T	**8.** T
10. F (126)	**12.** T	**14.** T	**16.** T
18. T	**20.** F (122)	**22.** T	**24.** T
26. F (126)	**28.** F (135)	**30.** T	**32.** T
34. T			

FILL-IN

2. numeric, alphabetic, alphanumeric

6. file

10. master

14. tracks

4. direct access storage device

8. file protect ring

12. interblock gaps

MULTIPLE CHOICE

2. b

4. b

CHAPTER 5

TRUE/FALSE

2. F (140)	**4.** T	**6.** T	**8.** T
10. F (153)	**12.** T	**14.** F (156)	**16.** F (158)
18. T	**20.** T		

FILL-IN

2. data; instructions
6. control
10. buffers

4. address
8. overlapped processing

CHAPTER 6

TRUE/FALSE

2. T	4. T	6. F (175)	8. T
10. T	12. F (170)	14. T	16. F (185)
18. T	20. T	22. F (192)	24. T
26. F (179)	28. T	30. F (185)	32. F (186)
34. T			

FILL-IN

2. microprocessor
6. word
10. virtual disk
14. motherboard
18. baud
22. speech synthesizer
26. assembler
30. mouse

4. hard
8. strong magnetic field
12. bus
16. interrupt
20. pixel
24. operating system
28. spreadsheet

CHAPTER 7

TRUE/FALSE

2. T	4. F (209)	6. T	8. T
10. F (220)	12. T	14. T	16. F (228)
18. F (234)	20. T		

FILL-IN

2. online terminals, real-time processing, and fast response time
6. bits per second, baud rate, characters per second, words per minute, and throughput
10. intelligent
14. wire pairs; coaxial cable; microwave; optical fibers

4. UART
8. point-to-point line
12. acoustic coupler
16. value-added network (VAN)

18. video conferencing, teleconferencing, and computer conferencing

20. keyboard, telephone, television

CHAPTER 8

TRUE/FALSE

2. T	**4.** T	**6.** T	**8.** F (253)
10. T	**12.** F (256)	**14.** F (251)	

FILL-IN

2. data dictionary
6. mainframe
10. schema

4. three
8. relational

CHAPTER 9

TRUE/FALSE

2. F (267)	**4.** T	**6.** F (270)	**8.** T
10. F (273)	**12.** T	**14.** T	**16.** T
18. F (274)	**20.** F (275)	**22.** T	**24.** F (281)
26. T	**28.** T	**30.** F (284)	**32.** T
34. F (279)	**36.** F (279)	**38.** T	**40.** T

FILL-IN

2. systems programs
6. command processor
10. programmer
14. single-task
18. RAM
22. MS DOS, or PC DOS
26. layered
30. COMMAND.COM
34. buffers

4. control programs; service programs
8. input/output control system (IOCS)
12. source language; machine language
16. portable
20. 4.0
24. command
28. menus; icons
32. background
36. 1 megabyte

CHAPTER 10

TRUE/FALSE

2. T	**4.** T	**6.** T	**8.** F (314)
10. F (308)	**12.** T	**14.** T	**16.** T
18. F (317)	**20.** T	**22.** F (322)	**24.** F (295)
26. T	**28.** T	**30.** T	

MATCHING

2. K, O, L	**4.** H	**6.** G	**8.** A
10. P	**12.** C		

CHAPTER 11

TRUE/FALSE

2. T	**4.** T	**6.** F (334)	**8.** T
10. T	**12.** T	**14.** T	**16.** T
18. F (341)	**20.** T	**22.** T	**24.** T

FILL-IN

2. manufacturers

4. algorithm

6. debugging

8. sequential

10. simple English

12. they are limited in their ability to understand language

14. reserved words

16. windows

CHAPTER 12

TRUE/FALSE

2. T	**4.** T	**6.** T	**8.** F (361)
10. T	**12.** T	**14.** F (375)	**16.** F (377)
18. F (380)	**20.** T	**22.** T	**24.** F (369)
26. F (378)	**28.** F (382)	**30.** T	

FILL-IN

2. display type; artwork

4. right justification

6. kerning

8. Aldus Corporation

10. leading

12. Times, Palatino, Schoolbook or Bookman

14. outline

CHAPTER 13

TRUE/FALSE

2. T	**4.** T	**6.** T	**8.** F (397)
10. F (413)	**12.** T	**14.** T	**16.** T
18. F (402)	**20.** T	**22.** F (413)	**24.** F (417)

FILL-IN

2. value

16. report generator

4. left
6. saved
8. BROWSE
10. slash (/)
12. user friendly
14. window

18. integrated software
20. index
22. mathematical, logical, and statistical functions
24. screen cameras; film recorders
26. protocol
28. enter all data
30. formulas

CHAPTER 14

TRUE/FALSE

2. T	4. T	6. F (435)	8. F (347)
10. T	12. T	14. F (441)	16. F (435)
18. F (436)	20. T	22. F (449)	24. F (452)
26. T	28. T	30. T	32. T
34. F (461)	36. F (466)	38. F (466)	40. T

CHAPTER 15

TRUE/FALSE

2. T	4. F (483)	6. T	8. T
10. F (490)	12. T	14. F (488)	16. T
18. T	20. F (497)	22. T	24. F (504)
26. T	28. T	30. T	32. F (506)
34. T			

FILL-IN

2. management information system (MIS, data processing (DP), information processing (IP), and electronic data processing (EDP)
6. time-consuming to prepare input, must wait for output, expensive process to prepare data
10. host
14. departmental or end-user support, more predictable response time, easier access to data, reduced computer workload
18. broadband coaxial cable
22. workstations
26. computer
30. dedicated; disk; software; telephone line

4. on-demand
8. remote batch processing; conversation
12. remote or wide area; local area
16. ring
20. expandable
24. terminals
28. real-time

INDEX

Atanasoff, John Vincent, 11
AT&T's UNIX operating system, 281
ATM (Automated Teller Machine), 235
Audit trails in management information systems, 465
AUTOEXEC.BAT, 276, 281
Automated teller machines, 235
Automatic computation, early history, 6–19
Automation, impact of, 19, 553–59
Auxiliary storage (*See* Secondary storage)

B

Babbage, Charles, 7–8, 11, 20
Background applications, 280
Balance sheet, 434
Bandwidth, 228
Bar codes, 94
Bar graph, 406, 458
Base of a numbering system, 564–65
Base sixteen (hexadecimal) table, 567
Base two (binary) table, 564
BASIC (Beginner's All-purpose Symbolic Instruction Code), 25, 172, 195, 337
Basic Input Output System (BIOS), 271, 275
Batch processing, 48–49, 62, 482
Baud, 173, 214–15
BCD (*See* Binary Coded Decimal)
Beginner's All-purpose Symbolic Instruction Code (*See* BASIC)
Binary Coded Decimal, 212, 569–72
Binary number system, 41, 563–66
    why used with computers, 41
Binary-to-decimal, 563–64
Binary-to-hexadecimal, 568
Biochips, 537
Bit, 15, 41, 142
    start and stop in communications, 213
Bit mapped display, 192
Block, magnetic tape, 118
Block, of text, 366
Booting the operating system, 274, 281
Branch connector, 299–300
Broadband communications channel, 229
Bubble storage (*See* Magnetic bubble storage)
Buffer, 160
Building a spreadsheet, 402–4
Bulletin Board System (BBS), 505–6
Burrough's Corporation, 18, 24

Bus, 183, 186
    LAN, 503
Byte, 41, 574

C

C, 249, 281, 335, 338
Cache memory, 141
CAD (Computer-Aided Design), 96, 103–5
CAD/CAM (Computer-Aided Design/Computer-Aided Manufacture), 96, 103–5
Caduseus, 545
CAM (Computer-Aided Manufacturing), 103–5, 526
Canned software, 360
Card reading and punching devices, 69, 106
Careers in computing, 517–25
Cartridge, mass storage system, 124–25
Cartridges:
    for magnetic disks, 124
    for magnetic tapes, 118, 173–74
CASE (*See* Computer Assisted Software Engineering)
Case structure, 320
Cassettes for magnetic tape, 173–74
Cathode ray tube, 70, 88, 106, 192, 449
CDC 6000, 14
CD ROM (*See* Compact Disk Read-Only Memory)
Cell, in a spreadsheet, 399
Cell pointer, 399
Census Bureau, equipment for, 9
Census tabulator, 9
Central host computers in DDP networks, 490–91
Central Processing Unit (CPU), 39, 62, 147–48
    arithmetic/logic unit, 39, 147–49
    control unit, 39, 151–58
    in a microcomputer, 183
Chain printer, 82
Channel, 159, 162
    communications, 228
    multiplexor, 160
    selector, 160
Character, 115, 410
Character-addressable display, 192
Character generator, 192
Character printers, 78
Character readers, 71–75, 106
Charge-coupled device (*See* Storage, charge-coupled)
Check bit, 213

O

P

S